*Also by Simon Louvish*

*nonfiction*

MAN ON THE FLYING TRAPEZE
The Life and Times of W. C. Fields

MONKEY BUSINESS
The Lives and Legends of the Marx Brothers

STAN AND OLLIE
The Double Life of Laurel and Hardy

*fiction*

A MOMENT OF SILENCE
THE THERAPY OF AVRAM BLOK
CITY OF BLOK
THE LAST TRUMP OF AVRAM BLOK
THE DEATH OF MOISHE-GANEF
THE SILENCER
YOUR MONKEY'S SCHMUCK
THE RESURRECTIONS
WHAT'S UP, GOD?
THE DAYS OF MIRACLES AND WONDERS

KEYSTONE

# KEYSTONE

*The Life and Clowns of
Mack Sennett*

SIMON LOUVISH

Faber and Faber, Inc.

An affiliate of Farrar, Straus and Giroux

New York

Faber and Faber, Inc.

An affiliate of Farrar, Straus and Giroux

19 Union Square West, New York 10003

Photographs courtesy of: the British Film Institute; the Museum of Modern Art,
stills archive, New York; the Academy of Motion Picture Arts and Sciences, Los Angeles;
and the author's collection.

Library of Congress Cataloging-in-Publication Data

Louvish, Simon.

Keystone : the life and clowns of Mack Sennett / by Simon Louvish.— 1st
American ed.

p.    cm.

Includes bibliographical references and index.

ISBN 0-571-21276-X (hc : alk. paper)

1. Sennett, Mack, 1880–1960.    2. Motion picture producers and directors—United
States—Biography.    3. Motion picture actors and actresses—United States—
Biography.    I. Title.

PN1998.3.S43L68 2004
791.43'0233'092—dc21
[B]

2003059923

www.fsgbooks.com

1   3   5   7   9   10   8   6   4   2

# Contents

# List of Illustrations

Photographs courtesy of: the British Film Institute; Museum of Modern Art, stills archive, New York; the Academy of Motion Picture Arts & Sciences, Los Angeles; Joel Finler and author's collection.

# That Rag Time Band

In Hollywood did Mack Sennett a stately pleasure dome decree: It was to be, in his own words, 'the greatest monument in the world . . . Lasting, made of granite and marble, and as big as all outdoors.' Three hundred and four acres on a mountaintop east of the Cahuenga Pass were purchased in 1925 and a top Los Angeles architect, John De Lario, was commissioned to prepare the plans. A blueprint and drawings were produced, and then a model, of a great mansion in the Spanish style, with white stucco walls and tiled roofs. A series of courtyard loggias were to be paved with handmade tiles, and the patio would have a stone fountain and brightly coloured Mexican tiling. The sloping hillsides on either side were to be landscaped into hanging gardens, with terraces, statues, waterfalls and paved walks. An ingenious irrigation scheme would utilize the water from the fountains to flow into the lower gardens and the forty- by seventy-foot swimming-pool. The interior would consist of a vast two-storey living-room with full projection facilities, a library, dining-room, conservatory, kitchen and servants' quarters, four guest rooms, each complete with its own fireplace, private bathroom and porch. There would be a special apartment for Mr Sennett's mother, Catherine Sinnott, of Danville, Quebec, who would move in during the long Canadian winter months, if not permanently. The house was to 'look well from all sides – there is no front of the house, and it can be seen from the entire San Fernando Valley and the country surrounding'.

This perfectly befitted a Hollywood legend, a man who had risen from the lowest ranks to become the master of the largest movie studio in Los Angeles, employer of hundreds of actors, film directors, camera and sound men, crew and staff, inventor of the most popular comedy brand in the world, producer, director, writer and, in the early days, actor in his own productions, possessor of a personal fortune claimed to be as high as fifteen million dollars in the mid-1920s. A man who had acted on the maxim he had declared in February 1917:

All creative intellectual work consists of the development of individuality. The very essence of motion picture making is to encourage originality. To bring out individual characteristics. The famous stars of the stage, film and literature have been great because, at some point, they differed from everyone else. They had a flavour all their own.

It was the very epitome of the American Dream, as it shimmered in the first and second decades of the twentieth century, an era of enormous change and dynamism, when cities began to rise in tiered skyscrapers, transport, subways and trams proliferated, the Model T introduced the affordable personal car, technology took to the skies with the Wright Brothers, women smoked in public, played tennis and agitated for equal suffrage, immigrants continued arriving from all corners of the globe, and a new medium, which had crept its way into the bottom half of vaudeville programmes in the last years of the previous century, leaped forward to become the nation's and the world's most popular entertainment, the motion-picture business. In 1917, it seemed at the height of its development both as an industry and an art form, and Mack Sennett was at its apex, having formed, in combination with two of the movies' biggest operators, D. W. Griffith and Thomas Ince, an amalgamation which was intended to dominate the entire industry and tie up the country's stage and film talent in an unbeatable cartel, the Triangle Film Corporation.

All was flux and flow. Sennett himself observed, in his house journal, the *Mack Sennett Weekly*, in April 1917:

There is no form of American industry which experiences such rapid and sensational changes as the motion picture business. There is no other business that has made such enormous strides in so short a time . . . Henri Bergsen [*sic*], the noted French philosopher . . . gave out one mighty thought that we can all understand and take to heart: that life is the process of changing. And when you stop changing you die and decay.

When Sennett wrote these words, the United States was entering into its major engagement with the global trauma known today as the First World War. And changes continued, for good and ill, throughout the decade of the 1920s. Today, in another era of dynamic change, opportunities and dangers, great hopes and setbacks, it may be salutary to look back on another era in which anything seemed possible, and to look at the world that Mack Sennett built in a small corner of Los Angeles, Calif. The world of the Keystone Comedies, the first enterprise in movies dedicated to comedy alone, in which chaos was order, action was non-stop and a host of multi-talented, eccentric and sometimes near-deranged people ran, jumped, cartwheeled, pratfalled, leaped off tall buildings, plunged down waterfalls and fell off a multitude of speeding vehicles on to the backs of their necks in the performance of their daily duties.

Some of these men and women became famous – and notorious – beyond the confines of silent comedy, such as Charlie Chaplin, 'Fatty' Arbuckle, Mabel Normand, Gloria Swanson, Harry Langdon. Others were as well loved in their day, the ubiquitous 'clown princes' and 'princesses' of comedy: moustached Chester Conklin, cross-eyed Ben Turpin, clumsy Louise Fazenda, Charles Parrott (later to be Charley Chase), Phyllis Haver, Mack Swain, Charlie Murray, Andy Clyde, Billy Bevan, Larry Semon, Al St John, Slim Summerville, Hank Mann, Jimmy Finlayson, Fred Mace and the Big Chief of the Keystone Kops themselves – among his many masks – Ford Sterling. Many were stars in their own right, in Keystone's prime, while others cavorted as eternal sidekicks, comic foils, kops and kaperers in the Sennett follies. Cigar in mouth, their employer and tormentor watched from his high tower in the midst of the lot, or often lay, buck naked, in his office bath-tub, thinking up new ways to make comedy pay and build up that great personal fortune.

The monument to his endeavours, alas, was never built. While Mr Sennett dawdled over architect De Lario's blueprints, dreaming his fond dreams of setting his life in stucco, the money drained away from his enterprise, as, in Hollywood's Bergsonian flux, it lost ground to competitors in the changing fashions and appetites of more sophisticated audiences than he had ever tried to please. Then, in 1929, the stock market crashed, and the fifteen million dollars gladly invested in the unstoppable future of American capital suddenly melted into thin air. The master dodged and weaved and manoeuvred to save his business, clawing his way back for a short while in the world of talking pictures before the market waves washed over his head once and for all, and bankruptcy finally beckoned. By 1933 there was nothing left of the empire that had been Mack Sennett's Keystone, and then Triangle Pictures, and then Mack Sennett Comedies.

The house on the hill remained a paper palace. All that remains atop the mountain today is a television transmission range and a sign, first erected in 1924 as an advertisement for real-estate developers Woodruff and Shoults to highlight their new planned neighbourhood – 'HOLLYWOODLAND'. The sign was constructed of letters 50 foot high, covered with four thousand 20-watt light bulbs. By 1949 it had become a ruin, and all the light bulbs had been stolen or smashed. It was rebuilt, with the last four letters shorn off, and then, in 1978, renovated again to attain its present iconic status.

'HOLLYWOOD' abides. But Mack Sennett's true monument lies hidden in history's shades . . .

As ever, a comment on sources: In 1954, Mack Sennett published an account of his own life, *King of Comedy*, compiled with Cameron Shipp. This has universally been enjoyed for the racy style of its personal stories but noted for its many inaccuracies, showbiz flimflam and chronological chaos. Self-evidently the image that Sennett wished to present of his life, it was close in approach to the only previous account of Sennett's life to have seen print, Gene Fowler's 1934 book, *Father Goose*. Fowler, ace Hollywood script-doctor and confidante of W. C. Fields and other exuberant stars, wanted to help Sennett financially in hard times, and adopted a type of narrative we might today call 'factual' but which was more suited to the tall tale than the facts. Nevertheless, there is value in *Father Goose* on two counts: first, this was the way Sennett wished to appear, in the full glory of his own reinvention, and second, Fowler had a knack for describing the surreality that was Hollywood and capturing the essence of places and times. Many years later, comedy historian Kalton C. Lahue published two books on the Sennett studios, *Kops and Custards* in 1971 (with Terry Brewer) and a more comprehensive account of the Keystone Studio, *Mack Sennett's Keystone: The Man, the Myth and the Comedies*, in 1972. Two other books by Lahue, *World of Laughter, the Motion Picture Comedy Short 1910–1930* (1966) and *Dreams for Sale: The Rise and Fall of the Triangle Film Corporation* (1971), are also invaluable. But although Lahue dug and delved into the tale of Keystone, he was frustrated by his lack of access to the immense archive of Sennett's personal papers, which had been bequeathed to the Academy of Motion Picture Arts and Sciences as far back as 1951 but were not actually collated, catalogued and finally made available to scholars until forty years later. The result of this massive task has been a dream collection which includes scripts, stills, biographical files, copies of contracts, financial records, e'en unto Sennett's liquor bills and the grocery invoices claimed by his mother when she sojourned with him in her winter escapes from Quebec.

Another obvious source for the saga of Sennett and Keystone is the films themselves, an astonishing number of which are today available on video from various US mail-order firms. The credit documentation from the Sennett collection of these films, compiled by Sam Gill and Warren M. Sherk, runs to 855 titles, and, frighteningly, these are far from all the titles produced by Sennett from 1912 to 1932. Films for which production files are missing are not listed. Some omissions, such as, oddly, most of the Chaplin films, are covered copiously by other research, but others are lost in the Great Film Mountain, the mound of silent movies, short and long, that have disappeared into the fog of memory, lost or melted down for their chemical constituents when talkies replaced the silents. All in all, Sennett is calculated to have produced, under one heading or another, over eleven hundred titles. Confusion is rife, with batches of old Keystones sold off to various distributors, receivers and brokers after the company's demise, to resurface with new monickers, many of which are on the video releases, so that it is sometimes nigh to impossible to track down original titles. These video copies and other film sources are, as one might expect, of varying quality, and often a boon to the occulist's trade. In fact, viewing several dozen of these old one- or two-reel movies in succession for long periods, with their frenetic, dazzling chases and capers, is much like being clapped over the head with a monkey wrench for hours at a time. These films were made to be taken in small doses, in moderation, and excessive abuse can lead to disorientation, the feeling that one has been transported into a madhouse where the usual rules of conduct and society have been completely superseded by the principle of anything goes. Therefore be warned: the world of Mack Sennett is not for those who want their entertainment refined, their comedy sweetened and their comedians properly house-trained. This is the crucible of comedy, the cosmos of pratfalls and 'slapstick', of lecherous husbands, unfaithful wives, pompous social parasites, mad lovers, moustache-twirling villains, flirtatious floozies, venal vagabonds and the ubiquitous inkompetent kops. And so – let the havoc commence!

*From the Mack Sennett archives (Academy of Motion Picture Arts & Sciences, Los Angeles, California):*

WESTERN UNION TELEGRAM – NIGHT LETTER

Los Angeles, Cal. May 23 1916

Campbell MacCullough
1457 Broadway,
New York City

Working title PLUMBER STORY revised title BATH TUB PERILS
directed by E. A. Frazee cast Fred Mace proprietor of hotel
Dale Fuller his wife Hugh Fay guest at hotel and his pretty
misunderstood wife Synopsis Mace and domineering wife run
seaside hotel Fay and wife come there to spend season at beach
Mace flirts with Fay's pretty wife Fay indignantly interrupts
him and takes wife to room Fuller reprimands Mace and takes his
clothes away and locks them up Mace escapes in pajamas, gets
caught in hall, dashes into Fay's room where he hides in wall
bed Fay enters accusing wife of being untrue discovers Mace in
wall bed chases him through hotel down dumb waiter to basement
followed by Fay with gun Mace hides in trunk, the trunk is
taken to Fay's room from which he just escaped and is again
discovered by Fay in wife's room and chases him out shooting at
him a bullet punctures water pipe almost drowning Fay when Mace
throws him out Unable to stop leak in pipe Mace goes to
basement to shut off water, breaks gas pipe. The room he has
just left fills with water and in trying to stop leak Mace
accidentally sets fire to gas excited he connects gas pipe to
water pipe This causes tank in Fay's bathroom where his wife is
about to take bath to fill with gas instead of water and
explode, blowing out walls and rooms filling with water,
carrying bath tub with Fay's wife in it out into hall, down
stairs, through lobby into street Mace follows her on a dresser
where he has taken refuge both float out into ocean motor cops
chase them Fay's wife grabs tail of kite to save herself and is
carried out to sea Mace still follows close The bath tub
strikes bell buoy sinking bath tub Fay's wife holds on to
bellbuoy Mace comes up and collides with same bellbuoy picture
fades out Mace is thought to be knocked out and is met under
water by sword fish and fight between Mace and fish all ending
happily with all rescued.

Hampton Del Ruth

Prepaid
Charge Keystone Film Co

# PART ONE

# *His Hidden Talent*

Starring:
Michael Sinnott – A Canadian Upstart
Mrs Catherine Sinnott – His Determined Mother
Mr John Sinnott – A Disillusioned Farmer
Mr D. W. Griffith – A Bold Dreamer

Supporting cast:
Family; Townspeople of Richmond County, Quebec;
New England Steelworkers; Calvin Coolidge;
Marie Dressler; Bowery and Broadway thespians;
players and crew of
the American Biograph Company, etc.

# CHAPTER ONE

# Trail of the Pioneers

The county of Richmond, in Quebec, is still today a sparsely populated region. Between Drummondville, to the north-west, and
Sherbrooke, in the south-east, the countryside rolls in pleasant hills
and long stretches of farmland dotted with small towns. Life is still
lived at a leisurely pace and the most obtrusive aspect of modern
globalized life seems to be the lapdancing parlour attached to the
roadside motel outside the village of Danville. A small main square
surrounds a central memorial to the region's contribution to the
Great War of 1914–18: 'We lie dead in many lands so you may live in
peace'. Quebecois, like their fellow Canadians, cast their seed out to
the world.

In the middle of the nineteenth century, however, they were taking
men and women and their children in, immigrants to farm the wide
open spaces and work the lumber mills of a growing economy. As a
contemporary local bard, Captain William Wadleigh, a newcomer
from Newcastle upon Tyne, expatiated:

> *Here, where for ages in the elder day,*
> *The red-man held an undisputed sway,*
> *Flowed then as now yon ever coursing stream,*
> *'Neath the sun's ardent or the moon's pale beam . . .*
> *So, whilom came to this fair continent,*
> *A hardy race for home and freedom bent . . .*

They came, these robust folk, mainly from Queen Victoria's Britain
and from British-ruled Ireland. While the French had been established along the St Lawrence River, the land to the north, once the
hunting ground of the Abenakis Indians, had remained largely unoc-
cupied for almost two centuries. But in 1854 the Grand Trunk
Railway connected Richmond County to Montreal. By 1861, the
population of Richmond County was 8,844, of whom 1,312 were

French Canadians and 7,532 British and Irish. Most were employed at the sawmills, pulp and paper mills near Danville and the village of Brompton. Land was still mostly in the hands of four owners of massive government grants – over 150,000 acres as against 113,000 allocated to settlers. The farming land was, however, most desirable, as described by the Surveyor General of Lower Canada, Mr J. C. Bouchette, in 1832: 'Well furnished by good maple, beach, elm, pine and oak timber. The soil is so good that it requires but little aid to become uncommonly fertile . . .' It was not, however, an easy life, as the pioneers had to haul their goods on sleds, drawn by oxen, using axes to clear the trees or stumps in their way. Winters were, as they are, harsh and long, but already in 1891 a Richmondian *émigré* to the United States, visiting his childhood home, could lament his lost youth: 'The beautiful little spring we drank out of in summer . . . the little trout brook and the old fallen log are now scarcely visible . . . Just below this place is where young Fowler, a fine lad, a son of Dr W. H. Fowler, of Melbourne, lost his life while skating. He ventured too near the edge of the open ice and skated off into the current . . .' There was always an edge to the idyll.

Irish families populated the towns and villages from the early nineteenth century. Sennett himself, in *King of Comedy*, claimed that the family had been in Canada for a hundred and fifty years before his own birth. Current local lore in Danville has both the paternal and maternal ancestors, the Sinnotts and the Foys, arriving in the mid-1840s. The earliest census record that can be found pertains to Sennett's mother's family, the Foys, who are listed at the Township of Tingwick, a few miles north-east of Danville, in 1861. The pater-familias, Michael Foy, is registered as 'Catholic, Farmer', though we are told by local historians that, despite his devout Catholicism, he 'donated all the logs needed for the Anglican church which the congregation was erecting in the neighbouring community of Trout Brook'. In 1871, we find the Foys still in Tingwick, as well as the Murphys, who were to produce the first husband of Catherine Foy, whose second husband, John Francis Sinnott, was to be the father of our hero. The Sinnotts themselves are to be found in force, in 1871, in the District of Shipton (today the Danville area), with John, nineteen, the eldest of four sons and four daughters of Michael and Margaret, Catholic Irish farmers. On 24 February 1879, John Francis Sinnott married Catherine Foy, widow of David Murphy, in the diocese of Nicolet, at Danville – many of these townships being connected to each other by the Grandes-Lignes, or roadways, along which the farmers worked their lands. There, at John Sinnott's farmhouse, gone today but survived by many similar old wood houses, along the Grande-Ligne stretching out from Danville, was born their first son, Michael, on 17 January 1880.

Sennett wrote, in *King of Comedy*:

The Sinnots and the Foys, like most of their neighbours, were 'mixed' farmers. They raised everything they consumed and were the most independent people in the world on their little holdings, which averaged about a hundred and fifty acres. When I was a small boy my family wove its own cloth and made its own clothes and shoes. Later, as the charms of Sears, Roebuck and Montgomery Ward catalogues influenced us, we had store-bought cloth and footgear.

My people – indeed, all the neighbours around us – were large, well fed, full-blooded, tough and pious . . . good, practicing Roman Catholics . . .

There were two younger brothers, John and George, and a sister, Mary. Sennett also reminisced about his Uncle Mike Foy, a big man who could outwrestle the French Canadian 'Canucks' and stir up a stormy jig at wakes. 'In our part of Canada,' wrote Sennett, 'there was a dearth of entertainment,' and the opportunity of a good send-off for the sadly departed was too good an occasion to miss. Indeed the annals of the pioneers record that 'in the old days . . . people made their own entertainment, with bagpipes, fiddles, mouth organs and dancing the reels of Scotland and the jigs of Ireland'. Unaccompanied singing was another heritage that was much appreciated. Sennett attributed his own dawning prowess with the voice box to his becoming a basso suddenly, at the age of fifteen. Not being the traditional Irish tenor, he recalled, his warbling was not popular:

I mooed on lonely roads in Canada. I was not encouraged to sing in public. Indeed I was not encouraged to sing in privacy. My father and my brothers gave out that my voice reminded them of a moose in a bog.

Throughout his account, Sennett is trying to reconcile two somewhat different images of his teenage youth and early manhood: The traditional stance of the manly Irish man, a true son of the soil, albeit of Richmond, not the ancestral County Wexford in Ireland, a good old-fashioned scion of a hard-working, hard-drinking, hard-wrastlin' clan, and the alternative view of a more pensive youth, dreaming of other climes and places, perhaps even a reader of books, though none are mentioned at this point – a closet intellectual. We are certainly told by Sennett that his mother, Catherine, née Foy, encouraged him in his later dream of becoming a professional singer, entailing, as was certainly popular among many Irish, learning to sing in Italian. Her motto, said Mack, was 'never step on my dreams'. And indeed, this was the first working title Mack later chose for his co-authored auto-biography.

John Sinnott, on the other hand, was a practical man, who favoured practical solutions to problems. A good carpenter – this was later to be one of his trades – he had, while Michael was still a small boy, decided to quit the hard graft of farming, and found money to open a hotel in Richmond town itself, named the St Jacob. In Richmond, Michael had his first, unexceptional years of schooling. Like another young scion of a boarding-house family, Oliver Hardy, he must have hung around the premises, observing the comings and goings of strangers, the various foibles and eccentricities of the human race on the move. He never mentioned this, but we can be allowed some speculation. He might have observed the first police-man in Richmond, a Mr Walter Scott, a photograph of whom, with neat cap and pointed moustache, can be found in the pioneer annals, and who was said to have designed the first fire engine in Richmond. An embryonic Keystone kop?

From his high tower at the apex of Keystone, two decades later, Sennett reflected on his own ideas about the origins of his most famous comic type, writing in *Motion Picture Classic*, in 1918:

There is no American who, as a boy, has not dreamed of caving in the hel-met of a cop with a mighty swat that will send it around his ears. Most of us have never gotten over the feeling. Nearly every one of us lives in the secret hope that some day before he dies he will be able to swat a policeman's hat down around his ears. Lacking the courage and the opportunity, we like to see it done in the movies.

We cannot be sure at what stage this particular idea, that police-men are comical rather than reassuring or oppressive, took hold of young Michael's mind (and we shall see, later on, how the young film-goer's appreciation of an earlier strand of film-making influ-enced him in New York City), but Sennett's thoughts on the psychol-ogy of comedy, and which human types one might lampoon or throw a pie at, and which not, must surely have been based on deep desires. At any rate, there is no indication that young Mack ever acted on these hidden impulses, under the watchful eye of Ma Sinnott and the proper sanctions of society.

Early schooldays were unremarkable, if arduous. Sennett recalled freezing winter walks to school with his sister and brothers, six or eight miles through ice and snow. He was fortified, he claimed, by Ma's '186-proof wine' which made him drowsy in class. 'As a result, I was not bright in school.' But Catherine's determination that her sons should better themselves in the world was evident in 1896, when Michael was sixteen, as she enrolled him at an especially progressive school, the Institut Française Evangelique at Point-aux-Trembles, due west of Richmond.

All three brothers were enrolled at this school (we assume Mary stayed home), which was situated about nine miles north-west of Montreal, by the wood of Belle Riviere (an area now blessed by Montreal's airport). Montreal writer Pierre Pageau, who has diligently researched Sennett's Quebec roots, has discovered that at that time the school, founded in 1846 by Swiss Protestants, was considered the most advanced in Quebec. The school was open to all, regardless of religion, language or culture, and it was co-educational, a revolutionary stance for the age. The school also accorded great importance to Bible studies, under the heading of 'Education as a Help to Evangelisation'. Profoundly Christian, if non-sectarian, ideals were espoused. Rules of conduct were strict, uniforms obligatory and, as it was a boarding-school, parents' visits were limited to Sundays between 2 p.m. and 4.30 p.m. Lights out at 9 p.m. As Pageau found, in the school's literature:

Naturally a great deal of attention is paid to the French language which is in each school the language used extensively in the primary classes . . . In addition to the regular class drills, rhetorical exercises are held. These are much appreciated by students, who learn thus how to become proficient in public speaking.

Half a century later, at the Cannes Film Festival in May 1952, Sennett joked that his French speaking had been marked by the formal training of these sessions.

Apart from rhetoric, training was also given in singing by Mme Rosa Raymond. Sennett's own recollections of his time at Point-aux-

Trembles presented a very contrary image. He complained that he had hated the school and was always involved in fights, sparked by his first realization of the drawback of his name: 'All the kids yelling at us: "Look! Here come the three S'nott brothers."' Probably the inevitable ribbing by city boys of their gauche country cousins. Nevertheless, three rough, tough Sinnott lads should have been equal to the opposition.

It is not difficult to imagine that the Sinnott brothers were also uncomfortable due to the distance between their school and home. At the time Ma enrolled her kids at Point-aux-Trembles, the family had moved from Richmond two hundred miles further east to Lac-Megantic, a beauty spot on the lake of the same name, where John Sinnott had opened another hotel. There was a direct rail link from Lac-Megantic to Montreal and the school, which the boys and their parents could travel by regularly, but nevertheless it was a long haul.

The nature of the school Sennett attended during at least part of his most formative years challenges the image he was later determined to present of himself: the uncouth, semi-educated, untrained youth, forged in hardship, a chip off the old block of Irish labourers, a true nephew of big Uncle Mike Foy, who, after hitting an opponent on the head with a three-foot iron chisel, would peer at it with affection and declare: 'Now, that's a handy tool!' In fact, Michael was well on his way to a level of schooling far above his class and patrimony. As he let slip later on, with his remarks on 'Henri Bergsen' and others, he was well read and musically literate.

But the path to Evangelization was curtailed, and the Sinnott boys were not to stay long with the pedagogic Swiss. Their restless father, observing no great profit in the Quebec hotel business, and none at all in a return to farming, had set his heart and mind, like many of his compatriots and millions of hopefuls across the Atlantic, on a move south, across the Canadian border. Catherine preferred Quebec and the consolations of her own country and family. But John Sinnott determined their fate. In 1897, the family moved to Connecticut and settled in the steelmaking town of East Berlin, in the industrial heartland of the United States.

# CHAPTER TWO

# 'You Mean the Sinnott House Is Noisy?'

'Well, it's a long story about these here Sinnotts. They came down from Canada a few months ago. Quebec. A town called Danville, I think the ole man said. He's a whale of a feller, six foot three and good-natured. The mother of the family – he calls her Catherine – is kinda partial to one of her sons, Michael. So there is some fights *oncet* in a while betwixt the boys. Michael is seventeen and can fight like hell. The other boys, George – he's the oldest – and John Junior, can fight like hell. Well, the ole man *lets* 'em fight. He sets on the cellar steps while they fight and umpires it. Oncet he got mixed up in the fight and one of the boys give him a lacin'. The ole man didn't resent bein' belted around, but he says to me: 'Leon,' he says, 'Leon, the saddest moment in a man's life is when his son gets big enough to lambaste him.' . . .

'You mean the Sinnott house is noisy? That what you mean?'

Leon looked down at his work. 'You'd think this grave was the middle of Lake Erie. Is the house *noisy*? You ain't heard the half of it. I can see you're a quiet man, not used to noise.'

'No? I'm a boss at a boiler factory,' said Mr Cabot, not without pride . . .

Gene Fowler, *Father Goose* (1934)

Mr Amos Cabot, 'the sensitive boiler maker', according to Gene Fowler's colourful reconstruction of Sinnott family life in Connecticut, was seeking bed and board in the town of East Berlin, and was thoughtfully directed by the gravedigger Leon, a 'Falstaffian Portuguese in fishermen's hip-boots', to the abode of Mr and Mrs Sinnott, who were seeking lodgers to augment the boys' salaries at the American Iron Works Company. Mr Cabot seemed a most amiable fellow, as he was also forewarned that the young man, Mike, 'a bull if there ever was one, thinks he'll be an opry singer'. A 'little dago' named Signor Fontana came once a week to give him lessons. 'Fifty cents a lesson, or I hope to drop dead.' Ole man Sinnott was dead agin' it, but to no avail, for what could he do if his son was big enough to 'lambaste' him?

Mr Cabot arrived in time for the Sinnotts' twentieth wedding anniversary banquet, which included the said Michael rendering 'In the Gloaming' while his brothers played cards in the corner. Mr Cabot commiserated with Pa Sinnott on his son's laryngital atrocity and was welcomed as boarder and family friend. To save John Sinnott the pain of his son's continual warbling, he found young Michael a job at the boilerworks, teaching him to hammer rivets rather than tunes, at one dollar fifty a day.

Whether this account emerged from the fertile mind of Fowler or Sennett or a combination of both and some good flasks of Old Bourbon we cannot know. The pedantic scholar can point out that the Sinnotts' twentieth wedding anniversary bash would have occurred in 1899, by which time the family had cleared East Berlin and moved on to Northampton, Mass. But clearly we are not intended to take it all for real, merely to absorb the flavour of the red-blooded Sinnotts at work and play.

Sennett's own account, in *King of Comedy*, omits the sensitive Amos Cabot entirely and claims his job at the American Iron Works was found for him by his mother's cousin, Pete Comisky, a 'rusher', or foreman, whose task was to get the maximum work out of the labourers, who were paid by the day. Work in this crucible of the American steel industry was dangerous and back-breaking, and men were men: 'In my day,' writes Sennett, 'it was commonplace for four men to hoist a four-hundred-pound rail, place it on the shoulders of a single man, and expect him to tote it a hundred yards. I was a big, black-haired boy standing six foot one and weighing 210 pounds, so a job in the ironworks seemed the most natural thing in the world.' Even having light hair, one might surmise, detracted from one's manliness here. Sennett despised his exploitative cousin and another slave-driver, a 'bucker-upper' named Smith, 'who caught white-hot rivets in a bucket as fast as he could – he was a pieceworker too – and ordered me to slam them home at high speed with a ten-pound sledgehammer. The faster I slammed, the more money Mr. Smith made.'

The heat and heavy atmosphere of the ironworks was debilitating. Back home, Sennett wrote, his mother took care of ten boarders at a time, paying seven dollars a week each, with prodigious appetites.

Here, little Signor Fontana was engaged by Ma to teach Michael singing. His ambition, or perhaps it was mother's for him, was to sing at the Metropolitan Opera in New York. This did not go down well in East Berlin, Connecticut, and was not well received by Pa Sinnott: 'This kid . . . will never be a singer . . . And we have to sit here night after night and listen to a good ironworker being ruined!'

Work in the ironworks, or even proximate to the white heat of heavy industry, was no more congenial to Pa Sinnott, however, than to his son, as – both personal accounts and hard data combine to show – the family only stayed one year in East Berlin. The first factual sighting of the Sinnott family, provided by our genealogical bloodhound Dave Rothman, occurs not in Connecticut but in Northampton, Massachusetts, in 1898. Local street directories list Sinnott, John F., running a restaurant on 15 Strong Avenue, and resident at the same address. This restaurant was operated by a Mrs C. A. Sessions in 1897, so the Sinnotts must have been recent arrivals. In 1899, Mr and Mrs John Sinnott were still at the restaurant, but the census of 1900 locates them at 29 Strong Avenue, with John F.'s profession listed as carpenter, and Michael and his brother George as 'Pulp Mill Employee'. (The third brother, John, is down as 'night watchman'.) In the 1901 street directory, both John F. and Michael Sinnott are registered as employees of the Mount Tom Sulphite Pulp Company.

Neither Sennett nor Gene Fowler make any mention of these posts, so determined are they to maintain our image of the Iron Boy Who Wanted to Sing at the Met. Local lore in Northampton has it that young Sinnott did indeed sing at the town's new Academy of Music, which had opened in 1891. Northampton was a very different environment from East Berlin, boasting several good educational establishments and New England's first women's school, Smith College, chartered in 1871. Concerts, lectures and 'dramatic events' were sponsored by the college and the academy, part of a social life which included bicycle riding, horse-trotting matches by the river at Hatfield, and trolley riding to neighbouring towns on hot summer afternoons on the brand new electric trolley lines which had replaced the horse-and-buggies. As their local history describes, 'The people of Northampton pursued the even tenor of their way, industrious, possessed of many of the good things of this world that go to make prosperity and happiness.'

The Sinnotts joined a community of about one thousand French Canadians in Northampton, one quarter of the 4,000-plus foreign-born residents (of whom another 1,800 or so were Irish) out of a population counted at 16,746 in 1895. The main industries of Northampton were tobacco farming and lumbering, including the large pulp mill at Mount Tom, some miles south of town, set up in 1889. As the local history has it,

Raw materials for the Mount Tom Sulphite Pulp Mill were logs cut in Vermont and New Hampshire and floated down the Connecticut River . . . The logs were kept moving by a gang of men with twelve-foot pikes whose job it was to pry out the key log of any jam and get the logs going down-stream again . . . boys used to walk out on the floating logs and use their jack-knives to pick out the spruce gum for chewing gum. It was a dangerous game.

Inside the mill, there was plenty of arduous work to do in a harsh setting, as a detailed contemporary account of the factory shows:

Several immense circular tanks, like upright boilers, rise into the upper glooms of the building . . . To visit this department suggests a descent to the infernal regions described in detail by Dante and certain theologians. The air is charged with sulphurous odors to an extent that very quickly brings the visitor to the sneezing point, and when the lid of one of the curious ovens is lifted a bit that he may look in and see the softly leaping blue flames, he finds it advisable to hold his nose. The fumes of the burning sulphur are passed through five great tanks of lime rock, one after the other, each twenty-two feet high, where they meet and unite with water trickling down through and thus form the bisulphite liquor . . .

We do not know what work Pa and Son Sinnott performed in this factory, whether they were labourers in the infernal regions, loggers or merely clerks. The available data suggests that prior to 1900 Iron Mike might have been spending the previous two years working at his father's restaurant, perhaps unglamorously waiting on tables. That would certainly not have fitted the myth. But whatever the work, it was certainly not advancing young Sinnott towards his artistic goal. (Local records show that workers at the pulp- and sawmills of Northampton endured a seventy-two-hour week until unionization in 1901 forced a few hours to be shaved off.)

At this point, as factual information recedes once more, legend kicks in again. Cue Sennett:

I said to Mother, 'I think I should get some stage experience before I sing at the Metropolitan Opera House. There is a show in town starring Marie Dressler in *Lady Slavey*. She's a Canadian, and I wish I could go ask Miss Dressler how to get on the stage.

Mother said that would not be easy to do. 'Miss Dressler is famous and busy,' she said. 'How are you going to get in to see her? You are an iron-worker, Mike. And to tell the truth, you look like one . . . Let me try to think up something.'

A few days later she said she had thought up something.

'The lawyer,' she said. 'He has influence. He is a Republican . . . Mr Coolidge is his name.'

Calvin Coolidge, future President of the United States, was then plying his trade as a lawyer in Northampton, but was also a city councillor. He was Clerk of the Court, and chairman of the Republican City Committee, a very solid citizen. Kind to his clients, or unwilling to face down Mrs Sinnott's determination, Coolidge wrote to Miss Dressler, according to Sennett, the following laconic note:

> Dear Miss Dressler
>   This boy wants to go on the stage.
>   Yours Truly,
>   Calvin Coolidge.

Mother took the note, with young Michael, to Miss Dressler; Miss Dressler wrote an introduction to impresario David Belasco in New York; Michael packed his bags and went to New York, introduced himself to Mr Belasco and was advised to start his long march to the Metropolitan Opera by enrolling at the lower rungs of burlesque.

Thus far, Sennett's own story. In Gene Fowler's *Father Goose*, the story of Coolidge and Dressler is omitted entirely, and Iron Mike simply chucks in his job at the ironworks one day, informs Pa Sinnott he's changing his name to Mack Sennett to avoid a repetition of the old S'nott jibes and leaves directly from East Berlin for New York in the year 1906. This chronology is clearly specious.

The transformation of Sinnott into Sennett is the key to appreciating the sixty-four-thousand-dollar question arising from our story: how did the gauche Canadian immigrant lad, whose sole ambition appeared to be to sing grand opera, mutate into the manipulating, all-powerful Hollywood boss, the archetypal movie mogul, the

'Father Goose' of his menagerie of mavericks, the ruthless business-man, the master of all he surveyed? How do we get from *A* to *B*?

As with so many showbiz personalities, we are in the presence of a prodigious mythmaker, a man intent on reinventing his past and, not to mince words, a shameless liar. Mack's reinventions kicked in at an early date, as emphasized in his story, published in the *Mack Sennett Weekly* in 1917, of the creation of the Keystone company, a tale we shall come to in due course, which was taken up and repeated in press accounts *ad nauseam* until recent times. The fantasies and tall tales were then exacerbated by the central theme of Sennett's person-al life as it unfolded, a theme which became codified in the annals and then recycled, in our own time, in the shape of a Broadway musical, *Mack and Mabel* – the love song of Mack Sennett and Mabel Normand.

The earliest Marx brother, Karl, coined a useful phrase: all that is solid melts into air. And Hollywood, the dream factory, embodies the sense that we live in a moral and mental environment that pits empir-ical observations about what is, was, and became against specula-tion, delusions and lies. As in politics, so in show business: it is not easy to unpick fact from fiction. Autobiographical and personal accounts are unreliable, oral histories and recollections of witnesses are often unsound, even archives can sometimes be suspect. But, in the absence of archives, we are indeed on shifting sands.

Iron Mike and Marie Dressler inhabited two different worlds. Miss Dressler was indeed at that time a highly regarded actress, who had succeeded on the stage despite the evident drawback of her physique, her large frame and a far from pretty face – as she described herself, 'an ugly duckling'. Born Leila Marie Koerbe in Cobourg, Ontario, she left home at the age of fourteen to join a stock company and later sang with the Starr Opera Company. Although she got no nearer to grand opera than Mike Sinnott, she was fêted on Broadway for a string of bravura performances that made her nationally famous. The play that would initiate her into the movies, *Tillie's Nightmare*, was not to come till much later. But Marie Dressler was the first of the stage stars with whom young Sennett touched base in his early years – if indeed the tale were true – and who later ended up working for him.

This became such a theme of Sennett's tales that we might suspect he added the primary link with Miss Dressler to his myth for this pur-pose alone. On the other hand, he did seem to be making an effort with Cameron Shipp, in *King of Comedy*, to offer some factual nuggets out of the dross. The whole tendency and tone of Gene Fowler's earlier account, *Father Goose*, is to present Iron Mike as evolving his theatrical life out of the standard school of hard knocks, describing his arrival in New York City in suitably intrepid terms:

Mack Sennett strutted into the West Forty-third street boarding-house of Madam Mamie Oakes, ex-wardrobe mistress of the *Black Crook* company. She saw a very cocky fellow who weighed one hundred and eighty pounds and was almost six feet tall. Her practised eye took in his dark hair, brown eyes and ruddy complexion with the quick appreciation of a woman facing the Indian summer of her libido.

Madam liked him at once. He reminded her of John L. Sullivan, the pugilistic champion, whose savage nature she had charmed with sentimental ditties played on the zither. This had been a long time ago and before her knight had embraced the canvas at New Orleans.

Fowler was a great admirer and friend of prize-fighters, and Mack would be flattered to be compared to these tough working-class heroes. Getting your first break in show business from a dame, and a homely looking one at that, however famous, was in conflict with this image. The introduction via Calvin Coolidge might have sounded equally wimpish – surely the tough boy would have had stronger nerves? The real story emerging from this might be a symptom of Michael Sinnott's most awkward character trait – his persistent and frustrating shyness.

He was certainly a strong lad, and a large man, as photographs and his appearances in movies show clearly. His self-presentation as physically clumsy, with 'arms like an orangutan', is misleading, since we can gauge his movements as a film actor by watching his development in the early Biograph films. But he could be ponderous, as well as mercurial, as he told of himself, in *King of Comedy*:

Charles Chaplin, when he was young and shy and working for me at Keystone, said, 'Mr. Sennett, do you think it will rain this afternoon?'
Three hours later I sent him a message.
'Looks like rain,' I said.
The story is true. I like to think things over.

Unlike Demosthenes, Mack Sennett did not put stones in his mouth to force himself to speak clearly. But he did endure a long, testing odyssey on his path to self-assertion.

Treatment: EXPRESS AGENT'S DAUGHTER (working title)
6 May 1915
Released as A VERSATILE VILLAIN, 20 May 1915,
with Charles (Charley Chase) Parrott, Harry Bernard &
Louise Fazenda

Open with Bernard and Parrott, Parrott swatting flies. Bernard
sends Parrott to books and exits into outer office. Parrott
gets idea, goes to phone and calls. Louise at home answers,
registers lunch and exits. Bernard in outer office is trying
to lift barrel, calls, Parrott hears and enters to help him.
Bernard exits to platform. Parrott sees chicken fly up in
window, having been scared off next by small boy. Parrott
calls small boy in, has biz with eggs, sleight of hand, throws
egg at door, another hits Bernard on platform . . . Bernard
enters outer office, sees kid, blames him and kicks kid out.
Train now arrives, Bernard exits to platform. The constable
strolls in and on to inner office, shows Parrott doing tricks,
calls his attention to desperado circular and hangs it up.
Parrott takes his watch, they have comedy biz. Outside Bernard
gets money package, signs for it and is watched from
another set by villain. Bernard goes in, puts money in safe,
sees constable and Parrott biz with his watch. Villain enters,
takes Bernard's watch and slips constable's watch in Parrott's
pocket. Bernard misses watch, accuses Parrott, they search
him, find watch, and accuse him of taking it. In the meantime
the villain has left.

Pick up Louise who is on her way to father with lunch and
has become caught on rock. She cries for help and villain
hears and comes to her rescue. Flash two or three times from
Louise and villain and back to Parrott and constable still
accusing him. Back to Louise, sees villain with father's
watch, she biffs him and exit, villain following . . .

. . . Villain shoots at Parrott again, Parrott exits.
Constable in shrubbery set hears shots and waits. Parrott
dashes by, constable tries to grab him, misses and starts
chase. Louise comes on meeting place, villain grabs her and
drags her off . . . Villain has dragged Louise to corrall set
where both mount the same horse and exit. Constable, Parrott
and Bernard enter meeting place, have biz and all exit. They
arrive at corrall set, Parrott and Bernard get on horses,
Constable exits to cowpuncher set, gets several cowpunchers
and exits. Villain and Louise arrive at exterior of house,

dismount, enter house, villain throws her into chair. He shows her the money in the coat, she tries to get it, he throws her back again and ties her in chair. Parrott and Bernard arrive at exterior house, villain sees, bars door . . . Constable and posse arrive and try to get in door. Parrott climbs to roof of house and into trap door. In loft he finds a rope, sees Louise, drops rope down, pulls her up, she knocking a candle over on a fuse connected to a can of powder . . . Villain and Parrott have biz about powder . . . Follow powder thru small window into house. Villain grabs bucket of water and throws at bomb, misses. Outside flash of constable, Bernard and Louise, look off sharply, as house blows up. Insert of villain in sky coming up into picture, umbrella opens, biz of him coming down. Flash of crowd pointing up. Have villain fall in their midst. Ad lib biz over coat, money with Bernard and Constable and money. Parrott and girl in embrace.

# CHAPTER THREE

# Ad Lib Comedy Biz

It was Mack Sennett's fond memory that his first role on the stage was as the hind legs of a horse. A young colleague named as Stu Krauss had snapped up the role at the front. This was, according to Sennett, at the Bowery Theatre, venue of the great star of burlesque, Little Egypt, America's first belly dancer. The fair lady's scantily clad bumps and grinds led, Sennett related, to a police raid, and his first recorded encounter with the kops he was to later lampoon so mercilessly. The judge, hearing his somewhat confused history, advised him to return to the ironworks.

His next job, proposed by a fellow boarder, a sword-swallower, was as a singer in the choir at the Fifth Avenue Baptist Church, frequented, it was said, by John D. Rockefeller himself, though Sennett confessed he never set eyes on the mogul. He resumed his singing lessons, with one Professor Waldemar, who had a studio at Carnegie Hall. But he quit after learning that one of the professor's star pupils, whose family had already spent fifty thousand dollars on his musical education, was currently exercising his larynx at a café uptown for thirty-five dollars a week.

The fond stories proliferate, but hard facts do not. The truth is that, as young Michael Sinnott reaches New York, we lose him in the city fog. In scholarly terms, we have no verifiable information about the entire period Mack Sennett spent on the stage. This period, lasting most probably from 1902 until the beginning of 1908, stretches from age twenty-two to twenty-eight, normally the most formative years of any person's life. We are forced to fall back on the dubious chronologies and tales of Sennett's *King of Comedy*.

Little Egypt was real enough, aka Fahrida Mahzar Spyropolos, supposedly of Armenian origin, though not, one might assume, with that name. She was hardly likely to have been hauled before the judge in 1902, as she had been bumping and grinding for American

The twentieth century arrives . . .

audiences since the Chicago World's Fair in 1893. She did, however, have legions of imitators, and Michael might have got entangled with one of those.

Burlesque was very much its own world, with its separate circuits, stars and theatres. The Bowery theatres, which had flourished since the 1870s, had spawned Weber and Fields, W. C. Fields himself, the Yiddish comic Joe Welch and a host of burlesque queens, ladies of ample flesh, and muscle, who were even showcased on playing cards. Audiences expected the rough and tumble, and the cops were there, with their truncheons, not to censor the acts, but to prevent over-enthusiastic gentlemen, emboldened by beer, from rushing on to the stage. The opening chorus introduced the girls, high-kicking their powerful limbs and warbling, and after that it was a case of anything goes: wrestlers, jugglers, knife-throwers, contortionists, lantern-slide singers and the ubiquitous ethnic acts which were variety's meat and potatoes.

In his own account of these days, Sennett mentioned touring with 'Frank Sheridan's burlesque show' around the East Coast and as far inland as Chicago. This particular claim is hard to pin down. There was a Frank B. Sheridan who had been a staple of the burlesque 'wheels' since 1882, in a host of combinations, notably with one Joe Flynn, in 'Irish comedy'. But the more likely candidate is the veteran character actor, Frank Sheridan (chronology suggests that this was a different person, possibly an offspring of Frank B.), who was a staple of Broadway shows from the turn of the century, reviewed by Percy Hammond of the *Chicago Tribune* as 'eminent in the delineation of brusque, virile, oof oof roles, worthy or otherwise'. Described in 1903 as 'actor and plunger', which suggests an acrobatic past, and 'possessed of the attributes of the average physical giant', an early photograph of Mr Sheridan shows him in typical Irish wide-boy garb of waistcoat, derby hat and teeth-clenched cigar, a probable role model for the young man from Northampton, who would later be seen in a very similar 'hard-man' pose. Apart from his roles in such plays as *Mills of the Gods*, *The Jungle* and *Wildfire*, alongside Lillian Russell, Frank Sheridan also had his own company, and it is this group that Sennett may well be alluding to, in the tale of his tours. Another act mentioned by Sennett is The Cloverdale Boys, a 'close harmony quartet' which played 'weddings in Brooklyn, funerals in the Bronx, Irish wakes all over town, and innumerable birthday celebrations. We charged higher for funerals. We would have sung at banquets for nothing.'

But, assuming we can take Sennett's word for it, and following the trail of the play titles he consistently provided as his sources of employment in this period, we can feel his frustration at being trapped by his roles in the male choruses of major Broadway shows. These choruses were uncredited, low paid and uncreative, reducing their members, men as well as women, to figures in the crowd, clothes-horses for the various *outré* costumes and funny hats thought up by Broadway's costumiers. On the other hand, given that this was his meal ticket for about five years, we can also safely assume that Mack's singing voice was at a professional level, rather than the 'mooing on lonely roads in Canada' that he professed as his standard.

His first employ, according to *King of Comedy*, was the musical comedy *King Dodo*, starring the veteran Raymond Hitchcock. A star since 1893, Hitchcock had excelled in eccentric and exotic roles, such as Fanfani Pasha in *A Trip to Africa* and Abajah Booze in *The Yankee Consul*. King Dodo presided over an imaginary kingdom, an ageing monarch searching for an elixir of life, which he finally finds in Spoopju Land. This was a far cry from East Berlin, Connecticut. Sennett claimed he was rapidly fired by Hitchcock, who quoth, as the young man clattered along the stage: 'Kindly remove this bumbler . . . The man is murderous and all theatrical life is in peril.' As he exited, Sennett claims he muttered to Hitchcock: 'The day will come when you will be working for me.' Which indeed would come to pass, in the fullness of time, though we might doubt our hero's prescience.

As *King Dodo* opened on 12 May 1902, we have a tentative date for Sennett's first named engagement. The second musical play Sennett named, *A Chinese Honeymoon*, might provide us his first review, as *The New York Dramatic Mirror* on 14 June 1902 stated that 'there was a very large chorus, not long on good looks, but costumed most tastefully . . . All the costumes are rich and colorful, and have been selected with a keen eye to color effect.' Was Mack mauve or yellow? History does not relate.

Sennett wrote that Fred Mace, another Keystoner-to-be, was a fellow singer in the chorus. Mace, in fact, was to be a keystone of Keystone, an ally and equal of Mack when he was planning his move from the American Biograph Company to form his own movie brand in 1912. If it is true that Mace was in the chorus of *A Chinese Honeymoon* in 1902, his subsequent rise was spectacular, as in 1904 he was already playing the lead role of Samuel Pineapple in the same show. This may well have encouraged Sennett to stick with show business, rather than return to the pulp mill in Massachusetts.

Fred Mace's background to a show-business career was as odd, in its own peculiar way, as Sennett's, since he had trained as a dentist, receiving his degree from the Jefferson Medical School of the University of Pennsylvania in 1898. He practised for two years in Erie, Pa., and then suddenly left town, the victim, he claimed, of a 'fractured heart'. Mace, by then an established star, told *The Billboard* issue of 18 August 1906:

I had met a manufacturer of a tooth-wash at one of our dental conventions in Philadelphia, and had written him some jingles advertising his tooth-wash, and he had offered me a position any time I wanted it. I went around to see him and he gave me a job at $40 a week. I held this a month or two, and then decided to go on the stage against the violent opposition of my mother, who argued that all the money she had spent to educate me would be thrown away. I said, 'Mother, if I don't get up in three years I'll quit the stage and start over again practising dentistry.' She wouldn't hear to this; but I went ahead, and now she's delighted, and I am still her unmarried boy.'

Mace also appeared in another show with Mack in the chorus, the eponymous *Piff! Paff!! Pouf!!!* The *New York Dramatic Mirror* expatiated about this popular hit, in April 1904:

This musical comedy of the uncommonly silly name is several degrees superior to many of the recent 'shows' of this kind, and is several degrees inferior to anything that warrants the name of art. It is not obscene and is not essentially vulgar. It is merely inane – and of the particular brand of inanity that is greatly relished by the large and liberal-handed class of citizens that considers Broadway at midnight just a shade better than paradise.

*Plus ça change* . . . The plot took almost as long to summarize as the duration of the play, involving such stalwart characters as Lord George Piffle, Macaroni Paffle and Peter Pouffle, played, at the opening, by another stage veteran who was to take the Sennett shilling many moons later, Eddie Foy. Two set pieces, the 'board walk at Atlantic City' and a 'country house on the Hudson', must have provided ample room for the anonymous chorus. The play ran for 264 performances and should have seen Sennett through 1905.

Other shows Sennett mentions are the short-lived *Md.lle Modiste*, of autumn 1906, whose co-actor, singer Fritzi Scheff, turned up to verify their appearance in a *This Is Your Life* programme decades later, in 1954, and another comedy operetta, *Wang!*, whose star, De Wolf Hopper, gave him some singing and acting advice: 'Never give away everything. Keep something in reserve. Try to be more than a mere bass, Mack.'

Was it Mack already? We simply do not know when S'nott was dropped and Sennett picked up. We do know that the name was in place in 1907, the only instance of a published credit for Mack in a Broadway show: *The Boys of Company B*, which opened at the Lyceum theatre on 8 April. This was 'another sweetly sentimental, mid-Victorian play of exuberant youth', with 'bursts of song' enlivening the scenes, a Fifth Avenue mansion and an encampment of the National Guard, to which the protagonists belong. There is 'much soldier-like horseplay', and 'slang and mild profanity interlard the youthful dialogue', which must have been at least a relief from the funny costumes and mock-oriental accents of previous gigs. But here he is at last: 'Servant . . . Mack Sennett', listed fourteenth in the cast.

This was as far as Sennett was to go on Broadway, though he claimed a brief stint in a company with John Barrymore, of which no details are offered. Offstage, life seemed to gravitate between Brady's saloon on Seventh Avenue, between 41st and 42nd Streets, where a stein of beer cost a nickel and free snacks consisted of large slices of cheese, thick ham, corned beef and bread (you can trust an actor's memories of food); the actors' boarding-houses – if not the Fowleresque Madam Mamie's, then similar places; and an apartment rented with three young unnamed friends up on 43rd Street. Both Sennett and Fowler recall, in varied detail, some flimflam involving a pretty hooker named Lucille whom Mack, in a platonic mode, was regaling with tales of Uncle Mike in his room when her pimp challenged him with a razor. A Keystone-type fight ensued: 'He came in more cautiously . . . I ran the gamut, parrying from prime to octave.' Mack held the pimp off with a chair – 'there's a handy tool!' – but was ultimately chased for eight blocks, outrunning his opponent towards the bar. This, Sennett wrote, ended his tenure at 43rd Street, then indeed a tough neighbourhood, the old tenderloin and 'Hell's Kitchen' of New York.

This activity passed the time, if it was short on advancement, but there was another type of entertainment available, for a nickel or, if you could spare it, a dime, if you economized on your steins of beer. Sennett was clearly not ignorant of the new form of mass amusement that was springing up all over town. Long before the Nickelodeons began operating, in the later months of 1905, moving pictures were being shown everywhere, in vaudeville theatres, storefront theatres, hotels and local halls. By 1906, the specialized theatres, showing only moving-picture performances, were becoming all the rage. Thousands of short films were being made and exhibited by a growing number of production companies. Edison and Lubin, Selig and Vitagraph pursued a fierce rivalry. The French company, Pathé, a pioneer of mass production, was aggressively targeting the US market for its moving pictures. And another company, the American Mutoscope and Biograph, founded as early as 1895 in Canastota, New York (as the American Mutoscope Company, changing to its full title in 1897), had already established itself as a major force. In 1903, the company built a brand new studio at 11 East 14th Street in Manhattan, and in 1904 it dedicated itself to producing 'feature fiction' products alone. These would be story films of six to fifteen minutes length approximately, lasting 500 feet to a full 1,000-foot reel. Stories with titles such as *The Chicken Thief*, *The Moonshiner*, *The Lost Child* and *The Gentleman Highwayman*. An amusing comedy, *Personal*, shot at Grant's Tomb, featured a French gentleman named Alphonse who is chased, in succeeding scenes, through the streets, by a mob of women, leaping over a stream, a rail fence and other obstacles. Audiences loved it, and called for more.

By 1907, the Biograph company had gone through a series of ups and downs, financial crises and ongoing conflicts over Edison's claims of patent rights to all movie equipment. There was even talk of liquidation. A new president, Jeremiah J. Kennedy, a civil engineer and ex-railroad builder and industrialist, was brought in to revive the company, with veteran Wallace McCutcheon as chief director. The company was taking on new actors, at the handsome fee of five dollars a day. Some time in January 1908, a thirty-two-year-old playwright and actor from Kentucky who called himself Lawrence Griffith presented himself at the studio and began to earn his daily bread. And it was here, at East 14th Street, that another hungry actor at about the same time – or just a few weeks later – gravitated in search of a job.

# CHAPTER FOUR

# The State of the Art

On 25 July 1908, the *New York Dramatic Mirror* published, in its 'Moving Picture Field' section, the following column:

### 'MIRROR FILM CRITICISMS'
**They Are Highly Commended by Prominent Moving-Picture Men**

The Mirror's innovation in the manner of handling moving picture news and film criticisms continues to attract wide attention in the moving picture field. The trade papers quite naturally and properly treat moving picture affairs from the commercial side . . . But there is another side to the subject – a side that must be cultivated and improved if motion photography is to occupy a permanent place as an art or a profession, and this side is the artistic, viewed from the position of the exhibition and the public. It has remained for The Mirror alone to recognize this fact, and to conscientiously endeavour to meet the requirements of the case . . .

It was the good fortune of D. W. Griffith and of Mack Sennett that they both entered the picture-making field at the historical time when it was becoming noticed and promoted as an art form. *Variety*, in fact, had been reviewing films, albeit selectively, since early 1907. And the *Mirror* continued to expand its innovative full-scale reviews of movies, commenting, on 8 August 1908:

*The Indian and the Child (Biograph):* The best Indian film we have yet seen was produced last week by the Biograph Company. In many respects it is one of the best handled subjects ever produced by any company. The scenery is superb, the photography perfect, and the acting, especially of the Indian character, is of the highest class. But chiefly the story is original and consistent, and the scenes follow each other consecutively and naturally . . .

Only weeks before, the *Mirror*'s reviews of Biograph films had been much gloomier: 'There is an excellent comedy story in this film, but it is dragged out too long with tedious details' (*At the French*

*Ball*); 'The story is not convincing, nor quite as well handled as we would like to see' (*Tavern Keeper's Daughter*). What had changed?

What the *Mirror* was highlighting, and the general public was hardly aware of at the time, was the primacy of the director, as well as the cameraman, in determining the artistic qualities of a film. The weekly journal, however, could not name the director or camera operator as, in keeping with the general practice of film companies at the time, no credits for crew or actors were provided either onscreen or in publicity handouts. The record tells us today, however, that *The Indian and the Child* (aka *The Redman and the Child*) was Griffith's second film as director for Biograph, and that it was photographed by Arthur Marvin.

Mack Sennett's period at Biograph, which lasted from 1908 to the summer of 1912, has been portrayed in film histories as a footnote to the career of the movies' grand innovator. Sennett himself credited Griffith with teaching him everything he was to know about motion pictures: 'He was my day school, my adult education program, my university.' The main way Sennett learned, he revealed, was in the course of long walks he shared with Griffith from the studio to Griffith's home thirteen blocks uptown, asking questions and listening to the master's thoughts about the art of the screen. Our only other recorded witness of Sennett's time at Biograph is Griffith's wife, Linda, née Arvidson, who published her account of the period, *When the Movies Were Young*, in 1925. Mrs Griffith's descriptions have been faithfully copied since then, to provide the accepted historical record of Mack and David at work and play.

Curiously, Mrs Griffith thought that Sennett had been a trainer for lightweight boxers before his chorus career, a tale Mack did not even try to foist on Gene Fowler. Mrs Griffith wrote:

One of our regular 'extra' people was Mack Sennett. He quietly dubbed along like the rest, only he grouched. He never approved whole-heartedly of anything we did, nor who did it. There was something wrong about all of us – even Mary Pickford! Said the coming King of Comedy productions: 'I don't see what they're all crazy about her for – I think she's affected.' Florence Lawrence didn't suit him either – 'she talks baby talk.' . . . But beneath all this discontent was the feeling that he wasn't given a fair chance: which, along with a smouldering ambition, was the reason for the grouch.

Clumsy, muscle-bound, unpopular with the extra girls for his constant clowning, tight-fisted with money and definitely no intellectual, this is the image reproduced in many accounts and Griffith biographies. Richard Schickel writes of his 'burly bear-like figure, long gorilla arms . . . a wide, good-natured grin on his face'; 'he struck Griffith as an interesting and photographically useful type and so he gave Sennett small roles on an irregular basis, allowed him to hang around.' Just a comic figure in the Biograph landscape.

The record shows, however, that this is yet another twist in the myth. Film historians Kemp R. Niver and Eileen Bowser, of New York's Museum of Modern Art, have collated and published the single-page Biograph Bulletins which accompanied each company release through the relevant years of 1908–12. Although no one was credited, early work in 1939 and 1940, with the assistance of sixty-seven-year-old Billy Bitzer, identified the actors in the accompanying photographs and verified Griffith's and Sennett's roles in the films. This shows that Griffith and Linda Arvidson appeared as actors in the Biograph 800-foot reel of *Classmates (A Stirring Romance of College Days)*, released on 1 February 1908. As Griffith is known to have appeared in his very first film, *Rescued From the Eagle's Nest*, made for the Edison Company, in January or February 1908 – it would have to be January to fit this scenario – this pins down Griffith's knock on the door at East 14th Street to January, too. The first Biograph film directed by Griffith was *The Adventures of Dollie*, released on 18 or 19 June. The first Biograph film in which Sennett is verified to have appeared, alongside Griffith, is *The Sculptor's Nightmare*, released on 6 May 1908. When Sennett was hired by 'Old Man' McCutcheon, therefore, D. W. Griffith was still just a fellow studio actor.

Let us put ourselves in Mack Sennett's oversize if battered shoes, if we can, and imagine his state of mind as he stepped up to the threshold of 11 East 14th Street to knock hesitantly on the door. He had spent around five years scraping about at the lower end of New York's thespian society, as a jobbing extra, wandering between shows, waiting in crowded booking agents' offices, quaffing steins of beer in tenderloin bars with his fellow extras, 'resting' between sparse engagements, chasing and being chased by various demons, telling tall tales about his past, his dreams about the Metropolitan Opera receding further into make-believe. All the braggadocio about chucking it in because singers make no money should fool no one. He may have written home, as he claimed: 'dear Mom: I am doing fine and making lots of money. I am not exactly a star yet and my name is not up in lights, but that will come soon.' But there would have been many hard moments of contemplation by the scuffed bathroom mirror. The stifling heat of the city in summer and the bitter, badly heated winters could sap anyone's morale. Strong liquor helped you through, and we know from later evidence that Sennett developed a mighty thirst for the sauce. That strong, patient farmer's heritage and Ma's stubborn strain of optimism would have sustained him in the hardest times. It was, perhaps, this adversity itself that bred the powerful urge to overcome and triumph against all odds. This was, after all, the America of opportunity and the city of Horatio Alger, who had captured the imagination a generation earlier with his iconic tale of Ragged Dick, the bootblack hero, who raises himself to a position of respectability and wealth. In the original legend, there was one Micky Maguire, an Irish tough who bullies the hero. The Irish working-class world, poised between exploitation and criminality – always tempered by the option of becoming a cop, or a priest – was another might-have-been for Mike Sinnott. He persevered with the male chorus and the warbling at Irish wakes and weddings, but there came a time when he had to throw in the towel and strike out for something totally new.

And movies were new, for an actor, because, as should be obvious, they were silent. Or rather, wordless, accompanied by the tinkle-tonk of the Nickelodeon piano (wielded, perhaps, at some dive Mack might have entered by the even younger Chico or Harpo Marx?). Many actors, as we shall see, spoke about the difficulty of adjusting from the spoken and sung stage to the world of pantomime gestures. A world befitting, perhaps, the physical comedian, but the dramatic actor? We are used to reading about the problems silent actors had adjusting to the talkies of the late 1920s, but during the long dawn of the cinema, the problem was the other way around. It was this, perhaps, that lay at the root of Sennett's predilection for movie comedy and his abiding belief, which so annoyed Mrs Griffith, that silent melodrama was inherently ludicrous.

At any rate, like so many of his fellow New Yorkers at the lower echelons of working-class society, he frequented these motion-picture parlours, although there is no evidence that he saw this world as his future. The unsophisticated prancing and gesticulating of the moving-picture actors in pre-1907 productions cannot have impressed him too much. Though the amount of nickels and dimes handed over at the box office by the increasing audiences, swollen by the hundreds of thousands of new immigrants for whom freedom from a specific language constituted the movies' prime attraction, might well have given him food for thought.

There was one movie company, however, whose slick, craftsmanlike approach to telling film stories was evident, even over the Edison, Biograph or Vitagraph films. This company was Pathé, the French upstarts, who had branched out from local distribution to mass bookings in the US. The 'Red Rooster' films, as they were known, after the distinctive mascot, were almost dominating American movie theatres by 1906. Pathé were pioneers in a factory style of production, with three studios in the Paris region, organized in 'director units'. Exhibitors and audiences alike praised Pathé films' technical superiority, their high-quality 'flickerless images'. By late 1907, the domination of Pathé became a serious national issue among American producers, with the Edison company in particular feeling that control of the medium was slipping out of its grasp. Rivalry with Pathé fuelled the American companies' own push to produce more, and better, films.

From 1905, Pathé were releasing comedies starring a minor comic star of the French music-halls, Max Linder. In his early films he was, like everyone else, unbilled, and it was not until 1909 that his character was openly called Max. From his earliest films, he had adopted the style of an elegant dandy, the man about town, often with top hat and tails, effervescent and full of tricks. His physical moves were magnificent, his mastery of gags absolute.

Gags, technical trickery and physical action abounded in the Pathé comedies. (Like other companies, they produced dramas and other subjects too, but comedy was their most popular form.) Another French comedy star was the clown André Deed, who began his 'Boireau' series in 1907, playing an idiotic, grotesque youth who causes havoc wherever he goes. Things fall apart, the centre cannot hold, and the contents of shops, kitchens and building sites tumble about in chaos. Historian David Robinson reports that there is even a custard pie hurled in an early Deed film. Was Sennett watching in the front seats?

Sennett admitted candidly in *King of Comedy*: 'It was those Frenchmen who invented slapstick and I imitated them. I never went as far as they did, because give a Frenchman a chance to be funny and he will go the limit – you know what I mean. But I stole my first ideas from the Pathés.' What he meant by the French penchant for 'the limit' was a tendency – which gave American puritans a chance to lambaste the 'Red Rooster' – to un-American activities like hysterical gestures, pathological itching, sneezing, vomiting, general naughtiness and amorality. All of which clearly impressed Sennett greatly in the matinées, deeply embedding the seeds of future mayhem. One Pathé film, released on 11 July 1908, practically concurrent with Griffith's first directed Biograph, was entitled *Contagious, Nervous Twitching* – 'This film appears frivolous in describing it,' quoth the *Dramatic Mirror*,

yet it is productive of much laughter on account of the excellent acting. A young man is afflicted with nervous twitching that proves to be contagious. Wherever he goes, his sudden fits of twitching and squirming force everybody else to do likewise. The episodes that follow are lively and novel.

It must surely be a Max Linder picture. This kind of thing has induced a recent researcher, Rae Beth Gordon, to publish a book eccentrically titled *Why the French Love Jerry Lewis*, an analysis of the early obssession in French theatre, cabaret and silent cinema with uncontrolled bodily functions induced by hysteria and hypnotism, linking up with concurrent medical theories about psychology and the unconscious. We shall return to this intriguing linkage later, when Keystone unleashes its own hysterics.

One Pathé film which Sennett must have viewed – at the risk of inducing my own wishful thinking – is a 1907 short attributed to Ferdinand Zecca, entitled *The Policemen's Little Run*. In the opening shot, a dog runs into a butcher's shop and steals a pork chop. Two cops rush up and chase the dog, joined by a host of other cops. Flailing truncheons, they pursue the dog down cobbled streets, across tram lines, in and out of a cellar, up and down the side of a building to the roof (a trick set obviously laid flat on the studio floor), through a sleeping man's bedroom, into the dog's kennel, from which the dog emerges to chase them back, down the streets, over a rail fence, up a lamppost, across the town square and back into their own station.

End shot: close-up of the dog, wearing a policeman's kepi, happily gnawing the chop.

So now we know: The Keystone Kops, the bumbling representatives of idiotic, inefficient authority, are, after all, French. Perhaps Mack, né Michael Sinnott, had a special affinity, from his Quebec background, with this kind of Gallic humour. In any case, it was highly popular with the working-class audiences of America. Comic policemen had, after all, been a staple of vaudeville for generations, if in a less spectacular form. The forces of commerce and probity eventually beat back the Pathé challenge, assimilating the company, so that it set up a US affiliate studio in 1910 to produce westerns and other suitably American themes. But its original spirit returned, soon enough, from an unexpected direction, to confound the puritans with renewed force.

# CHAPTER FIVE

# Beyond the Curtain Pole

One of the first extant films in which we can glimpse Mack Sennett is *Balked at the Altar*, of 25 August 1908. This is a country rube tale of an old maid whose crotchety father forces a hesitant suitor to a shotgun wedding, only to have the husband-to-be run off in an unenthralling countryside chase. He is brought back, but the old maid balks in return. Sennett appears in the background as one of the country loiterers, waving those 'gorilla-like' arms in a demonstration of 'what the hell am I doing here?' acting. In the 1 September movie, *Betrayed by a Handprint*, we can catch the briefest glimpse of him as a butler. A few weeks on, however, he is actually in the lead, in *Father Gets Into the Game* (released 10 October), playing an elderly pater, jealous at his son's philandering, who is convinced to have a makeover, shed his grey locks, put on a neat suit and saunter out into the park to woo the damosels. This is a sprightly Mack, more at ease by now in the cramped set and outdoor frolics – with some tantalizing shots of Central Park in that bygone age of long frocks and dandies with canes. It is already clear that Mack has adopted his comedy acting style from the boulevardier, Max Linder, albeit shorn of the latter's elegant grace.

The frequent appearance of Mack Sennett in these early Griffith films should not be surprising, as the practice at Biograph was for everyone to muck in and take part in most productions, on or off screen. This was a small unit with a high degree of camaraderie: Harry Salter, Charles Inslee, Frank Gebhardt, Florence Lawrence, Linda Arvidson/Griffith, Arthur Johnson, Mabel Stoughton, Dorothy West, Jeannie McPherson, Anita Hendrie and John R. Cumpson played most of the roles, sometimes doubling up in each picture. A twelve-year-old boy named Robert Harron, who was employed by Griffith as a 'gopher' and extra, would later be Griffith's lead actor in many of his major features. Billy Bitzer and Arthur Marvin were the cameramen. Del Henderson, Frank Powell and Christy Cabanne graduated from being Griffith's assistants to later directing some of the films. 'Old Man' McCutcheon and his son remained in the background, along with Henry Marvin, Lee Dougherty and other senior staff.

There was one indoor studio in the building, completely enclosed, unlike studios at other companies which were partly open to daylight. The lighting of these early films is fairly flat and uniform – experiments in more expressive use of lighting would be mainly pioneered by Scandinavian film-makers, from about 1911. Film technology historian Barry Salt reminds us that many things we consider innovations were present earlier than previously assumed. Many of Griffith's apparent inventions, like cross-cutting, can be found in earlier films, though the way Griffith utilized these techniques was what marked his particular genius. Apart from the scenes shot in the studio, there would be exteriors shot in Central Park, or further afield in New Jersey and Connecticut, when country scenes were called for. Griffith's first film as director, *The Adventures of Dollie*, was shot in Connecticut and reprised a common and popular theme of a child kidnapped by gypsies. The racial obtuseness that would disfigure Griffith's later *Birth of a Nation* was a common affliction among white Americans – and Europeans – for a long time to come. *Dollie* did, however, feature the heroine going over a waterfall in a barrel, the first sample of a woman-in-peril gambit that would become a Griffith staple. The film, like all those made at Biograph in 1908, was shot in the standard mode of the day, each scene taken in one shot from a fixed camera position, the actors shown full length, as on a stage.

Mack Sennett watched closely as Griffith developed his skills. Viewing these very early Griffith movies, one is struck by the director's steep learning curve. These films were shot at great speed, at rates of three, then two per week, to keep up with the incessant demand of audiences for new material. When one reads in the *Dramatic Mirror* that Griffith's second film, *The Indian and the Child*, 'was held over two days by special request', one realizes how ephemeral these short films were, projected, in most cases, once or twice, for one day, in any single theatre. New films were needed all the time.

*Romance of a Jewess*, released in October, already displays some of the major themes Griffith would develop throughout his work: A 'pathetic story of East Side life in New York', it features Florence Lawrence as the heroine, whose love for a poor bookstore owner – and gentile – is rejected by her pawnbroker father, who turns her out into the street. The man is killed by a fall off a ladder in his store, and the poor Jewess, now with a little daughter, is reduced to penury. The little girl takes her mother's locket to the pawnshop, where the pawnbroker, recognizing the portrait of his daughter, hurries to a deathbed reconciliation. The film features some fascinating documentary shots of the teeming streets of the Lower East Side. The harshness of convention, the power and pathos of love, and social deprivation are all condensed into one telling reel.

Sennett appears, in a cameo role, at the pawnshop, as a Frenchified performer, down on his luck, with a garish jacket, outrageous moustache and Cyrano de Bergerac nose. He is determined, in this tragic tale, to inject a note of comedy farce. He prances in, offering his hat, cane, jacket, dickey and tie in turn, but the hand pantomime indicates the price is not right yet. Having stripped down to his vest and pants, he turns the watching daughter's head round and proceeds to take off his pants, whereupon the pawnbroker capitulates and pays him enough to go away. Kissing father and daughter's hand in gratitude, he exits the scene, bowing gracefully. He then appears in another role in the film, Man in Bookstore, in a proper suit but with the Cyrano nose still tacked on.

Mack's clowning, noted by Linda Griffith, was becoming something of an obsession. Eventually Sennett, after 'much coaxing to get himself "starred"', as Mrs Griffith wrote in her memoir, convinced the director to give him a chance to air the zany French character in a leading role. The result was *The Curtain Pole* – the very first Mack Sennett comedy. It has been said that the idea and the script for this picture was by cameraman Billy Bitzer, though Sennett claimed he was mulling over his own script ideas by that time. However it came to be, the making of *The Curtain Pole* was an event for the Biograph company, as Linda Griffith described the ambitious set constructed for the shoot at Fort Lee, New Jersey:

Carpenters had been sent over a few days in advance, to erect, in a clearing in the wooded part of Fort Lee, stalls for fruits, vegetables and other foodstuffs. The wreckage of these booths by Mr. Sennett in the guise of M. Dupont was to be the big climax of the picture.

The story called for 'M. Dupont' to visit friends in a country house who are trying to put up a new curtain. Offering to help, Monsieur breaks the pole. No matter, he gestures, I shall go out and get you a new pole. He buys the pole but stops to imbibe with his pals on the way back, and his manœuvres with the long pole and a horse-drawn cab fill the rest of the picture, as Mrs Griffith explains:

I was a market woman giving the green cabbages the thrifty stare, when the cab with the curtain pole sticking out four or five feet either side, entered the market place. M. Dupont, fortified with a couple of absinthe frappes, was trying to manipulate the pole with sufficient abandon to effect the general destruction of the booths. He succeeded very well, for before I had paid for my cabbage something hit me and I was knocked not only flat but considerably out, and left genuinely unconscious in the centre of the stage. While I was satisfied he should have them, I wasn't so keen just then about Mack Sennett's starring ventures.

Nevertheless, Mrs Griffith sniffed, her being knocked cold by his new star did not prevent her husband from starring him again soon, in a less dangerous role, in *The Politician's Love Story*. Mack returned, however, to Monsieur Dupont in a half-reel oddity, *Those Awful Hats*, released at the end of January 1909. This was a promotional piece, presented entirely in one shot, set in a movie theatre, with trick photography showing a film within the film on the screen. Monsieur Dupont appears, in his checkered coat and moustache, protesting wildly about the women who keep blocking the screen with ever larger and more flowery hats. The ladies refuse the gentlemen's desperate pleas for unobscured vision, until a large iron claw emerges from the top of the frame and removes first a hat, then the lady herself, followed by the end title: 'Ladies Will Please Remove Their Hats'. The *Dramatic Mirror*'s review added a little anecdote:

After this picture was exhibited at the Union Square in one of the shows Tuesday there entered the theatre a tall woman with a hat nearly as large as those shown in the picture. As she majestically sailed down the centre aisle the spectators broke into laughter, which increased to an uproar when she sat down in front of a fat German, who moved over to the other side of the theatre in disgust. A lecture on Bermuda had commenced, but it had to be suspended until one of the ushers succeeded in getting the lady to remove the conspicuous hat.

*The Curtain Pole* had been shot in October 1908, but was not released until two weeks after *Those Awful Hats*, when Monsieur Dupont was already a familiar figure. Nevertheless, it was his swan song, so perhaps Griffith had not forgiven the cod Frenchman for knocking his wife cold with that pole after all. Sennett continued to appear in various standard roles in Griffith's Biograph films with the rest of the ensemble, including *The Vaquero's Vow*, *The Salvation Army Lass*, *Lucky Jim*, *The Violin Maker of Cremona*, *A Convict's Sacrifice* (as a prison guard, together with another actor who was to become a Griffith staple and major early star, Henry B. Walthall), and many more.

*The Lonely Villa*, 1909 – Mary Pickford top girl, left

In April 1909, Sennett managed to sell a script to Griffith, or a synopsis, which Griffith filmed as *The Lonely Villa*. This short film has become renowned in film history as the first to feature, full-blown, Griffith's innovative use of the technique of cross-cutting. Since the script has not survived, we cannot know if the idea of cutting between the family besieged by burglars in their own home and the friends rushing to their rescue was in Sennett's original text.

Cross-cutting – moving back and forth between scenes in different places – had been done before, by Griffith and others, but not with the same boldness and dynamism. To an audience used to seeing the action develop consecutively, scene after scene, it must have been a disorienting experience. As the scenes alternate, faster and faster, the cinema is decisively adopting a grammar that distinguishes it clearly from the stage. The penultimate moment, as the family hold a door shut to stop the invaders, would be repeated to powerful effect in a similar scene in *Birth of a Nation*.

It is easy in hindsight to see the product of genius, as the building blocks of an art form are put in place. At the time, it was just another short movie, and the actors and actresses who worked with Griffith simply took it in their stride. For Mack Sennett, probably piqued that Griffith showed no further interest in his ideas for zany characters, the coming two years were a preparation for something uncertain, a vision that was still extremely vague. Griffith increasingly focused on stories with a high moral purpose, refining his ideas of melodrama. Those social realities which Monsieur Dupont so wished to gallop through with his curtain pole were becoming Griffith's favoured subjects. Nevertheless, Griffith continued shooting stories of all kinds: period costume tales, comedies, thrillers. The demand for Biograph movies was growing, and Griffith could not direct them all. Comedies were his least favourite genre. Even *The Curtain Pole* reveals that, although the acting is manic, there is no great comic imagination in the individual scenes. Once mayhem is unleashed, the camera simply follows it, almost by rote. Clever experiments in cutting, composition and dramatic acting are of little use to comedy, which favours character, situation, gags and plot. Griffith had no interest in gags, but Sennett did.

And so, in the early spring of 1911, Mack Sennett became the director of American Biograph's comedy films.

*From the Mack Sennett Archives:*

Synopsis: MARRYING MONEY
Produced by Keystone, 26 May 1914
Released as FATTY AND THE HEIRESS (13 June 1914)

Story opens with the comedian and girl on a park bench in love
scene. Old maid passes, she nods, comedian and girl register
amusement at the giddy old girl; As she passes, she is tearing
a letter to pieces — the comedian gathers in one of the
largest fragments and reads thereon the information from her
lawyers that she has just 'fallen heir to a fortune of
$50,000.' As money is the first thought with him, he loses
immediate interest in his pretty companion, and goes over to
an adjoining bench where the old maid has seated herself, and
proceeds to successfully make love to her. (HIS WEDDING DAY)

He marries the old maid with an elaborate wedding — and just
as they have been pronounced man and wife, her lawyer appears
upon the scene, and announces that 'He begs to announce that
in case of her marriage, the money reverts to her niece,' the
former pretty sweetheart of the bridegroom, which strikes
constrination (sic) to his heart, as he is now bound hand and
foot to the old maid.

He now attempts to renew his attention to the pretty girl,
but his wife angrily drags him away and claims him as her own.
He creates a violent scene, shocks the guests, who leave the
house in disgust. Left alone, the quarrel continues and he
finally leaves the house in a rage.

He now conceives the idea of poisoning his wife, that he may
marry the girl with the money, and sets out to the drug store
and blandly asks for some arsenic. The druggist, who was a
member of the wedding party, and remembering the quarrel,
substitutes powdered sugar for the arsenic . . .

(and so forth . . . )

# CHAPTER SIX

# A Dash Through the Clouds
## (or *Mack and Mabel, Episode One*)

Much has been written about the impact and meaning of the thousands of short films produced by various companies in the twentieth century's first decade. From its earliest beginnings as a curiosity at the bottom of vaudeville bills in 1896, movie-making had developed by leaps and bounds to become an industry that, by 1909, was worth forty million dollars, with forty-five million people watching the movies every week. Historians of 'modernity' have descended on the phenomenon, examining the new century's urban obsession with rapid movement, hyper-stimulation and the contradictory fear of, and demand for, constant change. We have seen how the commercial realities of the movies required a continual turnover, the persistent call for new stories. But what kind of stories?

In the late 1890s, American newspapers and magazines were full of sensational tales about the perils of modern life: newfangled trolley cars were running amok in the cities, crushing innocent pedestrians under their wheels; 'the slaughter still goes on. What will Brooklyn do about it?' cried the Brooklyn *Standard* in 1896. In a cartoon entitled 'Broadway – Past and Present', *Life* magazine contrasted the sixteenth century – a noble Indian with pipe and child, in a wooded glade – against the twentieth century – a terrified woman and child running for their lives from the onrushing cable car. 'Moving Pictures – Open Sunday' says a billboard behind the car.

It was no accident that Griffith, his technical prowess aside, was best placed to portray the fear of modernity that troubled the same audiences that demanded its products. He was the contradiction personified: a man of nineteenth-century morals who was mastering the techniques of the twentieth. These techniques included not only his understanding of the movie camera and the editing bench, but also, as time went by, of the publicity and 'hype' which fuelled commerce in the new age. So many of Griffith's stories played on urban anxieties: the degradation of city life in *Romance of a Jewess*; the perils of crime in *Money Mad* and *The Cord of Life*; unbridled capitalism's greed in *A Corner in Wheat*; the evils of booze in *The Drunkard's Reformation*. On the other hand, Griffith sought rural idylls to film more nostalgic tales like his series of Red Indian dramas: *The Mended Lute*, *The Indian Runner's Romance* and *The Redman's View*. These were shot in a new location, in Cuddebackville, up in the Orange Mountains of New York State. This was also the location for *Pippa Passes*, a breakthrough film involving expressive lighting, based on a poem by Robert Browning. (It was supposed to star Mary Pickford, who had played a small role in *The Lonely Villa*, but instead featured Gertrude Robinson.) Another film shot in Cuddebackville, *In Old Kentucky*, prefigures *Birth of a Nation* with its Civil War tale, including a homecoming scene featuring Henry Walthall, star of the later movie. Exile from a rural paradise, the dream of a future return: these themes struck a chord among many first-generation urbanites who recalled slower, quieter days.

But where Griffith was becoming the Great Idealizer, the knight errant in quest of an old morality in the new world, Mack Sennett was becoming a kind of antidote, a sceptical voice in the embrace of old values, a Sancho Panza to Griffith's Quixote. In pursuit of this, he was also exhibiting a steep learning curve of his own, both as actor and movie director.

Sennett's first directing assignment for Biograph was *Comrades*, starring himself and Del Henderson, a new recruit and fellow Canadian, born in Ontario in 1883. Henderson was a bluff, large man whose career later embraced roles in comedy talkies with Laurel and Hardy and W. C. Fields. '"Comrades, comrades, ever since we were boys; sharing each other's sorrows, sharing each other's joys",' quotes the burbling Biograph bulletin for the movie. '[W]hat beautiful sentiment is expressed by the lines of this old song, but like many expressions of the poets, real life gives it a sad jolt.' In this relationship, in which Mack is the patsy to the more mischievous 'Jack', Sennett breaks away from Griffith's sentimentalism, as the two wandering friends, with a Laurel-and-Hardy type set-up, compete for short-lived advantage, such as 'Jack' impersonating a member of parliament, enjoying the good life while leaving Mack in the cold. Mack inaugurated in this film the good-natured but somewhat dim layabout that he would reprise quite often, with Mabel Normand as his ideal.

Mack Sennett (second left) in *The Italian Barber*, 1911

But Mabel, already appearing in Griffith's movies, was not yet a staple of Sennett's crew. In *The Manicure Lady*, released in May 1911, Sennett appears as a barber, with Vivian Prescott as the manicurist he loves but who flirts with everyone else, until he goes into action to win her. The role was something of a reprise of *The Italian Barber*, made by Griffith some months earlier. This is a very different Mack from the manic Monsieur Dupont. His acting is restrained and unmannered, as he reins in his passion for the girl until she drives off with her new boyfriend and he leaps aboard the spare tyre, plunging through the back window of the car into the seat and ejecting the boyfriend into the road. This is a manœuvre we shall become familiar with at Keystone, perhaps Mack's first brush with a runaway automobile . . .

The summer of 1911 marked the arrival of another new Biograph recruit, an old friend, stage comic and ex-dentist Fred Mace. Mace had been alternating his shrinking Broadway appearances with visits to the London stage, having spent a year in England from late 1907 (which might explain why he was not around to help his pal Mack out in New York). *The Toledo Blade* of 21 November 1908 captured his wisecracking reminiscences of the bizarre English: 'London's a strange place . . . I was going into a tea shop on the Strand when I saw the notice "Lyons Brand here". Well, you know the Strand isn't the place for wild animals, so I went inside and had a cup of tea. I told the girl I wanted a spoon. She said, "All right, I'll come and sit with you when the shop's empty." That girl will get on . . .' Mace returned to England for a brief while in 1910, but neither there nor back in the US was the stage offering him much of a break. 'I felt that I was filling the wrong cavity,' he told *Motion Picture Magazine* in 1913.

A March 1912 Biograph release, *A Spanish Dilemma*, twinned Mack and Fred Mace in a comedy farce about two young Spanish firebrands who love the same *señorita*. The *señorita* was played by Mabel Normand.

'The most important thing in my life', wrote Sennett in *King of Comedy*, 'was a girl.' And therein lies the tale, which became a lifetime pursuit, then a legend, and eventually a not very successful Broadway musical which tried to capture this saga of 'the days when movies were young'. 'Mack and Mabel' are the centrepiece of the Sennett myth – the love affair of the mogul and the star, two mercurial people who would not give way to each other, a salutary tale for those who worship or envy success, and a window into the scandals, murders and other murky affairs that blighted Hollywood a decade and more later.

Mabel Normand's early life was for long shrouded in even greater confusion than Sennett's. Sennett at least told the truth about his place of birth. Mabel could not quite settle even on that. She told the *New York Evening World* in 1918:

The wind blew me into pictures . . . It was when I came to New York from Atlanta, where I was born, to try and earn my living as an artist. They didn't approve of that at home, and when I determined to have a career, even if it had to be hammered out by myself, all I had to begin on was a small income inherited from an uncle enriched by oriental trade . . . I longed to paint stormy sea scenes of big sailing vessels battling with the waves . . .

But at other times she would claim Boston, or New York City, as her birthplace. Mack Sennett himself was convinced Mabel had been born in Providence, Rhode Island, though he could find no evidence, when he searched, of birth or baptism. Mabel's 1980s biographer, Betty Harper Fussell, found herself following a labyrinth of convoluted leads on her way to establishing some basic facts. Our own genealogist, Dave Rothman, has followed Mabel's trail way back to eighteenth-century Quebec, which makes her a compatriot, by lineage, of Mack. Her father, Claude Normand, and mother, Mary née Drury, did live in Providence, in poor conditions, but decamped to New Brighton on Staten Island, New York, where their third child, Mabel Ethelreid, was born prematurely, on 9 November 1892. Claude (Glodemir) Normand was a carpenter who had helped build the local music-hall at Sailor's Snug Harbor, and felt the theatre was 'in his blood'. All in all, there was a feeling, on her father's side, of gentility fallen on lean times.

Mabel's upbringing was relatively secure, if not wealthy, but she encouraged tales of early hardship. Hollywood chronicler and prime gossiper Adela Rogers St Johns even wrote about her 'struggles as an orphan, slaving in the hell-holes of the garment factories of New York, attacked by consumption before she was eight', with 'no mother, father, sister, uncles, aunts or cousins'. This was particularly odd, as one unsourced clipping in the New York Public Library's archive includes a vivid memory by Mabel of going to Fall River

to visit an aunt of mine. She lived in one of those old houses – they only have them in New England – where they seldom open the front room, and when you go in you get a curious, old, musty, bygone sort of smell. There were marble-top tables, low horsehair rockers and a horsehair sofa and a glass case with wax flowers and a stuffed dove in it. I hated to sit on the sofa because the horsehair stubs stuck through my stockings. When I scratched my legs they thought I was sick. Oh, I had oodles of aunts around there – all of them wore old fashioned bonnets and queer old velvet and jet things, and I really liked their clothes. They seemed so ladylike; much more so than old ladies' gowns do nowadays. As for the wax flowers, I got into a terrible mess because I always insisted on taking off the glass case and picking them to bits . . .

The above is interesting as evidence of the early sensitivity of the child to her surroundings, her observation – or invention – of detail, either of which stood her in good stead as an actress. She was certainly not short of siblings, although four of Claude and Mary's nine children died in childhood. Our genealogist has uncovered one sombre clue to future events which are still shrouded in mystery: the death aged one year and two months of a previously unmentioned brother, Walter (brother Harold and sister Grace had died before), in July 1898, of oedema of the lungs caused by 'syphilitic laryngitis'.

This meant that the disease, incurable in the medical circumstances of the day, was prenatally present in the parents. We cannot know if and when Mabel was informed of this family secret, nor when and how the condition originated, but reticence about the past and hereditary diseases might have been deeply ingrained.

Proving her physical fitness was certainly an issue for Mabel, as she became a powerful swimmer as a child, and she loved to make up stories, as we have seen. Her memories would often mix fact and fiction, as she told the *Toledo Times*, in 1919:

I don't remember much till I was seven. New York kids have uneventful lives. Anyway, when I was seven they sent me to North Westport, Mass . . . I attended St. Mary's seminary there till I was 13 . . .

I remember how I went way down to the Thalia Theater, on the old Bowery – and hung around there for hours just to see my childhood favorite, who was playing there – Vivian Prescott.

I knew a girl that had a sister . . . who was studying art at the Sargent school in Carnegie hall, and was paying for her tuition by posing for artists. She was earning $1.50 in the forenoon and $1.50 in the afternoon . . . This sounded good to me.

I wandered down to 28th Street, where E. Cole Phillips had a studio . . . I got a job posing at $1.50 a session.

I didn't have a lot of money in those days. We were living at Staten Island. It cost 30 cents to the wharf, five cents on the ferry and five cents uptown to 28th Street; so I had mighty little more to spend. But we used to go, walk up to 57th Street to lunch because it was cheaper there . . .

According to Betty Harper Fussell, Mabel set out at the age of sixteen in a quite routine way 'to seek her fortune'. Some time in 1908, she began to model for illustrator Charles Dana Gibson, becoming a 'Gibson Girl', posing for 'hats, cold cream, hairbrushes, shoes, stockings, combs, hair tonics, veils, gloves, satchels, lingerie, umbrellas, necklaces, frocks, evening wraps, furs, bracelets'. Posing for photographs and vaudeville lantern slides was seen as a somewhat more suspect livelihood, and some blurring of memories might have occurred in this episode. Another archive clipping describes the day, in 1909, that changed her life:

On that particular day I ran into Alice Joyce. She was then working at the Kalem Studios on Twenty-third street . . . She tried to get me to go over to the Biograph, where D. W. Griffith was working at that time. I didn't want to go there at first. I was fairly satisfied with $3 a day for posing, with an occasional $5 or $10 at the Fashion Camera studio. Besides, I wanted to be an illustrator . . . I went over to the Biograph studio. Griffith put me to work at once.

When Mack Sennett first came to me and said, 'How would you like to make $100 a week?' I said, 'Stop making fun of me.' You may believe it or not, but when I got a contract not for $100 but for $125 in my hands, I walked in a daze from Union Square to Times Square and back . . .

But this was to come later. Mabel's first stint with Griffith was short, as the Biograph company left New York in early 1910 to winter in the sun in California, leaving her behind in New York.

Areas around the boom town of Los Angeles were about to become a new home-away-from-home for film companies that wished to give the Edison patent warriors a wide berth and delight in the all-year-round sun. The Selig company's Francis Boggs and Thomas Persons had shot the first movie made in California in 1907, and two former New York film exhibitors, Adam Kessel and Charles Baumann, who had set up the New York Motion Picture Company, had arrived in Los Angeles in 1909, after allegedly having to flee for their lives from armed Edison enforcers during one fracas in New York. They set about converting an abandoned grocery store in the district of Edendale to a motion-picture studio, which began producing movies under the heading of 'Bison'. But Mack Sennett, on his first sight of California, was not aware of its part in his future.

For the moment, the living was easy, and Mack continued acting with the Griffith ensemble. 'I worked in whatever Griffith produced,' he wrote, 'including *Man's Genesis*, which was cave-man stuff and just right for me.' It was in California that Mack's first films as director were made, *The Manicure Lady* being shot in Glendale, just before the return of the Biograph crew to New York later in May 1911.

Mabel, meanwhile, had remained in New York, and then joined the rival Vitagraph Studios, in Flatbush, where she would work with their new comedy lead, John Bunny – who would become the American cinema's first comedy star – and Norma Talmadge, another young lady with a glittering future, who helped her learn the new skills of movie acting.

The lore has it that it was Sennett who convinced Griffith to rehire Mabel Normand for Biograph and cast her in *The Diving Girl*, shot at Coney Island. But Mabel appeared, in the next few months, in films directed both by Griffith and Sennett. She was with the company when they returned to California early in 1912 – her first visit to the West Coast. Her first film there was Griffith's *The Mender of Nets*, a joint appearance with Mary Pickford on the Santa Monica beach. But she soon became a 'steady' with Mack's comedy team.

Mack wrote of Mabel:

Mabel was like – she was like so many things. She was like a French-Irish girl, as gay as a wisp, and she was also Spanish-like and brooding. Mostly she was like a child who walks to the corner on a spring morning and meets Tom Sawyer with a scheme in his pocket . . .

Boys and girls were more innocent in those days than they are now and it was a long time before I even managed to kiss that girl.

For one thing, she never held still and it is difficult to kiss a girl who won't stand still for it . . . Mabel was frisky, as skittery as a waterbug and oh, my Lord, how pretty! She turned any place she was into an uproar and if she couldn't think up better things to do, she would pull the chairs from under fat men . . .

The idea of Mabel as child-woman obsessed Sennett from that point on, perhaps not surprisingly, as when he met her she was just seventeen. Like so many early screen actresses, she was quite small, about five feet tall (Mary Pickford and Gloria Swanson were likewise). But she was apparently not ethereal enough for Griffith, who cast her in 'voluptuous' roles. Sennett cast her as the eternal queen bee, around whom the hive always buzzes. In *Hot Stuff*, she played Mack's sweetheart, who is poached by his pal, Del Henderson. (A cigar-store owner in the film was played by William Beaudine, another Keystoner-to-be who would go on to greater things, directing, among countless titles, W. C. Fields's 1935 movie *The Old Fashioned Way*; he was even directing episodes of *Lassie* for television well into the 1960s!)

In *Oh, Those Eyes!* Mabel played the mischievous enchantress who agrees to marry several of her suitors 'if father agrees', till they all gang up to teach her a lesson. In *Helen's Marriage*, she would like to elope with her boyfriend Tom, but her Pop stands guard with a pistol. Tom sees a film crew shooting a wedding scene, and the two trick Pop into standing by as they fake a movie wedding only to reveal the truth to the fainting *pater*: an opportunity to glimpse Sennett himself, playing the director, with Fred Mace as a fake bride.

These early Sennett shorts reveal Mack learning not only to act, but to manage the craft of movie-making. Given the iconic speed and chaos of Keystone to be, it is interesting to see that his first directing efforts were more subtle, comedies of manners, with emphasis on character and situations, rather than action and gags. *Tomboy Bessie*, casting Mabel in the lead role, as the manic niece of the girl Mack wants to marry, shows Mabel in the full flow of her unstoppable energy, leaping, dancing, riding a bicycle to its destruction and shooting chickens with a catapult. In one scene, Sennett plays her horse, shuffling about as she pulls on his reins. Signals of things to come. The next film, *Katchem Kate*, begins to look like the Keystones we shall come to know, with Mabel as a fed-up laundress who signs up with Fred Mace's Alert Detective School and captures a gang of bearded anarchists before they can explode their bomb.

One can see, in these often faded prints, the nucleus of the force Mabel would muster as the screen's first great comedienne. Mabel, in Sennett's films, often initiates action, and is almost always a character in her own right, whereas Griffith's women, however powerful their performances, never quite escape the fate of being emblematic of the director's moral concerns. In June, Biograph released one of summer 1912's most distinctive Sennetts – *A Dash Through the Clouds*. It opens with the title:

DEMONSTRATING THE TECHNICAL PERFECTION OF THE MODERN
FLYING MACHINE . . . A FAR CRY FROM THE ORIGINAL INVENTION OF
WILBUR AND ORVILLE WRIGHT.

A somewhat startling statement, as the aeroplane featured in the movie, barely nine years after the Wright brothers' revolutionary first flight, looks a thing of shreds and patches, wooden slats and thin metal struts, a most fragile device, on to which Mabel scrambles eagerly, despite the protests of Fred Mace ('Chubby is fond of Josephine, but she is more anxious to be with Slim, the Aviator!'). Mace is a 'tutti frutti salesman' who goes to a neighbouring Mexican town and ogles the Junoesque Carmelita, only to be chased from the hacienda by her irate relatives. There follows probably the first shoot-out in movie history between an aeroplane passenger and Mexican cowboys, a perfect metaphor of the new versus the old. The *New York Dramatic Mirror* noted: 'The close views of the aviator and maid in their flight in mid-air are a notable feature.' And indeed there we have, with ingenious mounting of the plane showing its back rotor spinning, the medium shots of Mabel and her pilot taken from a camera placed on or just above the flying machine's frontal bar. 'Farce comedy', proclaimed the Biograph advertisement, 'of a melodramatic type that has thrill in every foot.'

Mack Sennett had found his forte. All that was required now was the opportunity to break loose from his subordinate status and find a commercial mechanism that could fulfil his own vision of what he would later call 'that Cloud-Cuckoo land of *laissez faire* and turvy-topsy'.

CHAPTER SEVEN

# He Goes Big

'Pioneers are seldom from the nobility. There were no Dukes on
the Mayflower.'

Mack Sennett, *King of Comedy*

On 1 January 1917, Keystone's house journal, *The Mack Sennett
Weekly*, began serializing the story of the creation of Sennett's dream
company, under the heading 'The Rise of the Keystone – An
Interesting Story':

Three men were sitting in a hotel in New York one day about five years ago.
They had decided to start a motion picture company. Not knowing as much
about the picture business as they do now, the fact that they didn't have much
ready money didn't bother them. Luckily they had a few family jewels. If it
hadn't been for a few diamonds that thereafter went with regularity to
'Uncle's' there wouldn't have been any Keystone Film Company today with
its sixteen companies and a plant covering twenty-two acres of ground. One
of the three men was Adam Kessel, Jr., now a well known yachtsman and cap-
italist. Another was Charles O. Baumann, and the third was Mack Sennett.

They were three interesting types. Baumann was an outdoor man, devoted to golf and hunting and a pal of his very charming young lady daughter.
Baumann, to this day, looks more like her brother than her father.

Kessel was a plucky fighter on the outside. At home his hobby was the
baby.

Sennett was a born organizer and actor.

Well, they sat there in the hotel looking for a name for the new company.

'How would Crown Comedy do,' someone suggested dubiously.

'Rotten,' replied the others in a chorus.

'Might call it something or about Vite,' ventured another of the group
timidly.

'Bunk,' chorused the other two.

They relapsed into silence. Just then a railroad train went by. On one of
the cars was the word 'Keystone' in big letters.

Without a word the three stood up and shook hands.

'If it's a good enough word for the Pennsylvania Railroad, it is good enough for us,' they said.

The tale of the creation of Keystone out of a whim and a handshake was an abiding myth that Sennett loved to repeat and embellish. The original story was that Kessel and Baumann were two small-time bookies who were hassling Sennett for a hundred-dollar gambling debt, and Mack weaseled his way out by offering to get them into the movie-making business. As we have seen, this was complete flimflam. Baumann had indeed been a bookmaker many years earlier, and Adam Kessel had once been a streetcar conductor, but they had been in the movie business at least since 1908. When the main picture companies, including Biograph, Vitagraph, Edison and Pathé, signed an agreement to form the Motion Picture Patents Company, which would monopolize the use of motion-picture equipment, companies left out of the deal were in trouble. Patent-company detectives dogged the footsteps of the 'independents', and even the favoured out-of-town locations of New Jersey were too close to escape their attentions. By the end of 1909, Kessel and Baumann's New York Motion Picture Company was operating out of its new California branch situated at Alessandro Street, Edendale, and soon functioning under a number of mastheads, including Kay Bee and Bison. In October 1910, another pioneer, Thomas Ince, joined Bison to make westerns, setting up shop further afield, at Santa Ynez Canyon, later named 'Inceville', and hiring an entire Wild West show, the '101 Ranch Circus', with its fifty genuine Indians, three hundred horses and buffalos.

The patent wars, however, spilled over to the West Coast, along with a host of complicated lawsuits involving Kessel and Baumann and Carl Laemmle's new Universal Company. Another of K & B's companies, Reliance, began recruiting actors from the Biograph Company, which continued to lose its cast and crew over the next two years. Biograph's policy of not crediting its on- or offscreen personnel was more and more irksome to the actors who had become famous by face if not by name: Mary Pickford jumped ship to Universal's Imp company, which proclaimed 'Little Mary is an Imp now'. (She was promptly poached by another company, Harry Aitken's Majestic, then returned briefly to Biograph before signing

Sennett, alias 'Walter Terry'

with Adolph Zukor's Famous Players company in 1912.) Biograph made matters worse by sending out portraits of its stars, but with made-up names, so that Mabel Normand was called Muriel Fortescue and Mack Sennett became Mr Walter Terry. This, too, fuelled their desire to jump ship.

Kessel and Baumann were waiting eagerly to catch them. Initially joined up with Lammle's Universal, which had also subsumed several other brands, they had fallen out with him over custody of the Bison imprint, and were about to lose their foundation stone. Ince was caught up in this imbroglio, which led to a stand-off between his Wild West cowboys and Indians and New York detectives, while the real battle was fought in the courts. Putting aside Sennett's Keystone 'creation myth' (Gene Fowler portrayed it in even more *schlemiel* terms, with the bookie Kessel asking, of a pile of flat round film cans: 'What's that? Herring?'), it may be that Mack's first meeting with K & B occurred much sooner than he claimed, back in Edendale, during one of the Biograph sojourns. But if we accept the New York meeting as the crucial foundation, and follow the wagon trail that shows that the Biograph company left California for New York late in July 1912, and that Sennett directed a little movie called *The Tourist* in Albuquerque, New Mexico, *en route* back east, we can date the famous handshake with Kessel and Baumann to late July or early August. Two later films, directed by Mack for Biograph, *What the Doctor Ordered* and *The Tragedy of a Dress Suit*, both featuring Mabel Normand, the latter definitely shot in New York, were released in August.

The point, beyond pedantry, is to locate the creation of Keystone in its commercial context: In 1912, as we can see from the foregoing flurry of companies, movies were a faster growing business than ever. Audiences couldn't get enough of them. Movie companies were like today's 'dot com' start-ups, with the difference that profits were immediate and tangible. As Sennett wrote: 'Anything on film made money. The only requirement was that it be reasonably new.' Companies like Comet, American, Thanhauser, Lux, Imp, Majestic, Champion, Eclair, Gaumont were all in the ring. In August, while Sennett was setting up shop with Kessel and Baumann, their own New York Motion Picture Company itself was being subsumed by another releasing company, the Mutual Corporation, run by ace wheeler-dealer Harry Aitken. The *New York Dramatic Mirror*

Mack Sennett with Adam Kessel on set

announced on 7 August that Mutual had acquired thirty-one 'exchanges' (or companies), including the Bison and Bison 101 imprints, Broncho and Keystone films. So the name of Keystone was already being traded, perhaps even before Sennett's famous hand-shake. The Mutual Company's films were reviewed by the *Dramatic Mirror* as separate items from the Motion Picture Patents Company's 'Licensed' movies as 'Supply Company Films', such as this early Keystone, puzzled over in the 6 November issue:

At It Again: This picture is poor, with few redeeming features. At no time is the story clearly presented. A young wife receives a letter in which she is told to watch her husband whom she accuses. That much we were able to under-stand. Just what she accuses him of does not appear. She hires two detectives who in various ways disguise themselves and supply the only humor. They finally arrest the chief of police. It is to be presumed that the wife thought the chief of police was her husband, and that she saw him with another woman. A tangle results with this arrest as may be imagined.

Sennett's tale of the first films shot by Keystone is an invention, involving a mythical Russian cameraman named Sergei who couldn't handle the camera at all and cranked its handle too slowly. As a result, the pictures he had taken were speeded up on the screen, and all the actors rushed about helter-skelter. And that's how comedy under-cranking was born. As Gene Fowler imagined it, 'Sergei was in a condescending humor . . . "You Americans are so impatient," said the lancer. "Everywhere I go, I see and hear nothing but 'Speed! Speed! Speed!' In Europe we take things more moderately and live longer."' While poor Mack was tearing his hair . . .

The other tale Sennett loved to tell was how the company first arrived with their camera to find a Shriners' parade marching just outside the train station. Mabel and co. rushed to take part in it, and their high-jinks formed the first Keystone film. This description does fit a Sennett film, but a Biograph one, *The Would Be Shriner* – 'a Comic Incident of the Shrine Parade at Los Angeles', shot previously in the summer. ('Hank Hopkins is a "rube" of the most extreme type, and on the morning of the great Shrine Parade in Los Angeles, he is met by a couple of friends, practical jokers, who make him believe they can effect his participating in the grand pageant. He telephones his wife to be on the grand stand to see him march by. Mrs Hopkins receives a great disappointment, but it is slight to what Hank receives when he attempts to get into line . . .')

Sennett was obviously determined to present the birth of his company as a maverick, pirate enterprise, a triumph of the individual over the forces of corporate enterprise. It was, in fact, a cog in an intricate set of machines, and destined to become a major part of the engine. *The Moving Picture World*, on 12 September 1912, announced that: 'Mack Sennet [*sic*], director, and Mabel Normand, leading woman, of the Keystone Company of the New York Motion Picture Company, arrived in Los Angeles August 28 as the advance guard of a new company which is to be located in the old Bison plant at Edendale . . .' The *New York Dramatic Mirror* put this arrival in context, having reported on 11 September:

Two Western reels, one new dramatic and two sets of split reels each week, is the new programme at the New York Motion Picture Company's plant at Edendale . . . President A. Kessel and Secretary Charles O. Bowman [*sic*] are here with Vice-President Fred J. Balshofer, who also is manager, putting the finishing touches on the plans.

An enlarged plant at Edendale is the result of the visit and the growing activity of the management. Max [*sic*] Sennett, recently comedy director and comedian of the Biograph, together with the clever Mable [*sic*] Normand, of the same company, Ford Sterling, and Henry Leherman [*sic*] all from New York, beat the officers of the company into Los Angeles by two days. The quartette represents the latest capture by the New York Motion Picture Company. Sennett will direct one of the split-reel comedies and Fred Mace the other. The other new reel will be straight drama, without Western flavor, to balance the work of directors Ince and Ford.

In October, however, Universal Pictures won the title to Bison, and half a million dollars' worth of stocks and bonds was ordered by the court to be returned by Kessel and Baumann, leaving Keystone as the most important component of K & B's operations. As no official incorporation documents under the name of Keystone have been found, it was probably, like all the other Bisons and Reliances, just another production masthead under which the two 'bookies" New York Motion Picture Company continued to function.

Thus far the legalities. Fortunately for Mack, Kessel and Baumann, unlike some other company owners, allowed their management team a relatively free creative hand in the making of their movies. As businessmen, they were as shrewd, ruthless, sometimes foolhardy, sometimes commercially suicidal, as any of their breed, as we shall see. They kept their hands firmly on the cash-box, but, following the motto of Sennett's mother, they didn't step on his dream. For the moment . . .

The first Keystone release, dated 23 September 1912, was a split-reel, i.e., two short films put together, the titles being *The Water Nymph*, with Mabel Normand, and *Cohen Collects a Debt*, starring the fourth leg of the quadruped formed by Mack, Mabel and Fred Mace – the equally roguish spirit, Ford Sterling.

Another early title, *Cohen at Coney Island*, released as *At Coney Island* on 28 October, was said to have been put together from footage shot by Fred Balshofer in New York before the company left for the West. This was part of a long running genre of 'funny Jew' films which was soon to fizzle out. The only title of this series by Keystone that survives is *Cohen Saves the Flag*, from 1913, a bizarre combination of Civil War anti-heroics and Ford Sterling's broad ethnic mugging.

*The Water Nymph*, fortunately, also exists, albeit in a form reconstituted many years later, in 1944 (with titles that may have been added at some date in between).

It opens on an idyllic garden scene of Mack wooing Mabel. A title proclaims:

TWO HEARTS SECRETLY PIERCED BY CUPID'S DART.

We are next introduced to Mack's Mama and Papa, the latter played by a Germanic-style Ford Sterling. Title:

MACK'S PAPA – A FAITHFUL HUSBAND WHEN LOCKED IN AT HOME.

Papa suggests imperially:

'LET'S GO TO THE BEACH.'

Mack has an idea to get Papa to like Mabel:

PAPA FEELS YOUNGER TODAY. VAMP HIM AT THE BEACH.

We switch to an area at the old Santa Monica beach where some of Griffith's old California Biographs were shot:

THE BATH-HOUSE, WHERE LADIES DRESS IN STRAITJACKETS, POPULARLY CALLED 'BATHING SUITS'.

A perfect opportunity to show off Mabel's athletic prowess, and lithe body, as she somersaults and backflips off the diving board into the sea, pleasure boats rippling in the background. Title:

OUT OF THE COCOON FLEW THE GRACEFUL MERMAID.

Papa emerges from the changing booths, arms akimbo, posing and posturing. Mabel emerges, joking with the other bathing girls. Later, at the café, he moves in on her, waving a thick wad of dollar bills. Mack saunters up, with Mama, saying to Papa:

'FOLKS, MEET MABEL, MY SWEETHEART.'

A flurry of consternation and embarrassed glares from Papa, a nudge from Mama, and Papa shrugs, as Mack kisses his girl.

THE END.

It was, of course, just the beginning.

# PART TWO

# *His Busy Day*

Starring:
Mack Sennett – A Man of Destiny
with
Full Supporting Cast

Synopsis, 10 January 1914: MABEL'S STRANGE PREDICAMENT
Released 9 February 1914;
Directed by Mack Sennett and Henry 'Pathe' Lehrman
Scenario by Mack Sennett
With Charles Chaplin, Mabel Normand, Chester Conklin,
Alice Davenport, Harry McCoy, Hank Mann, Al St John.

Husband and wife, and Mabel are staying at the same hotel.
Mabel is romping with her pet dog in hotel yard when her sweetheart comes on and talks with her. In next set husband and wife
are sitting. Wife leaves set for moment to get something.
During her absence Mabel's dog's ball rolls into husband's set.
Husband picks it up as Mabel comes on and takes his time in
presenting it to her very politely. Wife returning sees and
doesn't like it. Comes on to husband and Mabel and upbraids
husband. Lover from first set sees and comes on to husband,
wife and Mabel. Recognizes husband as friend and calms the
group down somewhat. Wife now takes husband into hotel and
Mabel bids lover good bye and also goes into building . . .

Mabel has prepared for bed and is in her pajamas. In playing
with her dog again, the ball rolls out into the public hall.
Mabel looks about and seeing no one goes after it. Dog inside
room in trying to follow her jumps against door, the spring
lock catches and Mabel is locked in hall in her pajamas. At
this point drunk comes along and tries to flirt with Mabel. In
a panic she tries the next room's door and enters husband's
room. Latter is standing at mirror and does not observe her.
She hides under bed.

Meanwhile Mabel's lover has taken notion to call and comes
to her room. Finds it locked. Looks through keyhole and sees
Mabel's dog. Passing janitor unlocks door for him and dog
emerges. As Mabel is not at home lover decides to call on
husband next door . . . Meanwhile in hall Mabel's dog has
found her trail and enters and goes to bed wagging tail . . .
Lover and husband notice dog and discover Mabel. Lover starts
to beat husband when the three of them hear wife and manager
coming. Do not want manager to know seeming scandal, so
husband and lover agree to keep quiet. Wife and manager enter.
Wife peeved at lover orders him out. He and manager exit. Wife
and husband alone. Wife calming down and almost reconciled
when she discovers Mabel under her bed in pajamas.

Consternation, etc . . .

# CHAPTER EIGHT

# Consternation, et cetera . . .

The one hundred and forty-odd short movies turned out in the first fifteen months of Keystone's production line were pretty ramshackle affairs. Many of them have not survived for viewing, but those that have exhibit the vigour, and the flaws, of that first flush of an enterprise whose ends often ran ahead of its means. Sennett wrote: 'We did the best we could with what we had. We made funny pictures as fast as we could for money.'

However experienced Kessel and Baumann were as financiers, and however eager the New York banks were to lend money for this new boom business, Sennett faced the obvious problem of setting up his company from scratch. Like the other movie start-ups, this was done by poaching personnel from other companies. From Biograph, Sennett recruited, as his main attractions, Mabel Normand, Fred Mace and Ford Sterling. Supporting actors came from Biograph and elsewhere: Alice Davenport, Dot Farley, Evelyn Quick, Victoria Forde and sufficient extras to fill the crowds on the beach, tailor shops or drawing-rooms constructed at Edendale. The legend had it that the studio 'was used chiefly as a place where actors could report mornings and collect their salaries on Saturdays', all movies being shot in the streets with the actors and crew 'hoofing it', as they couldn't afford motor vehicles. This is, of course, the usual nonsense, as a viewing of the surviving early films can reveal.

What is obvious is a total change of tone from the comedies made for Biograph and the new Keystone output. The comedy of manners is out. Observation of social reality, in any form perceived by 'normal' citizens, is abandoned. Cuteness is banned. Even the tame bear, which appears in a Sennett–Normand film for Biograph of 12 April, being patted and fed by Mabel, is assigned to barging into the Yiddish bath-house in April 1913's *Toplitsky and Company*, a farce–drama of adultery in the tailoring trade. General vulgarity,

*Toplitsky and Company*, 1913

biting of ears and noses in fights, and gags involving alleged body odours are in. In *A Strong Revenge* (probably aka *Schnitz the Tailor*, September 1913 – extant versions often have different titles tacked on in the confusing array of reissues later on down the line), Mack himself plays Schnitz, with Ford Sterling, the cobbler, as his rival, who sticks a piece of ripe cheese in the shoes he wears to the social ball. Much ethnic ribaldry is vented as the rivals, amid extraordinary displays of facial mugging, plant the cheese on each other, to the disgust of Mabel and her respectable family and friends.

In *Toplitsky and Company*, Ford Sterling is flirting with his tubby partner (William Hauber)'s wife, played by buxom Alice Davenport. Much is made of the ample dimensions of her bosom. Ford is chased by the husband, taking refuge in the bath-house (or *bech-hoiz*, as the Yiddish-Hebrew sign declares), with all its other seedy, mumbling patrons, until the bear, which has escaped from its handler, disrupts them, leading to much rushing about and climbing up lampposts. Ford is chased by the bear into his partner's wife's bedroom, and hides under her bed. Hubbie comes in to forgive his wife for doubting her, only to see Ford's bare legs sticking out. Confusion, beating, collapse of bed, fade out.

Fatty Arbuckle as *That Minstrel Man*, 1914

A far cry from Griffith, indeed. These ethnic comedies, appealing to immigrant audiences, are played with a minimum of intertitles, to an audience still unfamiliar with English, if not with jokes on wives, beds and breasts. Other transgressions included black-face comedies, such as *That Darktown Belle*, of April 1913, or *Rastus and the Game Cock* (June 1913). These risible 'coon' comedies had been a staple of movie cut-ups since the very earliest days, the late 1890s. Even Fatty Arbuckle, soon to join Keystone, made at least one of these, *That Minstrel Man* (August 1914), appearing in both boot polish and drag.

The 'Jewish Keystones', and many other early comedies, were directed for Sennett by Henry 'Pathé' Lehrman. Lehrman was Mack's chief recruit in the crew department of the new company, and between them they directed all the Keystone shorts made in the first nine months. Two other Biograph recruits, Wilfred Lucas and George Nichols, would then join the directors' roster, through to the end of 1913. After that, the system became more streamlined, as we shall see.

Lehrman is a peculiar figure in the cast of eccentric personnel that populate the early cinema story. He was said to have acquired his name because he approached Griffith, some time in 1908, claiming to be French and to have had experience of directing films for Pathé in France. In fact, he appears to have been born in Austria, in 1883, and educated at Vienna's Commercial University. He was said to have served as a lieutenant in the Austrian army, stationed in the city of Przemysl, according to a *Los Angeles Times* report of 1 January 1915. He came to New York, in this version, in 1907, speaking not one word of English.

Sennett claimed that Lehrman had been an usher at the Unique Theatre in New York, where Mack, engaging him in conversation, asked him his opinon of the movie then showing –

'It has an odor,' the usher said.

'You don't like it?' I scowled.

'*Mais oui*, the picture is all right, but the leading comedian, *sacre*, he is no good.'

'Do you know who he is?'

'*Certainement, absolument*, I know, *monsieur* – it is you.'

This turns out to have been more flimflam, as Lehrman assures Mack he was just joking and recognized the great Sennett by name – impossible, since Biograph's films bore no credits – but the story gets the two men off to a good mythical start. According to Sennett, they roomed together in the Alexandria Hotel at 210 West 5th Street. They appear to have got on well, despite later evidence that Lehrman would grow up to be the most hated director in the comedy business, becoming embroiled in lawsuits and conflicts involving even companies he himself had founded. He would use Keystone as a stepping stone, setting up his own L-KO (Lehrman Knock-Out Comedies), before moving to Fox to make 'Sunshine Comedies'. He would also play a major role in the murky tale of the Fatty Arbuckle scandal in 1921.

In early Keystone, Lehrman was indispensable, competently directing about half the output, churning the product out week after week. Equally indispensable was Sennett's main actor, Ford Sterling, who appeared in almost every movie until Fatty Arbuckle, and then Charlie Chaplin, came to displace him as comic leads.

Ford Sterling was born on 3 November 1880, in La Crosse, Wisconsin. His first stab at show business was with the Robinson

Circus, as 'Keno, the Boy Clown'. From 1897, he was with small-time vaudeville and burlesque, then played 'legitimate' supporting parts, in stage comedies such as *King Casey*, in which he was praised in 1909 for his part as 'Orphis Noodle, Prime Minister to King Casey . . . Ford Sterling does some clever work in the fantastic German role'. In May 1913, he told the *Denver Times*:

In the spring of 1912, while playing vaudeville in New York, under the name of McEvoy and Sterling, I was introduced to Mr Mack Sennett, who was then with the Biograph company. Mr Sennett prevailed upon me to give up the stage to join the Biograph company and when Mr Sennett went over to the Keystone company I followed with Miss Mabel Normand and Fred Mace.

Sterling's Germanic characterizations made him the perfect choice as the captain of Sennett's most enduring invention of the early Keystone years: the Keystone Kops. The Kops, who were often to feature Ford Sterling in command (or rather in total lack of command), seem to have made their début in *The Bangville Police*, completed in March 1913, a half-reel, six-minute picture. Mabel mistakes the cries of a cow giving birth in a shed for burglars, and calls the police, who tumble out of their rural headquarters in what would become a familiar chaos. The ensuing confusion between policemen, farmhands and Mabel's dad, each thinking the other lot are intruders, culminates in a shot of Mabel desperately holding the door of her room shut against her own gun-toting dad, in a clear spoof of Griffith's maiden-in-peril scene from *The Lonely Villa*, later to be made so much of in *Birth of a Nation*. Recalling the 1907 Pathé policemen, one can see the roots of the oafish coppers idea. The short was directed by Lehrman – raising the possibility that it was Lehrman, not Sennett, who suggested it, thus knocking away the foundations of legend!

The notion of krazy kops clearly did not resonate at that moment with the cry of 'Eureka!' as the studio then returned to its normal ethnic falderal during the following months. (Another short directed by Lehrman just one week previous to *The Bangville Police*, *Murphy's IOU*, featured Mack Sennett as a standard Irish policeman, adding fuel to the speculation of Lehrman as Kop-father.) The next iconic Sennett movie, *Barney Oldfield's Race for Life*, directed by Mack in person, in which Ford Sterling as a moustachioed villain ties Mabel to the railroad tracks as the train advances, in perhaps the

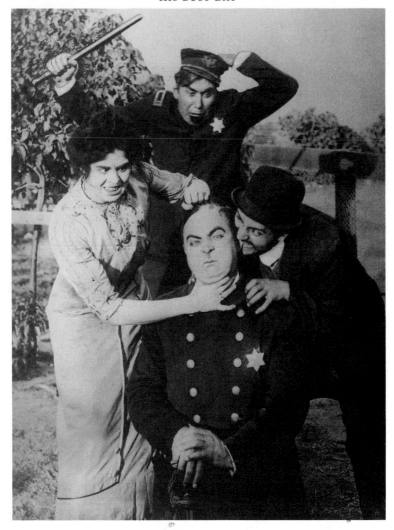

Mack Sennett (top) with Dot Farley and
'Pathé' Lehrman biting Fred Mace

most classic image of early silent comedy, did not feature the Kops at
all, as one might expect in such a tale had they been at the forefront
of Sennett's mind.

Barney Oldfield was a real-life racing driver, known as the 'Speed
King' – he had driven an automobile around a dirt track at a mile a

minute as early as June 1903. He featured in a number of Keystone movies, since car racing, and the crowds at the races, were tailor-made for Keystone's quest for ever-greater thrills and spills. As Barney races the train to save the girl, carrying Mack Sennett as the rube lover whom Mabel prefers, the movie camera fulfils its promise of the audience's release from mundane, plausible things. The whole affair is outrageously exaggerated Victorian melodrama, with the hirsute villain and his mad, destructive passion, but with the extrav-agant metaphors of modern machinery as the engines of death and liberation at the same time. It was, in fact, a kind of remake of a short Mack had shot a few weeks before, *Mabel's Awful Mistake* (working title 'The Saw Mill'), in which Mabel was strapped to the planing table in the equally classic image of ultimate peril. Mack arrives to hold back the machine, just in time.

The next extant film in which the Kops appear is *Fatty Joins the Force*, starring Roscoe 'Fatty' Arbuckle, made in October 1913; and their next full-blown explosion is *In the Clutches of the Gang*, made in December, which has left us the best-known still image of the Kops, with their original line-up, Ford Sterling with his goatee beard as the Chief (sometimes known as Chief Teheezel), a very young Edgar Kennedy, George Jeske, Al St John, Hank Mann, Rube Miller and Arbuckle. Neither of these movies were directed by Sennett, but by the new help, George Nichols.

By autumn 1913, the Keystone operation was buzzing at top speed, making funny pictures as fast as possible for money, as Sennett had set out to do. Kessel and Baumann could sit back happily in New York, counting their cash, and Sennett could begin withdrawing from the everyday direction of his pictures and attend to the overall strat-egy, which, in keeping with the whole idea of American capitalism, involved never standing still.

The original cast that Sennett had brought over from Biograph continued to frolic, but Mack was shrewdly aware of their limita-tions. His own rube character, with coyly humped shoulders, soft hat and mincing gait, wooing winsome Mabel, was phased out, the self-disparagement of his own talents as an actor becoming a convenient excuse. Mabel's star, on the other hand, continued to rise, her popu-larity increasing now that the fans knew her name and their curiosi-ty could be catered to by publicity in the motion-picture magazines. From *Motography* 19 April 1913:

Mabel Normand is all that the leading lady of the busy motion picture company is supposed to be and a good bit more. For besides being pretty and a real decoration to whatever picture she plays in she is also athletic and daring and provides the spectators of the silent comedy many a thrill in her performances. As a swimmer, she has scored her biggest successes, this accomplishment being her best beloved and best performed . . .

And one among many admirers could write:

> It's only a picture with a sweet, smiling face,
> But each lovely feature in my heart I can trace,
> With beauty and grace and eyes that outshine
> The stars as they twinkle – you are simply divine.
>
> I often have sat and watched you on the screen,
> In comedienne parts you are surely the Queen,
> Your admirers are millions, for such is your art,
> You have made us all lovers and won every heart.

*John McArthur, aged 12, of Los Angeles*

Press interest in Mabel was growing by the week. In March, the *Minneapolis News* had reported that 'Pretty, Dashing Mabel Calls Herself "The Airmen's Hoodoo" – her claim is based on the fact that the two men with whom she accepted invitations to "sky ride" were killed in flights made within a few weeks after they took her up.' These unfortunates were named as Horace Kearney and Philip Parmelee, the aviator with whom she had filmed her 'Dash Through the Clouds'. Mabel's penchant for dashing men, even if they plummetted terminally from the sky, could not have been welcome to Mack Sennett, already known as her 'steady', though the relationship between them was, as it was to remain, curiously undefined.

Although the first female movie star was the uncredited Florence Lawrence, known only as 'The Biograph Girl' until 1909, and both Blanche Sweet and Mary Pickford already had worshipful fans, Mabel Normand just pipped Mary to the post as the screen's first example of what we would today call a 'superstar'. She had the advantage of being a heroine to a wide audience, male and female, on several levels: As a big-eyed beauty, as an adorable child-woman, as a woman equal to men in her own right, an athlete, an adventuress, a connoisseur and daredevil driver of motor cars and, in just four years from her Keystone début, as the manager of her own movie studio.

The girl who couldn't stand still for Mack Sennett to kiss her was racing in her own trajectory to challenge him on an equal footing. When he was with her, Mack hinted, he could not quite convince her of his own imperial status, and reverted to the clumsy, shy, Canadian ex-ironworker of his not-so-long-ago past. But there might have been other obstacles, as we shall see . . .

While Mabel remained Keystone's mainstay, other pioneers became more stale. Fred Mace, who had been Sennett's equal as an actor at Biograph, was soon to be a second-stringer. At Biograph, he had inaugurated with Mack a double act as two detectives, incompetent 'Sherlocks', dressed in the Holmesian coat, pipe and deerstalker hat. In *Trailing the Counterfeiter*, of October 1911, they 'trail the wrong man, while REAL detectives run down the right one, and also arrest the sleuths for butting in'. A year later, they were reprising the roles for the Keystone *A Bear Escape*, an early sample of Sennett's own growing sense of press hype.

From *Motion Picture World* (26 October 1912):

Mack Sennett, director of the Keystone company, tells a thrilling story about a hair raising adventure that occurred to him and Fred Mace this week. The Keystone company was engaged in making a comedy in Griffith Park, which, by the way, is not a park in the sense ordinarily understood by the term, but a 4000 acre tract of mountainous territory located on the outskirts of the city limits and maintained by the municipality, to which it belongs, in its original, natural state. The services of a bear were required in the picture and Sennett had engaged one from a menagerie. According to his version the bear had a mean disposition and refused to be a motion picture actor. Instead it took after Mace and Sennett who started towards the top of the mountain. At length our heroes reached the summit. The bear was so close behind that they could feel his hot breathing. They ran out along a point and then discovered that they were on the brink of a precipice 1000 feet high. Behind them was the onrushing bear. Ahead of them yawned the chasm. There were only two things to do, and either one was certain death. Mace says that they turned back and were devoured by the bear, but Sennett insists that they leaped. The reader will recall that in the opening sentence of this paragraph it was stated that this adventure had occurred to Sennett and Mace. One suspects that it occurred to them when they were trying to figure out something for the press agent.

Keystone, however, had outgrown the original happy family of Mack, Mabel, Fred, Ford Sterling and Bruin the Bear. By the end of 1913, Keystone was no longer just a rickety machine for churning out funny pictures. It was about to become an industrial plant for manufacturing American dreams.

# CHAPTER NINE

# Love, Speed and Thrills – the Keystone Ethos (or *the Return of 'Contagious Nervous Twitching'*)

Before the movies, mass audiences had been prepared for amazing spectacles by the kaleidoscopic skills of vaudeville. Jugglers, acrobats, one-legged unicyclists, performing dogs, illusionists, tea-drinking monkeys, speaking automata, the freaks of the 'dime museums', Barnum's Jumbo, sketch artists, comedians of every ethnic stripe, monologists and assorted maniacs. The strange and the outlandish rubbed shoulders with the mundane, singers of familiar songs with contortionists and 'human fish' who read the newspaper inside tanks of water. Captain Spaulding ate molten lead nightly. Houdini released himself from handcuffs and chains. Burlesque queens jiggled their massive thighs.

Contrary to the view of many writers on cultural transitions, the movies did not inaugurate the mass consumption of transgressive notions and social subversion. The stage always provided a fair measure of topsy-turvydom and a vicarious rebellion against the modes and mores of the day. But the movies introduced a particular element: the disruption and disordered rearrangement of the apparent solidities of 'normal' life.

Cultural historian Rae Beth Gordon has quoted an early essay by the Russian writer Maxim Gorky about his first experiences of the cinema:

The strangeness of this world . . . devoid of color and sound (doesn't give) the movement of life but a sort of mute spectre . . . Everything moves, comes to life, and suddenly, having reached the edge of the screen, disappears who knows where . . . Nothing but shadows, spectres, phantoms . . . You end up being disturbed and depressed by this silent and grey life . . . You forget where you are. Strange ideas invade your mind; you are less and less conscious . . .

The audiences of the first Lumière films were said to have ducked when the train came into the station. Jean-Luc Godard satirized this condition in his 1962 film *Les Caribiniers*, when the rural idiot drafted to war rushes to the screen at his first view of a movie to find an angle from which he can see the lady bathing naked in her bath. The technique of the film – what we today call 'virtual reality' – called for a different way of seeing objects and people.

Eventually this became familiar, but even today movies are still seeking to find more effective means of causing the audience to lose itself in the illusion.

At the turn of the twentieth century, however, there were other phenomena that seemed to relate to Gorky's anxiety of dislocation. Psychological ideas about the loss of body control, hysterical conditions and techniques of hypnotism were fashionable and widespread. Pathologies of the nervous system were tied in with general anxieties about the modern world, as we have seen in New York with the fear of lethal mechanical vehicles. We have noted how early French comedy related directly to this 'modern condition'. One of the French cinema's early practitioners, Emile Cohl, dabbled often with the idea of finding a way to film the unconscious mind. He had, in fact, been a prominent member of an 1880s group called The Incoherents, graphic artists and cartoonists who developed grotesque caricatures of a mainly political bent. Cohl developed series of graphic images that we recognize today as comic strips, creating fantasy narratives out of linked drawings. When he discovered the cinema, he came across the idea of drawing simple pictures in sequence on film, thus becoming the father of animation. But he also developed, at the Gaumont studios, strange live-action grotesqueries, such as *Le Miroir hypnotique* of 1910, in which the thoughts of a person looking at a black box are reproduced as realized dreams: 'a thief robs and kills a sleeping woman . . . a schoolboy creates anarchy in the classroom . . . an unfaithful husband kisses a woman he meets at a dance'.

The hypnotic box is, of course, the camera, which can bring to life illicit desires. But the narrative itself is only part of the syndrome. The dislocation itself, Gorky's 'mute spectres' and the new techniques of cutting, changes of camera angle and the increasing pace of the screen's virtual reality contribute to the audience's nervous reactions.

From the start, authorities suspected movies. Moral guardians and anxious clergymen complained both about the content of films and

Ford Sterling conducts *The Ragtime Band*, 1913

the conditions in which they were viewed: young children and unaccompanied women mixing with disreputable single men in the darkness of the movie theatres. The Society for the Prevention of Crime
was reported by the *New York Times* (12 July 1911) to have 'probably
issued and circulated more pamphlets dealing with dangers incident to
moving-picture shows than any of the other humane societies'. As for
the content, the National Board of Censorship of Moving Pictures
had, by May 1911, after a mere two years of existence, already
destroyed, as 'unfit for public display', two million feet of 'objection-
able films'. The policy of the board, according to the *New York Times*
of 14 May, was that 'there shall be no sensationalism and no repre-
sentation of crime except with the object of conveying a moral lesson.
Certain socially forbidden themes are, of course, proscribed, and any
leaning towards oversensationalism is discouraged.'

Consider, then, these scenes and sequences from Keystone's May
1913 *The Ragtime Band*, starring Mabel Normand and Ford
Sterling: 'Mabel', the first title says, 'is very popular with the band.'
This introduces the vague plot line, which has Ford Sterling, the band
leader, Professor Smelts, and one of his band as rivals for her hand.

Smelts kicks out the rival, who reappears beside Mabel in the audience of the Amateur Show. As Ford waits impatiently in the wings, a succession of trashy acts cavorts on stage. 'Salome' performs her oriental gyrations, which climax in her reversing the sign indicating her act to show her address: '2 Rose Street'. The next act, the 'Fatima Sisters', also display at the end: 'Address 3 Flower Street'. They are hustled off the stage, the harassed manager furious at this obvious trick of hookers advertising their trade. 'Petite La Belle', who follows, is so massive that she cannot be pulled offstage by 'the hook'. The entire show is the acme of seediness and bad taste. When Ford's band eventually appears, the rival and Mabel begin throwing things. Pies are cast, and the band leader finally turns the firehose on the audience, Mabel, rival and all.

Mack pretended, just a few years on, to have set limits on what audiences would accept on screen in terms of 'The Psychology of Film Comedy':

There are certain characters whom the public wants to see roughly handled; there are others who are immune from rough stuff. It is not always clear why ... You can always be safe in hitting a policeman ... The copper is fair game for pies, likewise any fat man ... On the other hand, movie fans do not like to see pretty girls smeared up with pastry. Shetland ponies and pretty girls are immune ...

*Motion Picture Classic,* November 1918

But not Mabel, who was given the treatment many times. Classically brutalized and abducted by Ford Sterling's villain in the aforementioned *Barney Oldfield's Race for Life,* Mabel was chained to the railway tracks and generally treated like a sack of potatoes. The whole film is another direct spoof of the 'woman in peril' theme of Griffith's cross-cutting specials. It was as corny in 1913 as it is now, with its climax of Ford Sterling shooting dead five policemen and then trying to shoot and throttle himself. The extant version of *Barney Oldfield* is, incidentally, significant in terms of pace – if any movie shouts out for Sennett's famous under-cranked camera, it is this one, but in fact it appears to have been shot at normal speed. Given the way these movies were later reprinted or transferred at different projection speeds, it is impossible to pinpoint quite when this innovation was first used by Sennett. It is certainly not very evident in these early films, manic as they are. By 1915, the Keystone Kops and other chasers and chasees were routinely speeded up. There is nothing, alas, to support the primal 'Sergei the bad cameraman' story.

The censors were also increasingly unhappy at the Jewish stereotypes beloved by 'Pathé' Lehrman and Ford Sterling. Lehrman himself makes an appearance in the weirdest of these, *Cohen Saves the Flag* of April 1913. This was shot to take advantage of a Civil War picture Thomas Ince was shooting at Inceville. (One Kessel and Baumann hand washing the other.) Lehrman and Sterling enlist as Lieutenant Goldberg and Sergeant Cohen in the Yankee ranks when war breaks out, having already been introduced to us fighting over Mabel in the time-honoured fashion of eye-gouging and ear-biting. (This form of dental combat, as well as its corollary, nose-biting, appears to have died out of intra-Jewish conflict since then.) Cohen is sent into battle by Goldberg much as King David sent Uriah the Hittite, the husband of Bathsheba, to die at the front in biblical times. Cohen gets mixed up with the Union flag in battle and is seen by one soldier to have saved it, while Goldberg sees him running from another rebel attack and reports him to his commander as a deserter: 'Among the pigs he was hiding, the coward!' Cohen is sentenced to be shot, but, in another crescendo of Griffithian cross-cutting – and a very un-Griffithian inversion of the 'damsel in peril' formula – Mabel rides with the flag up hill and down dale to save him.

The amount of ethnic mugging conducted by both Lehrman and Sterling in this film could have fuelled the wrath of the Bnai Brith and other well-meaning Jewish organizations for decades and, as noted earlier, 'Jew' comedies disappeared quite soon off the screen. Even the black caricatures subsided somewhat, though this was more to do with the aftermath of Griffith's *Birth of a Nation*, in 1915, than any restraint among the comedy-makers.

The Kops themselves were an inevitable outgrowth of catering to immigrant and working-class audiences, who had all dreamed Sennett's dream of pulling the policeman's helmet down over his ears, and then some. Initially a rural, rube kind of force, they seemed incapable of coming through a door without collapsing in spectacular pratfalls. Beyond the oafishness of the Pathé originals, their entire existence seemed to be one huge, contagious nervous twitch. Their contagion spread to Keystone firemen, who were of course the last persons you'd wish to call when the flames began to lick out. Marionettes of some malign force of anarchy, the Kops would leap into their car only to fall behind and be dragged along in a meandering daisy chain. Called to rescue characters who had fallen off seaside piers – an inevitable fate, in Keystone movies – they could not lean over the railings without falling in, sometimes in their vehicle, or in motorcycle side-cars. The stunts the actors were called upon to perform were fearsome; broken bones were a normal daily hazard. No wonder they would later be portrayed asleep at their station, helmets over their eyes and blissfully impervious to the ringing of their alarm bell.

For Sennett, of course, putting aside the hindsight speculations on cultural trends and influences, the Kops were, in their clumsy movements, quite literally clowns, tumbling in the sawdust of the circus ring of Hollywood. Old Punch and Judy shows, familiar to all, could have provided him, or 'Pathé' Lehrman, with another convenient trigger for these droll monsters, whatever childhood fancies might have kicked in. All was of a piece with the frenetic ethos of Keystone. Love itself was mad, in Sennett's topsy-turvydom – villains snatching women from domestic bliss, only to have them snatched back by their husbands or lovers. Women often preferred the boldest flirts to their staider amours. Marital bliss was made to be disrupted, by crazy people jumping in through windows or coming up through the cellar.

Love did not necessarily conquer all, since chaos could always trump it. Happy endings were not *de rigueur*. Often the final bell would ring to a mêlée of beating and biting, the hero embarrassed or caught out in a folly, chasers and chased falling into a mud-hole. A standard formula of the chase would soon develop, with motor cars whizzing all over the streets of Los Angeles, displacing cops from their motorcycles, workers from their trenches, and upending women into wash-basins. It is probable that under-cranking developed specifically to make cars go faster, given the lethal nature of early motor vehicles, devoid of all safety features, with the Model T Ford already capable in 1911 of speeds of up to 45 miles an hour, even when not driven by Barney Oldfield. The 1890s warnings of the deadly dangers of horseless vehicles were magnified a thousandfold in the Keystones, although, like later cartoon characters, the Keystone clowns could fall on their heads, down ravines, be shot in the rear or blown up by dynamite, only to emerge unscathed. In the dream–nightmare of modernity, you could wake up perfectly safe, in your cinema seat, nothing permanently lost but your dimes.

But beyond the machinery, audiences still craved identification with the people they saw on the screen, the actors who went through the sawmill for them and represented their wayward dreams and desires. Sennett realized this, and began scouting for talent, once his conveyer belt was set in motion. At the end of his first full year of operation, he found, on a whim and an instinct, an English touring actor who showed promise. But in April 1913, he had already struck gold, engaging a young, if amply proportioned, comedian named Roscoe C. Arbuckle.

# CHAPTER TEN

# The Clowns: Fatty's Fickle Falls

From *Motion Picture*, November 1916:

> When I'm tired of watching 'vamping' by the mile,
> And I wish to clean my mind out and to smile,
> I go where that dimpled 'Fatty'
> Makes me laugh until I'm batty,
> With his innocent and cunning baby smile.
>
> *Mabel W. Burlestone, Temple, Texas*

From *Photoplay Magazine*, August 1918:

Mr. Arbuckle was born to fame, honor, and the power to rule over others. If newspapers, billboards or moving pictures were not invented, he would get before the public in some other way. He would make a splendid leader in war, as well as a good actor. He has more power for serious drama than comedies, but, if left to his own choice, the product of his brain would be clean and pure . . . He has so many good qualities that I have not the space here to enumerate them, but I will mention that he will always be inventing ways to make more money. He is saving but generous, and loves to give dinners for friends . . . Indications are that in 1920 he will be a 'bloated millionaire'.

And yet, at the end of 1921, 'Fatty' Arbuckle became one of the most reviled men in America, denounced from pulpits and political podiums as a monster in human form, accused of a horrendous rape and murder in a case that would be seen as a watershed, a before and after of Hollywood lives.

In the hall of mirrors of Hollywood history, Roscoe C. Arbuckle's hefty figure refracts in a cascade of distortions. His biographer, David Yallop, called his *dies irae* 'The Day the Laughter Stopped'. The laughter of course continued, but echoed thereafter with an anxious edge that had not been present before. Murky shadows gathered in

ROSCOE ARBUCKLE
KEYSTONE COMEDIES

Roscoe 'Fatty' Arbuckle

the sunny glades where the movie people had frolicked in their make-believe innocence in never-never land.

In truth, the shadows were present in Roscoe Arbuckle's life from the start. Despite a self-painted image of a happy childhood, he was in fact the son of an abusive father who beat him and then left wife and children to fend for themselves in the early 1890s in Santa Ana, California, while he ventured north to seek his fortune. After Roscoe's mother died, he sought out his father and had to endure the round of beatings again. In 1902, Roscoe's father, William, became a restaurateur, much like Sennett's father a couple of years earlier, and fifteen-year-old Roscoe waited on tables. Like Mack Sennett, a talent for singing drew him away from drudgery, and he found employment at a café in San Francisco, run by the theatre owner Alexander Pantages.

In April 1906, the devastating San Francisco earthquake tipped Roscoe out of bed and into the streets as corvee labour, clearing debris under army bayonets along with John Barrymore, another aspiring thespian caught in the city. His next break came when comedian Leon Errol took him on for his touring company of players. He learned his trade rapidly – singing, physical comedy, burlesque and vaudeville routines, black-face minstrel, whatever was called for. His first brush with the movies was with the Selig Company, the first film unit to open up shop on the West Coast, making a handful of films in 1909. The *New York Dramatic Mirror* wrote about the 'fat fellow, a new face in picture pantomime . . . the earnestness of his work adds greatly to its value'. But he soon returned to the stage.

In 1908, Roscoe had met a petite and pretty actress named Minta Durfee, whom he married soon after. David Yallop, who interviewed the ex-Mrs Arbuckle in her later years, quotes her somewhat alarming tale of the moment Roscoe proposed to her, overcoming her shyness by physically holding her over the edge of the Long Beach pier: 'You are either going to say yes or no, or I'll drop you in the water. Do you love me or don't you love me? I love you and adore you.' People were apparently more robust in their romance in those days.

Minta and Roscoe toured together from then on, in various shows – one archive clipping of 1910 from the *Los Angeles Examiner* reports tantalizingly on 'Roscoe Arbuckle, the German comedian of Taftian proportions', playing with a partner called Fred Ardath in *Spending a Million* at the Princess Theatre. In 1911, Roscoe and Minta undertook an arduous overseas journey with the Ferris Hartman 'Campus Company', covering, in his own words, 'China, Japan, India, Honolulu, the Philippine Islands, and even more civilized places'. The company returned to California in February 1913, just in time for Roscoe to hear about new opportunities in film comedy opening up in Edendale.

Stories about Arbuckle's introduction to Keystone vary, of course, with the teller. Sennett said he was in his office with Mabel when 'a tremendous man skipped up the steps as lightly as Fred Astaire . . . "Name's Arbuckle . . . I'm a funnyman and an acrobat. I bet I could do well in pictures. Watcha think?" With no warning, he went into a feather-light step, clapped his hands, and did a backward somersault.'

Minta Durfee, on the other hand, recalled to David Yallop that Roscoe had just entered the Keystone building when 'a man with a shock of grey hair and a mouthful of tobacco' spat tobacco juice at him and shouted: 'You! Be here tomorrow at eight o'clock! . . . How in hell do you know, you might be a star someday.'

For once, Sennett's account rings more true.

The Sennett studio was, at that time, in the midst of an expansion which would last through the next two years, adding more shooting stages, cutting rooms and workshops, filling up the land around the complex at Allessandro Street and Glendale Avenue with more buildings for the administration and crews. Eventually it was to cover thirty acres, with a special water tank for the girls' aquatic adventures, a great cyclorama that provided moving painted backdrops, living quarters for the Keystone bear and dogs, and electric generators that could power a small town of over ten thousand inhabitants. But in the early period, Minta Durfee recalled, 'we worked out on the streets, the fields, the lakes, everywhere'. The administration centre was not yet the high tower that Sennett was to construct later so that he could survey all that he owned. But the large bath, in which he liked to soak while thinking, chomping on his cigars, was already installed in his second-storey office, high enough to keep an eye on the mob of delinquents on his payroll.

Sennett put Arbuckle in a film called *Gangsters*, with Fred Mace, Ford Sterling, Hank Mann and Al St John, the main studio stalwarts. The director was Henry 'Pathé' Lehrman. The following week, Roscoe was in two more Lehrman films, *Help! Help! Hydrophobia* and *Passions, He Had Three* (oddly shipped as *Possums, He Had Three*), and from then on he was working constantly. His first film with Mabel Normand was *For Love of Mabel*, made in June. The first that gave him the name he was famous for was *Fatty's Day Off*, in July. He was roped in to join the roster of Kops, becoming, at first, just one of the gang. This included the usual suspects, with the steady support of such Keystone staples as Hank Mann, Slim Summerville and Al St John. St John was Roscoe's nephew, and was pursuing a career as a trick bicycle rider when his uncle roped him in as an extra. He was soon pratfalling all over the place, with his rubbery limbs and even more rubbery face. Hank Mann had been a sign-painter and a 'high lofty boy', working on tall buildings before becoming a vaudeville acrobat. Slim Summerville, born in Albuquerque, New Mexico, was shunted about as a child between his father in Canada and an aunt in Oklahoma, before setting off on his own to work in 'coffin factories, brickyards, lumber mills and machine shops . . . [riding] the rods over practically every railroad in the country', playing small parts in amateur shows. He was recruited for Sennett, the legend goes, by Edgar Kennedy, one of the earliest Keystoners. These were the men who were to take the hardest falls, outdoing each other in visual gags.

A summer Keystone, *Mabel's New Hero* (aka *Fatty and the Bathing Beauties*) shows Roscoe at his most playful, as a suitor wooing Mabel at the beach. Prancing about in striped bathing costume, he appears jaunty as an overweight elf. A rival villain sends Mabel up into the sky under a balloon, which the jittery Kops try vainly to pull down by its rope. In the finale, Mabel shins down the rope into Fatty's waiting arms.

At the end of 1913, the lot was so busy that Sennett began to allow his stars to direct themselves in their own movies. Mabel was the first, with *Mabel's Stormy Love Affair*, in December. In the spring of 1914, Arbuckle directed himself in *Barnyard Flirtations*, although he was assisted by Keystone staffers, as were his other colleagues. From the beginning, there had been writers and gag-men on the payroll, despite the mythology that Keystone films were made up as they went along. Nevertheless, in the first year, the scripts were fairly basic, and few have survived, mostly one-page synopses. By 1915, however, these scripts would be much longer, more detailed, often extant in several drafts. As Arbuckle told *Photoplay* magazine in a revealing piece in 1916, entitled 'Why Aren't We Killed?' ('A Keystone Confession Which Must Not Be Read by Insurance Agents'):

'We figure it out on paper, and if it looks as if it will work we do it . . . Now and then it doesn't work, and we either have to plan it a different way, or do it over again until we get it. Naturally I figure pretty carefully, because I don't want to roll off a roof more than seven or eight times just for a foot or two of film . . .'

In 'Fatty and the Broadway Stars' he dropped through a skylight and fell about ten feet upon a table, with nothing to ease the percussion [*sic*]. In 'The Village Scandal' he rolled down a roof and dropped fifteen feet into a trough of water. In 'Fatty's Tintype Tangle' he walked along a bunch of telephone wires thirty feet above the ground, and dropped through the roof of a house, lighting upon a bed eighteen feet below. In 'Fatty's Jonah Day' he dived seventy feet from the top of an electric light mast above a bridge in Hollenbeck Park, Los Angeles, into twelve feet of water.

*Fatty's Tintype Tangle*

The basis of Fatty's enduring popularity was precisely his paradoxical skill as an overweight acrobat. The more spectacular the feat, the better; although for *Fatty's Tintype Tangle* he did allow, according to David Yallop, a suitably padded stunt man to take his place on the wires.

Often, the newspapers reported, the whole Keystone lot would look more like an open-plan hospital ward than anything else, as the *Toledo Times* wrote in July 1914:

Roscoe Arbuckle is doing some tremendous tumble acts these days, and a thirty-dollar preservation harness, made of the same material as a horse's girth, has been constructed to eke out his native padding. Nick Cogley is still on crutches from a compound fracture which he got last fall in a movie

Fatty, Mabel and Luke in *Fatty and Mabel Adrift*, 1916

race, and Charles Murray, lately of the team of Murray and Mack, in his own words, is 'all bunged up' from getting hit with bombs and tank explosions and jumping off bridges. But Miss Mabel Normand, the phenomenal comedienne of the Keystone, is still intact and as dainty and cool-headed as ever.

It was the teaming of big 'Fatty' and small Mabel which was to make Roscoe the most popular draw for Keystone, in films such as *Mabel's Wilful Way*, *Mabel, Fatty and the Law* and *Fatty and Mabel Adrift*. The latter, made in 1916, begins as a farmyard triangle between Fatty, Mabel and Al St John as the jealous but moronic boy on the next farm. Fatty and Mabel are married and their parents buy from a city slicker a cottage perched precariously by the sea. Al plots revenge, with a criminal gang led by 'BRUTUS BOMBASTIC: Abductions – Robberies – Murder – Lowest Rates'. The crooks cut the cottage loose in a storm, and Fatty and Mabel drift out, their house afloat among the ocean-going liners.

The scene is embryonic of the disaster-thrill scenarios which Buster Keaton, still at that time in vaudeville, would be learning from Arbuckle a year or two down the line. The movie also features Luke, Roscoe's dog and Keystone's first full-fledged canine star. The dog rustles up the Kops, who rush into their motor boats and capsize, as is their wont. Nevertheless, Mabel and Fatty are rescued in the end, while Brutus Bombastic and his gang are blown up in their cave by their own dynamite and poor Al St John is felled by a rock.

There are some moments of lyrical tenderness in the film which are not wholly played for jeers. It opens with Fatty and Mabel in heart-shaped frames, shot through by Cupid's arrow, while Al sees his own heart collapse about him. The closing shot is of Luke, in his own frame, with a look that speaks volumes of the inanity of humans who require dogs to look silly. On the way, there are some poignant sunset shots of Fatty fishing for Mabel's dinner during their brief night of wedded bliss, before the storm and the criminal classes float them off on separate beds.

By the time this film was made, Keystone had mutated into the Triangle Film Corporation and Fatty Arbuckle was planning his own independent production company. But much transpired before that point, as Roscoe steadily developed his skills.

Arbuckle was the first true pantomime genius discovered by Sennett. Unlike Fred Mace or Ford Sterling, he never mugged or relied on exaggerated gestures. His facial expressions were subtle, often set in the 'stone face' of heightened concentration that Buster Keaton would deploy so effectively. And his body could do wondrous things. In *The Waiters' Ball*, he plays the cook in a seedy restaurant who tosses pancakes, produces cups of coffee, wrestles with limburger cheese and duels with Al St John with a broomstick, with great panache and dextrous ease. The movie, directed by Arbuckle and his old stage boss, Ferris Hartman (also swooped up by Sennett), conjures up the world of downmarket eating houses and their grotesque customers that Chaplin would portray more ruthlessly. Sennett himself lends a hand as a spaghetti-eating lout, under the sign 'NOT RESPONSIBLE FOR CHEWING GUM STUCK UNDER TABLES'. Pork and beans is referred to as 'one grunt with a thousand on a plate', and a fish which is not quite dead is mourned on its final passing by all the diners. An undercurrent of social reality not common to Keystone is apparent, the seam that Chaplin mined to great effect.

As Keaton would recall about his great mentor, whose partner he became at the Comique company from 1917, Roscoe taught Buster all there was to know about making movies, and not only on the acting side. Keaton wrote: 'Roscoe . . . took the camera apart for me so I would understand how it worked and what it could do. He showed me how film was developed, cut, and then spliced together.'

In the authentic mode of the old vaudevillian, Roscoe left little to the ad lib. The *New York Sun* reported in 1917:

Mr. Arbuckle has probably the most complete joke library in the world. It is being scientifically indexed and edited under the personal direction of the screen's funniest fat man . . . Every joke that appears in the weekly and monthly publications is clipped and placed on Mr. Arbuckle's desk and then classified in the library . . .

Arbuckle built himself up as an encyclopedia of comedy, with a mastery of gags and of structure. He was also, of course, a great thrower of pies, that perennial comic gag Sennett claimed to have discovered when Mabel once threw a pastry on impulse into the cross-eyed face of Ben Turpin. As Turpin did not arrive at Keystone until 1915, and Sennett dated his e-pie-phany to 1913, this puts the kibosh on that story. Arbuckle, it seems, became the champion pie-thrower – able to throw two pies in different directions at once. Sennett quoted his later chief director, Del Lord, as the philosopher-king of pie-lobbing:

'You don't throw like a shortstop rifling to first base. You push the pie towards the face, leaning into your follow-through. Six or eight feet is the limit for an artistic performance.

'You must never let the actor know when you're going to give him the custard in the choppers. Even the most skillful actor . . . finds it difficult to conceal anticipation.

'The wisest technique is to con your victim into a sense of security and then slip it to him.

'In my day . . . I developed a prejudice for berries with whipped cream. After the actual whomp in the face, the berries trickle beautifully down the actor's shirt and the whipped cream besplashes his suit. This is muddy, frothy and photogenic.'

Students take note. In fact, despite the favoured image of pie mayhem, pastry-tossing was a relatively rare form of Keystonery. Smashing an entire room, or motor car, was much more satisfying for the company's raucous master.

As time passed, Roscoe Arbuckle sought to broaden not only his ambidexterity but his character, playing an unshaven tramp who is mistaken for a mad bomber in *Fatty's New Role* (Headline: 'THREE SALOONS BLOWN UP BY MAN ENRAGED AT BEING REFUSED SERVICE'), an upper-class doctor who has a mad adulterous dream after a lobster dinner in *He Did and He Didn't*; and, in *Miss Fatty's Seaside Lovers*, an obese heiress harassed in 'a hotel lobby infected with mashers'. These pests include a very young Harold Lloyd, eking out his brief tenure at Keystone before an offer of $50 a week, which Sennett reputedly refused to match, sent him scuttling back to Hal Roach studios, from whence he had come. Miss Fatty, in striped bathing suit, blonde curls and tiny twirling parasol, was a sight indeed, ever apt to turn on her admirers, grab them by the neck and toss them half a hundred yards off in the surf.

As it turned out, Arbuckle and other recruits were serving their apprenticeship at Keystone before moving on to construct their own lucrative careers. As Mack himself oft repeated, ruefully: 'Start with Sennett and get rich somewhere else!'

It was not so much that Sennett was too stingy with money, though he was not keen to toss his gold doubloons about, but that the fame of his new employees spread much faster than his own capacity to keep up with the game. In 1918, *Photoplay* journal was to write, of the crowds surrounding 'Fatty' on location on one of his own productions:

These people adored 'Fatty', I soon discovered – young and old. They felt that somehow he was a rock to cling to, a prop against the shadows that are falling all too heavily in these days of stress. He represented the way of escape – he and his merry-making crew – the defiance that we humans must hurl at woe; in a way he typified the happy, serious spirit of the American: the ability to see the funny side of anything, however seemingly tragic . . .

When this was written, in November, American troops had already been fighting and dying for over a year in the trenches of France, and the need for comedy was taking on a new desperation. But in the halcyon year of 1913, before the war in Europe had begun, the Keystone kavorting seemed devoid of melancholy, fuelled chiefly by the rough energy generated by actors, crew, gagsters, directors and the mercurial boss, soaking in his office tub, chewing tobacco and underlings alike, demanding more, more, more, faster and funnier, by the barrelful. Lest things go stale, new blood was sought. Among the newcomers, two more veterans of the American vaudeville circuits, Chester Conklin and Mack Swain, were also signed on in 1913. And at the end of that year, Sennett's freshest recruit, the young Englishman from the Karno touring company, arrived to begin his movie career.

# CHAPTER ELEVEN

# Charlie's Strange Predicament

One of the many features written about, or supposedly by, Charles Chaplin in the first decade of his fame was a serialized account in the *Chicago Herald*, published in July 1921, of his first days at Keystone:

I left New York for California under the flattering and delightful impression that in the movies I was to play romantic and serious roles . . . On arriving at Los Angeles I reported for duty at the producing studios . . . the out-of-door surroundings, the sight of 'interior' scenes open to the sky, the view of distant mountains and the breezy flashes of western life were all amazing to eyes accustomed only to the world behind the footlights and the confining brick walls of the New York and London stage.

I shall never forget my first day as a moving picture actor. I reported for work at an intolerably early hour – it was at least 9 a.m. As I stood in the awesome presence of the stage director my heart beat high and I was thrilled with curiosity as to the type of romantic youth I was to play in the forthcoming film. Somehow I had an idea that it would be a drama of the Elizabethan period, and that I would be called upon to wear doublet and hose and wield a rapier on behalf of my lady love.

The stage director's first words stunned me.

'Good morning,' he said. 'Can you fall off a stepladder?'

I fell back a few steps, open-mouthed.

Unbelieving, I asked him to repeat the question.

'I mean, can you do a funny sprawl off a stepladder without breaking your bones?' he demanded.

An hour later I was falling off the ladder – with frills and variations . . .

Despite Chaplin's early attempts to kid the good citizens of Chicago, he was, of course, never so green. He had been touring America since late 1910, his first US tour with the Fred Karno company, mainly playing the drunk in the perennial 'Night at an English Music Hall' sketch. Another tour, from the autumn of 1912, had repeated the company crossing of the United States, from New York over the Rocky Mountain states to California and back. Everywhere, Chaplin's observant eye had taken in the sights and sounds of frontier and urban life, the rumbustious audiences, seedy burlesque theatres, cheap restaurants and dives that would feature so often in his films.

Chaplin's early life has been covered copiously, most thoroughly in David Robinson's comprehensive biography, *Chaplin, His Life and Art*: his childhood in Kennington in London; the death of his alcoholic father, Charles Senior, also a 'well-known mimic and music-hall comedian'; the incarceration of his mother as a 'pauper lunatic' when he was aged fourteen; and the life of the two teenage brothers, Sydney and Charles, as juveniles on the English stage until both found their place with 'Karno's Speechless Comedians' at different times (Sydney joined Karno in 1906, Charles in February 1908). Karno's companies were the perfect school for pantomime, playing their crazy sketches up and down the British Isles. Even the more obscure shows, like *Early Birds*, provided Charlie with ideas and plots that he would later use on screen: the lurid tale of mayhem among East London's Dickensian underclass would turn into 1917's *Easy Street*.

How Charlie Got to Keystone is another tale with many variants. It was in the fall of 1912, at the American Theater in New York, when Mack and Mabel caught Charlie's performance as the drunk with the Karno troupe. Or it was Adam Kessel, or Baumann, who caught the performance and spotted the 'limey' who was getting the laughs. Or it was their third partner at the New York Motion Picture Company, Harry Aitken, who attended a matinée show. In the spring of 1913, a legendary telegram was sent to Karno manager Alf Reeves:

IS THERE A MAN NAMED CHAFFIN IN YOUR COMPANY OR SOMETHING LIKE THAT IF SO CAN HE COMMUNICATE WITH KESSEL AND BAUMANN 24 LONGACRE BUILDING BROADWAY NEW YORK.

Chaplin signed a standard contract with Kessel and Baumann in September, for an initial salary of $150 per week. He reached Los Angeles in early December and met Mack and Mabel by chance on a visit to the Empress Theater. Sennett was supposedly taken aback by the new boy's youth, although Chaplin was only two years younger than Arbuckle had been when Sennett hired him. Thus far the accretions of legend.

Mack Sennett (centre) with Charles Chaplin and D. W. Griffith

Much has been made by Chaplinologists of the circumstances of his first screen appearances, and of his choice of the costume and make-up that would become so iconic – recognizable even to people who had never seen a movie, let alone a Chaplin one. Argument swirls over whether it was in *Kid Auto Races at Venice* or in *Mabel's Strange Predicament* that the tramp's costume was born. Before these shorts, Chaplin had appeared for the very first time in *Making a Living*, directed by 'Pathé' Lehrman and released on 2 February 1914. This film was shot some time in the first week of January, and so Chaplin had to cool his heels at Keystone for a month while he hung about the studio and learned the ropes, watching other films being made. He might have been in time to glimpse the filming of the Kops special, *In the Clutches of the Gang*, but would most likely have seen the making of *Mabel's Stormy Love Affair*, *A Flirt's Mistake* and an educational short called *How Motion Pictures Are Made*, which must have been timely. *Mabel's Bear Escape* immediately preceded *Making a Living*. In Chaplin's first film, he is dressed as a drunk upper-class spiv, or Sennett's idea

of what 'an English Lord' might look like. A long drooping moustache, grey topper, spotted cravat and monocle grace this graceless
character who touches rival Lehrman for a loan, flirts with his girl
and in general behaves obnoxiously for no reason. As Chaplin had
been a drunk for Karno, neither Sennett nor Chaplin seemed to see
any good reason for making him sober in any but a few of his first
tranche of films.

Contrary to the claim that *Making a Living* was an 'elaborate'
Keystone production, it was run of the mill, and the next, *Kid Auto
Races*, is so perfunctory as to seem no more than an extended screen
test. One of the many Keystones shot to fit in with an existing event,
it simply consists of Henry 'Pathé' Lehrman as a director trying to
shoot a car race while the tramp keeps intruding into shot. Pushed
out of the way, he keeps coming back. And that's it.

Chaplin's own recollection was that *Mabel's Strange Predicament*
was the first movie in which he used the tramp costume, although
research beyond the call of duty performed by film historian Bo
Berglund, tracking down the weather pattern in Los Angeles on the
days in question, proved that *Kid Auto Races* was shot first, on
Saturday, 10 January. In fact, this is also the date of the archive synopsis of *Mabel's Strange Predicament*, reproduced at the start of this
section, which shows the drunk as a minor character appearing, on
paper, in only one scene. As the film features the drunk as its main
character, it becomes clear that this change was applied in the filming,
to give Chaplin his first stab at a lead in a proper farce–drama, and
therefore the synopsis precedes the shooting, which is not always the
case in these early Keystone documents.

Chaplin wrote, in his autobiography:

I had no idea what make-up to put on . . . However, on the way to the
wardrobe I thought I would dress in baggy pants, big shoes, a cane and a
derby hat. I wanted everything a contradiction: the pants baggy, the coat
tight, the hat small and the shoes large. I was undecided whether to look old
or young, but remembering Sennett had expected me to be a much older
man, I added a small mustache, which, I reasoned, would add age without
hiding my expression.

I had no idea of the character. But the moment I was dressed, the clothes
and the make-up made me feel the person he was. I began to know him, and
by the time I walked onto the stage he was fully born.

Chaplin omits the tryout at *Kid Auto Races*, as it doesn't fit into this myth. He clearly had a day or two to sink into his costume before the shooting of his third film. Most of these Keystone shorts took between one and three days to film – though *Kid Auto Races* was said to have been shot in under an hour! – and 'Pathé' Lehrman told a later friend, the director Robert Florey, that *Mabel's Strange Predicament* had been shot in one day. That would not have been difficult, as it was set entirely on the indoor stage, comprising a hotel lobby, two rooms and a corridor between them, in which Mabel gets caught in her pyjamas outside her room while trying to follow a ball thrown for her dog. Husband, wife, stranger, girl caught under the husband's bed: Keystone staples with which the drunk tramp is entangled. During the shooting, stage hands were in fits of laughter at the new boy's antics, something not seen at Keystone since the early tricks of Ford Sterling. Clearly there was a new prince in the kingdom.

Things did not go completely smoothly for Chaplin, however. He did not get on with his directors, complaining that Henry Lehrman butchered his work in the cutting room, destroying the rhythm of his gags. He was not in tune with director George 'Pop' Nichols, either, who directed him a few weeks later in *A Film Johnnie*, a basic 'new boy screws up the studio' type of plot which nevertheless gives us a fascinating glimpse of the Keystone stages, all hustle and bustle and knocking over scenery. As Mabel had directed *Mabel's Strange Predicament*, he was uncomfortable with her command too, probably on the basis of standard male prejudice but ostensibly because, as he told Sennett, 'She's very young.' Mabel was three years younger than Charlie, but had been acting in movies for over four years. Other sources relate, accordingly, that it was Mabel who taught Charlie his first lessons in film-making, showing him what the camera could do and how an actor could relate to that piece of glass at the end of the box.

Chaplin's problem was a familiar one of stage training, longing for the linear continuity of acting, building the pantomime gag and following it through without interruption, as against the stop and start of the films. Lehrman's brief, as a Keystone director, was to keep the action moving, but Chaplin's speciality was the expression of ideas by means of his body language, as befits the proper mime. It would take time before he could work out how to deploy the camera so as to express his skills just as he wished on the screen, but once he discovered this, he never looked back. By April, he had convinced Sennett to allow him, too, to direct himself in his films, thus freeing himself from the onerous control of others.

Before this, there was *Tango Tangles*, directed by Sennett, with Charlie, Roscoe Arbuckle and Ford Sterling all playing 'straight', without their usual masks. Roscoe is a musician, Sterling the band leader and Charlie a drunk who disrupts the dance hall. This is the only movie in which Chaplin appeared without appreciable make-up, *sans* moustache, large or small. The film also features a cameo appearance by Chester Conklin, as a guest in cop uniform, his second part in a Chaplin movie, after another cop role in *Between Showers*. He was to crop up often in Charlie's subsequent Keystones, with his great moustache and apoplectic manner. When Charlie left, Conklin was to continue a long starring run in his own right, often twinned with Mack Swain as 'Ambrose and Walrus'.

Conklin's trajectory followed another singular and convoluted path to the movies from the vaudeville ranks. Born to a building contractor in Oskaloosa, Iowa, he won an elocution prize at a church speaking festival at the age of twelve, then upset his father by declaring his wish to become an actor. 'Father urged me to stay at home and make a man of me,' he told the press many years later, 'and he kept saying that he had never seen an actor who was worth a row of beans.' At Fruitvale, California, eking out a living as a 'monologuist', he was told by the manager: 'Conklin, you're a nice young feller and I like you . . . but, for heaven's sake, cut out this acting stuff. You're the rottenest monologuist I ever saw – and that is saying considerable.' A spell in musical revues and the circus followed, and his arrival at Sennett's is subject to the usual piquant tale, according to the *Cleveland Leader*: 'For three weeks he hung around the Mack Sennett studio. At last one day Sennett said to him: "Say, are you funny?" Chester sighed deeply. "There is some difference of opinion as to that," he said. Which tickled Sennett so much that he told him to go make up.'

Chester is most recognized by fans of classic films for his great double act with Chaplin in the non-talking talkie *Modern Times*, of 1936, as the co-worker who gets Charlie caught up in the factory machine when both are sent to restart the idle works. His hallmark moustache was of course a prop, which meant he was never recognized

CHESTER CONKLIN WAS SUPPOSED TO STAR IN
THE FIRST KEYSTONE PICTURE THAT OUR HERO
APPEARED IN — **BUT** —

Chaplin entering legend . . .

in his own clean-shaven face when he clocked off work at the studio. The great 'tache, he said, was adopted in imitation of a man back home in Oskaloosa: 'I used to hang around his shop waiting for him to talk so I could watch it move up and down.'

It does a lot of moving in *Mabel at the Wheel*, in which Conklin plays Mabel Normand's excitable father in a tale of skulduggery at the racing-car track. Charlie Chaplin plays the villain, a strange character in coat and top hat, much like his get-up in his very first movie, *Making a Living*, with a bizarre goatee beard and a Ford Sterling-like gait and facial mugging. Charlie and his crook friends kidnap Mabel's boyfriend, a racing driver played by Harry McCoy, and Mabel 'takes the wheel' and wins the race in his place. Mack Sennett himself contributes a cameo, as a rube spectator who spits tobacco juice all over Chester and ogles the women in the seats behind him.

Obviously Charlie was not quite ready to adopt The Tramp as his absolute stock-in-trade, though the character was immediately popular. Mabel was co-directing *Mabel at the Wheel* with Mack Sennett, and Chaplin staged an on-set rebellion against her instructions, sitting down in the road and refusing to work. This might have ended Charlie's stint at Keystone prematurely, David Robinson has recounted, but for news from the financial office back east that audiences and bookers were clamouring for more Charlie Chaplin pictures. Both Charlie and The Tramp went back to work.

In all, Chaplin appeared in thirty-five films at Keystone, of which he directed twenty-one, beginning with *Twenty Minutes of Love*, made in April. He appeared with most of the stock company: Arbuckle, Minta Durfee, Conklin, Swain, Alice Davenport, Edgar Kennedy (another 1913 recruit), Hank Mann, Al St John and Fred Mace. Chaplin was steadily honing his skills, learning to craft scenes with quick cuts and frenetic action, and other scenes in which the camera would hold in one shot to allow his comedy 'bizness' to unfold at its own pace and flow. Anything was ripe for experimentation, including the old vaudeville cross-dressing act, as used in *A Busy Day*, a kind of extended *Kid Auto Races*, with Charlie as an alarmingly violent lady spectator, wife of Mack Swain, who lashes out right and left with her parasol in a parade crowd until Mack shoves her over the pier.

On 9 August, four days after the declaration of war in Europe, Charlie wrote to his brother Sydney, back in England:

My Dear Sid,

You are doubtless realizing who is addressing you. Yes. It really is your brother Chas. After all these years, but you must forgive me. The whole of my time is taken up with the movies . . . Well, Sid, I have made good. All the theatres feature my name in big letters, i.e. 'Chas. Chaplin hear today' [*sic*] . . . All the managers tell me I have 50 letters a week from men and women from all parts of the world. It is wonderfull [*sic*] how popular I am in such a short time and next year I hope to make a bunch of dough. I have had all kinds of offers . . .

Charlie was already plotting to move on to a studio with a little less ensemble and a lot more Chaplin in the foreground, for a lot more dough. But he had also been convincing Sennett that if one Chaplin was an asset, two would be better, and he warned Sydney not to accept an offer at Keystone for less than $175 a week. In the event, Sydney would join Keystone in November, just before Charlie began negotiating with the Essanay Company of Chicago.

The late autumn of 1914 spelled disaster for Europe, but in California, comedy had never had it so good. America had not been at war since 1898, and had no intention, at that point, of being sucked in. In September, Charlie romped with Roscoe Arbuckle in *The Rounders*, as two late-night revellers, and in October he was mixed up in a bakery plot with Chester Conklin, *Dough and Dynamite*. Both films featured a young twenty-one-year-old extra named Charles Parrott, who had joined the studio as early as March 1913, but his future antics as Charley Chase are not yet apparent on screen.

Chaplin's next two films, *Gentlemen of Nerve* and *His Musical Career*, highlight his partnership with Mack Swain, another stalwart who would return to glory in a later classic, *The Gold Rush* of 1925 – as the starving prospector who chases Charlie around the snowbound hut with an axe under the mistaken belief that he is a chicken.

Mack Swain, born in Salt Lake City in 1876, of English–Norwegian ancestry, had worked for twenty-two years, since the age of eleven, in theatre, vaudeville, black-face minstrelsy and 'almost every line except grand opera'. He was to create, at Keystone, a heavyweight character called Ambrose, a vainglorious braggart who gets embroiled in various scrapes. In *His Musical Career*, he and Charlie are professional movers, given an assignment to deliver a new piano to a rich client and to repossess another piano from a poor musician who has fallen behind on his payments. Off they go in their donkey cart, in scenes which clearly inspired Stan Laurel, who, as Stanley Jefferson, had accompanied Chaplin on the two Karno tours and was still, at that time, touring with Karno's *Night at an English Music Hall* act. Mack pulling the piano with Charlie sliding behind it, Charlie dropping the piano on Mack's prone body and their tussle to haul it up a flight of steps, look forward to Laurel and Hardy's classic short, *The Music Box*, of 1932. Charlie and Ambrose even outdo Stan and Ollie in their climax, a spectacular slide of the piano down a steep road to sink into a lake.

Chester Conklin and Mack Swain

Midway through Chaplin's Keystone trajectory (though the film shot in the summer was not released till November), he participated in Mack Sennett's boldest project to date: the production of the cinema's first long-length comedy feature, *Tillie's Punctured Romance*. Full-length features, lasting four to five reels (each reel running eleven to fourteen minutes depending on the camera cranking speed), had been appearing since 1912, with even longer films coming from Europe in the form of Scandinavian dramas and Italian epics such as the eight-reel *Quo Vadis*. D. W. Griffith had shot his four-reel *Judith of Bethulia* in 1913, and in the summer of 1914 was about to commence a massive project, *The Clansman*, which would become *Birth of a Nation*. All these were dramas, but why should comedy be left behind?

Historian Kalton Lahue writes that Sennett's financial backers, Kessel and Baumann, were at first appalled by the idea of Sennett risking a budget of $50,000 on a single film, long as it might be. They demanded a star with a clout beyond Keystone's rowdy ensemble. Sennett chose the person who had given him his introduction to show business a dozen years earlier, the theatrical diva, Marie Dressler. The movie would be an adaptation of one of her great stage successes, *Tillie's Nightmare*. The show was the tale of a drudge who dreams that she visits her lover in New York, whom she weds in a sumptuous ceremony, after which they both fly off in an airship. Dressler told Hollywood columnist Louella Parsons in 1915:

'I loved Tillie . . . she was so human. She was my idea, and that is why I dragged her into the movies. Through the screen I am taking her to the human people, the people I could never reach, because they never had the price. There never was, in my estimation, a show worth $2 . . . I wanted to come to the "movies" with a 10 cent to 50 cent performance, and I intend to remain with them, watch me.'

This tug of war, between Dressler's desire to enhance her theatrical creation's appeal to working women everywhere and Sennett's co-option of her into the Keystone gang, would cause business headaches and lawsuits later. But for the moment, Sennett poured all his resources into the pot. Chaplin, Dressler and Normand would be the leads, and everyone else piled in after. The story was altered, while keeping its initial rube background: Tillie, 'the pride of Yokeltown and the apple of her Papa's eye', has some money stashed in a jar. Charlie – not playing the tramp, another sign that he was not yet ready to settle on the mask – is 'The Stranger, a wise guy who sought country lanes when city streets became too hot for him'. Mabel is his floozie back home. Attired in frock coat and straw boater, with cane, Charlie flirts with Tillie and entices her to the city in the hope of getting his hands on her cash. ('From the pure breath of the open spaces to the fetid atmosphere of the wicked city is but a step – and what a step!') She gets drunk in a restaurant, slaps everyone around and ends up in jail. Meanwhile, Charlie has rejoined

Mabel. Tillie is released, destitute, into the streets, and gets a job as a drudge in the restaurant. Wealth beckons, however, because her millionaire uncle has gone mountain climbing and fallen into the snow. Charlie sees a newspaper item about the missing heiress and rushes her into marriage before she finds out about the inheritance herself.

This leads to the grand party in Uncle's swank mansion, now taken over by Tillie and Charlie. Mabel follows, dressed as a maid. Tillie tangoes, sweeping all before her. Much pratfalling and slapping-about of flunkeys ensues. Then news comes that Uncle Banks is not dead after all, and he turns up to chase them all out. Bullets, mayhem: the Kops are called, and the denouement has all and sundry falling over the pier. Mabel and Tillie both reject Charlie and embrace, tearfully declaring that 'he ain't no good for neither of us'.

For our present tastes, the film hardly stands the test of time. Sennett directed personally, in a convention based on the old 'one shot, one set-up' format, with almost no close shots. Three-quarter long shots dominate in all scenes. Marie Dressler was not a born pantomimist, although she could match anyone else in a pratfall. Both Dressler and Chaplin do a great deal of mugging, Ford Sterling style. Nevertheless, the movie was a box-office smash, and Chaplin became even more of a bankable Hollywood name.

Sennett, however, had his eye on other matters besides the success of one of his stars. The production of the feature was already tied in with an idea germinating among his financial backers and between himself and his fellow producer, Thomas Ince. *Moving Picture World*, in August 1914, got a whiff of this possible seismic shift:

INCE AND SENNETT COMING EAST
*Their Visit May Mean the Two Men Are to Manufacture for Themselves –
and It May Not.*

The two chief directors of the New York Motion Picture Company – Thomas H. Ince, director general of the Kay-Bee, Broncho and Domino brands, and Mack Sennett, creator and director of Keystone comedies – left Los Angeles early in the week, and will arrive in New York Monday, July 27 . . . their sudden coming to the metropolis has given rise to a variety of rumors.

One report had it that there had been a disagreement between Ince and Sennett and their employers and that the directors were preparing to cut loose and go on producing independently . . .

Kalton Lahue, in his book *Kops and Custards*, stated that the visit was made primarily to show Sennett's bosses, Kessel and Baumann, the finished print of *Tillie* and discuss its marketing strategy. There were all kinds of financial obstacles. K & B's normal contract with its distributors, the Mutual Film Company, was arranged for a multitude of short subjects, and the payment for a single film, albeit a longer one, would not cover the production costs. Marie Dressler's fee alone had been $2,500 a week, and her husband, James Dalton, was party to an arrangement with Sennett that, she believed, would give her a stake in the exploitation of the film. Kessel and Baumann brought in another businessman, Al Lichtman, who had formed his own company, Alco, to distribute the film exclusively, for $100,000. Kessel and Baumann were happy, but Marie Dressler sued. Then Alco went bust. The Mutual Film Company were left muttering and grumbling, and their chief executive, Harry Aitken, began to formulate a plan which could bypass these endless wrangles, soon to be exacerbated by disputes over Griffith's new epic, which Aitken was also financing. In early January 1915, Kessel and Baumann travelled from New York to Los Angeles to examine Keystone's operations.

But by January 1915, Chaplin had gone from Keystone, having decamped at the end of his year's contract to Essanay in Chicago. He had demanded $1,000 a week from Sennett for a new contract. Sennett offered a three-year deal, with a salary rising from $500 a week in the first year to $750 for the second and $1,500 for the third. Chaplin suggested reversing the fees, taking $1,500 the first year, and so forth. Sennett passed.

'Start with Sennett – get rich somewhere else!' Chaplin certainly fulfilled that promise. By the summer of 1915, his first Essanay films, *His New Job*, *A Night Out*, *The Champion*, *In the Park*, *A Jitney Elopement* and particularly *The Tramp*, which cemented the character that was to penetrate so deeply into the twentieth century's psyche, would make him world famous, hyped and interviewed endlessly, merchandized and sung about in the streets.

Without Keystone's rickety sets, the pre-existing world of its eccentric characters, bums, ne'er-do-wells, violent philanderers, innocent young swains, rude women and social braggarts, however, Charlie the Tramp would never have been born. For while Chaplin brought the form of Karno pantomime to his new world, the content was Sennett's own America, contagious, nervous, always at high speed.

It was a world, too, of cruelty and ruthlessness. In *His Trysting Place*, shot in September 1914, Charlie is married to Mabel and living in a cramped, poor apartment, with a squalling baby whom Charlie holds over the oven like a sack of lard, looking forward to the brilliant tropes of 1917's *Easy Street*, when Charlie the cop feeds the poor family's brood of children like chickens. The Diner, where Charlie encounters Mack Swain's Ambrose, is a place of frenetic hurry, in which soup-eating is a contest almost of mortal combat, and Charlie wipes his dirty hands on a customer's beard. All the little bits and pieces of business that made up The Tramp's many mannerisms, his cane-twirling, ear-picking attention to small details, were a realization in depth of Keystone's external chaos. Chaplin's gestures expressed his thoughts and feelings about the tumult surrounding him, and it was this that enabled him to communicate with audiences of any background, universally. But though he slowed down his character, the New World surged on around him at its urban whirlwind pace.

Charlie's last film for Keystone was *His Prehistoric Past*, a vintage tale of men in animal furs and a bevy of 'caving-beauties'. Ambrose and Charlie knock each other happily over the head with clubs, only for Charlie to wake up from his dream at the end on a park bench, with a policeman's stick beating time on his cranium.

He saunters out of the frame, leaving the Kops and other assorted riff-raff in charge of the Keystone Sennetorium.

# CHAPTER TWELVE

# Love and Money
## (or *Mack and Mabel, Episode Two*)

From an interview with Mack Sennett, in the *Toledo Blade*, 23 January 1917:

### WORDS MEAN NOTHING IN LIFE OF FUNSTER MACK SENNETT

A Seeker of Information interviewed Mack Sennet [*sic*], the Keystone comedy maker, the other day. He went away much wiser than when he came. The conversation follows:

**Seeker of Information** – How do you get the effect of a man flying through space propelled by his own momentum? Everybody knows that can't be done.

**Mack Sennett** – If it can't be done, why ask me how I do it? You saw him fly, didn't you?

**S of I** – Apparently your men are thrown or projected through brick walls. How do you do that?

**MS** – Have you heard of the Fourth Dimension? Maybe we have found the secret.

**S of I** – In your automobile and taxicab smashups – how do you manage them? Every one is apparently killed, but we know you cannot do that.

**MS** – That is a simple trick – the machines just run together – you read of it in the papers every day.

**S of I** – I have seen your men jump off 10 story buildings into tanks of water.

**MS** – Yes, we have some divers on the lot . . . .

**S of I** – I know that a man can't swing off a 20 foot bridge by his heels and grab a girl out of a rowboat, but you apparently achieved that.

**MS** – Oh, yes, we have some acrobatic performers among our comedians – that is simple.

**S of I** – You know and I know that the wind can't blow the feathers off a hen and leave her stripped for the skillet – yet I saw you pull off that stunt all right.

**MS** – We have wind of unusual strength and velocity switched on to order.

**S of I** – I saw one of your fellows flying over the city attached to an umbrella. How'd you manage that?

**MS** – Easy. He just held to the umbrella and it did the rest . . .

**S of I** – How do you pull off those train wrecks? They can't happen, of course.

**MS** – There are train wrecks occasionally. We try to have a man with his camera on all trains in case of accident.

**S of I** – Do you really burn buildings?

**MS** – Oh, yes. No Keystone day is complete without a fire . . .

**S of I** – How do you manage those explosions where the fellows are blown to smithereens and a whole house is wrecked?

**MS** – Well, every now and then somebody gets careless with dynamite and accidents will happen. We regret wrecking the homes of prominent citizens – but if the homes get in the way we can't help it. Our fellows are used to being blown up; it's part of the game. They expect it.

Unsourced, 1915:

'SUPERVISED BY SENNETT' *Full meaning of the phrase illustrated at the taking of a film . . .*

On the mammoth stage of the Keystone Studios at Edendale, California:
The stage was set for a large ballroom scene. The orchestra had taken their places at the foot of a great staircase leading to a landing where a number of young men and women in evening clothes were chatting. A hundred couples stood in little groups around the polished floor. Three cameras were trained on the set and the director, megaphone in hand, stood ready to begin the rehearsal.

A man sat behind the piano at the rear of the set. He did not look at the scene and did not appear to be listening to the words of the director. His derby hat was well over on his forehead and his hands were buried deep in his pockets. No one seemed to pay any attention to him. But when the scene had been rehearsed two or three times, lights had been called for and the camera man was preparing to get busy, the man behind the piano quickly rose and walked to the director's chair.

It was Mack Sennett. Apparently he had not paid the slightest attention to anything that had gone before, yet he knew every situation and every move of the actors. With his first words his face relaxed, and from that time on the famous director acted as if he enjoyed the work, the extras caught his spirit and did better than they knew. This was an illustration of what has been called Sennett's magic . . .

From the memoirs of Gloria Swanson:

The following Monday I got on a streetcar and took the long ride to the Keystone studio in Edendale (from Cahuenga Boulevard) . . . The building was a large, sprawling shed with slanting glass roofs, topped by a big printed sign that said MACK SENNETT STUDIOS. When I entered the tiny office, which stood beside the shed, it was absolutely mobbed with people trying to see producers. There was no place to sit or stand. I tried to explain to several people that I had a letter of introduction, but they looked at me as if I were crazy. I was on the verge of leaving when someone called out my name.

'Gloria Swanson, what are you doing in California?' . . . It was Frank Hayes, from Key West . . . 'Hampton!' he called to a strange-looking man hurrying past. 'This young lady has a letter to Mr Sennett.'

The other man sized me up and said, 'She doesn't need a letter. What a crazy day.' Then he said to me, 'I'm Hampton Del Ruth. Come with me.' He grabbed me by the arm and dragged me down a corridor to an office with Mr. Sennett's name on it. Mr. Sennett was not there. So Mr. Del Ruth dragged me outside to a back lot. 'Wait right here,' he said; 'I see him.' A few minutes later he came back with a man of about thirty in shirt sleeves and suspenders. 'What about her?' he asked the man.

I smiled sweetly, but Mr. Sennett didn't say a word. He raised the brim of his hat an inch, chewed on his cigar, spat out the juice on the ground and studied me as though I were a pony at a country fair. 'The clothes are terrible,' he said . . . 'and that make-up is a joke . . .' As he walked away, he called back over his shoulder to Mr. Del Ruth, 'Have her call on Thursday.'

And they kept calling, every day of the week. Kessel and Baumann's visit of January 1915 had resulted in another expansion of the Edendale studio facilities. These included a new 155-foot indoor stage, with full lighting equipment, a new building for the actors, with seventy-five dressing rooms, showers, baths and lounges. An artificial lake, forty feet by twenty, was built outside the stage, along with new administration buildings and garages for the studio vehicles. A whole new roster of directors and writers joined the ever-growing list of players. Del Henderson, Charles Avery, Fred Fishbach and Frank Griffin were behind the camera, as well as Mabel Normand and Roscoe Arbuckle, who were directing their own titles, and Charles Parrott, who had graduated from the extras pool. On the acting side, Ford Sterling, who had left with Henry 'Pathé' Lehrman for other pastures early in 1914 (they created Sterling Comedies, then had a bust up, and Lehrman went on to found his own L-KO company), returned, resuming his post as the Chief of the Keystone Kops, as well as other apoplectic roles. Fred Mace, who had left in 1913 to make films with other companies, also returned in 1915. Mack Swain, Chester Conklin, Slim Summerville, Bobby Dunn, Bill Colvin, Nick Cogley, Earle Rodney, Eddie Ring Sutherland (listed on his own card as 'Juvenile', but later to become one of Hollywood's stalwart producer–directors), Joseph 'Baldy' Belmont, Harry Williams ('I love old Tin Pan Alley – But this is the life, boys!'), Shorty Hamilton and Frank Hayes were only some of the featured male actors. Della Pringle ('The Woman of the Smile and a Million Friends'), Polly Moran, May Emory, Cecile Arley, Claire Anderson and Louella Maxam formed the nucleus of the Sennett girls, not necessarily restricted to bathing.

Peggy Pearce, Vivian Edwards and Dorothy Dufee added more comic skills, as did Dale Fuller – 'Eccentric Comedienne' – who added her slinky and sometimes sullen presence to many titles, and Ora Carew, a Griffith dramatic soubrette who exchanged the Fine Arts studio film company for the madhouse. Julia Faye was another Fine Arts graduate who, in the words of the *Dramatic Mirror*'s roundup of Keystone starlets, 'is a fearless little lady . . . it was only the other day that she worked in a burning set until the wrap was taken from her shoulders by the flames, and Julia . . . dashed out just in time to escape the falling wreckage'.

Louise Fazenda was another 1915 addition to the roster, and quickly became a leading lady. A tough and athletic comedienne, described as having 'light hair, hazel eyes, weighs 138 pounds and . . . double-jointed from the neck down', she came to be cast in the role of the gawky, simple girl who wins through despite all the odds.

Like so many of our subjects, she told various conflicting stories of her life BK – Before Keystone – telling one correspondent (from *Motion Picture Classic*):

I was raised in an atmosphere of roasts on Sunday, starched calico dresses that scratched, and missionary meetings. My rather lonely girlhood has bred in me an absolute frankness towards myself and other people which made it difficult to understand the little peculiarities of folk in general . . . It was daily instilled in me that life was a serious proposition – there was no such word as humor, and comedy consisted only of black-faced clowns and medicine fakers.

Charlie Murray and Louise Fazenda

But another press story constructed her childhood as a tomboy:

the boys seemed to Louise to have the most fun, playing ball and duck on the
rock and other manly sports adapted to their years. So Louise left the little
girls and their dolls and learned to swat the horse-hide sphere . . . She has
remained a ball player ever since, and recently took part in a match in Los
Angeles, amazing the beholders with her skill and speed . . .

Fazenda's first work for the screen was in westerns for a small
company called Joker, before she ignored warnings of Keystone's
'raucous' reputation and walked up to 'a fierce-eyed individual', who
turned out to be Mack Swain.

Was he using any people today?

'Can you shoot a gun?' he roared back . . .

I should say I could, without batting an eye . . .

Keystone provided young women like Louise with a perfect anti-dote to the conventional female roles. Neither child-women nor *femmes fatales*, they could muck in, indulge in the rough stuff with the male of the species, hammer people over the head and be hammered, giving as good as they got. Sennett teamed Louise up first with Mack Swain in his 'Ambrose' series, but she was later paired most often with Charlie Murray, one of the veteran troupers on the Keystone lot, whose previous career in vaudeville as half of a double act, Murray and Mack, had lasted over twenty years. Murray had his own starring series at Keystone, as Hogan, a clumsy and workshy, if sometimes resourceful, working man, in titles such as *Hogan the Porter*, *Hogan's Mussy Job*, *Hogan Out West* (all 1915) and so forth. Louise Fazenda stayed with Sennett well into the 1920s, and Charlie Murray soldiered on into talkie times.

Other names that have vanished into the scratches of old films, but who were stalwarts of the Keystone family, were Harry and Eddie Gribbon, Wayland Trask, Hugh Fay, Victor 'Slippery Slim' Potel, Fritz Schade, James Donnelly, Harry Booker, Raymond Griffith (eventually to become the most neglected star of silent comedy movies), Blanche Payson (Oliver Hardy's harpie wife in *Helpmates*), et cetera, et cetera, et cetera. The bevy of beauties, Gloria Swanson, Phyllis Haver, Mary Thurman, Vera Stedman, Eleanor Field, Mae Busch, kept calling, the latter – recruited in 1915 – destined to play a legendary role in Mack Sennett's own personal saga.

For 'Father Goose', however, Mabel Normand remained his favourite gosling. Now that Chaplin had gone, Mabel was the most prominent presence on the lot, and the favourite of Hollywood's press corps, who voted her a close rival to Mary Pickford as their top actress of the day. In August 1915, she was on the cover of *Photoplay* magazine, which recorded 'some impressions of a girl who has made the world brighter for millions'. Writer James R. Quirk did not stint on hyperbole, as he described a gloomy day on the Sennett lot:

The clouds rolled by. The sun burst forth. Joy and Cheer made a bayonet charge on the Gloom trenches . . .

Mabel Normand had arrived.

'Hello, fellers,' yells Mabel – just like that, as she flashed her great, laughing eyes around in a general greeting, and everyone drinks in the smile.

'Hello, Mabel,' they all yell back: and inside five minutes five cameramen are winding the five funniest film comedies in the world into black boxes, and half a hundred high salaried fun makers are seriously at work manufacturing laughs for the movie millions.

Well, it's not the real world, after all. In the real world, the romance between Mack and Mabel had already entered stormy waters. The legend recounts Mack's own version:

Mabel and I were engaged and unengaged more than twenty times . . . and once or twice we set a date. But things being like they were around Hollywood, she would hear stories about me and I would hear stories about her, and our affair was a series of fractures and refractures . . .

And therein lies a convoluted tale . . .

In order to put together the puzzle picture of the story of Mack and Mabel from its scattered fragments, we have to delve a little deeper into the shadowy corners beyond the sunshine of all that make-believe. Hollywood's happy mirror would be shattered some years later, in 1921, by the Fatty Arbuckle scandal, to be followed barely a year after that by the murky murder case of William Desmond Taylor, involving Mabel and a host of other happytown habitants, and even that was only the beginning of the end of the myth of primal innocence among the fragrant orange groves. In 1922, an anonymous booklet was published by 'A Hollywood Newspaper Man', later to be revealed as Ed Roberts, once the editor of *Photoplay Journal*. The booklet was called *The Sins of Hollywood: An Exposé of Movie Vice*, and it portrayed, in lurid terms, a place of coruscating hypocrisy, in which the cynical propagandists of the press – presumably including himself – had imbued Hollywood's movie people 'with every ennobling trait', while 'privately they have lived, and are still living, lives of wild debauchery'.

Licentiousness, wild parties, orgies, 'hop' and 'dope', openly illicit liaisons, yachting parties, the secluded road houses and private residences at which drunken revels were held regularly, all undermined the innocent faith of 'the boys and girls of the land' in the popular idols whom they 'applauded, lauded and showered with gold'. Roberts does not date the start of these Bacchanalian revels, but puts the blame squarely on those new denizens of the California paradise who, unlike an earlier generation of theatrical stalwarts, who had 'held their wits' in the temptations of the entertainment gold rush, were 'the upstarts, the poor uncouth, ill-bred "roughnecks", many of whom are today famous stars, and who never knew there was so much money in the world, who made the Sins of Hollywood the glaring, red sins they are today'. In other words, the lower classes who had made good.

Both Mack and Mabel could be said to belong to this new upstart group, or could be seen as its typical exemplars. In the sunshine world, Mabel cavorted with her motor cars, exemplifying the modern 'liberated' woman, riding horses, pursuing all her outdoor sports, ecstatically happy both in her private and working life. Despite the fact that her salary remained at $500 per week from Keystone, not quite a queen's ransom, she lived a life that many young women, and men, envied and aspired to, buying jewellery and furs, taking a chauffeured Rolls-Royce to a party, then getting bored and riding home in a milk wagon. Mack, on the other hand, was the quintessential 'man of the people' who had picked himself up by his own bootstraps and fulfilled the American Dream of the self-made entrepreneur, never happier than when at work, presiding over his buzzing brood of employees, making decisions, overseeing all the fine detail, the Man in Control of His Destiny.

To Mack, the official story was still the old tale of the shy, somewhat clumsy boy and the pretty dynamic girl who wouldn't stay still to be kissed. He was not, of course, the only boy on the lot who wanted to kiss her. Chaplin made his play, but was rebuffed, and another rival, playing Toplitsky to Mack's Schnitz the Tailor, was none other than his chief director, Henry 'Pathé' Lehrman, who, according to Gene Fowler's jaunty tale, revealed his true feelings to Mack while the mogul luxuriated in his iconic thinking bath:

Pathé blurted out: 'You may as well know the truth. Mabel and I are in love. Now you know.'

Sennett sat up and stared hard at Pathé. 'Take your jokes somewhere else.'
Pathé was pale. 'It's no joke. I meant to tell you before.'
Sennett gripped the side of the tub. 'How long's this been going on?'
'Since Tia Juana. It began down there.'
Mack was dazed. 'You and Mabel!' he said. 'You and Mabel in love!'
Pathé started for the door. 'I'm quitting.'

Mabel Normand in glamour days

And that's why Lehrman left Sennett, if you wish to believe it. Mack himself claimed that he was often insanely jealous of Mabel, and followed her boyfriends around, hiding behind a tree, a tale more Keystone than kredible. A tussle with another suitor, actor Jack Mulhall, led to an unseemly brawl at Mabel's apartment, leaving the suitor with a black eye. Eventually, his story went, Mack plucked up courage and got her to name a wedding day, 4 July 1915. He had already bought her a shining five-thousand-dollar diamond ring, which she kept for the day.

But Mabel, too, was intensely jealous of the many starlets who pranced and preened for their priapic boss. Just before the wedding date, Mack related in *King of Comedy*, he took one of these ladies to dinner and then to his apartment to discuss her coming roles. Mabel broke in upon them, got the wrong idea and stormed out. The wedding was off.

Mack did not name the lady, but the unfolding legend has named her as Mae Busch, an Australian-born brunette who had just joined the Keystone company. The story was that, as Mabel had introduced Mae to the studio, she felt doubly betrayed. The story behind the story, which has since become the accepted version, was that Mabel returned to her own apartment to find Mack in his underpants and Mae Busch naked in the bed. Mae panicked and smashed a vase over Mabel's head. A version of this tale was told by Roscoe Arbuckle's wife, Minta Durfee, to Arbuckle's biographer, David Yallop, claiming that Mabel had been out driving with Minta and another actress, Anne Luther, when Anne told her that if she went home, 'she would catch her lover with another woman', naming Mae. Later that night, the Arbuckles found Mabel on their porch with blood pouring from her head. Two weeks after this, Mabel tried to commit suicide by jumping off the Santa Monica pier.

The dates of these tales do not gel. In July 1915, Mabel was being voted 'Best Comedian – Female' in *Motion Picture Magazine*'s 'Great Cast Contest', and on the ninth of that month she appeared at a benefit at St Catherine's Church in Los Angeles, together with a whole Keystone crew. In August, the 'Girl on the Cover' article appeared in *Photoplay*, celebrating anti-Gloom Mabel and the sunshine. Evidently neither wedding nor head injury and suicide attempt had taken place then. On 10 September, *Variety* reported that 'Mabel Normand defeated 20 others in a five-mile swim at Santa Monica recently'. On 30 September, though, the *Los Angeles Herald* reported:

## MABEL NORMAND FIGHTING DEATH

While medical science waged a desperate battle for her life, Mabel Normand, famous film star and comedy queen, was unconscious and rapidly sinking today.

Her physician, Dr. O. M. Justice, early today stated that the chance for her recovery was slight . . .

Miss Normand's illness is attributed to an accident in the studio of the Keystone company . . . a little more than a week ago. It is stated that the beautiful star fell, sustaining injuries to her head.

Other papers added that the injury had occurred during a wedding scene, featuring Roscoe Arbuckle, at which 'a general bombardment of old shoes and rice' had taken place, with misthrown footwear hitting Mabel in the head as Fatty dodged it. Sennett was reported to have said that 'the accident was unavoidable and that no one could be blamed'.

Mabel's biographer, Mary Harper Fussell, plumped for the version she was told by Hollywood gossip queen Adela Rogers St Johns, who claimed to have been present when Mabel jumped off the pier – 'the Nat Goodwin Pier in Santa Monica where there was a big restaurant called the Sunset Inn'. Mabel said: 'This is doing nobody any good. If he loved me he wouldn't have gone to bed with Mae.' Then she jumped, and was rescued by two life-guards on the spot.

So what are the facts? Putting aside the recollections of senior citizens, the primary source for the Mack, Mae and Mabel imbroglio appears to be the aforementioned Ed Roberts' exposé of Hollywood's sins. In a section headed 'A Battle Royal That Led to Stardom', 'Anonymous' recounted the tale with loosely concealed pseudonyms – 'Molly' for Mabel and 'Jack' for Mack, though Mae is named Mae – setting the event in a 'love nest' Mack had set up for Mabel. 'Molly', Roberts wrote, had befriended Mae on the lot and 'frolicked' with her, though he does not elaborate on that word. As for Mack, Roberts writes: 'Temptation tossed her curls and beckoned him to come and play along the Highways of Immorality.' Roberts writes of a succession of parties, of which Mabel was ignorant. Returning from an out-of-town trip ahead of time, she chanced upon the two lovers in her own 'love nest'. Mae battered her rival's head against the window sill in the ensuing fight.

The result, Roberts claimed, was a ruthless payoff for 'Molly'. Calling 'Jack' to her sickbed, as she lay with her head swathed in bandages, still atwixt life and death, she gave him her ultimatum: exposure, or a movie deal. Instead of her weekly pay, he would procure for her her own studio, with his best director, and a feature drama project that would be all her own. In fact, Roberts wrote, Mabel was faking it, and her injury was not life-threatening at all.

The upshot is history: Mabel got her own studio and made her feature film, *Mickey*, in 1917. She never married Mack, and never forgave him. Finis of Mack and Mabel Romance.

We are, indeed, totally lost in this hall of mirrors. As Chico Marx once asked: 'Who do you believe? Me, or the evidence of your own eyes?'

But there are other ramifications to this story that lead us even further into the fog of assumptions and speculations about the goose that was laying the golden eggs of comedy. The plot had much more thickening to undergo.

# CHAPTER THIRTEEN

# Of Mabel, Mammon and Mamma

Mack Sennett had many other concerns, apart from his love life, in the spring and summer of 1915. The expansion of the studios set in motion by Kessel and Baumann was the first part of a strategy which was to culminate by July 1915 in the setting-up of a new motion-picture company, the Triangle Film Corporation. This was the brainchild of the third party in their business, Harry Aitken, then chief executive of their distributors, Mutual. His idea was simple, and in line with the trends occurring in the contemporary development of American industries: get away from all the squabbling of small independent companies and their distributors by amalgamating the strongest and most successful forces in the business, which were already loosely affiliated – i.e., D. W. Griffith's feature-film operation, Thomas Ince and the Sennett Keystone studios. The initial name for the corporation was 'SIG' or 'Sig', for Sennett–Ince–Griffith, but this was too silly and became Triangle.

If capitalism tends to monopoly, as not only Karl Marx asserted, why buck the trend? The boldness of the idea is made explicit in a long and revealing letter sent by Charles Baumann in New York to Mack Sennett at the Los Angeles Athletic Club, dated 4 June 1915:

The new contracts beginning as of September 1st will be made with the Distributing Company, which is being formed, after having had two days discussion here with Aitken and Griffith . . .

We are working hard in landing and lining up all of the stars for Griffith and Ince, such as Billie Burke, Maud Adams, Grace George, Francis Star, Nazimova, David Warfield, Henry Miller, Otis Skinner, Southern & Marlowe, Nat Goodwin and in fact all of the stars on the legitimate stage . . . Regarding the Keystone Company, we are negotiating and hope to close contracts in the same way as with the people above referred to, with Montgomery & Stone, Eddie Foy, Weber & Fields . . . and all of the biggest people in the comedy line . . .

The plan was to draw together not only production but a line-up of stars with which other film companies couldn't hope to compete:

It has also been decided that the Motion Picture stars be corralled, such as Mary Pickford, Marguerite Clark, Charley [sic] Chaplin, and in fact any of them that may come up very strong in the next few months. We have decided in view of our new plan to corral both the legitimate and Motion Picture stars, regardless of cost, for the reason of taking the props right from under any other Motion Picture concern right in America, and we being then absolutely in a position to get the very best theatres in America right off the bat . . .

The flaw in the plan was glaringly obvious, as Chaplin, comedy's greatest star, was signed for a year to Essanay in Chicago, but Baumann did not let this daunt his ambition:

Be sure to make new contract with Sydney Chaplin if you believe him to be of a value that will fill the bill for the big scheme, and use your own judgement in getting him at the best figure, but at any rate get him, especially if it will help you to get Charley back at the expiration of his contract. We have decided that we can go as high as $3000 a week for Charley Chaplin if it is absolutely necessary, but be sure to get him signed up and contracted for beginning immediately at the close of his present contract with the Essanay. This is very important. We are all of the opinion here that if we have to pay him $3000 a week and he *doesn't even appear in pictures*, we have accomplished a great deal by getting him away from a competing Company, thereby leaving no competition in the field for the Keystone films, and it will also help us to get higher prices from the exhibitors . . .

The new plan and organization is so well laid out and founded that we are all in common now for one another, and we now have the big three taking care of the producing end, and confidentially Aitken intends to resign from the Mutual after June 16th and will begin activities with us to get ready to open the big show about September 1st. So in view of all this be sure to add Charley Chaplin, even if you hate his guts [sic], for the reason that he must be gotten out of the market and competition in that line killed.

Nothing becomes America so much as capitalism untrammelled, and as Kessel and Baumann were plotting to monopolize screen acting, Harry Aitken, the money man, was moving in on his Wall Street bankers, an investment firm called F. S. Smithers and Company. Aitken was riding high, as his gamble on backing Griffith's epic *Birth of a Nation* had paid off in huge profits. The film had opened in February 1915 and was packing in audiences, pro and con, at prices

The Keystone–Triangle ethos

that ran to two dollars a seat. Theatre owners and exhibitors were rolling in dough. The bankers were, despite their caution, impressed.

Aitken's financial methods were of a kind that present-day high flyers would find familiar, as Kalton Lahue explained: 'He owned many pieces of various organizations on paper, but then again, he really didn't – one had been mortgaged to buy another which in turn was used as collateral for a third and so on.' In short, a classic scam. As Baumann explained to Sennett, 'SIG' would be formed for five million dollars, consisting of one million preferred and four million common stock:

We have already arranged with Aitken to have the financiers take $1,000,000 preferred with $4,000,000 common stock as bonus in consideration of their financing and putting up $1,000,000 in cash, which we will get within the next thirty days . . .

Believe me, the new scheme is the last thought and the biggest improvement the Motion Picture Industry has ever known . . .

I believe all of the stock we get out of this particular Distributing Company will be actually worth to each one of us concerned half a million in cash . . .

We must again impress upon your mind the importance of getting Charley Chaplin regardless of cost, when his contract expires . . .

There being no further business to speak of at the present time, we close with the best wishes, hoping to hear from you at the earliest possible moment, particularly in regard to Charley Chaplin, and your approval generally.

Yours sincerely, CB

Sennett would have liked the bit about the half million in cash, but he must have known that he could not satisfy Baumann's Chaplinosis, as The Tramp was firmly set on his own path, and would move on, in 1916, after his Essanay contract, to the de-Aitkenized Mutual Film Corporation, for the staggering sum of $10,000 a week and a signing bonus of $150,000, the highest fee for anyone in the film business at that time. Chaplin was twenty-seven years old.

At any rate, the comings and goings, letters and telegrams and conspiracies involving the setting up of Triangle, and the 'coralling' of talent before rivals became aware of what was going on, occupied much of Sennett's time in the first half of 1915. Secrecy demanded that all parties meet up neither in New York nor California but in La Junta, Colorado, to sign the deal, on 20 July. The day before, a Certificate of Incorporation was filed in Richmond, Virginia, far enough from prying movie moguls. The new company was to have ten directors: Harry Aitken and his brother Roy, Ince, Griffith, Sennett, Adam Kessel and his brother Charles, Baumann and two bankers. The key structural component of Triangle was to be its own chain of theatres, situated in every major city, with the right to first-run exhibition of every Triangle film. The Knickerbocker Theatre in New York, at Broadway and 38th, would showcase the first Triangle programme, which would be Douglas Fairbanks in *The Lamb*, supervised by Griffith, Ince's production, *The Iron Strain*, and Keystone's *My Valet*, a four-reeler starring Raymond Hitchcock and Mabel Normand. The première screening took place on 23 September.

Just one week after this event in New York, Mabel was reported to be languishing close to death in Los Angeles. The press reports suggest, however, that her recovery was pretty rapid, *Photoplayers Weekly* of 16 October announcing that 'she is out of danger and well on the road to complete recovery. During her illness bulletins were read in cafes, theatres and other public places not only in Los

Angeles, but in many other parts of the country . . .' Even in her crisis, the studio press publicists, ruthless then as now, lost no chance to highlight her fame.

Having looked at the events that were distracting Mack Sennett during this crucial time, we might backtrack and glance at Mabel's activities over the same period: On 1 April, the *Los Angeles Times* reported a rumour that Mabel Normand and one Bert Levey, a manager of vaudeville circuits, then twenty-five years old, had plighted their troth and were about to wed. 'It is further reported that Miss Normand will desert the films for the fireside.' Nothing more was heard of this, so perhaps it was only an April Fool piece. Later in April, Mabel and Roscoe Arbuckle left for the grand World's Fair exposition in San Francisco, which resulted in a rare Keystone newsreel-type item, *Mabel and Fatty at the World's Fair*. On 23 April, *Photoplayers Weekly* announced that Mack Sennett was resuming work on 'a six reel feature' with Mabel, presumably *My Valet*.

Mabel's private life seemed to be dogged by the intrusion of what we would today call 'stalkers'. On 30 April, it was reported that 'Miss Mabel Normand, "Queen of the Movies", was greatly annoyed a few days ago by a "nut", who followed her to her home and later to the Keystone studio. He informed the gardener at her home that he was the "King of the Movies" . . .' The 'King' was arrested by the studio gatekeeper. On 24 June, *Photoplayers Weekly* stated that 'Mabel Normand has engaged a cottage at Venice and spends much time there. Her town house is not closed for the summer, however, as she motors back from beach to city and back daily.' The same issue announced the death of Miss Normand's 'blue-ribbon' cat, with the statement that 'henceforth Miss Normand will purchase nothing but stuffed cats'.

On 8 July, our favourite fan magazine told us that Mabel owned a summer home in Bear Valley, 'where she takes parties of friends on weekends, although she is busy this summer shooting her many two-reelers, so she has taken a cottage closer to work, in Santa Monica'. On 22 July, we are told that 'last winter Miss Normand purchased a sixty-foot yacht' which was 'thoroughly overhauled and refurnished'. On her three-day summer vacation, she took her friends to Catalina for a quiet cruise and fishing. On 29 July, the press agents decide that 'Mabel Normand killed a five foot rattler last week'. The snake had leaped in her path and she had dispatched it with a stick and a stone. The same issue told us that Mabel had routed another intruder, a burglar, at her home. She 'picked up a heavy medicine ball which was lying in the room, and flung it at the man, striking him on the chest'. The man skedaddled sharply.

While making allowances for the over-active imagination of the Keystone press agents (in September, they revealed that when shooting beachside scenes for *My Valet*, Mabel was seized by an octopus while being tied to the rocks), it does appear that Mabel was living the most typical life of a Hollywood film star that money could buy. This would not preclude her feeling trapped and depersonalized in a gilded cage, or being besotted with her boss, though all the evidence points to the fact that it was Mack who was crazy about Mabel and not the other way around. She was having a good time and he was breaking his head trying to take over the movie business in his conspiracy with Aitken, Kessel and Baumann. The dalliance with Mae Busch can be seen in more than one light: either as run-of-the-mill Hollywood casting-couch action, or as an uncharacteristic diversion by a business workaholic who took a night off from worrying about money and love. Either way, it is difficult to believe that Mabel was so shocked by this event, if it ever occurred, that she flung herself off the Santa Monica Pier.

But there are yet more angles, and more faces in the distorting mirrors . . .

Mabel biographer Betty Harper Fussell subscribed to the view that Mabel was, in Mack's own words, 'the most naïve person that ever lived', who was passionate, but, in the words of Adela Rogers St Johns, 'unusually pure', with 'no desire, no sex, no nothing'. Ms St Johns' insights were, as we know, highly suspect, but if she were right, Mabel's 'purity' might have had another cause, if we recall our genealogist's findings about the death by congenital syphilis of her baby brother, Walter, in 1898. There might have been a reason for Mabel to shun sex, and this might even shed light on the particular circumstances of her death at the age of thirty-seven. Proof of these matters is hard to come by, at a distance of well over eighty years.

Turning to Mack, Miss Harper Fussell interviewed a one-time companion of Sennett, one Lonnie D'Orsa, who, Miss Fussell states, was

'Mack's production manager in the twenties . . . who lived with him in the mansion . . . that Pickford and Fairbanks vacated when they moved to grander quarters at Pickfair'. D'Orsa claimed that Mack was in love with Mabel but 'didn't want to marry anybody. He was "a man's man". A health nut and a chronic athlete. He got his kicks by walking to work every morning over the top of his 300-acre mountain . . .'

Another 'Sennett contemporary, now in his nineties' told Ms Fussell that 'Mack didn't marry because he was "queer as a coot", just like William Desmond Taylor'. Trotting along this somewhat smudged trail, our genealogist's research informs us that Lonnie D'Orsa, a respected production manager, producer and assistant director, died in 1993, aged ninety-six, and was survived by a wife, although in the 1920s he was unmarried.

Mack's private life, Mabel apart, is, in one regard, not in doubt: he never married, never sired any children, and never, as far as one can ascertain, resided with a female companion, married or not. Mack's residential address during his Keystone–Triangle period is given in city directories as 431 West 7th, abode of the Los Angeles Athletic Club, which had moved into its new purpose-built premises at the corner of Olive Street in 1912. (Mack's first domicile during Keystone's first formative year was at another hotel, the Van Nuys.) Chaplin was another famous resident of the LAAC, where Mack remained through 1920, after which he gives us the slip for a while, to reappear at 141 Westmoreland Place, the multi-roomed mansion which became his personal court. Apart from the Athletic Club, Mack clearly maintained another residence, which we cannot pin down, as described by *Photoplay Journal* in May 1920 under the heading 'What Kind of Man is the Laugh King?':

Personally Mr Sennett is not a 'cut-up'. He enjoys a good story and the companionship of good fellows . . . But to meet him, one is impressed rather with the fact that he is like a successful, dignified man of affairs.

Like most such men, he is simple, unaffected and with a rather attractive shyness that almost approaches bashfulness. Strange to say, he has a horror of having his picture taken. Also, like most successful business men of the day, he gives very careful attention to his physical welfare. He rides every morning, his steed being a mean little wall-eyed broncho whom no one else can ride. He works out in his private gymnasium in the studio and takes a Turkish bath every day. He employs a famous prize fight trainer as his valet . . .

In private life, Mr Sennett lives very quietly – he is a bachelor – in a big house at the beach near Los Angeles. He reads a great deal and, following the peculiarity of many men who live strenuous lives of intense effort, likes detective stories. It is a curious fact that nearly every prominent public man whose life is a storm of terrific effort turns to sleuth stories for relaxation.

At the 'house at the beach', Sennett could be as discreet as he wished. But gossip about Mack's sexuality has percolated down the years, albeit of the most inconclusive kind. A recent book by a Canadian author, Charles Foster, *Stardust and Shadows*, which chronicles Hollywood's Canadian *émigrés*, quotes a Chaplin account of 1958 in which Charlie confronts Sennett with the tale of the 'gambling syndicate that tried to estimate the day and month when Mack and Mabel would get married'. Charlie and Slim Summerville were the only ones who bet the marriage would never happen. When Sennett asked him about this, Charlie replied, '"Because we think you are queer, Mack." He went white as a sheet . . . "How did you know, Charlie, how did you know?"' This unsourced tale, however, sits uncomfortably in the midst of a plethora of gossip and factual errors about other aspects of Sennett's life.

On the other hand, we have an interview conducted by Hollywood historians Joe Adamson and Carlton Moss with veteran director Stuart Heisler, an editor at Keystone from the early days, relating incidents during a later period (the early 1920s), in which he could hear, from his editing room, Sennett making hay with star Phyllis Haver in her adjacent dressing-room: 'He gave Phyllis a little hump. And here I was! The walls were so goddamned thin . . .' Heisler concluded that 'Sennett was one of the greatest cocksmen that was ever in the business. Nothing slipped by him.'

The affair with Phyllis Haver, the only other woman linked with Mack apart from Mae and Mabel, well into the talkie era, will be discussed anon. The evidence, such as it is, is most patchy. Was Sennett, despite Heisler's admiring testimonial, bisexual, or gay? And might the necessity to conceal this explain his insistent self-presentation as the rugged, unintellectual rough diamond? Or is this an unwarranted speculation, assuming that lack of evidence should suggest guilt?

Intimations of homosexuality in Hollywood, even today, can be a source of lawsuits and box-office panic. But the word 'gay' belies the reality that confronted any gay person in the first half of the twentieth century, and the movie colony was, as it remains, a classic model of denial and subterfuge. Even the dirt-flinging Ed Roberts with his *Exposé of Movie Vice* shied away from the 'love that dare not speak its name'. Exposure meant shame, shunning and oblivion. Even the merest hint of bisexuality would be destructive.

The intrusive biographer is pressed to a decision, but must remain, for the moment, still on the fence. Experience suggests that oral tales can mislead, and the archive often confounds recollections. The paper trail leaves us with no indication of the truth or falsehood of any of the versions of what occurred late in September 1915 between Mack, Mabel and A. N. Other. The archive does provide us, however, with another facet to the story of Mack Sennett's personal life and his deepest affections, involving the most biased witness of all – his mother.

Enter (or rather, re-enter) Mrs Catherine Sinnott.

From *Photoplay*, January 1920:

I've already broken it to you as gently as I know how that Mrs Sennett destined her son for the ministry. Well, who knows, they say the church needs rejuvenating and we believe he could have done it. But think what the world may have missed without the Sennett bathing girls.

The resemblance between this mother and son is more distinct and noticeable than any other than [*sic*] I found. For the white haired old lady has the same squareness of build, the same quick, telling smile, the same forceful shape of head and forehead.

'Mack was such a funny boy,' she said reminiscently. 'How he did hate girls. Never would even speak to them. Always getting sent home from school for deviling them. Once he tied his little cousin to an oak tree, and left her all day because she wanted to follow him around while he was playing. He couldn't see any use in girls.'

Which may well indicate, as any red-blooded boy finds out, the opposite of what Mama assumes.

Mack's relationship to his mother remained close throughout her life. The Sinnotts had remained in Northampton, Massachusetts, until Mack's father, John, died in 1904. We do not know if Catherine Sinnott visited her son in New York during his five years in Broadway shows, but she was certainly present at some point during his work with Griffith at Biograph. By then, she had returned, with some of her children, to Danville, Quebec, to the old family farm. From Danville, she followed the progress of her son as he formed his own

Mack Sennett and Mamma, on set

company and climbed to success. From an early stage, she discovered that while winters in Danville remained as harsh and cold as ever, winters in California were paradise. She accordingly adopted the habit of decamping from Canada every November, often with other members of the family in tow, and remaining a guest of the Keystone Company at least until the beginning of March.

In 1925, the *Los Angeles Examiner* featured Mack in its essay, by Florence Lawrence, on 'Four Famous Sons Devoted to Their Mothers'. The roster was Al and Charles Christie, Sid Grauman and Mack Sennett. Mrs Sennett, said the newspaper,

passes each winter with her son here, and his beautiful home in Westmoreland Place is the scene of many charming dinners and luncheons where she is surrounded by women friends of her own age. Mrs Sennett, a handsome and robust woman, also presides at the head of the Sennett dinner table on those occasions when her son entertains the film celebrities who gather so often at his hospitable board. But whatever her other engagements she makes a daily visit of an hour or more at the studio. She enjoys watching the comedians at work, particularly, and is an excellent judge of their 'gags'.

The Sennett archive contains a bulging file packed with the invoices of Mrs Sinnott's expenses, from the train ticketing to the rented furnished house at South Manhattan Place, down to the merest grocery bill at Young's Market store – 'I lge bread; I pt green olives; jello; strawberries; I can tomatos; I currant jelly' – all billed to Keystone studios. Not to speak of the liquor bills to see her through the spring of 1918 in Danville, from the Wholesale Liquor House in Sherbrooke, Quebec: 'Five gallons high wine, one case De Kuypers gin, five gallons Port wine, ten gallons Canadian Club rye, one case each Three Star Hennessy brandy and white whiskey, prepay and charge Mack Sennett Comedies'. To Mrs Sinnott, Mack always was her favourite child, and he repaid her with equal devotion.

Many witnesses attest that it was Mrs Sinnott who most pressed Mack to marry Mabel, whom she saw as a most suitable catch, although this, too, may obscure the ways mothers have of blowing hot and cold on a marital prospect. We cannot know how much of the underbelly of Hollywood's happy cavorting Mother was aware of, or what part it may have played in her decision to keep her son under iron surveillance for at least part of each year. But we can safely surmise that whatever less than decorous activities Mack was up to in his – not very extensive – hours off work, he would have been at great pains to keep them concealed from her of all persons, and therefore concealed, period.

In the years of scandal, Fatty Arbuckle's fall and the Taylor affair that dragged Mabel into its murky whirlpool, Mrs Sinnott could reflect that, after all, her son's bachelor life was a comforting and unmixed blessing. Hollywood's unholy brew of immorality, drug addiction, 'perversion' and murder had, like the Angel of Death, passed her beloved son over and merely brushed his brow. Or so it seemed, and Sennett succeeded in keeping it so.

Whatever happened in September 1915 might have frustrated and banished love, but it did nothing to stop the march of money. The Triangle Corporation had been launched in triumph, and Sennett and his clowns could continue the pursuit for which the public paid them cash – their non-stop trade of being funny.

Back to the Plumber Story:
*Mack Sennett Archive, 1916:*
*Rehearsal script:*

1. APARTMENT HOUSE LOBBY:
   Insert of Fred Mace (hotel manager) talking to pretty
   bather – his back to camera
2. Insert of Miss (Dale) Fuller (his wife) watching same
3. Insert of Mace and bather; draw out to full set
4. Miss Fuller in some manner turns Mace around showing his
   face – bather exits, Mace receives chastising from wife –
   cut
5. EXTERIOR:
   Taxi arrives with trunk – Hugh Fay and Miss Luther get out
   of taxi – look up and see side of apartment – exit inside
6. INTERIOR OF LOBBY:
   Miss Fuller on – Miss Luther and H Fay enter – biz of
   registering etc. H Fay exits
7. INTERIOR: H Fay enters – biz with driver about trunk and
   baggage
8. INTERIOR APARTMENT LOBBY: Miss Luther on – Mace enters a
   flirtation with Miss Luther.
9. EXTERIOR: After having trunk put in basement Fay exits
   inside
10. INTERIOR: Mace and Luther on – Fay enters – sees Mace and
    wife, starts to clean up Mace.
11. DESK SET: Fuller on – seeing Mace and Fay fighting exits
12. LOBBY SET: Fay and Mace arguing – Fuller enters, tells
    Fay that is her husband and separates them, taking Mace
    upstairs by his ear
13. HALL: Mace and Fuller enter and exit into room
14. BEDROOM: Mace and Fuller enter – Fuller makes Mace
    undress
15. LOBBY: Flash of Fay and Luther arguing
16. UPSTAIRS BEDROOM: Fuller takes Mace's clothes – locks
    them in trunk – gives Mace pajamas or bathrobe and tells
    him to stay there and behave himself. Fuller exits . . .

(et cetera . . . )

# CHAPTER FOURTEEN

# Bath-tub Perils – Back to the Clowns

The *Plumber Story*, released as *Bath Tub Perils*, was one of sixty-six films shot by Keystone for the Triangle Film Corporation in 1916. The movie featured Fred Mace, Dale Fuller, Hugh Fay, Anna Luther and a bunch of other company regulars. Running two reels, about twenty-three minutes, it was directed by Edwin Frazee and photographed by Hans Koenekamp, a major pioneer of Hollywood special effects and later cinematographer for such as William Dieterle and Howard Hawks. A routine production, it pulls the bells of all the stock domestic comedy situations: the newlyweds with flirty bride and jealous husband, the philandering hotel owner and his harridan wife, people in pyjamas in the wrong rooms, and a favourite Keystone gambit – mixing up the water and gas pipes so that the house is first flooded and then burned down, leading to a spectacular finale with the young wife careening in her detached bath-tub out of the bathroom, down the flooded hall and stairway, into the street and out to the sea, firemen and Kops in motor boats in hot pursuit.

Contrary to myth, Keystone movies were, by 1915, extensively scripted, the synopses and treatments running to about seven or eight pages, though later scripts for a two-reeler could run to as many as seventeen pages. As we can see, directors and actors were left to sort out their little bits of comedy 'biz' on the set, but the scenes and movements of the characters were blocked in. Sometimes a synopsis would say some thing like: 'After a few comedy incidents in a café, the proprietor goes to sleep and dreams that he is doing a rushing business in sausages in many funny situations' (*A La Cabaret*, August 1916). But the bath-tub scene above was fully scripted:

136. LOBBY: Water thru lobby – crowd all scramble in water – bath tub thru followed by Mace.

137. EXTERIOR: Firemen up ladders trying to climb in windows – gush of water thru bath tub thru – smoke – ladders down – letting firemen fall

138. STREET SCENE: Water rushing down street with bath tub – followed by Mace

139. STREET SCENE – Men digging manhole for trunk water overflow – gush of water coming down thru water hole carrying bath tub – followed by Mace on furniture . . .

*Bath Tub Perils*, 1916 – Fred Mace is tickled

And so forth. This scenario is followed closely in the movie, and the breakdown of shots shows that the text preceded the shoot. Other 'script continuities' in the Sennett production files are clearly illustrative of the finished films, some running to over 650 shots! (*A Social Cub*, with Bobbie Vernon, July 1916, two reels – 656 shots; this may well reflect a longer version than the one released.) As early a film as *Crooked to the End*, a Fred Mace vehicle, shot in November 1915, boasts 389 shots on paper. This reflects Sennett's adage, explained to *Photoplay Journal* in April 1917, that:

CUTTING IS REAL SECRET OF SUCCESSFUL MOTION PICTURE MAKING: NOT
WHAT YOU TAKE BUT WHAT YOU ELIMINATE THAT COUNTS
By Mack Sennett.

Successful motion picture direction in the larger sense, consists very largely in having an organization big enough and comprehensive enough to provide for your failures.

To say this in another way, it isn't so much what you take as what you cut out and what you retake that makes a great picture . . .

I ascribe much of the success of the Sennett–Keystone comedies to the fact that we take plenty of time in their preparation . . . No comedy goes to the director who is to film it until I have personally gone over the story – usually many times. A fresh exuberant young idea comes in at the front door of our scenario councils; it staggers out from our council of war a thing of war torn wounds. Before we are through, we all take a swat at it.

While the comedy is actually in process of filming, it is brought many times to the projecting room to be shown in fragment form. There it is torn to pieces again. Sometimes we reject the whole thing and it is re-taken from the beginning. Our organization has been so arranged that the directors are under no special time limit. They take as long for the production of a comedy as it is necessary to get out a good one.

The fact is, they are allowed time enough and money enough to get out a long six or eight reel comedy; every comedy that is filmed at this studio is of that length when it comes to the projecting room.

Indeed, we are in much the same position as is a great newspaper. Their problem is not 'how can we fill the paper' but 'what can we best leave out'.

This expresses an obvious fact of motion pictures as well as the usual Sennett flimflam, since his directors were not always, and probably not often, given 'no time limit' for their assignments, as we shall soon see. But the files leave no doubt that Sennett did indeed involve himself in the fine detail of most, if not all, his productions, particularly in the cutting and titling stage. Later on, there would routinely be lists of options and alternatives for every intertitle sent up to Mack so that he could choose from up to forty different versions of a line. Editor Stuart Heisler recalled, however, that many initial ideas for the movies came from a variety of sources in the studio:

Heisler: [The story lines] came from everywhere – writers, title writers, property men, cameramen or actors – whoever came up with an idea they felt would make a funny picture, they would tell it to somebody, or go to the Story Department and say, 'Is this a good idea for a picture?' . . . The writers in those days were mostly just idea men. They were not supposed to be finished writers. Some of them turned out to be damned good directors . . . Many times the basic story was suggested by the director . . . In a comedy studio, every time somebody got something they thought was funny, they went around and tried it on everybody, and lots of that stuff got into the films.

However much trust and leeway Sennett devolved to his directors and actors on the shoot, he was a tyrant in the presentation: Every Keystone film, he knew, carried his personal imprint, and would be judged as a Mack Sennett film.

The enhanced resources provided for Keystone movies by the Triangle deal, and the production values achieved, can be gauged by another routine farce–thriller of early 1916, *Dizzy Heights and Daring Hearts*. A two-reeler starring Chester Conklin, it co-stars Cora (Claire) Anderson, who plays the Mabel-like role of a daring aviatrix. Chester is an agent for a 'Royal nation' out to bid for a new-fangled aeroplane from the Eagle company, against a tricky rival with a different kind of moustache. A barrage of trick aerial shots, which must have involved early experiments in optical effects, as well as model shots of some sophistication, follows, as Chester steals the new plane with the girl, who is the company magnate's daughter, on board. Her lover, a pilot, follows in a second plane, an even ricketier affair than the one in Mabel's *Dash Through the Clouds*. The world's first movie aerial chase ensues. The plane flips over several times in a loop. In one shot, the plane hovers a few feet over a car. Chester throws aerial bombs down which wreck a bridge, but the car leaps over the gap. After landing, Chester is unmasked as a fraud and the rival takes the plane up, only to wreck it, leaving part of the wing lying on a factory chimney. The company pilot climbs up a ladder to free the wing and is trapped on top of the seventy-odd-foot chimney by Chester pulling down his ladder. The girl flies the second plane up and plucks the pilot off the chimney, as he clings to the wing, just as Chester blows up the chimney from below.

The pace is relentlessly fast, even factoring for the inevitable uncertainty about the original camera cranking speed. Shots are quick and short, cross-cutting feverish. The combination of stunts and camera effects is astonishing. In one shot, Chester turns the aeroplane propeller to start it and is twirled around with it at top speed, the next shot showing his figure twirled round the propeller in flight, presumably replaced by a dummy. Sennett had elaborate mechanisms erected to hold the aircraft upside-down, or suspend it from wires, which he used in other productions.

Oddly enough, the press suggested that it was Mabel who was playing the female lead in this film, which was apparently shot in November 1915. *Photoplayers Weekly* announced that Mabel had been injured 'when a runaway monoplane got beyond the control of its amateur driver', and 'was dragged along the rough ground for nearly 100 yards' (20 November). It is possible that scenes were reshot, explaining why Miss Anderson is the lead in the picture. Mabel was certainly becoming a regular visitor to the emergency ward. Later press reports and production records place her on the East Coast a few weeks later, shooting *Fatty and Mabel Adrift*, with Roscoe Arbuckle and his own quasi-independent unit which was based at Fort Lee, New Jersey. In April 1916, however, she was presenting herself as 'an aspiring dramatic star', having returned to Los Angeles 'to begin her new duties as an artiste under the supervision of Thomas H. Ince'. These new duties, however, would not be performed at Inceville or Keystone, but at a brand-new studio which Sennett was erecting at a separate location, off Sunset Boulevard. Her visits to the main Keystone plant at Edendale, as reported by *Photoplay*, were, it was reported, merely to cheer up the boys.

Whether Sennett set up this separate studio as a result of her blackmailing pressure over the Mae Busch incident, as 'Anonymous' of the *Exposé of Movie Vice* alleges, or because she was the company's biggest box-office draw, is a question we can now begin to address. Certainly Sennett did not stint in his support. 'THE DREAM THAT CAME TRUE', it was called by *Motion Picture*, which related that:

All of you who have for years been laughing with Mabel Normand, talking gaily of her funny exploits, would never believe that those long, silky black curls covered anything more than a brain devoted to creating laughs. That she could be serious; that she could have keen ambitions; that she could cherish for years a thrilling and eminently sober dream, would never occur to those who know her only from her screen frolics. But she has guarded that dream, and every movement has been an effort towards making that dream come true. And it has. She has a studio all her own, on which her name, in four-foot letters, smiles at the passers by on all four sides. The studio has been built as she wanted it built, and it has ever so many pretty little, feminine touches that make it artistic as well as businesslike, comfortable as well as efficient.

We were talking, one morning, on the tiny, vine-hung balcony outside of her dressing room, where we could look down on the busy scene below. She sat in a big, wicker, chintz-cushioned chair, and sighed blissfully as she looked up at the backs of one of the signs that spells her name.

'At last,' she breathed, 'I am almost thru with the first picture of the new series, a second play chosen and being prepared for production, and still I can hardly realize that my dream has come true. If I hadn't worked so hard and planned so hard these years to attain just this end, I'm afraid I would have my head turned by it all. But I know a cure for that – hard work! There's plenty of that ahead for me too!

'. . . The men tease me, or try to, about the "woman's touch," . . . but . . . you see . . . I have a hobby that dovetails beautifully with my work here. It's studio housekeeping. I was allowed to plan a great many of the details of the studio here, and it has been my ambition to make it, in its own way, a model plant. Efficiency comes first of course, but I didn't see why a studio should be a huge, unlovely barn of a place, just because it was built of wood. So I planned for comfort and beauty, as well as efficiency. That explains the rugs downstairs, the adorable balcony and the attractive dressing-rooms.'

The *New York Dramatic Mirror* described the place as 'independent and feminine, looking for all the world like a Japanese structure, its base and top of restful green, and its walls of cool white. Across its top runs a big black-lettered white sign announcing "THE MABEL NORMAND STUDIO".' The movie project that Mabel had set her heart on was a feature-length film, which would finally be released as *Mickey*.

Mabel's biographer wrote that Mack had initially offered this project to another actress, which was the cause of Mabel's quitting Keystone. The usual confusion of facts and gossip persists. In reality, the whole point of the Triangle operation was that it could link the operations of its tripartite units, and there were sound economic reasons to hive off Mabel's productions to a new venue. The contract between Keystone and Triangle, agreed on 30 July 1915, had committed Sennett to producing two two-reel 'photo-plays' every week for exclusive distribution by the Triangle Film Corporation. A further clause to the contract allowed Sennett 'the privilege of supervising the production of 2 photoplays during each year which shall in no wise be included or governed by any of the terms of the agreement', probably referring to the early planning for Mabel Normand features. Over a year later, a revised contract, signed on 29 September 1916 by

Mack and Mabel do business

Aitken, Kessel and Sennett, committed Sennett to producing one two-reel comedy and two one-reel comedies per week. A new clause gave Triangle, the Buyer, the right to reject any Keystone product, so that Sennett would be obliged to have further 'photoplays' ready to offer in such circumstances. The Buyer had exclusive rights to 'all the photoplays and the negative and positive prints thereof produced by the Seller'. (The Buyer would have to buy up any rejected photoplay for half the actual price of production.) The Buyer would pay Keystone $7,500 for each one-reel film and $20,000 for each two-reel film, rising slightly in 1917. This would include forty copies of the one-reelers and twenty-five of the longer items. This meant that Sennett was bound, more than ever before, to a factory style of production, turning out his movies like sausages. The contradiction between this requirement and assuring quality for each film, with adequate rehearsal and shooting time, must have been evident at the time. But once again, capitalism has its own logic.

It seems abundantly clear, looking at the documents, that Sennett was tied to a production line at Edendale that could not sustain the extra burden of feature films – though more expansion would take place in later years. It made sense, therefore, to make Mabel Normand a separate franchise under the Triangle heading. In any case, while her studio was being built, Mabel began rehearsals for *Mickey* on the old Keystone stage, among her many friends and admirers. The idea that Triangle might foot the bill for all this merely because Mack had been blackmailed by Mabel into building her a studio cannot therefore be tenable. Yet another building block of the great Mabel–Mae prize-fight proves to be of shoddy construction.

The Triangle contracts highlight another dilemma: The fees payable to Keystone for each one- and two-reel subject cannot possibly have been enough to cover the costs of production, upkeep of the immense studio complex, and the salaries of cast and crew. A letter from Aitken to Sennett on 28 September 1916, the day before the signing, states that:

In order to induce you to enter into (the) agreement . . . I agree that upon the extirpation of the term of the agreement whereby 65% of the capital stock of the Triangle Film Corporation is deposited with Title Guarantee and Trust Company, I will transfer to you Twenty-three Thousand (23,000) shares of said stock, provided that at that time you are supervising the production of Keystone pictures for the Triangle Film Corporation.
Very truly yours,
H. E. Aitken

Another addendum to the 29 September agreement gave Sennett 25 per cent of 'what is known as the Mabel Normand picture', with 75 per cent going to the Keystone Company.

A detailed analysis of the financial shenanigans of Harry Aitken, the Kessel brothers, Baumann, Ince, Griffith and all can be found in Kalton Lahue's *Dreams for Sale, The Rise and Fall of the Triangle Corporation*, published in 1971. Lahue had access to Aitken's personal papers, but, as stated before, the Academy of Motion Picture's Sennett archive was not available at that time. It is an elaborate – and familiar – tale of creative accounting and high-wire finance that parlayed imaginary assets into the illusion of sound profitability and inevitable growth. The big carrot, the fantastic proceeds of *Birth of a Nation*, was gnawed to its roots by the poor box-office of Griffith's follow-up epic, *Intolerance*, although that picture was not directly distributed by Triangle. Ince's rival epic, *Civilization*, set in a mythical kingdom, with a similar anti-war theme, was more successful and was also credited with helping to re-elect Woodrow Wilson, who campaigned on the motto 'He kept us out of the War'. Ince's series of westerns, starring W. S. Hart, were probably Triangle's biggest earners.

The Keystone comedies were doing well, but not well enough. The root of the problem lay in the Triangle concept itself. The Big Idea of Monopolization, 'corraling' big-name actors from the legitimate stage, was palpably not working. Aitken corralled the great English stage star Sir Herbert Beerbohm Tree, promising him $100,000 for thirty weeks' work, but the great thespian could not perform for the silent screen to save his life, nor would the American audience have cared if he could. On the comedy side, Triangle swept up Eddie Foy, who appeared with his stage brood, the Seven Little Foys, in Keystone's *A Favorite Fool*, shot in September 1915. Mae Busch, Polly Moran and Charles Parrott provided support, but Sennett clashed with Foy and fired him. Foy refused, it appears, to take the Keystone pie in the face, and even rejected Sennett's kind offer of a substitute – limburger cheese. Foy sued Sennett for $7,000, which included $1,000 for 'humiliation', citing 'walking on limburger cheese and riding a locomotive attired in a night shirt "with a hose on him"'. He won the suit.

Joe Weber and Lew Fields, veterans of vaudeville and pioneers of stage slapstick from the 1880s, might have seemed a much safer bet. So many of Keystone's regulars – Chester Conklin, Mack Swain, Roscoe Arbuckle et al. – had started out in vaudeville and had learned the wordless craft of pantomime. But Weber and Fields were particularly wedded to their tit-for-tat, German dialect act, a kind of precursor of the nonsensical Groucho–Chico dialogues: 'If you luffed me like I luff me, den no knife could cut us togedder.' The physical knockabout derived from their characters, which required the speech. By 1915, Weber and Fields had gone far beyond their original acts into the realm of musical production, but, for $3,500 a week, they were willing to regress. They were, however, a bit old for the more extreme mayhem. In their first movie, *The Worst of Friends*, they were almost killed when a stunt car crash went wrong and they were thrown on to the ground. A subsequent script, working title 'Weber and Fields Story', featuring the duo threshing about in a river, trying to drown a cat for an old lady (titles: 'How will we know if the cat is drowned?' 'Put me in the bag; When the cat is drowned I'll pull the string and you can drag me out.' The joke is still verbal) was probably never filmed. Weber and Fields returned to the New York stage in April 1916.

It was back to the stalwarts. Roscoe and Mabel, as recorded, Mack Swain and Chester Conklin as Ambrose versus Walrus in a dozen or so films (*When Ambrose Dared Walrus, The Battle of Ambrose and Walrus*, et cetera, et cetera), or Ambrose alone, as in *Ambrose's Rapid Rise* (archive synopsis, September 1916):

Ambrose, a tramp, while trying to steal a ham, is chased by two dogs and finds safety at the top of a high fence. The Sheriff in the shade of the fence meets the bandit. The meeting is interrupted by the sudden appearance of Ambrose, on the fence. The Sheriff pulls Ambrose off the fence and tells him to get out of town.

The Sheriff and the bandit part. The Sheriff goes to meet the school teacher. He waylays her on her way to the school and tries to make love to her.

Meanwhile, Ambrose sees a stage coach held up. He takes a horse from the coach, pursues the bandit, captures the bandit and brings him to town . . .

*(The sheriff is caught out and deposed, Ambrose becomes the new sheriff . . . )* The deposed Sheriff gets jealous and tries to get Swain in bed with a tribe of nearby Indians. He sets fire to the school house, with the hope of saving the teacher and winning back her favor. Ambrose escapes from the Indians and rescues the school children. The old Sheriff, seeing that his plan has failed, enters the burning school house from the rear and kidnaps the teacher, after a struggle in the fire with Ambrose. Ambrose gives chase with posse . . . Posse and Indians engage in fight. Ambrose pursues the old Sheriff, gets girl and shoots the bandit, who, horse and all, fall into the water. Swain gets the girl.

It appeared to be business as usual, but not for very long.

# CHAPTER FIFTEEN

# Mack Sennett and the Triangle of Doom

In January 1917, the Keystone company began publishing a regular bulletin called the *Mack Sennett Weekly*. It might as well have been called the *Mabel Normand*, or the *'Mickey' Weekly*, since every issue carried a plug for the feature-in-progress and a picture of Mabel on the front page. Little boxes giving news of the movie appeared in the inside pages:

MISS MABEL NORMAND IN 'MICKEY': 'Mickey' is a quaint little mountain girl who runs the gamut of life. Laughter and tears take their turn in the unfolding of the story . . . A vivid and appealing comedy drama with real living characters, told without squash pies, battles or the seduction of the innocent heroine . . . No padding. When the story is over the curtain goes down. Method and date of release will be announced later.

This went on for months and there was still no sign of the picture. Meanwhile, the squash pies, battles and seduced heroines got their plugs inside the bulletin, along with portraits of the artistes and features on the Sennett Bathing Beauties, or 'Splash Me Girls' as they were then referred to. Sennett's version of the 'Rise of the Keystones', the potted history according to Mack, written most probably by the *Weekly*'s editor, H. C. Carr, ran for several weeks. The front page in every issue carried a long piece by Mack himself, possibly also ghost-written by Carr, on such subjects as 'A Frank Talk to Exhibitors', 'Writers of Funny Scenarios Are Not Very Plentiful', 'You Can't Put a Stop Watch on Brains' and 'Why Not Let Pa and Ma Be the Censors on Moving Pictures?', a sentiment that was not echoed by the State and National Boards which were closing in even on comedy mischief:

BOARD OF CENSORS IS A NEEDLESS INSTITUTION
By Mack Sennett.
When I was a boy, there used to be a number of respectable old ladies who delighted to go to funerals to compare notes on the behaviour of the widow.

Funerals are a little out of date now as a form of popular entertainment so the old ladies of both sexes censor motion pictures instead . . .

And so forth. The same issue of the *Weekly* highlighted, as well as *Mickey*, Keystone's latest novelty two-reeler, *Villa of the Movies*, a bizarre concoction shot on the Mexican border with, it was claimed, the tacit approval of the legendary freedom fighter himself. Pancho Villa was played in the movie by young Glen Cavender, who 'personally met the elusive Mexican, studied him, equipped himself with photos of the bandit chief taken from every conceivable angle, and with the aid of his make-up kit, transformed himself into such a close replica of the bandit chief that you are defied to tell them apart'. The film itself, the *Weekly* hurried to assure its readers, was nevertheless a comedy: 'From start to finish it is a laugh, with most of the characters in hot water all the time.'

Plugging the movies apart, Mack clearly enjoyed using his *Weekly* as a soap box to hold forth on all his bugbears. Inveighing against factory-style 'Efficiency Experts' in the 12 February issue, he wrote:

Commercial efficiency demands that all men should be poured into the same mould. Artistic efficiency demands that they be moulded according to their personalities . . . You can make a million ten penny nails by pouring hot metal into a machine. But you have to carve statues by hand . . .

The temperament of actors seems to worry the outside world considerably more than it does us. Those who see some actors doing childish things, such as applauding their own pictures on screen; trying to dodge the letter R and talking the way people in New York are supposed to talk do not quite realize the situation.

Everyone with much force and originality somewhere has this same characteristic concealed. An actor who doesn't secretly believe he is the best one in the world couldn't succeed . . .

When the brash young efficiency expert arrives to iron out these eccentricities, he will find that he is in the midst of a tolerably large job. Should he succeed in 'systematizing' the pictures to the extent that he hopes, he will find that he has nothing left but system . . .

However, all these high-minded defences of art and individual initiative could not conceal from the people in the movie business itself, and those who followed the ups and downs of the movie companies, that all was not well in the supposedly happy Triangle–Keystone kingdom. One early homily in the *Weekly*, addressed by Sennett to the movie exhibitors, and pledging a solemn oath of fair dealing and commercial honesty and honour, elicited a sarcastic response from a theatre owner in Erie, Pennsylvania, Mr Frank E. Wood of the Strand Amusement Company, who wrote to Sennett on 15 January 1917, accompanying his letter with a plethora of poignant little drawings illustrating the exhibitors' true and sorry fate:

Dear Sir,

Mack Sennett   W.J. Hayes

Bomb.

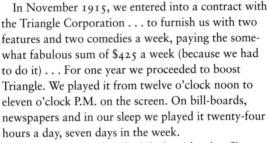

EMPTY IS THE CRADLE
KEYSTONE'S GONE.

July weekly #17
Dec weekly #10

In November 1915, we entered into a contract with the Triangle Corporation . . . to furnish us with two features and two comedies a week, paying the somewhat fabulous sum of $425 a week (because we had to do it) . . . For one year we proceeded to boost Triangle. We played it from twelve o'clock noon to eleven o'clock P.M. on the screen. On bill-boards, newspapers and in our sleep we played it twenty-four hours a day, seven days in the week.

During this period we had deals with other film corporations, and gradually we learned that this so-called fifth industry in the United States was largely in the hands of thoroughly incompetent, irresponsible, or a worse class of men at the executive end of the business. Old 'Billy Dutch' never disregarded 'a mere scrap of paper' with easier conscience than does the producer in the film business disregard a contract, if it is not to his advantage . . .

Contract
Triangle
Strand
#1200

One of the key problems that dogged the Triangle Film Corporation was the scheme to tie up movie theatres to special first-run deals. By the end of 1916, however, only 1,500 of the country's estimated 20,000 cinemas had signed up. Even with these theatres, the internal financial crises of Triangle led to severe conflicts, when the supply of films was suddenly curtailed, reneging on contracts that had promised four weeks' discontinuance notice, as Mr Wood pointed out:

Now, Mr. Sennett, we understand that the Triangle Corporation was not able to pay you for your comedies, and therefore you did not deliver them . . . (But) was not the Triangle . . . included morally, legally and honourably to carry out your 'philosophy of playing fair' bound to deliver us two Keystone comedies a week according to contract? . . .

There is one possible explanation of the producers' treatment of the exhibitors with whom they have contractual relations, to wit, if the producers carried out the ordinary liability contained in a contract with the exhibitors, the shock would be so great that we would all drop dead.

Mr Wood did not refer to another practice of those piratical days – most notoriously used by Paramount, which handled the films of Adolph Zukor and Jesse Lasky's Famous Players Company – of offering a product to one theatre in a particular town at a higher price than the competition, accompanied by the open threat to set up a new theatre which would play the Paramount product exclusively. The chief enforcer of this kind of gambit was one Stephen A. Lynch of North Carolina, who cut a swathe through the South, terrorizing small theatre owners into taking Paramount's block bookings. In 1916, Lynch was recruited to the Triangle company and later headed its distribution.

The basic problem of Triangle films could not be finagled or ignored: the production costs of the corporation's movies were too high to ensure a profit. Cash flow had become more and more erratic. By the end of 1916, Kessel and Baumann had been forced to sell their own New York Motion Picture Company. To avoid it falling into rival hands, Harry Aitken raised more money to buy it off them. But in March 1917 Griffith jumped ship and signed with Zukor's Artcraft Pictures, taking another major figure, Douglas Fairbanks, with him. In June, Thomas Ince, too, went over the side, retaining his own production business.

Now Sennett had to move quickly. A flurry of telegrams to Keystone general manager John Waldron reveals the ruthlessness with which he moved to rescue his core of operations, leaving Triangle with the empty shell of the company to which they held title. The essential strategy was to move all his production assets into his own name, as Mack Sennett, while abandoning the brand name of Keystone. The telegrams refer to various other conflicts that appeared to be raging within the ranks:

KEYSTONE FILM CO LOS ANGELES CALIF JUNE 16 1917

I AM INFORMED THAT CLINE RECENTLY REMAINED AWAY FROM STUDIO FOR SEVERAL DAYS ALLOWING HIS COMPANY TO LIE IDLE ASCERTAIN FROM HIM ON WHOSE AUTHORITY HE DID THIS ALSO FIND OUT FROM HIM AND WIRE ME AT ONCE WHAT HIS POSITIVE AND NEGATIVE FOOTAGE WAS ON LAST STORY ALSO NUMBER OF DAYS OCCUPIED IN

PRODUCTION WE ARE AT PRESENT IN COUNCIL ON SUCH MATTERS AND I
MUST HAVE FULL INFORMATION ON THIS SUBJECT.

This cable refers to one of Sennett's youngest directors, Eddie Cline;
the next refers to managers who may have got wind of pending
changes:

June 19: AM SURE WATSON, HALL AND EMERY WISH TO BE RELEASED.
WANT YOU TO TAKE NECESSARY STEPS TO DO SO DO NOT STAND FOR ANY
ARGUMENTS OR CONVERSATION WHATSOEVER FROM THEM IN FACT
THINK IT NECESSARY FOR YOU TO MAKE EXAMPLE OF THEM
IMMEDIATELY.

Three hours later, he instructed Waldron:

YOU UNDERSTAND MY WIRE REGARDING PEOPLE MENTIONED WANT YOU
TO MAKE IT APPARENT BY ALL MEANS TO GET INTO AGREEMENT WITH
THEM AND FORCE THEM OUT AND GIVE UP THEIR CONTRACTS.

and on 20 June:

SEE THAT ALL THE WOODLEY WEEKLY NEGATIVES AND POSITIVES WITH
KEYSTONE GIRLS ARE IMMEDIATELY TAKEN TO SAFE DEPOSIT VAULT FOR
SAFE KEEPING AND ARE PLACED THERE IN MY NAME.

25 June:

REGARDLESS OF PREVIOUS INSTRUCTIONS PREPARE ALL COMPANIES FOR
IMMEDIATE PRODUCTION OF CHEAP AND SPEEDY STORIES REGARDLESS
OF QUALITY BUT HOLD ACTUAL PHOTOGRAPHING UNTIL RECEIVING MY
NEXT WIRE TODAY.

Later that day came the clincher:

HAVE JUST CLOSED DEAL SELLING MY INTERESTS IN KEYSTONE
RETAINING STUDIO AND ENTIRE PROPERTY AND CERTAIN NUMBER OF
PEOPLE LIST OF WHOM WILL REACH YOU BY MAIL TUESDAY OR
WEDNESDAY . . . WILL REPORT AT STUDIO TUESDAY TO TAKE CHARGE OF
FINISHING PRODUCTION NOW UNDER WAY AND WILL POSSIBLY PUT ALL
COMPANIES IN PRODUCTION IMMEDIATELY PROVIDED THEY CAN FINISH
BY JULY FIFTEENTH.

A cable of 26 June speaks of releasing 'great numbers of people'.
Then, on 29 June:

INSIST UPON CAMPBELL DOING SINGLE REELERS IMMEDIATELY OR QUIT-
TING. DO NOT TAKE UP BOOKERS OPTION. LET LYNN OUT IMMEDIATELY IF

SHE IS UNRULY. REMOVE MY NAME ENTIRELY FROM ALL PICTURES. TRY TO STRETCH ALL SINGLE REELERS POSSIBLE INTO TWO REELERS REGARDLESS OF QUALITY. MOST ESSENTIAL THING NOW IS SPEED AND QUANTITY . . .

and on 30 June:

I WILL TAKE OVER ENTIRE PLANT ABOUT THE FIFTEENTH . . .

There is a kind of chill in seeing Sennett unmasked by these brief and brutal messages, stripping away the veneer of paternal concern and artistic integrity he was so careful to nurture for the motion-picture fans. But if Sennett was baring his fangs, he was doing so in a cage packed full of even more desperate wolves. When the saga of Triangle came to an end, four years later, executives of Triangle and other companies caught in its financial snares brought suit against its founder, Harry Aitken, alleging a stock fraud which had left Aitken holding the lion's share of the company's money while the company itself, and other stockholders, were starved of funds. The whole affair had been a boondoggle from the start, akin to W. C. Fields' imaginary 'beefsteak mine' shares. No wonder all the producers jumped overboard, every man for himself.

The Triangle crisis was, in retrospect, more damaging for Mack Sennett's general outlook on life and his own self-esteem than the alleged love-nest bust-up with Mabel. His initial deals with the two Kessels and Baumann had been, in comparison, Sunday-school outings. It is possible that Mack's original myth, presenting his two partners as simple bookies tricked into investing in movies by the wily Irish Canadian, was a wistful attempt to separate them in his mind from the sharks he already knew had their jaws clamped on his groin. Adam and Charles Kessel and Charles Baumann had, after all, enabled some of the most significant forces in the early film industry, Ince and Sennett included, to experiment and flourish with the new medium. They deserve better from posterity than just being the butt of his jokes.

Sennett's only hope of financial survival, however, lay with embracing the new corporate breed of movie entrepreneurs, hitching his post to winners, instead of losers. A capping telegram to Waldron on 1 July reads:

HAVE SIGNED UP WITH PARAMOUNT RELEASING ONE MACK SENNETT COMEDY EVERY TWO WEEKS STARTING RELEASING SEPTEMBER 15TH. HAVE MADE VERY FINE CONTRACT. FIGURE STARTING FULL SWING JULY 15TH.

The *Mack Sennett Weekly* announced the change with its usual upbeat approach: 'GREAT PARAMOUNT COMPANY WILL RELEASE MACK SENNETT COMEDIES'. Sennett assured the press and the fans on 30 July:

There will be no difference except the trade mark. The comedies will be made by the same actors at the same studio under the same supervision.

Since the earliest days of motion picture comedies I have made a practice of personally supervising the making of every comedy turned out at this studio.

I have superintended the making of all the scenarios; supervised the finishing of the picture and finally have cut it in the projecting room.

I will do exactly the same with all the Mack Sennett Comedies; many of the directors who have been my associates and co-workers in the making of comedies will still be with me in the making of the comedies under the new trade name.

The same comedians you have laughed at and the pretty girls you have admired will still be there.

It will be the same old rose which the late Mr. Shakespeare assured us would smell as sweet under any other name . . .

Under the wise guidance of Mr. Adolph Zukor, the Paramount has justified its name. It is pre-eminent in the motion picture world.

Mr Zukor is an illustration of the old saying that the best goods come in small packages. The 'Little Napoleon of the Films' stands about five feet high and weighs about 130 pounds, but he is a veritable dynamo of action. There isn't an angle of the business of motion picture production that he has not mastered. Mr Zukor is the 'Man Who Does' . . .

It will be a matter of pride for me to produce my comedies under the releasing banner of this great organization.

Then, as now, Hollywood could outdo the applauding claque of any totalitarian dictator in its rank obeisance to its own power and glory. Sennett had, after all, hitched his wagon to the very mogul whose company had, by its own ruthless and monopolizing tactics, ensured that Triangle's would-be monopoly failed. 'A great new day is dawning in the picture world,' Sennett summed up. But in an adjacent column, one of his actors, Charlie Murray, at least got in a contrary dig in the regular slot of rhymes and one-liners:

> Ashes to ashes,
> And dust to dust,
> If the Triangle don't get you
> Mack Sennett must.

The front page of the *Weekly* featured a photographic spread of Sennett surrounded by his star actors: Chester Conklin, Bobby Dunn, Glen Cavender, Wayland Trask, Slim Summerville, Mack Swain, Charles Murray and Jack Dillon. Mabel had finished *Mickey* but had also quit Sennett's companies. Ford Sterling was still aboard, though very much a second stringer. Fred Mace had died in New York in February 1917. He had been found lifeless in bed at the Hotel Astor, having expired of an apoplectic fit. This was not surprising, as he had resigned only a month before from the vaudeville actors' association, the White Rats, in a patriotic protest against 'anarchic foreigners', such as its English International Executive, Harry Mountford, whose sin was to 'dictate to real American citizens . . . managers who have their good money invested how to run theatres'.

Mace died before he could see America deeply embroiled with foreigners, as it joined the war in Europe in April, committing hundreds of thousands of troops to the bloody trenches of France. A new mood of fearfulness about the world could not fail to affect even California's factories of dreams.

On the more cheerful side, Sennett had signed up a new employee in March 1917, who was also featured on his July *Weekly* cover – a comedian who would rapidly become a mainstay of his studio and one of the most recognizable faces in the cinema – the cross-eyed king of clowns, Ben Turpin.

# Mack Sennett-Keystones

Chester Conklin and Mack Swain in Their Dressing Room          —By Mal St. Clair

# PART III

# *His Ups and Downs*

Co-starring:
The Happy Hooligan
Post-Keystone Mabel
Teddy & Gloria
A Posse of Hard Boiled Yeggs
Frank & Harry, Happy Dreamers,
Billy, Sally, Carole &
The Sennett Girls

# CHAPTER SIXTEEN

# The Eyes Have It:
# Case History of a Clown – Ben Turpin,
# Episode One

Once upon a time . . .

From the pen of Agnes O'Malley, chief publicist for Mack Sennett Studios:

Drowning out the screeches of agitated ladies having their teeth pulled was the way Ben Turpin, the Mack Sennett comedian, broke into the world of art.

Ben says he is proud to have assisted at the wedding of art and science. He provided the art with a big base drum. The proprietor of the medicine show with the glittering tooth yanker provided the science.

'That was my first job,' said Ben. 'And I got ten whole dollars a week for doing it.

'I think we were what you would call a versatile company. We sold patent medicine guaranteed to cure all human ailments. We sold a renowned soap; gave beauty concerts to establish the high tide of pulchritude in the different sections through which we passed. But tooth pulling was the grandest thing we did.

'Usually we travelled from place to place in an old-fashioned covered wagon, with our advertising signs plastered all over the sides. On specially grand occasions we went on the train and slept in the day coaches.

'Whenever we would set up the platform and light the old kerosene torches, I always went on in black face.

'After I had charmed the multitude with a song, the medicine man would come out on the platform to show the hicks the soap.

'This stunt was so easy it was foolish. He would first rub his hands over with soap bark which they couldn't see. Then he would pick up a bit of soap so tiny you could stick it in your eye.

'Now ladies and gents,' he would say, 'I will show you what this wondrous soap will do.' He would soak his hands with the speck of soap; then throw it away with a great gesture. When he put his hands in the water, the soap bark would make a lather that looked like an Alaska snow bank. The hicks never failed to fall for that. He usually finished the demonstration by publicly washing the lamp black off my face, turning me to white as it were. It was guaranteed to cure man or beast with one bottle. That one bottle consisted of colored water and eight cents worth of salts; he sold it for a dollar a bottle.

'The beauty and popularity contest never failed to bring in the dough. We always bought a pair of lace curtains from a mail order house for forty-nine cents. This magnificent article of art we agreed to give to the most popular maid or matron in Bingville. The votes cost ten cents each. The voting results, as the totals magnificently rose, were written by me on a blackboard that we carried. This was our dramatic suspense.

'The hicks from the farms and the shieks from the village livery stable would contest furiously, buying votes for love and honor – for ten cents per vote. We never failed to clean up $20 to $30 on each forty-nine cent curtain.

'For obvious reasons we always saved the tooth pulling to the last. The medicine man, by use of a marvelous unction, invented by a famous Indian chief, guaranteed to yank the hugest and most vicious tooth absolutely with [sic] pain – payment strictly in advance.

'There wasn't any pain that anybody heard about. The people always yelled bloody murder; but I stood up on the front of the platform and drowned them out with my big base drum.

'I need not say that we did not tarry for them to compare notes. After the last tooth was yanked, we stood not on the order of our going; we scooted.'

Bernard Turpin was born in New Orleans on or around 19 September 1869. His father, Ernest, born in Mexico, was a wholesale confectioner who was said to have pioneered the use of 'taffy' candy in the 1880s. As a result, his son developed a distinctly unsweet tooth, and the famous eyes were apparently quite normal as they appear in an alleged portrait of the youth at the age of eighteen. When Ben was still a child, his father moved to New York, and the Manhattan census of 1880 lists ten-year-old Bernard, and daughters Ernestine, thirteen, and Octavia, nine, as attending school in the city. Father Ernest resided in New York for some years, but seems to have been back in New Orleans by 1892.

Ben's own story, told to *The American Magazine* in 1934, fits in, for a change, with the record. He tells how he went to school on the East Side, an area mostly Irish and German, above the Lower East slums. He claims to have nursed a burning ambition to be a fireman. Perhaps he gave up when he discovered that firemen were not actually supposed to fall off their ladders on to their heads. He told his interviewer, Neil M. Clark (whose piece was called 'The First Fifty Years Were the Hardest for Ben Turpin'): 'I joined the Fourth Street German Turn Hall and became a very good acrobat . . . When I quit school I went to work for a company that made trunks, jeweler's sample trunks, Crouch and Fitzgerald. I was the shipping clerk.' A very similar job to those another teenage youth, Adolph 'Harpo' Marx, would take on a few years later. When his father decided to return to New Orleans, he gave his son a hundred dollars to get a proper job and earn his own living.

And so the daring young man went on the road:

'I went as far as Jersey City, or some other place – I can't remember just where it was now – and got into a crap game with some fellows. In no time at all I'd lost the whole hundred dollars!

'Then I was in a fix! I was only a few miles from New York; but I didn't dare to go back home.

'I had never ridden a freight train up to that time . . . But I saw a train in the yard and climbed on, and the next thing I knew I landed in Chicago!

'I got off and brushed myself, but I didn't have any more money than when I started. My stomach was aching for food. I saw some fellows who looked friendly, so I decided to get some advice from them.

'"How does a fellow get something to eat in this town?"

'"Hit the back doors!" one of the bunch replied.

'I did, and I got enough to eat pretty quick. It looked like an easy life. I didn't feel any wish to go and hunt a job and start work as long as food came free.'

For four years, Turpin claimed, he lived as a tramp – 'Mulligan stew was my daily bread . . . It taught me human nature.' One night in Chicago, Ben said, he did a few stunts, and people said, 'Say, you'd ought to be an actor!'

At the age of twenty-two, he first walked out on stage:

'I began to do any funny things I could think of – stunts with chairs and furniture, comic tumbles – what they call silence-and-fun. Pantomime, that's what it was. I got away with it, too! The house liked it, and gave me a big hand . . .

'I improved my stuff, invented some stunts, and borrowed some from other actors . . . I got bookings pretty regularly, and traveled everywhere – riding passenger trains now! As I got better, I made more money – twenty-five dollars a week, thirty, forty, fifty, sixty; but never more than sixty.

'That was good wages in those days . . . When you got it you were rich. When you didn't get it, maybe you pretty near starved. Traveling and living expenses and everything had to come out of it.

'One night I happened to see a fellow doing Happy Hooligan on the stage. It was a new act. "I could do that," I said to myself. "I'm a long-necked guy, and kind of funny looking."

'So I got me a wig – bald you know – down to the fringe around the edges. I fixed up a tin can on my head and began to practice making Happy Hooligan faces, crossing my eyes and all the rest of the business. I was a knock-out! I *was* Happy Hooligan!'

The Happy Hooligan was a cartoon character introduced in the Hearst newspapers by artist Fred Opper in 1900. The strip ran for over thirty years and was a perennial American hit. The carefree bum who keeps screwing up while trying to do good inspired a whole slew of comedians, from Oliver Hardy to W. C. Fields. Turpin dated his début with this character to 1902, which sounds about right. Ben was playing the raucous houses of burlesque as well as so-called 'dime museums', essentially freak shows, America's most popular entertainment between the minstrel era and 'polite' vaudeville.

It was playing the Happy Hooligan, Turpin insisted, that made him go cross-eyed:

'My eyes were straight when I started, perfectly straight. I wasn't such a bad looking fellow. But all this practicing and acting Happy Hooligan, crossing my eyes to look the part, strained them pretty bad. One morning I woke up and looked in the glass. My right eye was crossed, and I hadn't crossed it!'

The Hooligan was certainly optically challenged in the cartoons, and so life once again imitates art.

In 1905, in Chicago, Turpin married Carrie Le Meaux, a French-born actress, which might suggest that the Eye Event occurred after that date. This marriage was long-lasting, and became the most vital part of Turpin's life, a poignant love story unknown to the many fans of the funny-looking actor and tumbler. An accident in 1917 left Carrie injured and partially deaf. In 1924, she was struck by virulent influenza from which she never recovered properly. A series of strokes left her house-bound, and Ben abandoned his acting career for months to look after her. They were both intensely religious and he took her to various Catholic shrines in the hope of a miracle cure that was never found.

The private life of Ben Turpin, as of so many actors, was completely subsumed by the mask. By the time he appeared in his first film, in 1907, he was thirty-eight years old. His film début, for the Essanay company in Chicago, predates both Sennett and Griffith. Of these early efforts, only two, *Mr Flip* and *A Case of Seltzer*, made in 1909, are known to have survived. Like Sennett's own early cut-ups, the character of Mr Flip is a straight Pathé take-off. Flip is a flirtatious pest, who keeps chasing the ladies and gets chased in turn out of their shops and offices. At a lunch counter, he gets a pie in the face, several years before Mack Sennett was supposed to have invented the trick. Turpin told *Motion Picture World*, in April 1909:

'This is a great life. I have been in the motion picture biz . . . for two years, and I must say I have had many a good fall, and many a good bump, and I think I have broken about twenty barrels of dishes, upset stoves, and also broken up many sets of beautiful furniture, had my eyes blackened, both ankles sprained and many bruises, and I am still on the go.'

Turpin's speciality, in a trade full of masterful tumblers, was the sheer panache of his pratfalls, his contortionist skills, the way his limbs seemed to fly about in all directions at the same time, like a straw doll. He was famed at Sennett's for his '108's, a form of pratfall in which the actor twisted forwards to end up on his back. He could do a complete forward or back flip at the mere tap of a hand on his shoulder. And above all, the moment he walked into frame, he could reduce an audience to howls of laughter. He was never a great actor, like Chaplin or Keaton, or a master of character, like Lloyd or Laurel. He was, quite simply, funny.

Around 1910, Ben left Essanay, refused a pay rise by the boss, George Spoor. He claimed to have then joined a circus as a 'producing clown', honing his physical skills. After three more years in variety, Essanay took him back at his old salary of twenty dollars a week.

This placed Turpin in the right place at the right time, when Charlie Chaplin was signed up for Essanay at the end of 1914. For it was his roles as Charlie's foil, in Chaplin's first Essanay classics, *His New Job*, *A Night Out* and *The Champion*, that made Ben's cross-eyes and floppy body world famous. Chaplin reputedly said, upon clapping eyes upon Turpin: 'Haw! . . . what sort of funny-looking egg is this I've got to play against?' Soon after, Chaplin called him to join the unit he was forming to shoot away from the cold winds of Chicago, in sunny Niles, California.

Ben and Charlie fell out, however, according to Chaplin's cameraman, Rollie Totheroe, over Turpin's request for parity. Chaplin was not interested in double acts. So Ben continued working at Niles with the second stringers, Harry Todd, Victor Potel, Lloyd Bacon and the company's two directors, Broncho Billy Anderson (the A in S & A) and Wallace Beery, soon to become another Sennett recruit with his young wife, Gloria Swanson.

Chaplin's fame was always giving other actors ideas of stardom, just as it drove his junior Karno partner, Stan Laurel (then Jefferson), to paroxysms of irritation. Finding himself a business manager, Turpin parted with Essanay and joined the small Vogue Comedy company, becoming one of its mainstays, in April 1916. The Vogue company was not very distinguished, and its movies were often slack imitations of Keystone–Triangle's hits. One of Ben's efforts, *Doctoring a Leak*, was our familiar chestnut, the plumber story, Ben prancing about with his tools, mincing with the maid and slipping on flooded stairways. Sennett, however, always on the look-out for talent, finally enticed him away from Vogue, despite their reluctance to answer his calls. The legend is that Ben turned up in 'civilian' garb at the office of Sennett's manager, George Stout, minus his toothbrush moustache, and Stout, failing to recognize him, took him on as a carpenter–janitor. This strains the imagination. However, Turpin told *Picture Play* magazine in 1920:

I sat and sat and sat in Mr. Sennett's office until I noticed he began to wiggle and twitch in his chair. Then he turned to me and exploded: 'Well, what do you want?'

'I want a contract,' I said.

'All right. But take those eyes out of here and stick 'em in a bucket of water or something until we're ready for you.'

Gene Fowler's fanciful version claimed that Sennett was superstitious about Ben's cross-eyes and was fearful of bad luck if he employed him. If 'twere so, it was a curious fright, as Sennett employed Ben Turpin, off and on, for the next decade, right through to the triumph of the talkies.

Turpin's first leading role for Sennett was in *A Clever Dummy*, a two-reel extension of an original one-reeler called *The Automaton*

*Figure*. Ben is a janitor for an eccentric inventor and his partner who have developed an electronic dummy that can move its head and limbs. They are made an offer of sale by the Spotlight Vaudeville Circuit (manager Patrick Cohen – that takes care of the ethnic niceties). Both the partner and Ben are in love with the inventor's daughter, played by Claire Anderson. In order to get in good with the daughter, Ben exchanges himself for the dummy (motivation was becoming a flexible term at Sennett's). In reel two, at the vaudeville theatre, two big hitters of the Sennett roster have been added – Chester Conklin as a frustrated stage hand and Wallace Beery as the vaudeville manager. Ben is 'made' to do a trick counting the manager's money, only to pocket it with sleight of hand. Consternation, et cetera, as the dummy escapes on a motor cycle, pursued by Beery et al. in a car, smashing through walls and beer halls *en route* to a rising bridge over the river, where the cops catch up and fall on the dummy with their clubs.

The movie was almost tailor-made to exemplify the core of Ben's clowning: his capacity to cause mayhem wherever he goes. He never fitted into the customary category of a movie clown, since he was neither handsome nor too thin, nor fat or menacing, too tall or too short; he was simply Ben. His appearance alone is enough to disrupt the course of normal life, such as it is in the world of pantomime comedy. In our own day, he would be classified with those elements that are not allowed to be objects of fun any more. When his eyes became crossed, Turpin said, he was offered a simple operation to uncross them, but as he was busy on the road, and possibly too poor to pay for it, he finally decided, 'Aw, what's the difference . . . Now I look more like Happy Hooligan than ever!'

In essence, Ben was just that – a cartoon character in human form. Like so many of his peers, he was a craft comedian *par excellence* – his wife's troubles apart, he lived for his work. 'Since I've been with Sennett I haven't missed a day,' he told Neil Clark, 'haven't been late to an appointment, and haven't had any spells of "temperament". Just work – that's me!' The Sennett publicity department responded with a concerted campaign to talk up their new star and his unique asset: 'They say that when Ben cries, the tears roll down his back,' they burbled; 'when you see Ben, you'll laugh till you cry'. A major publicity stunt involved insuring the famous cross-eyes for twenty-five thousand dollars with Lloyd's of London, 'to pay loss providing the eyes of Ben Turpin become straight from any cause whatsoever'. Looking down the rest of the text, however, it turns out this coverage was to run 'commencing at noon, November nineteenth, Nineteen twenty-one and ending noon on Monday November twenty-first, Nineteen twenty-one', so the premium for this policy couldn't have given Sennett any sleepless nights, unless Ben had chanced to knock his eye out with a fishing rod that weekend. But Agnes O'Malley, Sennett's head of publicity, worked overtime to promote Ben's peculiarities and his supposed philosophies of life:

### THE PHILOSOPHY OF BEN TURPIN

In the old days when I had a horse and buggy, I used to take tremendous excursions five and a half miles and back again. There wasn't anywhere to go because you couldn't get anywhere and back. Then a feller came along and invented an automobile and in three or four Sundays I had been everywhere and now it's worse than it was before. I not only have nowhere to go; but I know now that there isn't anywhere to go anyhow. When I had the old horse and buggy I used to think 'I bet it's great over the other side of those hills.' Now I know there's nothing only some more hills.

The only difference between a horse and buggy and an automobile is that you don't have to change tires on a horse and an automobile doesn't have colic.

I never knew, however, until I went automobile riding around through the traffic jams on Sunday that everybody in the world is a darn fool except me.

But this was to come a little later, when Sennett had segued Ben Turpin's character into a different kind of clown: the satirical epitome of the inversion of heroes, in spoof characterizations like the mock-debonair Rodney St Clair in *A Harem Knight*, the fake Von Stroheim in *Three Foolish Weeks*, the Latin lover in *Romeo and Juliet*, or the cod-Valentino of *The Shriek of Araby*. In 1917, Ben Turpin was still himself, the real, live Happy Hooligan, running, jumping and falling over with the rest of the mad Sennett crew.

# CHAPTER SEVENTEEN

# Mabel's Wilful Way

In April 1918, the United States had been involved in the war in Europe for one year, but Mack Sennett Comedies was soldiering on in its own universe, releasing *The Battle Royal*, with Ben Turpin and Polly Moran. This co-starred 'Charlie Lynn', a pseudonym of the actor Heinie Conklin, who is often confused with his colleague Chester but was neither *alter ego* nor relative. Ben is dumped by his landlady and taken in by a stranger who brings him home to be nursed by his winsome wife, Polly. Ben flirts with Polly, is chased out by 'Charlie', and they both end up in the ring of a prize-fight. Another participant in this imbroglio is billed as 'Abdul the Turk', who was Sennett's personal trainer. This was, after all, a year of some austerity, and everyone had to pull their weight. The 'Battle Royal' of the title also involved a number of black fighters, who got involved with Ben and Abdul in black-face. Old comedy habits died hard.

Abdul the Turk was not the only Sennett veteran to cross over from the ring to the screen. The most frightening actor on the Sennett payroll was without doubt Kalla Pasha, a bear-like individual who appeared with a huge beard and beetling eyebrows as an all-round heavy, working-class ruffian, foreign anarchist or half-man half-animal type. His real name was Joseph T. Rickard, and he was a New Yorker born in 1877. Before joining Sennett, he had spent over twenty years in carnivals, circuses, burlesque and wrestling circuits. Oddly enough, he was buried as Kalla Pasha, which had been his wrestling *nom de guerre,* in a Russian Orthodox cemetery in California in 1933, after appearing in over forty Sennett movies.

The director of *The Battle Royal*, as of around ninety Sennett movies, was F. Richard Jones, Sennett's star director and one of the most prized assets Sennett managed to preserve from the Keystone–Triangle period. From a $250-a-week post in 1917, he eventually drew $15,000 a picture for his features of 1920. When

Jones was being wooed by Pathé Lehrman at the peak of Sennett's escape-from-Triangle saga, Mack wired his manager, John Waldron, on 1 July 1917:

IT IS NECESSARY THAT WE TRY AND KEEP JONES . . . IN TALKING WITH JONES AND OTHER IMPRESS UPON THEM THE WONDERFUL OPPORTUNITY AND PRESTIGE THEY HAVE BY BEING WITH ME AND BEING ON THE PROGRAM WITH ALL THE LEADING ARTISTS . . .

Jones resisted the Lehrman call and remained with Mack for the next seven years.

Jones was Mabel Normand's choice for director on her first feature, *Mickey*, the bane of Sennett's life for two years. The actual filming appeared to be over by the spring of 1917, but post-production dragged on for ever. Mack invented his own myth, as usual, about this phase of the movie. No distributor, he said, would have faith in the movie, until a small movie theatre in Bayside, Long Island, which was stuck for a feature, put it on at Sennett's prodding and, lo and behold, it was an instant hit. 'I hollered, "I told you so!" and "I knew it all the time!" . . . Money rolled in so fast we had to hire educated men to count it,' he wrote in *King of Comedy*.

But by the time *Mickey* was released, Mabel had been with the Samuel Goldwyn Studio for almost a year. The circumstances of Mabel's professional split from Sennett are shrouded in the usual confusion of facts and gossip, but there is little doubt that the production itself was an unhappy experience most of the way. Shooting had stopped several times due to Mabel's sickness, a hacking cough and haemorrhages, much later diagnosed as tuberculosis. Biographer Betty Harper Fussell writes that Mabel scorned doctors and took to using a cough syrup laced with opium, which led to a later addiction to cocaine. This raises the question of the whole concealed morass of Hollywood's love affair with drug addiction, and leads us into a necessary digression:

Drugs and Hollywood have been a favourite theme of gossip since time immemorial, but some context should be provided. In the early part of the twentieth century, in the United States as in Europe, addictive drugs were not illegal. Cocaine was praised as therapeutic by Sigmund Freud and acceptable in literature as used by Sherlock Holmes ('a seven per cent solution, Watson!'). Cocaine Toothache Drops were advertised openly in the 1880s ('Instantaneous Cure!

Mabel with her favourite director – F. Richard Jones

Price 15 cents'). Coca-Cola, marketed from 1886, was said to contain cocaine until 1903. Heroin, a brand name of the Bayer company, was introduced in 1898 and used to counter the addiction to morphine, which was becoming a growing social problem in the early 1900s. Opium, as smoked by Chinese labourers, became common as what we would today call 'blowback' from the British-inspired opium wars of the early nineteenth century. The Harrison Narcotics Act outlawed cocaine in 1914, though it was still widely used. (Marijuana was not criminalized in the United States until 1937.)

The main focus of reformers in the US was alcohol, the Prohibition of which was widely discussed and was imminent in the period of our story. The use of the other drugs above was at this time limited among white people, and therefore considered more of a social transgression than a matter for the law. In the world of silent comedies, drugs of this sort were widely lampooned: *The Mystery of the Leaping Fish*, a Fine Arts film for Triangle in 1916, starred young

Douglas Fairbanks as a spoof sleuth, Coke Ennyday, who is on the trail of a gang smuggling his favourite substance. Chaplin's *Easy Street*, released in January 1917, featured Lloyd Bacon (later a major Hollywood director) as the dope addict on whose needle Charlie sits when slapped down, galvanizing him to leap up and demolish all the villains in a superhuman assault. In 1918, Charley Chase (still as Charles Parrott) played a character conned out of his 'coke' by Billy West in *Playmates,* released by the King Bee company. The character is also gay, and West (in his trademark Charlie Chaplin imitation) sneezes and blows away his white powder.

Ed Roberts' *Exposé of Movie Vice* abounded with allegations of drug addiction, traced in his book to the pioneer explorations of movie idol Wallace Reid, who ended up in a private sanatorium in 1922, a declared morphine addict. A more recent 'exposer' of Hollywood vice, Kenneth Anger, described, in his lurid tome, *Hollywood Babylon* (1975), how the *nouveau-riche* Hollywood folk escaped to the '"joy powder", as cocaine was called in those free-and-easy days, for a sure-thing-pick-you-up. In fact, a "joy powder" manic movie comedy style rapidly evolved . . .'

The idea that the Keystone comedies, as a genre, were launched on a sea of cocaine, with the crazy antics of clowns leaping on their heads and falling out of aeroplanes induced by a non-stop orgy of 'nose-candy' is attractive, but somewhat far-fetched, as we have traced other sources for this conduct. Movies were more apt to ape other movies than to follow the contours of drug hallucinations, though even Sennett referred to 'every fool thing you might think of under the influence of hashish or a hangover', in the most metaphorical sense, of course. And so underground Hollywood could not fail to have had some effect on its overground façades, on the warp and weft of its dreams.

The lid, however, was soon to come off this particular basket of snakes . . .

Mabel's troubles with *Mickey*, however much they had to do with secret transgressions, illness and temperament, had more to do with the financial shenanigans over Triangle–Keystone's 're-arrangements', which caught the movie up in their swirl. While Sennett was manœuvring like mad to break away from Triangle and set up on his own, he was also trying to keep control of *Mickey*.

Mabel Normand as Mickey, 1918

Matters were complicated further because director Jones had 'kid-napped' some reels of the negative 'in lieu of unpaid bonuses'. *Mickey*, however, belonged to Triangle, who would not release it for their own reasons, probably in order to maintain some pressure on Sennett, after he had left them with the empty shell of Keystone. The film fell under the control of one of the Triangle shell companies, Western Imports, which swindled Sennett out of his own share of the picture, cut it without his involvement or consent and released it in

August 1918. Despite the terrifying influenza epidemic that was gathering force at that point, the film was indeed a hit, though neither Mack nor Mabel shared in the box-office profits.

*Mickey* was a sentimental 'Cinderella' tale of an orphan girl brought up by a prospector whose gold mine has fallen on hard times. She is brought up by an Indian nanny, played with some dignity by one Minnie Ha Ha (otherwise known as Minnie Devereaux). To have a better life, she is sent off to relatives in the city, who soon discover her guardian's gold mine is played out and treat her as a servant. George Nichols, Minta Durfee and Tom Kennedy were in the cast, along with a young energetic actor, Lew Cody, who years later would become the partner of Mabel's only marriage. In the movie, he plays a would-be rapist, who chases her viciously from room to room.

The film has its modicum of rural charm and some tender moments with Mickey's lover, played by Tom Kennedy. On the whole, it became the embodiment of the idea of Mabel as the child-woman, tomboy and free spirit. The American woman can be free, it suggests, as long as she does not become an adult. Being the child-woman allows her to flaunt her voluptuous charms, bare her thighs and even dive, apparently nude – although in appropriate 'fleshings' – into a lake in the woods.

Although Sennett laid claim to *Mickey*, it was Triangle that marketed the film successfully, as its publicists 'saturated the country with sheet music, vaudeville lantern-slides . . . "MICKEY" shirts, sox, flowers, sundaes, phonograph records'. In a country undergoing the gloom both of war and influenza, some months before the armistice that would end the Great War, the film's simple romance, recognizable heroine and villains, the triumph of the downtrodden and the virtues of rural against city life struck a familiar chord.

For Mack, Mabel's success was a bitter irony. He had, in that fateful summer of 1917, amid all his other telegrammed orders to manager Waldron, tried to intervene in the negotiation between Mabel and the Samuel Goldwyn company: wiring her lawyer, Arthur Butler Graham (who was conveniently his lawyer as well), that she would do well to insist on a better contract and ask Goldwyn for $5,000 a week. He may have hoped to keep Mabel on board, as he tried to convince producer Charles Baumann to help her 'stall a little longer and you keep up the negotiation with Goldfish'. But Baumann wired him back: 'Client absolutely unmanageable and unalterable she refused absolutely to have anything to do with me or yourself in connection with any business proposition whatever she is determined to go through with the contract.' On 23 July, Mabel wired Mack:

LOS ANGELES ATHLETIC CLUB LOSANGELES CALIF

SIGNED TODAY . . . I YEAR AND OPTION GRAHAM VERY SATISFIED SAID MUCH BETTER THAN EXPECTED START WORK SEPT I COMPANY SAID I DIDN'T LOOK WELL MUST REST AND GO AWAY UNTIL THEN WINTER STUDIO FLORIDA SO I WON'T BE ABLE TO PEEP AT YOU EVER AGAIN WANTED YOU TO KNOW I SIGNED ALTHOUGH YOU NEVER WIRE.

M

And that, for the time being, was that.

In September, Mack leased 'that certain Motion Picture Studio known as the "MABEL NORMAND STUDIO"' to Thomas Ince. It had been built, equipped and used for just the one movie, and then transferred for the making of William S. Hart's westerns.

Mabel's career at Goldwyn's seemed to be a fulfilment of all her dreams and desires. Goldwyn, ex-Goldfish, had been bought out of Adolph Zukor's Famous Players–Lasky company and used his $900,000 pay-off to set up on his own. Rivalling Aitken's Triangle, he too tried to woo famous names to his movies, though he wished his product to be more refined. Mabel was to appear in his publicity not as the simple country lass of Sennett's imagination but as a glamorous star, to rival Mary Pickford, at that time Hollywood's favourite. In November 1917, she toured the New York theatres, to speak for the war's Liberty Loan. She gave interviews which emphasized her new serious character, speaking about her private intellectual life, reading Strindberg, Ibsen, Shaw and the 'Russians', and carrying about volumes of Nietzsche and Freud. Her movies for Goldwyn, however, were mostly in the *Mickey* mode, after a disastrous first attempt at a flag-waving Jeanne D'Arc type – *Joan of Plattsburg*. There followed *The Venus Model*, *Back to the Woods*, *Peck's Bad Girl*, *Jinx*, *Pinto*, *The Slim Princess* and *What Happened to Rosa*, made very quickly over the next two years. By 28 December 1918, the *Los Angeles Times* was reporting:

Just as Mabel Normand, Goldwyn star, was happily settled in her Hollywood home, and was planning a nice house-warming party, along came the flu and not only threw cold water on all her nice little social plans, but stopped work on 'Sis Hopkins.' Miss Normand is reported to be seriously ill.

This was, of course, the height of the killer influenza epidemic, but Mabel's 'flu' was her recurring illness. Biographer Fussell has claimed, in the recollective fog of elderly witnesses, that Mabel had miscarried a child by lover Sam Goldwyn, her new boss. We might recall, too, our own genealogist's discoveries concerning the death of her baby brother, Walter, and the possibility of congenital syphilis. The medical history of that disease reveals it to be the 'great imitator', regularly capable of causing the symptoms of other chronic illnesses. This, too, can neither be proved nor completely discounted, along with the tales of Mabel's deepening cocaine dependency. The one fact we can glean from this is Mabel's increasing distress, and her desperate effort to keep up the appearance of joy and glamour and her pursuit of the higher matters of life, as she told Grace Kingsley of the *Los Angeles Times* on 12 January 1919:

'Why, all my friends are out here, and they've been just too lovely to me for anything. Even when I had the "flu" they kept me jolly with letters and telegrams and flowers and candy . . . But I'll tell you a secret. I got a chance to read a lot of books I've been wanting to read for a long time. Just as Carlyle used to read yellow-backed novels as a rest from serious labors, so the joyous comedienne as tragedy relief, so to speak, turns to highbrow literature. So I've been reading history and all kinds of stiff things, with H. G. Wells as the very lightest one of all!'

While Mabel was stretched on the rack at Goldwyn's, Mack fretted in his own office bath-tub, never giving up his plans to somehow woo her back to his fold. In the acres of speculation, ploughed here and elsewhere, one might add, even within the swill of ambition and avarice, the sweeter possibility that Mack Sennett actually felt responsible for Mabel, whom he had wooed from Biograph and others to build into America's star. Beyond love, affection and the desire for a jewel in the box-office crown, there might well have been an old-fashioned impulse from an old-fashioned sort of man.

He could certainly console himself with many other fish in his water tank: the Sennett belles or 'Rosebuds' – whose great dilemma was, according to the *Mack Sennett Weekly*, 'Shall I Get Wet Or Not?' – Marie Prevost, Mary Thurman, Ora Carew, Maude Wayne, Peggy Pearce, Harriet Hammond, Virginia Warwick and Phyllis Haver. The girl who was destined to outshine them all – Gloria Swanson – was already oozing her own brand of slinky glamour. From *Motion Picture Classic*, March 1918:

Here is Gloria Swanson, famous beauty in Mack Sennett comedies, rigged up like Egypt 30 B.C., playing the Honolulu musical importation (*the ukelele, ed.*) and wearing 1917 pumps. If it weren't for such oddities we might think her Cleopatra herself, instead of only a comedy queen.

Posing at first nights in spectacular costumes, coats of 'Ville de Paris importation . . . the color raspberry, the material panne velvet . . . the bottom of the coat elaborately trimmed with marabou . . . an adaptation of a style from the Louis Ouinze [*sic*] period . . .', Swanson was by far the press agents' favourite. Sennett, however, seemed to see her as just another comedy asset in the barn. He kept teaming her with Teddy, the studio dog, who was photographed endlessly with Swanson, exhibiting his own patrician disdain. Teddy had his own niche in the publicity department, reputed to be a 'one-take' dog. A Great Dane, he tended to do his bit and then curl up in a corner, oblivious to all the other frenzied thespians. This melancholic demeanour may have been due to a less than happy childhood, as his trainer, Joe Simkins, once revealed that 'I kept Ted half starved when he was a pup. He didn't get a good square meal until he was about two years old; the consequence is that he is like a trained athlete.' *Photoplay* interviewed him in July 1917:

'Who's your friend, Teddy?'
'Woof, waff, wuff!' (Translation: 'Gloria Swanson.')

Teddy earned $50 a week and paid $25 annual income tax, according to a later *Photoplay* issue. But he was in good athletic shape in *Teddy at the Throttle* (1917, directed by Clarence Badger), rescuing Gloria from a band of ruffians and stopping the runaway train just short of canine and human disaster. The villain of the piece, Wallace Beery, was Gloria's new husband, who got caught up too enthusiastically in the action:

Wally, in full villain's make-up, let out a roar and grabbed me, but much too hard, it seems. I panicked and he got carried away . . . He leered at me, I

*Teddy at the Throttle* with Gloria Swanson

started hammering on his chest, and he raced with me to the tracks. He threw me down and tied me to the tracks with a length of chain. The more I pounded him with my fists, the more he laughed. Then he tied my hands together, much too tightly. I tried to kick him but I couldn't move my legs. The chain was cutting me. Suddenly Mr. Badger yelled, 'Cut! That's it! Wonderful!' He came over himself to untie my hands, and as he did so, he could see the red marks on my wrists and feel me shaking like a leaf.

This presaged similarly robust trouble in the Beery–Swanson marriage, but Gloria was to go on to husbands two, three and four in due course – she was only eighteen years old, after all, when she plighted her troth with Wally – number two being restaurateur Herbert K. Somborn and number three the marvellously titled Henri, Marquis de la Falaise de la Coudraye. She was demonstrably unhappy, she claimed, to be cast at Sennett's as a 'pie-in-the-face' girl. 'I hated the vulgarity,' she wrote in her autobiography, *Swanson on Swanson*:

It was a world of falling planks and banana peels and wet paint and sticky wads of gum, of funny-looking fat men with painted moustaches blowing the foam off beer at each other, of stern battle-axes wielding rolling pins . . . and of cute giggly hoydens being teased, tickled and chased.

Start with Sennett, get rich somewhere else. Gloria moved on, to one of Triangle's drama companies, making *Society for Sale* with director Frank Borzage, in 1918. In 1919, she joined Cecil B. De Mille, to begin the career that would ensure her lasting fame and fulfil her penchant for exotic costume to the utmost.

Teddy the dog remained behind loyally, the least likely of Sennett's star cast to make trouble over pies, rolling pins and moustaches, or to make unreasonable demands for a pay rise.

# CHAPTER EIGHTEEN

# He Did and He Didn't
## (or *Drowning Mack's Sorrows*)

The end of the War, in November 1918, brought a great surge of patriotic relief to Americans, along with an overwhelming desire for a 'return to normalcy'. The idea that the war was fought and won for Democracy ushered in a new period of official self-congratulation, though this too could be undermined by the severe employment problems facing the hordes of returning soldiers, the new paranoia of Russian-inspired subversion and the empire of crime that was about to be sparked off by the Prohibition of alcohol.

Comedians, though, continued their gambols. The only major comedian of the silent screen to enlist was young Buster Keaton, who interrupted his partnership with Roscoe Arbuckle at Comique Films to ship out for basic training on Long Island, reaching France in the late summer. Fortunately for him, the war was over within a few months, though he was kept in the army for a while longer as an entertainer with the Sunshine Division.

Harold Lloyd, another comedian soon to be of note, had spent no more than a few weeks playing an extra at Keystone before finding a niche with producer Hal Roach, creating his Lonesome Luke character from mid-1915, before discovering his classic 'Glasses Character' in 1917. The Roach operation, however, was not yet a rival to Mack Sennett's sprawling studio.

Chaplin, on the other hand, was carving his unique space, moving from Essanay to Mutual, then to First National Films. In early 1918, he had shot the three-reeler *A Dog's Life*, his first masterpiece, linking the comedy of his gags and character to the tragedy of life in America's tenderloin. *Shoulder Arms* and *Sunnyside* would follow, taking him through into 1919.

Among Sennett's great dramatic contemporaries, D. W. Griffith had recovered from the box-office drubbing of his most ambitious epic, *Intolerance*, to shoot *Hearts of the World*, a love story set against the background of the war. One of his alumni, Erich von Stroheim, was about to shoot his first feature, *Blind Husbands*, and would be casting Mack's alleged nemesis, Mae Busch, in his second film, *The Devil's Passkey*, shot in November 1919. From Germany, in the same year, would come a film that would introduce new and strange ideas into the cinema: *The Cabinet of Doctor Caligari*.

The movies were moving on, but Sennett remained at Edendale, presiding over and protecting his kingdom. It was now a well-oiled machine, though it was turning out fewer films than before, reflecting a general economic downturn. To the outside world, Sennett was the same Sennett, the same authority on the business and art of comedy, as he expatiated to *Motion Picture Classic*:

Gozzi, the famous Italian dramatist, demonstrated conclusively, as the result of examining thousands of plays, that there are only thirty-six possible dramatic situations. There are only a handful of possible jokes.

The chief members of this joke band may be said to be:

The fall of dignity.

Mistaken identity.

Almost every joke on the screen belongs, roughly, to one or other of these clans.

All jokes are old, and there are only a few of them. One of the earliest inscriptions found in Egypt was a joke about a mother-in-law told in hieroglyphics . . . Like a diamond, a joke depends very largely upon the setting. Nine times out of ten if a gag fails it is because of the poor paving of the way up to it.

This is true of any joke. How many times have you seen a good story ruined because the teller chose a time when his audience was not in the mood to pay attention!

The mood for comedy had not dimmed, and the king of comedy was settling down to an administrative routine, pursuing his bachelor life after work, and spending more and more of his office hours in a strictly supervisory role. Gone was the Sennett who appeared in his own movies, happy to be just one of the gang (although he would do cameos on occasion). Now he was 'the Old Man', ensconced in his tower, keeping his eye on all that occurred beneath him, and on the unruly gag-writers and scribes who were not apt to keep to office hours. Legend had it that he had a creaky board on the steps that led down beside his office from the cubbyholes in which the writers were supposed to do their stuff, so that he could hear them if they skived off. But they fooled him, removing and replacing the step, breaking free from their rattling chains.

Our one reliable insight into the life of the boss in this period is a curious file in the Sennett archive. It contains, in copious detail, the personal accounts of Mack Sennett's purchases of liquor, dating from July 1917. The Booze File is a thing of wonderment, bulging with orders and offers from such vendors as the Sonoma Wine Company, Capitol Liquor, the Santa Rosa Vineyard and various San Francisco vintners. As the policy at the Sennett studios was one of strict abstinence, apart from an alleged dispensation for stage comedian Joe Jackson, who could not function without his tipple, it follows that the somewhat prodigious amounts of alcohol ordered were for the boss's own use (or reasonable entertainment of guests thereof), in one instance: '2 cases Haig and Haig, 1 case King Wm Scotch, 3 cases Cliquot Champ., 1 case Ripy qts Bd. 6 yrs old'. From Imperial Vineyards on 28 November 1918: '4 cases Sanderson's Port, 3 cases Pinch Bottle, 5 cases XXX Hennessy', totalling $524.50. Another requisition note from the Los Angeles Athletic Club on Sennett's account, dated 8 January 1919, added up to $1,149, a pretty hefty New Year's party.

But what Sennett was already concerned with was the onset of Prohibition, signalled by the passing of the Volstead Act, and prompting an urgent wire from the Santa Fe Avenue Mercantile Corporation, dated 15 June 1919:

MACK SENNETT MACK SENNETT STUDIOS

UNITED STATES POSITIVELY DRY JULY FIRST WE HAVE THE LARGEST AND MOST COMPLETE STOCK OF IMPORTED AND DOMESTIC WINES AND LIQUORS ON THE PACIFIC COAST EXTRA SPECIAL PRICES ON QUANTITY ORDERS SEND US YOUR REQUIREMENTS AND WE WILL QUOTE YOU OUR BEST PRICE

Sennett's obsession with his supply in these desperate times is highlighted by a letter on 23 June from an agent of a freight company presenting a standard loss claim for 'one bottle of American Picon' apparently missing from a shipment from M. M. Loewenthal in San Francisco, literally a drop in the ocean. But subsequent notes reveal that all was not yet lost, as long lists of inventories of 'Private Vaults Nos 7, 8 and 9' show how stockpiles were built up for the drought

years, and a smoking-gun form marked 'Order on Prop Department, The Keystone Film Co.' shows the method of the subterfuge: fifty-one cases of booze – 'Champagne, Gordons Gin, Vermouth, Caloric Punch, Apricot Cordial, Hennessey, Haig, American Picon, Paul Masson, Bacardi Rum, French Claret and two barrels of Schlitz Beer', with the pencil scrawl: 'Sent to Mr. Sennett's house'.

Another source of consolation for Mack, as he pondered his commercial blessings and his private sorrows, was the continuing presence of his mother, Mrs Sinnott, as she spent more and more time in the California winter sun. Given her own proclivity, as we have seen in a previous cutting, for the balming fluid, we might speculate on quiet nights by the fireplace with the contents of Private Vault Number Seven discreetly decanted in the salon.

Sennett's withdrawal during the war seemed to reflect not only the commercial changes that had taken up his energies during the crucial summer months of 1917. While there was little enough enthusiasm for the bloodletting in Europe among the population at large, actors and comedians in particular found themselves uncomfortable with the idea of armed conflict. Sennett's only apparent reference to the war, apart from some reassuring comments about the continuing box-office success of his product at the British box office, was a full-page spread in the *Mack Sennett Weekly* of 31 December 1917, presenting Adolph Zukor's appeal for help for starving Jews caught up in battles in Poland. Eschewing his usual lectures about comedy, the film industry and do-gooding censors, he contributed a column entitled 'Don't Let These Poor Women and Kiddies Starve':

When you sit down tonight and are trying to decide between a Manhattan and a Bronx; when you are having to debate with yourself as to whether chicken a la Maryland or roast duck will tease your fastidious palate, just remember that a child is starving to death and half the price of your dinner would have saved his life . . .

Not only the Jews of Hollywood were concerned at involvement in a war between the different ethnic groups that made up the warp and weft of America: English, Irish, Germans, Italians and so forth. Virulent anti-German propaganda was unsettling to many who felt that their own background was obliquely seen as suspect. Everyone in Hollywood was, in a sense, engaged in inventing their own identity, and comedy especially enjoyed its parade of masks, its principle of cocking a snook at authority, knocking off the policeman's helmet. Chaplin and everyone else advertised for the Liberty Loan, but when Chaplin captured the Kaiser in *Shoulder Arms*, all of war was made to look absurd. Mack Sennett comedies simply ignored the war, insisting on their own timeless chaos.

Sennett was still at heart a subversive, one of Ed Roberts's 'upstarts, the poor uncouth, ill-bred "roughnecks"' who had disturbed the balance of good and evil, propriety and licentiousness that pure-bred America might desire. But he was also now one of its self-made entrepreneurs, the very epitome of what a true American should be. The problem was to keep running on the perpetual tread-mill. Had he not himself written, in his own *Weekly*: 'Getting Into Rut and Routine Would be Fatal, Says Man Who Knows'? As he had fondly paraphrased Henri Bergson: 'When you stop changing you die and decay . . .'

Mack had installed, at his studio, the great 'cyclorama', a massive revolving drum on which painted backgrounds could whip by while drivers in cars, trucks or motorcycles could pretend to be rushing through the landscape. All in movies is illusion. Wherein, therefore, lies the truth?

As the American teens flipped into the twenties, standards and mores were indeed changing. Young people were becoming more assertive. Women's skirts were edging up, up, up. Mobility was assured by the accessibility of the personal motor car. A new tech-nology, radio, was about to connect people and homes in an unprece-dented way. People would soon be able to 'Dash through the Clouds' faster than Mabel Normand. Black jazz was being interpreted to white audiences on a mass level. The age of the 'flapper' had arrived, with its own slang, talking of 'the cat's pajamas', 'apple-sauce', 'dumbdoras', 'dropping the pilot' – for getting a divorce, 'alarm clock' – for chaperone, 'tomato' – for a dumb good-looker, 'cake basket' – for limousine and 'Father Time' – any man over thirty years old.

Against this stood Prohibition and the backlash of old-style puri-tanism, the determination of the good and the godly to maintain authority at all costs. In May 1920, in the wake of a small-town payroll robbery in which two men were shot dead, two Italian-American anarchists, Sacco and Vanzetti, were arrested, and became the perfect scapegoats for America's fear of supposedly alien social ideas. In the same month, a young writer, F. Scott Fitzgerald, published his first book, *This Side of Paradise*, revealing the casual way young men and women embraced the impulse of having fun with each other.

Meanwhile, in California, Mack Sennett was still planning to bring Mabel Normand back to the fold. He was preparing a property, a script written ostensibly by himself, but farmed out to scenarist Jane

Murfin – *Molly O'*. If *Mickey* was a hit, *Molly O'* would be bigger – 'the most costly production that has been produced in the world'. (Sennett claimed it eventually cost half a million dollars.) This would be another Cinderella story, with Mabel as the classic Irish working girl, a washerwoman's daughter, once again placed in the rough care of a rich family who abuse her, until the tables are turned. As Sennett described the film on its release:

Molly O is the personification of optimism; its heroine is so full of 'pep' that there wasn't any actress in the world that could play the part except Mabel Normand, who came back to the Sennett regime a greater, finer, more brilliant and winsome star than ever. And one purpose animated her: It was to see whether Mack Sennett could produce another 'Mickey.'

We have reason to believe that 'Molly O' is a 'greater-than-Mickey' picture. It ought to be . . . It covers a deeper range of emotions and it tells a keener story. Molly O, the embodiment of the spirit of 'I Will', struggles up from the dreary clums [*sic*] of society, and by virtue of that which is within her, assumes her rightful place in the universe . . .

The hell with Hollywood's new mood of serious drama, the *Blind Husbands* and *Foolish Wives* of von Stroheim's attempt to take movies down the path of sordid realism. *Molly O'* would return to basics, the tried and true sentimental formula derived from Griffith's own work.

Sennett's tale of his wooing of Mabel from Sam Goldwyn was his usual spin and myth: '"Sam," I said, "you have Normand under contract, but you haven't got any work for her for a long time. She's a pretty expensive luxury, isn't she?"'

Goldwyn demanded $30,000 to release Mabel from her contract, Sennett said, but Mabel turned his tailor-made script down. He tried again, and convinced Goldwyn to release Mabel. In fact, Goldwyn had wrung as much out of Mabel as he possibly could. When Sennett saw her, Mack claimed: 'All those years of neglecting herself, of fun for fun's sake and ice cream for breakfast, of driving herself to be gay and amusing, had left a mark on a girl who after all was very small.' But it was a very different white stuff than ice-cream that Mabel was taking to make it through the day.

Mack's offer was a lifeline to Mabel, and she grabbed it gladly. It reunited her once again with director Dick Jones, who did his best to make her shine in the old way. Once again, he demonstrated

Sennett's dependency on him as the studio workhorse, as the *Los Angeles Examiner* would later relate (6 May 1922):

A day's work with F. Richard Jones . . . would permanently fatigue the average labouring man. His day begins at sunrise and ends when the moon is swinging high and the last street car is clattering over the Broadway crossings.

After spending the daylight hours directing on the set, he passes into the projection room in the twilight and reviews the footage shot that day. Quite often there are night scenes to be filmed, keeping Richard on the job until the milk is being distributed among the nearby bungalows. But he'll be back at work at 8 a.m., and expects his company to do likewise . . .

Sennett kept a close eye on the movie as it went into the cutting room in the spring of 1921. The film was completed and made ready for its première in October in Los Angeles. All was primed for a return to the old-style movie, the story of laughter and tears, with lovely, pristine, innocent Mabel brought back to her glory days.

But on 10 September, the roof fell in on Hollywood, its pretence of happy-go-lucky innocence and its delusion of invulnerability from the pressures of the real world.

# CHAPTER NINETEEN

# Fatty's Fatal Fun

In February 1919, *Photoplay* journal published an essay entitled 'On the Advantages of Embonpoint', by Roscoe 'Fatty' Arbuckle, in which he offered the following reflections:

If you are gifted with avoirdupois you are always a welcome guest at a party, because you're supposed to be funny and everybody sits up and simpers as you enter with incomparable grace, nudging neighbouring elbows and observing *sotto voce*, so you can hear them: 'Oh, here comes that funny Mr. Arbuckle . . . now the party will wake up.' Then it's up to you to be funny. If you can't they'll laugh anyway, because anything you do will seem funny to them.

A fat man stays young when his cadaverous brothers have become like wrinkled mummies. He is ruddy-cheeked when his hair is like silver, and everybody loves him, despite that old saying, which has long since been disproved, to the contrary. He is regarded as harmless and innocent just because he looks so solid and easy-going. He may be harboring the most malicious thoughts, but he is disarmed by his own fat. Nobody suspects him. There was only one fat villain in fiction – that was in Wilkie Collins' 'Woman in White.' The exception proves the rule. Wasn't it the Bard of Avon who observed, 'Let me have men about me who are fat', or words to that effect? He knew. He realized that a fat man couldn't be evil, because no one would believe it of him.

A fat man makes a comfortable person to have around the house. His lap is a favorite perch for young and beautiful debutantes and sub-debs. They call him Uncle and punch him in the solar-plexus and generally kid him along. What fat man could fail to be happy under such circumstances?

It's no use a fat man being serious; he won't be taken so by his friends or enemies . . .

Alas, Fatty, too, was deluded, perhaps most of all. How could he imagine the scale of the cataclysm that was to focus all the fury and hatred of the reformers and scourgers of 'vice-ridden' Hollywood on his own 'comfortable' self? On 10 September 1921, Americans woke to the newspaper headline:

FATTY ARBUCKLE SOUGHT IN ORGY DEATH.
ACTRESS DIES AFTER HOTEL PARTY.

On 5 September, Roscoe Arbuckle had attended a Labor Day party at the St Francis Hotel in San Francisco, motoring up there with Sennett director Fred Fishbach and actor Lowell Sherman. Roscoe had just completed three feature films shot in a row, and was well disposed to celebrate. Illegal booze flowed freely in 'Fatty''s suite, and his friends gathered there during the day. Another visitor to the suite was an actress, Virginia Rappe, who was the somewhat part-time girlfriend of Henry 'Pathé' Lehrman, still running his own comedy company. Virginia Rappe had worked as an extra at Keystone during Roscoe's tenure there. She had a reputation as a fun-loving girl. Several other showgirls and some prominent San Francisco citizens, who later successfully covered up their own presence at Roscoe's party, also showed up.

What happened at the party became the subject of three sensational trials and endless speculation, gossip, accusations and inventions. Virginia Rappe became violently ill, frothing at the mouth, tearing off her clothes and screaming. Roscoe and his other guests tried to minister to her or at least get her to stop screaming. They took her to a separate room in the hotel and called a doctor, who found her lying exhausted but quiet, and decided she was only drunk. The hotel detective then called the house physician, who called four times during the night and was then replaced by a third doctor. It was only two days after the party that Miss Rappe was removed to a hospital, where she died on the Friday, 9 September. The doctors at the hospital found that her bowel had been ruptured, and also diagnosed gonorrhoea. She had died of peritonitis.

Miss Rappe, however, had been accompanied by a friend, Maude Delmont, who had begun complaining at an early stage that Roscoe Arbuckle had assaulted Virginia. It was her complaint, made to the District Attorney, which placed Roscoe on the rack. Maude Delmont claimed that Arbuckle had grabbed Virginia, shouting, 'I have been trying to get you for five years'. She saw Arbuckle drag Virginia into his own room and heard her screams as he was abusing her. The details of the abuse grew more and more lurid with the telling:

Roscoe had jumped up and down on Virginia's stomach with his great weight, rupturing her insides. He had thrust ice cubes and then a Coca Cola bottle into her vagina, ripping the poor girl apart. He had raped her in the most bestial manner, and was a monster who should not be allowed to live. 'Fiancé' Henry Lehrman weighed in, giving a vitriolic interview to the press in which he went down on his knees and begged God for justice, telling the newsmen:

That's what comes of taking vulgarians from the gutter and giving them enormous salaries and making idols of them . . . Such people don't know how to get a kick out of life, except in a beastly way. They are a disgrace to the film business. They are the ones who resort to cocaine and the opium needle and who participate in orgies that surpass the orgies of degenerate Rome. They should be swept out of the motion picture business.

Sweeping the degenerates out of the motion-picture business was a welcome project to the forces that had made Prohibition a reality and were ready and waiting to clean up the 'sewer' of Hollywood. Roscoe was arrested, despite all the pleas from friends and colleagues that he was the gentlest of men and couldn't hurt a fly. Buster Keaton, his regular film partner, weighed in with strong support. Mack Sennett, according to author David Yallop, tried to come to Roscoe's aid, stating: 'In all the years that Roscoe worked for me, he didn't do a thing anyone could point a finger at . . . I never knew him to be mixed up in any brawls or to do an ungentlemanly thing toward any girl. He was a kind, good-natured fat man and a good comic.'

Mack Sennett understood America's comic fantasies, and the anarchistic, anti-authoritarian impulses of its working-class audiences. What he did not fathom were the darker fantasies of the guardians of America's moral gates, and the extent of the power and malice of those who could profit by whipping up fear and hatred. Sennett's comments, and those of other friends and defenders of Roscoe Arbuckle, were not printed in the newspapers controlled by William Randolph Hearst, who adopted the case as an ideal circulation-building scandal. Hearst's Americanism was of the familiar xenophobic and flag-waving kind, and Orson Welles's later satirical portrait of his career in *Citizen Kane* in fact erred on the side of kindness towards Hearst's ruthless pursuit of power. Chaplin, too, declared his support for Roscoe, but not a word was printed.

The Arbuckle case caused panic among his producers at Paramount and throughout the industry. The case was being prosecuted by an ambitious San Francisco District Attorney, Mathew Brady, who seized on it as an ideal ticket to fame. Difficulties arose from the beginning, with evidence suggesting that Roscoe had spent no more than ten minutes alone in the room with Virginia Rappe and that she had a medical history of venereal disease and acute abdominal pains which amounted to a chronic type of cystitis. Several young ladies who were called as witnesses for the prosecution resisted the DA's efforts to fit their testimony to the preferred murder charge, and the whole process, as it unfolded, constituted one of the most prejudiced, deceitful and fraudulent attempts to secure a conviction in the history of American justice. Fingerprint evidence was fabricated, witnesses were intimidated, pertinent evidence was disallowed and the initial complainant, Maude Delmont, was never brought to the witness stand in any of the trials. An illegal initial post-mortem carried out on the dead girl, resulting in the destruction of her reproductive organs, was covered up. Zukor and his colleagues secured an excellent legal team to defend Arbuckle, but they were no match for the vultures of the Hearst press and the Reformers' brigades: the Anti-Saloon League, the Moral Efficiency League and the Women's Vigilant Committee.

Roscoe Arbuckle was tried three times for the same crime. At the first trial, during which the prosecution's case seemed to fall apart as it was being presented and Roscoe presented a convincing account of his innocence on the witness stand, the jury was hung ten to two in favour of acquittal, forcing a retrial. At the second trial, held in January 1922, defence attorney Gavin McNab made the mistake of having Roscoe's testimony read into the record, instead of putting him again on the stand. The jury was hung again – nine to three for a conviction.

By this time, the movie moguls were in total rout. Various censor boards had pulled Arbuckle films from distribution, although the few theatres that showed his films reported a roaring trade. The leaders of the movie industry felt their entire business was in jeopardy. Their first move, immediately following the first trial, was to appoint, on 8 December 1921, their own internal censorship guardian – ex-Postmaster General William Hays. Offered $100,000 a year for three years, Hays vowed to clean up Hollywood's act. A devout

Presbyterian and chairman of the Republican National Committee, he was ideally placed to protect the industry against its detractors, at the price of formalizing the process of keeping sex and vice off the screen.

There was not a trace of sex and vice in Roscoe Arbuckle's movies, and the heyday of comedy vulgarity, at Keystone and elsewhere, had come and gone, with surreal action gags replacing Yiddisher jokes about bosoms and adultery, but the movies and their practitioners were to be purged by Will Hays of anything which might sully 'that sacred thing, the mind of a child . . . that unmarked slate'. Movies should have the same responsibility, Hays declared, as the 'best clergyman, the most inspired teacher of youth'.

In his third trial, in April 1922, attorney McNab put Roscoe on the witness stand again, and most of the prosecution witnesses self-destructed almost before any cross-examination could begin. The invisible complainant, Maude 'Bambina' Delmont, was busy elsewhere, presenting her account of the 'Arbuckle–Rappe murder case' as a vaudeville act – 'a story for every father and mother, every young man and young woman. No increase in prices.' The jury acquitted Arbuckle in five minutes, adding a signed unanimous statement deploring the 'great injustice' done to him, to wish him success and 'hope that the American people will take the judgement of fourteen men and women . . . that Roscoe Arbuckle is entirely innocent and free from all blame'. Roscoe Arbuckle walked out of the courtroom, a free and relieved man. But six days later, Will Hays handed down his first decision as Hollywood's morals czar – banning Arbuckle's films from being shown on any American screen.

During the entire period of 'Fatty''s trials, Mack Sennett and Mabel Normand had been reduced to the level of helpless onlookers at a train wreck. Mack made his statement and stood aside, attending to his own flock at Edendale. Mabel, acutely aware of her own vulnerability to the crusaders against 'the scourge of drugs' in Hollywood, rallied round to the support of Minta Durfee, who had been estranged from Roscoe for four years but nevertheless came to his aid. 'Pathé' Lehrman's diatribe was an early warning of the hammer which was about to descend. The Arbuckle case did not come out of the blue, as far as Hollywood's public sins were concerned. Just one year before, in 1920, young Selznick Pictures star Olive Thomas was found nude and dead in a hotel room in Paris, having taken her own life with poison. Rumours of orgiastic carousing and drug-taking flew about. Jack Pickford, Mary Pickford's brother, was the dead girl's husband.

The fatal Fatty Arbuckle party was in fact prefigured by another party allegedly featuring Roscoe Arbuckle that had taken place four years earlier, on 6 March 1917. A dozen 'movie moguls', unnamed in reports but later known to include Adolph Zukor and Jesse Lasky, capped a banquet in Roscoe's honour in Massachusetts by driving to a house in nearby Woburn, Mishawum Manor, in effect a high-class brothel, at which twelve fun-loving girls were on hand. There followed a somewhat crude 'shakedown' operation, in which a number of the men involved received accusing letters and demands for payment from husbands of some of the girls. The moguls paid hush-money to the local District Attorney, Nathan A. Tufts, but this leaked out and he was charged with corruption. Roscoe had not in fact attended the party, as he was suffering at that point from an infection of his thigh which nearly caused doctors to amputate, but gossip nevertheless insistently named him as one of the Mishawum orgiasts. The case against DA Tufts dragged on and he was found guilty of corruption in October 1921, during the run-up to the first Arbuckle trial. The movie moguls had good reason to dread further scandal, and Arbuckle became their scapegoat.

By the time of Roscoe's acquittal, however, their worst fears were confirmed, as on 1 February 1922, towards the end of 'Fatty''s second, inconclusive trial, scandal struck Hollywood again, in an event which blew open Pandora's Box, and this time drew both Mack and Mabel directly into its sordid spill.

# CHAPTER TWENTY

# Isn't Love Cuckoo?
## (or *Who Murdered Whom?*)

From the *Los Angeles Record*, 12 November 1921:

In spite of the fact that November 10 is known to Mabel Normand and her intimates as her birthday, it made little difference to that young lady when she arose to greet the day that meant the beginning of a new year in her life. She received and accepted an invitation from her producer, Mack Sennett, to take dinner with him and a friend, at his home. The hour was set for 7 and as usual Mabel was on time.

As Mr. Sennett escorted Miss Normand to the dining room, which was darkened at that time, the lights were turned on and eleven of Mabel's friends rushed to wish her many happy returns of the day.

A beautiful three-piece silver tea set was the gift of the entire company. Many less pretentious gifts were presented from the people who worked with her on her last picture, 'Molly O", including an alarm clock from her director, Dick Jones.

Those who helped toward making the party a complete success, were Mabel Normand, William D. Taylor, Mrs. Catherine Sennett, Fay Borden, Mack Sennett, Mr. And Mrs. E. M. Asher, Dick Jones, Mr. And Mrs. Earle Mueller and John Grey.

While Roscoe Arbuckle awaited his first trial, besieged in his home by reporters, life in Hollywood nevertheless tinkled on. The appearance of glitz and glamour, and friendly dinners in paradise, was kept up. Beside Mack and Mabel and their fair and liberal friends, William Desmond Taylor had mounted a vigorous defence of the movie colony in his capacity as the President of the Motion Pictures Directors Association, assuring the censors that, though 'we have not been cleaning house for very long, just a few months', nevertheless 'in those few months we have cleaned house with a vengeance'.

A debonair Englishman, forty-nine years of age, tall, lean and deeply tanned, Taylor had a distinguished record as a director, having directed over forty films since his début in 1914, including several films for Mary Pickford. He was well liked, though some considered him haughty and ascetic, while others thought he gave Hollywood a touch of class that some of the 'vulgarians of the gutter' demonstrably lacked.

Some time during the night of 1 February 1922, however, someone shot William Desmond Taylor in the back, between his neck and shoulder, leaving him dead upon the floor of his duplex at the Alvarado Court Apartments. The sequence of events that followed the shooting was merely the prologue to a long and bizarre saga of investigation, obfuscation, revelation and disclosures, each stranger than the one before, involving a growing cast of characters and more suspects than could fill the Hollywood Bowl. News reports, journalistic exposés, pamphlets, books and counter-books have flowed to this day, and many fine minds have gone to the brink of dissolution in the maze of speculation on the events of that night. (The most exhaustive source for the study of this seminal Hollywood moment is the massive web site compiled by Bruce Long, Master of Taylorology, whose hypertext study winds through the labyrinth of news reports and almost infinite sources on any person even remotely touched by the affair.)

The first, and almost only, fact agreed upon by most commentators is that Mabel Normand was the last person known to have seen William Desmond Taylor alive. She claimed she had dropped in briefly in the evening to pick up two books Taylor had found for her, one of which was a literary study of Friedrich Nietzche's *Thus Spake Zarathustra*. Taylor had become Mabel's literary mentor some time before, and what else he had become was to be a matter of high, and low, conjecture. Taylor had mentioned, in this brief meeting, problems he was having with cheques forged by his vanished secretary, Edward F. Sands. His other woe that evening was his butler, Henry Peavey, whom he had had to bail out of jail that morning after he was arrested for soliciting boys in the park. Taylor walked Mabel down to her car and noticed her copy of Sigmund Freud's *The Interpretation of Dreams*, which lay on the seat. Thus both Nietzsche and Freud were tied neatly into the tale.

Next morning, at 7.45, Mabel's fellow actress Edna Purviance, who lived at Alvarado Court, telephoned her to say that the butler, Peavey, was rushing about the building shouting that his master was dead. When the police called, Taylor had been dead for over twelve hours. There was no sign of a break-in or robbery; jewellery and cash were found on the body. A neighbour reported hearing a car backfire or a gunshot only a few minutes after Mabel left with her chauffeur. The neighbour had seen a mysterious man on the porch at Taylor's apartment.

A crime of passion was immediately assumed. Mabel was in the hot seat, as was a younger actress, Mary Miles Minter, who later confessed she had been in the apartment the afternoon before the murder. The missing secretary and the child-molesting butler were also instant suspects. But the plot thickened rapidly.

William Desmond Taylor, it was revealed within two days of his killing, was not William Desmond Taylor at all. He was in fact one William Cunningham Deanne-Tanner, one-time travelling thespian, Yukon prospector and antiques dealer in New York in the early 1900s, who was prominent in society and appeared to have money from Ireland. He was married to one of the Floradora Sextette, Ethel May Harrison, who was now, the *New York Herald* revealed on 5 February, 'the wife of E. L. C. Robins, owner of Robins Restaurant and other hostelries'. They had a daughter, Ethel Daisy, born in 1903. Mr Tanner had deserted his wife on 23 October 1908 and she had neither seen nor heard from him until a chance viewing of a movie in 1919 revealed to her that the actor named in credits as William Desmond Taylor was her missing husband. (Our genealogist's research turns up a William C. Deanne-Tanner in New York in 1905, married to one Florence and engaged in the lumber business, so there may be even more facets to the man than previously realized.)

Ethel Robins's husband, Edward, recalled meeting Tanner, whom his wife contacted after the shock movie epiphany and whom Edward insisted for some reason on calling 'Pete'. To make things worse, or better, there was a brother, one Dennis (or Denis) Deanne-Tanner, who had been William's business partner but had disappeared from New York in 1912.

Speculation that Dennis Deanne-Tanner and Edward Sands, the missing secretary, were one and the same, followed. Sands also had another name, Edward F. Snyder, under which he had once been court-martialled by the US Navy for petty pilfering of ship's stores. Many more revelations were to come. This was even better than Fatty Arbuckle. Going to the murder house with the police to reenact her movements, Mabel searched for a bunch of letters she knew Taylor had kept in a drawer, but they were gone. These became known as the 'Blessed Baby' letters, as Mabel wrote to Taylor as 'Dearest Daddy' and signed off 'Blessed Baby', a private joke between them, she said. Butler Peavey testified that Taylor had been in love with Mabel.

Inevitably, Mack Sennett was hauled in. The roster of suspects and suspicious circumstances was growing by the hour. The press reported on 15 February:

MACK SENNETT QUESTIONED IN TAYLOR KILLING.
*Producer-Director is Asked Concerning Slain Man's Companions in Search For His Unrevealed Foes.*

Los Angeles, Feb. – Stories broadcasted early today that District Attorney Woolwine had restored the 'Blessed Baby' letters to Mabel Normand . . . were denied this evening. The District Attorney intimated that he might want to question the film actress again.

Information came to hand tonight that Mack Sennett had talked with the District Attorney although, it was said, he was not connected with the case . . . Miss Normand is reported ill at her home. Mr. Sennett is also ill and is denying himself to reporters.

Clearly a wise course. Adolph Zukor, for whom Taylor had made many of his movies, offered a reward of $2,500 for information, not a massive sum. Mr Zukor arrived in Los Angeles to comfort the colony, along with another arrival, Mr Pinkerton from San Francisco, who had come on his own account because, he said, he had 'a financial interest in Southern California studios and a keen interest in clean pictures'.

The Hearst press was having a host of field days. Yellow journalist Wallace Smith was in full flood of invention in the *Chicago American* on the fifteenth:

William Desmond Taylor was playing his last love scene, his final 'fade-out' locked in the embrace of one of screenland's favored beauties, when the slayer's shot in the back ended his eccentric life.

This spectacular theory of the weird murder, reinforced by the latest developments in the sensational case, was played before the district attorney today following the report that, within a week, the actress and her newest mate would be arrested and charged with the crime . . .

District Attorney Thomas Lee Woolwine, scanning the latest reports of his operatives, declined to comment on the 'kiss of death' theory . . .

The arrests, it was declared, would loose a mighty volcano of scandal that would bury Hollywood in its burning ashes and arouse the entire nation . . .

What was being 'unloosed' was without doubt the biggest lava flow of drivel that Hollywood had ever seen. Half-facts tumbled over hearsay, rumour tripped on innuendo and every morsel of gossip was relayed as fast as presses could roll. On 21 February, Wallace Smith was weighing in with butler Peavey's tales about the victim and Mabel:

'Sometime ago I guess they had a quarrel or something. She came in one night, tore down two or three of her pictures off the wall and sat down on the floor with a scissors and began cutting the pictures into bits . . . But they made up again, I reckon. Because after that I saw him take her in his arms and hug her and kiss her. They kissed like that when they were in his study, the night before Mr. Taylor was killed . . . Oh yes, he was in love with her all right. And I'm sure she is the one who killed him.'

Mabel was clearly not the only one seen 'hugging and kissing' with the deceased. The aforementioned Mary Miles Minter would soon take centre stage in the quest. She, too, was an invented person, though the inventor in this case seemed to be not herself but her mother, Charlotte Shelby. Mary herself was born Mary M. Reilly, though that was not quite certain either.

Sennett was reported to have hired his own detective to look into the case, one Charles Jones (not the famous cartoonist and chronicler of Bugs Bunny). Snoopers of all kinds were proliferating. The mystery man seen by a neighbour segued into a possible woman clumsily dressed in man's clothes. Two gas-station attendants were said to have been spoken to by a mysterious man who asked them for Taylor's address. A citrus grower in Orange County said he had picked up two rough-looking hitch-hikers on the day of the murder who said they were going to settle some account with a certain 'Bill' in Los Angeles. The simple 'burglar caught in the act' scenario was examined, but discarded as too tame. Other rumours involved a collection of lady's lingerie found in Taylor's closet, one item inscribed MMM. The most colourful speculation involved the Drug Theory: Taylor was helping Mabel Normand fight her drug addiction and became involved with her suppliers, either as a client or, an angle favoured by Hollywood defenders, a brave warrior against the drug pedlars' interests, which led them to contract a hit. Alternative stories abounded that Taylor had been known to frequent 'hop' parties and opium dens, all-male affairs where men dressed in kimonos smoked the pipe and had sex with each other. Two suspects named as Harry the Chink and Wong Wong Lee were given special mention. Other suggestions tied Taylor in with the occult practices of the 'Ordo-Templis-Orientis' cult created by drug fiend and Satanist Aleister Crowley. The *Detroit News* of 10 February reported that 'a famous motion picture actress, whose name has been mentioned in the Taylor investigation' – a clear hint at Mabel – had subscribed to the cult's journal, *The Equinox*.

Did Mabel Normand kill William Desmond Taylor, enraged at his other affairs? Was it Mary Miles Minter, or her mother Charlotte Shelby, who was seen to have been taking shooting lessons with a .38, the same calibre as the murder weapon, or any one of a dozen other women or their boyfriends? Did Mack Sennett kill Taylor, in jealousy over Mabel? There were some who thought this plausible, but he was lost in the blizzard of other candidates. In the mass hysteria that followed the avalanche of publicity, over three hundred people from all over the United States wrote or turned themselves in to their local police station, each confessing to the murder. Despite all this, no suspect was ever charged, let alone convicted, for the killing.

Sennett himself desperately tried to steer the press away from the 'kiss of death' theories and towards the more mundane solutions: 'There are only two tenable theories,' he told the *Chicago Herald-Examiner* on 21 February: 'either Taylor was killed by Sands, his former valet, or by somebody who held an ancient grudge against him. Find Sands, he holds the key to the murder . . . Taylor was not killed because of a love affair . . . Mabel Normand was not in love with him.' To another Chicago paper, *The American*, he said: 'I would be no more surprised if this building collapsed on me than I would be to learn that a woman did the deed. It is a ridiculous theory – one entirely unsupported by the facts.' Sennett was *en route* to New York, together with Thomas Ince, but both denied the New York papers' insinuations that they were doing a little detective work of their own, looking for the elusive Sands.

Whether they were or not, Sands was never found.

The bald fact about the William Desmond Taylor case is that it was never solved. Years later, director King Vidor claimed to have irrefutable evidence that it was indeed Charlotte Shelby who had killed Taylor, in her rage at his ravishing of her daughter. All of Hollywood knew this and connived at a cover-up, because it was still considered, in near-frontier society, that a mother's outrage at her daughter's ruination was a moral act that should be supported. Once again, and not for the last time, the Los Angeles police excavated a mountain and produced a molehill. But Hollywood was once more condemned:

Speaking on the sanctity of human love last evening at the Central Presbyterian Church, the Rev. Dr. Robert J. MacAlpine, the pastor, said:

'Untainted love is the divinest thing this side of heaven. But tainted love is born of Hades. It has disgraced Hollywood. It threatens the very life center of the film world . . . Did physical conditions exist with such destructive virulence, the state would long ago have quarantined the infested quarters and restricted the liberties of the infected parties. Public sentiment itself would have demanded it as a necessary protection to the health of society. Worse than such a pestilence has been running rampant in Hollywood. By accident, or incident, it has only recently been brought to light. And now no less is it necessary to protect society from its contagious germ. The whole cinematic bottom needs thorough house-cleaning and disinfecting. If it doesn't get it, nothing short of moral disaster will follow . . .'

*Buffalo Express*, 20 February

During the winter of the Fatty Arbuckle trials and the Taylor affair, when in Los Angeles, Mack Sennett lived at home with his mother. No one has recorded Mrs Sinnott's opinions about the explosion of unpleasant events and the terrible allegations about people she had known and met at her son's dinner table. She might have considered that life in Danville, Quebec, was not as disadvantaged as might be thought. Or it could have crossed her mind that she might best stay the rest of the year and keep an eye on her son on a permanent basis. At any rate, she did return to Quebec and awaited her return to the west at the end of the year.

Mabel's anguish at the unfolding events clearly hurt Mack deeply, although his fears that the release of *Molly O'* would be fatally affected were not borne out. The film was a hit and audiences did not desert Mabel. The murder had caught her mid-way through the filming of her next Sennett movie, *Suzanna*, a comedy drama set in the Spanish California of the 1830s, co-starring her Indian sidekick

Minnie Ha Ha and directed by Richard Jones. Once again, Mack had contributed a script idea that might remind Mabel of the good old days at Biograph, when they were shooting such feather-light concoctions as *A Fickle Spaniard* and *A Spanish Dilemma*. Shooting was interrupted as both Mabel and Mack were besieged by the press, but resumed in March and the film was finished in May. It would not be released, however, until February 1923. When filming was done, Mabel left in June on her first trip across the ocean, to Europe. This took her away for a while from the forces that were already eyeing her as one of the 'contagious germs' that needed to be disinfected from Hollywood.

Mabel's persona, the feisty heroine, Hollywood's first 'I Don't Care Girl', put her in the forefront of the Reformers' attention. After Fatty Arbuckle, she would be the next to be restrained so that Hollywood's moguls could be saved. Hearst's vultures even picked up on the books in her possession on the night of the Taylor murder, the works of Freud and Nietzsche: two Germans, one a Jew obsessed with sex, the other a declared enemy of God Himself – both un-American to the bone.

The Troubles of Mabel were far from over, and another hammer blow would be delivered in the New Year of 1924. But in the wake of the Taylor affair, Mack Sennett himself was beginning to wilt in his support under the continual pressure of media and Mammon. A future project which might have been tailor-made for Mabel, about a girl who seeks her fortune as an extra in the movies, was prepared for a replacement, Phyllis Haver, long a favourite of Keystone–Sennett fans, as well as, recalling editor Stuart Heisler's testimony, a favourite of Mack himself. The script was germinating in the summer of 1922, as the 'Phyllis Haver Story', or *Millie of the Movies*. By this time, Gloria Swanson had long gone, but Teddy the dog was still on paw to provide his stalwart support to whichever Sennett beauty the gods might favour.

Comedy, despite the shadows, had never ceased at Sennett's studio. Stepping over the bodies of Hollywood's fallen soldiers, it carried on with as much zest as before, and in a manner that was, if anything, even more zany than in Keystone's halcyon days.

*From the Mack Sennett archives:*
Unfilmed (?) treatment, working title: Chinese Story.
Undated.
Intended star: Ben Turpin?

Comedian's flirtation with woman across back fence results in trouble with his wife - she bangs him up and chases him out into back yard, where he goes to sleep on saw horse, bench, etc.

He is awakened by two mysterious Chinamen who sit on either side of him. They salaam and hand him a parchment, which gets over that he is the son of the long lost priest of the Temple of Kuku and that he is to accompany them. He goes with them to the temple where he receives homage from all and is then invested with the robes of state. He carries on a flirtation with two pretty wives of the Sub-Priest (Heavy) who denounces him and is thrown from the temple for his pains. The heavy swears vengeance and goes to the wife of the comedian, to inform her that her husband is trifling with another woman.

She goes with the heavy to the temple, where they gain access by a secret passage. Comedy business with guards, etc., until she finally gets to her husband, then is overcome by guards, who capture her and the Heavy and carry them to the roof of the temple, from which they are catapulted into another set.

The Heavy schemes a plot for vengeance and they go to load a sceptre which they send to the new High Priest. Comedian gets the sceptre - has business of brandishing it around because angered at Celestial, chases him around trying to hit him on head - finally throws it at him - misses and it goes out of the window, lands near heavy and comedian's wife, and explodes, throwing them into another set. Heavy's henchmen come to his aid and they go to headquarters of the Tong, where they arrange for a siege of the Temple. Business of battle from Temple set with cannons which shoot blown bladders (bouncing cannon balls).

After much fighting, the Temple guards win the battle and a big parade is planned to celebrate it. Comedian in elaborate costume and swell looking Oriental girls beside him, rides down street in big parade. Business of the wife and heavy getting into an aeroplane and hovering over parade where they drop bombs. After one or two bombs explode, Comedian orders servants to get a bathtub of water, which they mount on wagon and carry in line of parade and when bombs are dropped from the aeroplane they are caught and thrown into the water.

The Heavy's bomb plot is foiled. Comedian's wife drops anchor and hooks Comedian. Girls grab him and endeavour to keep him there and all three are drawn into the air. Chinamen jump in auto, chasing aeroplane — shots exchanged — girls drop off one by one from aeroplane and are picked up by pursuers. Aeroplane goes on the bum — turns over — woman and the Heavy are thrown out into the water but Comedian is still hooked at the end of the anchor rope and being snapped through the air by the wild aeroplane. The rope finally breaks — comedian also falls into the water where the wife commences to beat him up, with the aid of the Heavy.

He wakes up on the saw horse — his wife having thrown a pail of water over him, pulling at his hair and banging him, etc.

Ad lib finis.

# A Small Town Idol
## (or *Ben Turpin, Episode Two*)

Just before Christmas 1920, Mack Sennett announced that in the coming year he would make

> six big productions of romantic comedy, but I will not neglect the demands of those who want light-hearted, irresponsible farce and hilarity. Instead of making twenty-six pictures of this latter type, I shall make but twelve. In this reduction in quantity I pay my respects to the public's discriminating taste and seek in the future, as I have done in the past, to lead and direct that taste to higher levels of comedy appreciation.

Sennett had already been cutting down his output from 1918, when about thirty films were produced by his studio as against the 120-plus movies made in 1917. Sennett's distribution deal with Paramount related to his two-reel comedies only, so other companies, including United Artists and First National, were roped in to deal with the longer five-reel films (running fifty-plus minutes). One of these, *Yankee Doodle in Berlin* (1919, also known as *The Kaiser's Last Squeal*), distributed by Sol Lesser, was a kind of spoof of Chaplin's own war spoof, *Shoulder Arms*, featuring Ben Turpin, Ford Sterling and Chester Conklin as nutty generals, with the Sennett beauties – Marie Prevost, Phyllis Haver and Juanita Hansen – in full support.

Other mad Turpin spoofs of 1919 included the two-reelers *East Lynn with Variations*, *Salome Versus Shenandoah* (with Ben doubling as John the Baptist and a Confederate spy) and *Uncle Tom Without the Cabin*, which speaks for itself. *Down on the Farm* (also 1919) was another five-reeler, with Louize Fazenda, Ben Turpin, Teddy the dog and the Sennett cat, Pepper, who was eulogized when she died in 1924 'of old age at the Cat and Dog Hospital of Los Angeles' as 'the most talented of felines appearing on the screen . . . Pepper boasted no pedigree, neither did she carry off any ribbons at cat shows.

She was just a plain Maltese, but . . . was the only cat ever known to actually take direction.' Even the animals were of sturdy working-class stock at Sennett's.

The latter two films were among the first to feature another new actor on the Sennett lot, the Scot Jimmy Finlayson, later to find immortality as the finest foil to Laurel and Hardy. Finlayson joined Sennett on an initial contract (dated 8 October 1919) for a mere $95 a week for the first three months and $120 a week thereafter. (He was allowed to take a month's vacation from 28 February to 26 March without pay.) This rose in October 1920 to $230 a week. Few rose swiftly to riches with Sennett at this time. Ben Turpin had joined at $195 a week in 1917, rising to $420 a week in 1919 and a more substantial long-term contract signed in March 1920 giving him $1,000 a week rising to $2,000 over two years. It was not yet the point for Ben to rush into the street, as he was said to be prone to do in Mack's *King of Comedy*, squeaking, 'I'm Ben Turpin, three thousand dollars a week!' (Chester Conklin, in comparison, started in 1915 with Keystone at $150 rising to $250 a week; fees for the regular actors were clearly higher then.)

Finlayson, already sporting that irascible look that James Agee defined as if 'eternally tasting a spoiled pickle', continued to be cast with Ben Turpin through 1920 and into 1921, when both starred in Mack's longest feature since *Tillie's Punctured Romance* of 1914: *A Small Town Idol*. This cast Turpin and Finlayson as rivals, while Ben's adoration of a movie actress gets him into hot water with his fiancée, played by Phyllis Haver. The villainous Finlayson has Ben run out of town on a trumped-up charge and Ben goes to Hollywood, meets his dream actress and acts in a western, only to come home and be a victim of false charges again. The film, written by Sennett with Raymond Griffith and John Grey, was directed by Erle Kenton (who would tussle with W. C. Fields in *You're Telling Me* in 1934). Kenton, cinematographer Fred W. Jackman, the art designers and costumiers excelled in creating an idyllic small-town-America setting, with its rich cast of eccentrics, tenderhearts, home-town gals and schemers. The backlots of frenetic Hollywood are vividly rendered in their shoot-'em-up glory, and Ramon Novarro makes one of his earliest appearances as an exotic hunk ogling the slinky Marie Prevost. The whole imbroglio ends with a classic chase, Ben breaking out of jail one jump ahead of a lynch mob and battling to save his girl from Finlayson's clutches.

Kalla Pasha and Ben Turpin in *A Small Town Idol*, 1921

Ben's escape from jail is a particularly fine gag: the log brought by the lynch mob to batter down the jail door actually precipitates him through the outer wall of the cell and on to his horse. The *National Board of Review Magazine* wrote that:

We have so often seen Mr. Mix or Mr. Hart enter light-heartedly into a tough saloon and lick ten or twenty men without any trouble that we accept the scene almost without protest. Mr. Sennett makes Ben Turpin, a little shrimp of a man, do the same stunt while giving us a cross-eyed wink. Ben can twiddle his gun and shoot backwards like Bill Hart, or make perilous rescues of maidens from waterfalls and precipices in a way that will perhaps jog Mr. Griffith's sense of humor.

It was precisely the point, as Sennett knew, that Griffith lacked the sense of humour that would see the joke in the lampooning of his famous cliffhangers. Sennett was in fact indulging in some playful rivalry with his old mentor, as Griffith had complained to their joint distributor in 1919, United Artists, about low advances for his film *The Love Flower* while Sennett's *Love on the Farm* was getting more dough. This was continuing the old joust between D. W. Quixote and Sancho Sennett which had fuelled Mack's zeal in Biograph days.

In Ben Turpin, Mack had found his ideal anti-hero. The 'little shrimp of a man' was better suited even than Chaplin or Arbuckle to represent the idea of the inherent absurdity of melodrama and the clay feet of the traditional champion, the all-American Man of Destiny with his white hat and six-shooting justice. Even his mother in *A Small Town Idol* was cross-eyed. Sennett continued to apply his old maxim that 'We Americans like our humor laid on thick. There is considerable of the child left in every normal American. We have a childish fondness for telling tales in which a lot of big things happen. We want our jokes to be jokes of action and motion . . .'

This Ben Turpin continued to deliver, in spades, in *Love's Outcast, Love and Doughnuts, Bright Eyes, Step Forward* and *Homemade Movies*, made in 1921 and 1922. Most of these co-starred Billy Bevan, who had joined the studio as a supporting actor in 1920 and was soon to be a star in his own right. These two-reelers also specialized in presenting Turpin in love, a strabismic *amour fou* even more incongruous than his heroics.

Over the ocean, in Paris, a group of intellectuals, writers and poets were soon to create a movement which they called 'surrealism', to counter the hegemony of conformist art. One of their mentors, the Rumanian–French poet Tristan Tzara, had defined a movement called 'Dada', whose principles, he wrote, were that

Beauty and Truth in art don't exist; what interests me is the intensity of a personality, transposed directly and clearly into its work, man and his vitality, the angle under which he looks at the elements and the way he is able to pick these ornamental words, feelings and emotions, out of the basket of death.

The surrealists came to worship Chaplin, Keaton and Harry Langdon, and later the Marx Brothers, but they could well have adopted Ben Turpin as the purest sample of their ideals. When, in *Bright Eyes*, Ben looks at a clock, it breaks down, and when he sits down at a dressing-table to comb his hair, the mirror shatters. Indeed, the most important film-maker-to-be of the surrealist movement, Spain's Luis Buñuel, wrote in his autobiography, *My Last Breath*, that the movies that he and his student friends most adored in Madrid of the late teens and early twenties were American comedies:

'We loved Ben Turpin, Harold Lloyd, Buster Keaton, and everyone in the Mack Sennett gang. Curiously, Chaplin was our least favourite.' Buñuel's fetish for disability in movies had an appropriately eclectic origin.

Although Sennett had lost both Chaplin and Arbuckle – who was himself lost to pictures entirely by this time (only to return under the assumed name of William Goodrich) – Turpin was to be a money-spinner for the studio. In late 1922, production began on the first of a series which would define Ben's style from that time on: a spoof of Valentino's 1921 box-office smash hit, *The Sheik*, entitled *The Shriek of Araby*. Valentino had created, in Hollywood's most orientalist fantasy, the figure of a man who eschewed the tedious business of seducing women and proceeded directly to abduct his beloved and lay her out in his tent, ready for ravishment. This behaviour was tailor-made for Ben Turpin.

The archive has provided a curious artefact of this project, a fifteen-page telegram containing a treatment by writer John Grey, sent to John Waldron at the Sennett Studios on 19 June 1922. In pre-fax days, this was the only, if expensive, way to transmit a script quickly. The outline was followed quite closely in the movie:

THE STORY OPENS WITH AN ARAB ON HORSEBACK GIVING THE IMPRESSION THAT HE IS ON DESERT AGAINST SKYLINE STOP AS IRIS OPENS IN REALITY HE IS IN FRONT OF MOVING PICTURE THEATRE STOP THIS ARAB IS REAL THING AND HAS BEEN ENGAGED BY OWNER OF THEATRE TO ADVERTISE PICTURE SHOWING AT THEATRE THE SHIEK HE CARRIES BANNER WHICH IS HELD IN PLACE IN STIRRUP OF HORSE HE RIDES STOP BANNER READS EXTRAORDINARY ENGAGEMENT MONDAY TUESDAY AND WEDNESDAY AT PALACE THEATRE THE SHIEK STOP WE DO NOT SEE BANNER UNTIL IRIS OPENS IN FULL STOP BEN JUST FINISHED PASTING UP THREE SHEET IN FRONT OF THEATRE . . .

And so forth for 3,963 words. By this time, there was little place for improvisation at Sennett's and director Dick Jones assured him that the action would gallop swiftly along (though not as swiftly as the surviving video version of the film, which is condensed into thirty-eight minutes). Ben Turpin takes the place of the Arab on his horse and enters into a fantasy in which he gets shipwrecked on desert shores and ends up in the Arab's tent, enthroned in oriental splendour, surrounded by lissom oasis beauties and all. The scene is set for all manner of nonsense, with Ben kidnapping the heroine, played by Kathryn McGuire, capturing her as she sits painting portraits in the desert and giving her the Valentino treatment. Of course, she resists at first but falls for Ben's evident charms.

Sennett continued to keep a close eye on all his productions, and his meticulous attention is evident in archive notes of 'Additional Suggestions by Mr. Sennett (for) "The Shriek"', including such detailed touches as:

* Moving pillars and posts are all in the harem or throne room. Have a couple of Turkish poles with funny faces on them and funny shaped heads like totum [sic] poles so that when Kal [Kalla Pasha] sweeps his broadsword he frequently cuts off a head. During the fight between Ben and Kal just before Ben conquers him, Kal runs his blade through the center of one of these posts where it is held fast. Ben then comes from behind with his small sword and gets him.

* Before Ben has the difficulty with the lion have the magician meet him as they agreed over the 'phone. They are sitting on a rock talking, Ben toying with his fishing pole and line. Ben says to magician 'You're a nice fellow and I'd like to do a little trout fishing but there isn't a stream within one thousand miles.' Magician starts working with wand, tells Ben to close his eyes and the rock dissolves into a pretty little round stream of water with fishes. Ben starts fishing. Seated, still on the rock Ben shows his astonishment. 'My goodness!' Ben says. 'I'll make you my Prime Minister for this.' Ben goes on fishing then says to magician if I happen to get thirsty can you produce something a little stronger than water? Magician gets over that he can. When Ben is finished fishing the magician restores the desert to its natural form.

These 'suggestions', which could not be refused, were duly incorporated by director Jones into the film.

*The Shriek of Araby* and the other Turpin lampoons continued a long vaudeville tradition of spoofing successful 'legitimate' productions (the Marx Brothers' uncle, Al Shean, had produced *Quo Vadis Upside Down* in 1901) and of course Ben had acted in Chaplin's extended *Burlesque of Carmen* in 1916. But Sennett was to make this into a whole mini-genre. *Yukon Jake*, *Romeo and Juliet* and *Three Foolish Weeks* were to follow in 1924, and *The Marriage Circus* in 1925, all of them two-reelers. Most of these films involved scenes of trick photography, much more sophisticated now than in the days of yore, though not in these pictures! A lion is turned into a harmless black cat in *The Shriek* and *Yukon Jake* used a split-screen trick in

*The Shriek of Araby* – tender hearts and dodgy backdrops

which Ben stepped over from the 'South of '54' to the 'North of '54' line to pass from the wild west to the frozen north. Animation was used to make Ben, entangled with a bear, into a great snowball; and when he hits a tree, Sennett Beauties emerge from Igloo Town to frol-ic with him.

Eventually, in the fullness of film history, Ben would be replaced by Mickey Mouse, Donald Duck, Popeye and Bugs Bunny, who could do much weirder stuff both with the cinema frame and with their own bodies. This would, as Gene Fowler claimed, present Mack Sennett with a challenge even his India-rubber heroes could not match. But as yet, in the mid-1920s, in the world of farce–fantasy, Ben Turpin could not be surpassed. And cartoon characters could not recapture the sexually subversive effect of ugly Ben fawned over by so many beautiful women, a deliberate affront to America's cherished proprieties, even in the realm of Hollywood dreams. As the script treatment of his burlesque of Erich von Stroheim's *Foolish Wives*, *Three Foolish Weeks*, exemplifies:

Open on an Alpine skyline with Ben dressed in an Alpine costume. He is hunting the edelweiss or the source of the Yodel, seeking freedom from feminine pursuit. Other women are seen in the neighborhood, peeing [*sic???*] from behind snow banks, houses, etc, perhaps a group following with longing tender looks. Ben however is bored with females and shows it.

From the windows of the Royal suite in a neighbouring Alpine hotel, the Queen sees Ben and falls in love with his manly beauty. She determines to snare him for herself and starts out.

Ben has climbed higher to avoid the following females. He stands on the brink of a precipice admiring the view when from behind a bank comes an Alpine goat. The goat socks Ben and hurls him over the cliff.

Ben falls into a snow bank. He lies there struggling for an instant when there enters a St Bernards dog from the monastery with a cask of three star Hennessy around his neck. He goes to Ben and stands beside him. Ben looks up and then turns on the little faucet of the cask and fills the little attached glass. Drinks. The dog beats it and Ben throws another fit. The dog looks back sees Ben, hesitates then rather doubtfully comes back. The dog pauses by Ben, doubtful, Ben throws another fit to reassure the dog, the dog finally comes close and Ben gets another. The dog goes away again. Ben tries it the third time, but the dog's suspicions are now too strong. He looks for a minute then shakes his head and beats it.

Ben rises refreshed and starts off.

The queen comes to a spot in the mountains where she sees Ben. She takes some rouge from her lips and smears her temple with it, then lets herself over a cliff and begins to scream . . .

[*The Queen tries to entice Ben along with the Bathing Beauties and eventually throws off her robe to show Ben her figure. He follows her into the bathroom. The King's spies meanwhile rouse him with the news of his wife's infidelity . . .*]

The queen and Ben are about to embrace when the queen says, 'My God, my husband.' The king comes to Ben and asks what the hell he's doing there. Ben tells him to go chase himself and the king points to his crown and says 'How dare you, can't you see I'm the king.' . . . Ben punches the king in the nose and knocks his crown off, both reach for the crown but the king gets it and the fight is on again. They fight all over the place, the girls shriek and run out, the queen is trying to interfere. The two men fight all around the pool and finally into the other room. They fight all around the throne, up and down the steps, knocking the ministers about, etc. They fall over a sofa and disappear, when they reappear, Ben is wearing the crown . . .

Later, Ben is sentenced to be shot, but the firing squad is distracted by 'a dame starting to undress' up in the palace window – 'she takes off her hat and her waist etc as far as the censors will permit'.

Ben continued to cock a snook, when he returned to the screen in 1926, with his most dashing characters, the playboy Rodney St Clair ('Kiss Them, Love Them, Then Detour') in *A Harem Knight* and, later, the white-uniformed 'Baron Bonamo – International Ladies' Man', in *Pride of Pikeville*. Dapper and irresistible, perhaps these charlatans stood in for Sennett's own secret self-image as a clumsy rube trying to fake it in a society composed entirely of fakes. Like Mack Sennett, Ben Turpin rarely got his girl.

In his own private life, Ben's marriage to Carrie Le Meux continued to plough its way towards tragedy. Carrie became completely deaf, despite a trip she took with Ben to the miraculous shrine of St Anne de Beaupre near Quebec in April 1924, which he forlornly told the press had restored her hearing. Later in the year, she suffered a series of strokes which left her paralysed. In early 1925, Ben took a long leave of absence from film-making to tend her personally at home, as she could not bear being with a professional nurse alone. 'What's the good of all the money I got if it can't make my wife well?' he told the newspapers. 'She's all that counts. As long as she needs me the movies can go hang.' But in October 1925, Carrie died. In a kind of tribute, or exploitation, during the year of her decline, the Sennett publicity department issued a supposed essay by Mrs Ben Turpin, presumably written by chief publicist Agnes O'Malley:

I read in the magazines that comedians are always serious and thoughtful and tragic away from their work. Ben isn't. He is always carrying on at home. He has more pep than most men half his age . . . Maybe his good health is the reason for his good spirits. He is never sick and is always alive with energy.

Off the set: Mr Ben Turpin with Mrs Turpin

If Ben were the serious and tragic type of man, my illness of the past year would have been unbearable. His good humor and clowning have made me forget for hours.

You might think I would get used to Ben's antics and cease to be amused by them. I don't. When he flits through my room doing a scarf dance with a bath towel, it is as funny to me today as it was fifteen years ago.

Ben's clowning at home mostly takes the form of dancing – any kind of dancing. And he is more graceful than many girls. He can kick high, and he loves to dance to the radio music. Ben's burlesque of Rudolph Valentino doing the tango is one of the funniest things I have ever seen. I wish Mack Sennett would put it into one of Ben's comedies.

We have taken an apartment since I've been ill, and keep no servants. So Ben washes the dishes, and entertains me with the juggling act he used to do in the circus; only now it is my best Haviland ware he uses instead of the circus china.

Ben is seldom serious before people. They always expect him to be funny and he never disappoints them. He likes to show off like a little boy, and loves an audience. I am the only one probably who sees him when he isn't cocking his eyes at somebody for a laugh, or doing his '108' fall. When we have guests Ben loves to startle them by suddenly doing this fall. To the onlooker it appears and looks as if he has cracked open his head as he strikes the floor. But the awful thud is made with the palms of his hands and heels of his shoes striking the floor as he falls prone. For a moment he lies there and you are convinced he is unconscious – then he pops up his head, cocks his eyes at you and grins.

There is one hour of the day, however, in which Ben utterly relaxes. This is after dinner in the evening. He will go to the front porch of our apartment and sit in the twilight with his cigarette, watching the people thronging into the neighborhood theatre around the corner.

Even in the most private moments one does not know, as W. C. Fields once famously said, 'where Hollywood ends and delirium tremens begins'. Even the standard observation about the tragic life of the clown is belied by Ben Turpin's long epilogue. Following Carrie's death, Ben went into hospital for an appendicitis operation and during recovery he met a nurse, named Babette Dietz, whom he married in July 1926. She would remain with him till his death. Contrary to reports, he never became poor, but dabbled in real estate and owned several apartment houses. He was therefore protected from the stock market crash which destroyed so many investors. Like so many other silent comics, however, his career faded away with the coming of sound. His last appearance was in Hal Roach's Laurel and Hardy feature, *Saps at Sea*, in which he turns up briefly as the janitor of an apartment building, who has mixed up all the pipes. He says nothing, but just sits in his chair and glares at us – or at the great unknown, who knows where: Here I am, Ben Turpin – three thousand dollars a week!

# A Lover's Lost Control
## (or *Mabel's Unkind Fate*)

In 1923, Sennett was consolidating, repositioning himself within an industry that now included much bigger and more ambitious enterprises. The great studios, Metro-Goldwyn-Mayer, Paramount and Universal, were providing audiences with the high drama and top-budgeted productions to which they were becoming accustomed. In comedy, Hal Roach was prospering at Culver City, producing the highly successful kid's series 'Our Gang'. Roach was recruiting like crazy for his 'All-Star' slate of comedians, and would soon poach the pride of Sennett's behind-the-camera talent, director F. Richard Jones.

After the demise of Triangle–Keystone, Sennett had to set up his various financial and distribution deals himself. Kessel and Baumann were out of the picture, though they were still involved in the industry in New York, opening and closing distribution companies such as the short-lived Kessel Baumann Pictures Corporation. Mack's pictures were being produced as 'Mack Sennett Inc.', but in 1923 two other corporations, 'Mack Sennett Pictures Corp.' and 'Mack Sennett Color Film Co. Ltd.' were registered. Both appeared to exist only on paper, however, the former ostensibly to produce Mabel Normand pictures and the second as an enterprise which in due course was revealed as a one-film production company, that film being a two-reeler, *Radio Kisses*, made in 1930. In 1923, Sennett also switched his distribution to the Pathé Exchange, which handled all Sennett two-reelers until 1928.

Sennett was constantly manoeuvring to keep control of his enterprises and there is no doubt that there was money in the bank, though how much of this was Sennett's personal fortune is hard to say. Sennett's continued claim to have amassed fifteen million dollars cannot be verified, and certainly a large amount of whatever he did earn was spent in preparing the mountaintop in Hollywoodland for

Sennett beset by directors

his projected Xanadu mansion. He also owned a ranch in the San Fernando Valley, another adjoining Griffith Park, a couple of gold mines and a quartz claim in Deadman Flat Field near Grass Valley, according to Gene Fowler. Other tracts of land obtained in Burbank and Studio City were mentioned as possible sites for a new, multi-million-dollar studio.

Earlier, in 1922, Sennett had restated his wish to make

only big films . . . to make pictures just as I want to make them; to spend just as much money on their production as I want to spend; to produce just as good a picture as I know how to produce and then sell it in an open market on its individual merits as a box office attraction.

*Suzanna* had been the first release under this standard, and for the next 'big film' in this series, *The Extra Girl*, Mabel would once again be the star.

As we have seen, this project was not originally developed as a vehicle for Mabel, but as the 'Phyllis Haver Story'. Nevertheless, Mabel returned from her high-flying European vacation raring to go back to work. She had apparently recovered from illness by the time-honoured method of indulgence in extravagant shopping, spending tens of thousands of dollars on *haute-couture* gowns and coats and gallivanting about with Prince Ibrahim, nephew of the Khedive of Egypt, who also seemed to have a bottomless purse. As Betty Harper Fussell writes, 'he followed her to Paris with four tur-banned genii bearing rare perfumes, Kashmiri shawls, and talismans of gold. The genii would stand, arms crossed, in the corners of her hotel suite while she and the prince conversed on a divan.' It was enough to make even Ben Turpin jealous. The gambit certainly worked with Mack, as the *New York Morning Telegraph* reported on 22 April 1923:

*Hollywood, April 21* – Announcement was made today that Mabel Normand is to play the title role in 'The Extra Girl', which Mack Sennett is now pro-ducing. This settles a much discussed question, as Phyllis Haver, who was promoted to stardom by Sennett for this production, resigned her association with the producer last week. Rumor has it there was a disagreement over the story.

There certainly was. July 1923's issue of the gossip sheet *Capt. Billy's Whizz Bang* (unearthed by the prodigious Bruce Long) report-ed that

Mabel Normand must have renewed her hold on Mack Sennett. When Mabel recently returned from Europe she managed to kick up such a didoe that the Phyllis Haver–Mack Sennett love affair was broken off. Phyllis disappeared from the lot, and Mabel was given the lead in 'The Extra Girl' in spite of the fact that Phyllis already had done two weeks' work in the picture. Bernard Shaw and Hall Caine, who were so keen for an introduction to Mabel in London, might find a plot in this.

We can note that Phyllis Haver was only the second woman, after Mae Busch in 1915, to rate a press mention as a Sennett *amour*. There was not a peep from the mainstream papers despite the fact that, Mabel apart, this appears to have been the most long-lasting of Mack's female relationships.

However it came about, Mabel was back in the studio but still plagued with misfortune: A horse-riding accident put her in hospital in August and Mack noticed her continued coughing, wondering if she would complete the movie on time. There was a new melancholy in the Normand that appeared on the screen, a sense, in retrospect, of time running out. It was becoming more and more difficult for thirty-one-year-old Mabel to represent the child-woman of Sennett's dreams.

*The Extra Girl*, nevertheless, turned out well, arguably the best of Sennett's vehicles for Mabel. Director F. Richard Jones, ever Mabel's favourite, produced as well crafted a picture as any in the canon of light-romance Hollywood tales, far removed from Ben Turpin vulgarity and the tumbling of fake bears into snowdrifts. This time, at least, Mabel was no Cinderella but the spunky daughter of a gentle old couple living in the classical small town of River Bend, 'between the Rocky Mountains and Pittsburgh, but a long way from Hollywood'. Mabel, as Sue Graham, dreams nevertheless of movie stardom and practices innocent movie kissing with her childhood sweetheart, David, played by the personable Ralph Graves. George Nichols, ex-Keystone director, is the shambling father, with dimpled dumpling Anna Hernandez as Mother. Sennett stalwart Vernon Dent is the bulky fiancé-by-order-of-Pa, Aaron Applejohn, a 'well-to-do-druggist'. Boyfriend David is being eyed by Belle Brown, a 'grass widow in the field again', who takes Mabel's portrait out of the envelope she is posting to Hollywood as part of a movie competition and substitutes one of a glamorous cover girl. Mabel runs away on the day of her expected wedding to drugstore-boy, but when she gets to Hollywood they realize she's not the girl in the picture and her acting career is nipped in the bud.

There follow vintage scenes of the Sennett studio at work, as Mabel takes a job in the costume department. 'Hollywood – Any Day' says the title preceding a manic shot of a camera crew filming mayhem and smoke bombs on the back lot, shades of Turpin's entrance in *A Small Town Idol*. The most noted moment in the film is

Mabel going off to find some water for Teddy the dog, who has been dressed in a lion suit for a scene, only to return after the real lion has been substituted. Mabel then leads the beast through the studio on a rope, everyone panicking, before she realizes her error. This scene nearly came to grief when director Jones, standing by with a pitchfork, fell over, alarming the lion and stabbing Mabel in the rear instead. Lions were clearly not the most dangerous creatures on the lot. (Sennett made great play of this idea in a subsequent short made in 1924, *The Hollywood Kid*, which shows him at his desk when the same lion barges in, only to be ordered out through the window by the boss.)

The movie is then sidetracked into a mundane plot of Pa and Ma selling their home to be with Mabel, only to fall for a crook who gets them to 'invest' all their cash in a phoney oil deal. David, who has taken a stage-hand job to be near Mabel, joins her to foil the crook and save her parents' future.

At the centre of the film, Teddy and the lion apart, there is a screen test which Mabel fumbles, a mock-period sequence with leading actor William Desmond (not the murdered director) and Mabel in a crinoline skirt which reveals her bloomers when she bends over, marked with an oily stage hand's glove that she had sat on a moment before. Mabel as Sue doesn't get to be an actress, but an epilogue, 'four years later', shows her with husband David and a precocious child in their home, watching the dud screen test on a home projector. Mabel squints at the scene, then hugs her hubby and baby: 'Dearest, to hear him call me Mamma means more to me than the greatest career I might have had.'

One wonders how much this expressed the poor little rich girl's deepest and most poignant desires. Or how much, given Sennett's authorship of the script and his known control over every individual intertitle, might it have expressed Mack Sennett's idea of her deepest and most poignant desire that could not have come to pass, given all the impediments and obstacles in the way of any fairy-tale ending to the saga of 'Mack and Mabel'?

Mabel Normand belonged to the first generation of film actors, the very young men and women who felt their way through the craft of screen acting helped by the tutelage of directors like Griffith, Ince or Sennett. Frustrated by the anonymity of Biograph and other companies' presentations, they had no compass to orient themselves in the

storms of movie-goers' curiosity and adulation. They had no prede-
cessors from whose experience they could benefit. This was more difficult for the women, in an age not far past the Victorian. There were,
of course, stars of the theatre, like Sarah Bernhardt or Eva Tanguay,
but they still subsisted at 'ground level', their greasepaint and sweat
palpable to the audience. The idea of 'screen gods' or 'goddesses'
existing in the world of shadows and spectres of Maxim Gorky's early
movie reflections was totally new – giant luminescent faces beaming
down upon the great unwashed. Were these people real? In days long
before television, at the dawn of radio, only the newspapers could
feed the rapacious appetite of fans for the 'true facts' behind the idols
of the screen. And the newspapers, then as now, were cannibals.

And so Mabel pranced and preened for the watching world, alternating between her screen fantasy and the genii of the magic lamp.
Glamorous clothes, jewels, diamonds, big gleaming cars, luxury
suites, salons of ocean liners, wild parties and heavy potions to
smother the pain. Some weathered these storms better than others:
Mabel's contemporary and friend, Mary Pickford, succoured by her
marriage to fellow star Douglas Fairbanks and shrewd enough to
manage her finances, become a founder, with Fairbanks, Griffith and
Chaplin, of the United Artists distribution company. But somewhere
in the journey from obscurity to the blinding glare of nationwide
fame, Mabel Normand got lost. And Mack, who had cast himself as
the guardian angel to watch over her, fumbled, prevaricated and was
continually repulsed by the swirl of calamitous events, clashes of
opposing temperaments, the secrets and lies that bedevilled so many
movie entanglements and the sheer pressure of business and work.

*The Extra Girl* opened on 28 October 1923, to mixed reviews, but
Mabel and Mack were satisfied. Critics noted that Mabel looked less
buoyant, 'a little too old', said *The New York Times*, 'to play the
screen-struck daughter', but the movie was doing well at the box
office. Mabel toured and gave reassuring interviews. Mack spoke
about future Mabel films. At New Year's Eve, Mabel came to Mack's
party. Mother Sinnott might have begun hoping again. Then, on New
Year's Day, 1 January 1924, the roof fell in yet again.

On the afternoon of that day, Mabel claimed, she had been called
by her friend and colleague, Edna Purviance, to the house of one
Courtland S. Dines, described in the press as a '35-year-old oil operator and clubman of Denver', with whom they were both friendly.

Whether matters between these three were more intimate is the usual conjecture. Mabel and Edna were helping Dines to clear up the mess from his own New Year's Eve party. They were dressing for dinner when, Mabel said, she heard the sound of 'firecrackers' exploding. Dines staggered forward, shot in the chest.

'Honest, I never saw the shooting,' Mabel was quoted as saying in the *Chicago Tribune*. 'I didn't know nothing about it. I was in the other room, putting some powder on my nose, or maybe smoking a cigarette or something. And Edna was with me – see?'

The shooter was Mabel's chauffeur, one Joe Kelly, who, in the mode of these affairs, was actually someone else, namely Horace Greer, a fugitive from a chain gang who had been eking out a living in Hollywood since escaping from Oakland City Jail in 1914.

The next thing anyone knew, both Dines and Mabel were in hospital, he 'fighting for his life' from his bullet wound, she either 'suffering from what her physicians term a nervous breakdown brought on by excitement and worry', or pursuing her appendectomy, depending on which version you read. And the press made hay again:

MABEL'S CHAUFFEUR WANTED TO BE HER HERO, POLICE THINK
*Miss Normand's Host says Driver Who Shot Him 'Must Have Been Full of Hop.'*
. . . Horace A. Greer, the chauffeur, also known as Joe Kelly, still insists that he put a bullet through Dines in self-defense. The police are equally positive that infatuation for Miss Normand, coupled with an ambition to be her hero and protector, led Greer to shoot . . . Miss Normand, ignoring her chauffeur's self-defense plea, ridicules the police theory of infatuation with: 'Impossible! The man must have been insane.'

The chauffeur's story was that Dines had got Mabel blind drunk and was about to assault her: 'This guy Dines has got a lot of booze . . . and he's keeping poor Mabel so bleary-eyed that she can't do anything. I felt sorry for the kid, and I determined to put a stop to it.' The gun, it seemed, was Mabel's own, but the housekeeper, Mrs Edith Burns, had asked him to keep it as she was afraid 'Miss Normand might use it', though she hadn't said upon whom. Edna Purviance admitted that Dines was her fiancé, sort of, although 'he never gave me an engagement ring'. The chauffeur denied that he was 'full of hop'.

It was all the familiar mix of 'loose living', money-mad movie stars, drugs and, almost, murder, with shady types hiding in the closets.

This time round, Hollywood gave no quarter. By 4 January, the press was declaring that

Charles Chaplin, who starred Miss Purviance recently in a picture of his direction and who was reported to have decided to use her as feminine lead in his next comedy, announced Thursday that it was possible someone else may take the role, but denied that the publicity arising from the Dines shooting would influence his choice.

On the same day, State Censor Boards in Kansas and Tennessee declared their states would bar Mabel Normand's films 'permanently as a result of the connection of her name with the shooting Tuesday night of Courtland S. Dines'. John M. Dean, chairman of the Memphis Board, said that the members of the board were agreed that the Normand films would 'have a disastrous effect upon the youth of the community'.

Other states followed suit. In Ohio, the Toledo Temple theatre pulled *The Extra Girl*, which was due to open on 2 February. Another local theatre was running the Edna Purviance film, *A Woman of Paris*, Chaplin's drama of a woman brought to despair by a rich Parisian playboy. It was to be terminated at the end of its first week and not renewed. The film that Chaplin was casting, and poor Edna lost out on, was his masterpiece, *The Gold Rush*.

'As long as Fatty Arbuckle is banned', said the Toledo theatre manager, J. B. Hardy, 'Mabel Normand should be, because she has been in more trouble than he.' Guilt or innocence played no role here. There was no need for a formal Hays office ban on Mabel. The public, whipped up by the press, responded as expected and, state by state, the Union crumbled.

Mack's effort to relaunch Mabel had, again, come to nought. *The Extra Girl* was Mabel's swan-song as a Sennett star. She took time off from the movies again, took an Advanced French course, a new date, director Paul Bern, and an 'Italian bungalow' on Camden Drive in Beverly Hills. In June she announced that she was leaving Hollywood and going 'back home East'. Sennett, on the other hand, made a public statement that he was not willing to write her off. In the words of publicist Agnes O'Malley:

Mack Sennett, producer of Sennett comedies, returned yesterday from a fishing trip in the Santa Barbara Channel. Upon taking up his work again at the Sennett Studio, he issued the following statement relative to the future relations of Mabel Normand and his company:

'A misapprehension has been brought up by the publication of a story to the effect that we have cancelled Mabel Normand from all our motion picture plans and have rescinded her contract.

'The fact is, we have no contract with Miss Normand. About once a year we have made a picture with Miss Normand as the star. Each of these pictures has been a matter of separate and independent negotiation between ourselves and Miss Normand. She has never been under contract except for the period of each of these pictures . . .

'Miss Normand is possibly conceded by the world to be the greatest comedienne on the screen. She has a remarkable sense of humor; an original and unhackneyed method, and is in every way a great actress.

'Just as long as the public continues to demand Miss Normand, this company will continue to employ her services whenever possible, and as often as we can find suitable vehicles.'

This somewhat mealy-mouthed endorsement was in effect a goodbye kiss. The second film mooted in the new Mabel series, *Mary Anne*, which had been scripted by Sennett and writer Bernard McConville, was never made, and production records show its story development costs were written off several years later as an 'old scenario' loss.

In September, as a coda to Mabel's troubles of 1924, she was even named as a co-respondent in a divorce suit brought by the wife of a millionaire, Norman Church, who had been a patient at the hospital which had taken out her appendix, on the grounds that the two had been in and out of each other's rooms in their nightwear, and had shared drinks, kisses and 'naughty stories'. By June, however, the press had already written her career obituary. From the *Sunday News*, 29 June:

THE INSIDE DOPE ON MOVIE STARS.
*Mabel Normand Victim of An Unkind Fate*
By Julia Harpman.

Poor Mabel! All Hollywood is trying to save Mabel Normand. Mabel, the versatile; Mabel, the generous, all-forgiving and much-suffering . . . charged with many sins of which she was not guilty . . . She has known the height of success and the depth of disillusionment. She has been the favored of princes and the plaything of tragedy. Twice, when she had climbed to the apex of public commendation, a crime, in which she took no active part, besmirched her reputation because of her friendship with the victim. The fickle public, outraged by a supposed affront, then turned its back on the girl whose comic antics on the screen had cheered multitudes . . .

... Shortly after the Dines affair Mabel was operated upon for appendicitis. She is still under the care of a physician and she appears very ill. Her eyes are bulging and they have lost their old luster. Her voice is dull and at times wandering. She is still pretty. Her clothes are in beautiful taste. Recently she bobbed her hair in a spirit of mischief, when a friend dared her to have it cut. She loves the theatre; she still studies and infrequently writes a bit of verse ... She has a new chauffeur for her big limousine. She lives in a pretty little house in Hollywood and occasionally visits her parents in Staten Island.

Mabel Normand has asked a square deal of the public which she amused and which condemned her. She expects to work again, but the old Mabel Normand, of the serio-comic smile and the quick wit, is gone.

Mabel would not work in the movies again until 1926, and her return was to Hal Roach Studios, for which she made five films: three two-reelers; a four-reel picture, *Raggedy Rose*; and a three-reeler, *The Nickel Hopper*, which co-starred Oliver Hardy as a drummer and was part-written by Stan Laurel. Thus do the scattered skeins connect, as one star wanes and another two rise and twinkle.

Hollywood's scandals, as is their wont, did not end with the Dine case. On 19 November 1924, producer Thomas Ince, pioneer partner of both Mack and Mabel, died mysteriously aboard a yacht belonging to press tycoon William Randolph Hearst. Hearst's mistress, Marion Davies, and fifteen guests, including Charlie Chaplin and a young Hearst movie columnist, Louella Parsons, were on board. The official cause of death was announced as a heart attack, but rumours abounded that Hearst had shot Ince in the head in a scuffle that erupted when he found Charlie and Marion in the lovebird position, Ince having taken the bullet intended for Chaplin. Ince was cremated, as was the story. Louella Parsons became Hollywood's premier gossip columnist.

Mercifully, Mabel was not tangled up in this one.

'I never hold a grudge,' she had told Miss Harpman of the *Sunday News* – 'Life is too short.'

# His Lucky Star: the Quiet Clown –
# Harry Langdon

Some time in 1924, a young man who had begun his professional film career as a prop man and climbed to the heady heights of gag writer for Hal Roach's 'Our Gang' series presented himself at the Mack Sennett studio, hoping to make his decisive mark there on the way to becoming a movie director. The young man was named Frank Capra, and forty-six years later he was to describe his impressions of that day:

The Mack Sennett Studio in Edendale was as unplanned and chaotic as the Keystone chase: twenty-eight acres of hovels, shacks, offices, shops, and open stages, all huddled crazily on the rising flank of a hill. The roofs of the tired wooden shacks had begun to sag and slant at odd angles. Here and there, more imposing new buildings had been added. But as happens to the invaders of China, the new buildings soon looked slant-roofed, too. Not even stone and mortar could remain sane here.

I parked on Allessandro Street and walked towards a large sign: MACK SENNETT COMEDIES, which arched over a wide, swinging iron gate – the auto entrance, used only by Sennett. Alongside this big gate was a pedestrian portal, guarded by a studio sentry . . .

'Mr Hugunin's office is on the first floor of the tower,' said the gateman, handing me a pass and pointing up the raunchy studio street, 'that high building up there'.

I looked – and gaped for the first time at King Mack's Tower, more famous in comedy circles than the towers of London or Babel . . . Its first three stories were solid concrete with small windows, its fourth and top floor was all windows – like the control tower at the airport . . .

Workmen, comics and pretty girls scurried in all directions. A leather-coated animal trainer came walking toward me hand-in-hand with a chimpanzee. With his free hand the trainer was eating a half-peeled banana . . . When the chimp got alongside me it grabbed my leg and tugged, with demanding chatters. I got the shivers.

Harry Langdon and wife Rose Frances in vaudeville

'Well, come on, come on,' said the annoyed trainer, 'ain't you gonna give it to him?'

'Give him what?'

'Where ya from, Iowa? The cigarette.'

The trainer munching his banana, and the chimp puffing away happily, all was as normal on Sennett's lot. Executive Felix Adler introduced Capra to number-two man John Waldron, who gave short shrift to Capra's demand for a starting fee of forty-five dollars a week instead of thirty-five, the Sennett standard. Up they went to Mack's office:

Mack Sennett lay prone and naked on a rubbing table. Abdul the Turk was kneading his buttocks. Two sharp, nattily dressed gentlemen were acting out a scene for Sennett. Otherwise, the room was cell-like and bare except for a big leather chair and a large brass spittoon . . .

The gentlemen were director Harry Edwards and leading man Raymond Griffith, another stage veteran who had been in and out of Sennett's enterprises since 1916. After a Capraesque rapid-fire exchange about money and pratfalls, Sennett approved a deal for Capra to begin at thirty-five bucks a week, rising to the asking price the following day. Edwards then gave Capra the Sennett 'commandments':

'Thou shalt punch the time clock at nine, twelve, one and six.
   Punishment – half a day's pay for a ten minute delay.
   Thou shalt not speak to directors without permission from the name on the gate.
   Punishment – the gate.
   Thou shalt not feed Pepper the Cat.
   Punishment – wash Anna May the Elephant.
   Thou shalt not be seen carrying a book.
   No gags in books, saith the Lord.
   Thou shalt not gurgle the grape on these holy premises. Nor shalt thou ogle or pinch the Bathing Beauties . . .'
   'Okay. Out! OUT! Everybody,' snapped Sennett, hopping off the rubbing table. 'Ten minutes and not a laugh. Abdul, a steam and a bath.'
   The Turk ran into the Tub Room, turning on steam and water. The naked Sennett followed him in. There it was! The Tub! The biggest in Hollywood – eight foot long, six wide, and five deep. I was so fascinated with it Adler had to pull me away. As we were all going out the door, Sennett called out: 'Ray, Harry. Come back here and tell me how a guy with T.B. can play Camille. I can think better in a bathtub.'

Capra joined the 'prisoners of Edendale', the writers Tay Garnett, Brynie Foy, Vernon Smith and Arthur Ripley, in their eyrie up a flight of stairs with the famous raised step to make Sennett stumble if he tried to creep up on his gagmen unawares, to try to catch them sleeping or playing cards on the job. At story conferences,

Sennett sat in the big leather chair, suspenders over his undershirt, under which a large paw scratched his hairy chest. Down low over his eyes he wore a straw hat with the top cut out – to ventilate his luxuriant mop of hair – a forerunner of the hatless fad in Hollywood. And with the wad of bitten-off cigar in his cheek – and the handy spittoon alongside – this was his listening attitude. If he laughed it was thunder in the peaks, followed by rolling echoes.

The writers apart, Capra was working with two of the best comedy directors in the business, Del Lord and Dick Jones, still working all hours, always ready to be roused from bed to discuss a new gag for Ben Turpin. The construction of comedy, its timing, the building of gag upon gag to reach the 'topper' – Jones was peerless at this. It was overwork, his peers often claimed, that was responsible for his early death, in 1930, after five years' work at Hal Roach Studios, launching Laurel and Hardy among others.

Disagreeing with Sennett was a taboo, even if one was right. Capra related his clash with the boss over a gag he was sure would work but Sennett was equally sure would not. Sennett allowed him to shoot the gag and then fired him, but let him back after the gag worked with the audience and Capra had observed the studio ritual of 'walking the gate', hanging around the studio entrance with a dismal look, trying to catch Sennett's eye as he breezed in in his car. 'Whose name is over the front gate?' was Sennett's query to rebels, and the answer was clear.

But Mack was, as ever, master of contradictions. The whole balancing act of creation at Sennett's was to fill the place with rebels, then control them. If they moved on, that was their affair. There were plenty more fish in the sea. And so Capra, director Harry Edwards and writer Arthur Ripley were soon roped in to produce ideas for the latest catch in Sennett's comedy trawl – a very strange aquatic creature indeed.

His name was Harry Langdon. For almost twenty years, he had been presenting an act in vaudeville, together with his wife, Rose Frances. It had begun in 1906 as 'A Night on the Boulevard', and then mutated into 'Johnny's New Car'. Before that, as a teenager, having run away from home, Harry had worked at circuses, medicine shows, black-face minstrel acts and on the small-time circuits. A strange, baby-faced clown, born in Council Bluffs, Iowa in 1884, he had never seemed to grow up. Both Capra and Sennett pretended that

Langdon had been picked up from 'honky-tonk' vaudeville, but in 1923 Langdon was a veteran headliner, who had played the main Keith and Orpheum circuits for many years, to enthusiastic reviews.

Langdon's act with his wife was a curious blend of a simple activity with complex scenery. On a painted backdrop of a city avenue with trees and street lights, lit from behind, the Langdon couple entered with a prop car, backfiring and breaking down. Harry was the 'moon-faced' driver, with the sharp, harridan wife. Harassed by her all the way, Harry's attempts to get the car started again were the entire ten-minute act. Then the car started and made off down the boulevard, appearing to go over the horizon.

As George Burns observed, in the heyday of vaudeville you could play the same act in a different theatre for years without touching the same venue twice. Hundreds of acts, like the Langdons', eked out a living doing exactly the same thing, night after night, for five, ten, twenty, thirty years. By 1911, the Langdons' act was famous and the *New York Telegraph* wrote that the sketch 'has been a riotous laugh from its first presentation and bids fair to obtain for itself a special niche in the hall of vaudeville comedy fame'.

Film scholar and writer Joyce Rheuban has demonstrated in a detailed study, *Harry Langdon, the Comedian as Metteur-en-Scene*, that Langdon's comic stuff, the fine points of the characterization that Capra claimed he and his Sennett colleagues cooked up to create Langdon's peculiar persona on the screen, was present in his vaudeville act, since, apart from the specific body language and child-like personality of the clown, there was nothing else in the act to distinguish it from half a thousand others. Sennett did not snap up a clown he thought might be moulded from scratch into something new, but an existing property.

The plucking of Langdon from the vaudeville stage was proof, if proof were needed, that Mack Sennett's business sense remained subordinate to his instinct for, and love of, comedians. Capra describes how the directors and writers at Sennett's sat in on a projection of the Langdon act as captured on film, Dick Jones saying, 'Well, there he is, fellas. And we're stuck with him. I don't know what, but the Old Man sees something in this Langdon . . . Any ideas, anybody?'

Langdon had acted in two short films before his move to Sennett, for a small company, Principal Pictures (*Horace Greeley, Jr.* and *The White Wing's Bride*), but Sennett acquired them and they were not released until 1925. Jones described Langdon's performance in these films as 'just another fresh little guy'. The writers scratched their heads, puzzling over the slow, hesitant pace: 'This Langdon's no cure for insomnia. Takes him five minutes to blink.'

In fact, the record shows that Langdon was making films for Sennett some months before Frank Capra came on board. Although Dick Jones was supervising Langdon's pictures from the start, it was only from the eighth, *Luck of the Foolish*, that Harry Edwards became his regular director. Writer Arthur Ripley was not hired by Sennett until November 1924 and his first credit on a Langdon film was on *Boobs in the Wood*, released in January 1925. Capra's first credit was on *Plain Clothes*, released two months later, in March. Just another small reminder to take oral and personal memories with the usual pinch of salt.

Langdon's first film for Sennett was *Picking Peaches*, shot in late 1923, a typical domestic farce based on a pre-existing script not tailored to his own character. This was followed by *Smile Please*, *Shanghaied Lovers*, *Flickering Youth* and a few other movies made in the more standard Sennett mode. Directors Erle Kenton and Roy Del Ruth, and their gag men, had not yet found a way to fit Harry's pace into the frenetic world of Sennett chases, mix-ups and mishaps. In *The Sea Squawk*, directed by Harry Edwards, old formulas are still apparent. Langdon is cast in a somewhat Ben Turpinish role in a typical spoof, subtitled in the script synopsis 'The Ruby-At of Omar Macpherson':

While gaiety prevails on the main deck of the Three Star Liner, 'Hennessy', Saturday is going on in the steerage. Many future bank presidents are being bathed in a large wooden tub while Harry Langdon, a Scotch immigrant, entertains his fellow steerage passengers with a tune on his bagpipe. Another immigrant, Eugenia Gilbert, is swinging in a hammock nearby admiring Harry.

While Harry pauses for breath, his pipe falls into a milk bottle nearby, and the bagpipes suck in the milk, so that when he blows again the milk squirts out in the face of another passenger. The fellow chases Harry . . . [*and so forth*]

Harry crawls into a stateroom and begins to undress. His room mate is a mysterious looking Russian fellow. He is writing a letter, or a note, and asks Harry how to spell 'assassinate'. This frightens Harry somewhat but not nearly so much as when he notices the fellow carrying an immense revolver in his back pocket.

Harry Langdon in *The Sea Squawk*

(*Meanwhile*) the Captain of the boat receives a stranger who proves to be a detective. A certain famous jewel, a ruby, has been traced to the boat and the detective is on the trail . . .

(*Harry dons 'woman's masquerade costume' and the heavy flirts with him*) A chase ensues, in which Harry climbs the rigging followed by the crook and detective. Eugenia tells the detective that the Russian has the jewel. They fall off the rigging into a stateroom below and are caught. The crook tells them Harry swallowed the ruby. Eugenia speaks out and says Harry swallowed paste, and produces the real jewel. The thieves are taken out, and Harry takes Eugenia in his arms. She holds up the famous jewel for him to see. The sight of it is too much for Harry, and he seeks relief through the porthole.

The film strikes a balance between Harry's slow-burn responses and the mad pace of the usual ensemble business. The most striking scene is Harry-in-drag dancing in the ballroom while a monkey climbs into his dress and glides across the room, with its tail sticking out behind, jumping nervously at the ape's constant tickling. The ship's band plays on, oblivious to the hairy tail flicking across the trumpeter's nose. Typical Sennett, though not yet typical Langdon.

In *Boobs in the Wood*, we are getting closer, with Harry as a pretty effete lumberman pursued by pretty Marie Astaire but bullied by her boyfriend, heavy Vernon Dent. Chased out of the work camp by Vernon, he turns up in the town, where Mary is tending bar, and becomes the dishwasher, who, as a result of a series of misunderstandings with soup accidentally laced with lighting oil, wins a reputation as the 'Crying Killer' and ends up as a fearsome bouncer. In an early scene in the woods, Mary flirts with Harry, who exhibits a whole series of disconnected reponses: She approaches, he kicks his legs in the air, she retreats, comes forward again, he raises his axe to chase her off, she retreats again, mortified, he puts out his hand, she comes towards him, he runs away. She leans on a tree, saddened, he approaches, pokes his head between her and the tree, gives her a quick peck and faints.

Harry's bizarre responses to the threat of love, commitment or any emotion whatsoever were to be the basis on which his screen character would develop. As with Laurel and Hardy, the characterization has been often misunderstood. The traditional assumption was of Langdon as 'a child-like man who is lost in a sophisticated world . . . a sexless baby who concentrates on his bag of popcorn when a woman of ill repute makes eyes at him'. Rather a wise course of action, one might reflect. Like Laurel and Hardy, the basic idea of the child-as-adult has been overlaid with much more complex elements. Joyce Rheuban cites the surrealists' adoption of Langdon as 'the model of one who has attained the surrealist ambition of reconciling the states of sleeping and waking'. This is a return to our old idea of the movies as a hysterical excitation – but inverted: the other side of 'contagious nervous twitching' is somnabulism, the state of walking in dreams.

To some extent, of course, all movies are dreams, but some are more dreamlike than others. In *The First Hundred Years*, an early Langdon directed by Harry Sweet, Harry and his new bride, played by Alice Day, find themselves in a house full of devilish goings-on at night. Mysterious bearded men flit in and out; a seductive maid and a crooked rival figure in a plot which turns out to be a matter of (literally) undercover policemen. In *All Night Long*, Harry falls asleep in a cinema only to awake to find himself alone in the theatre. The appearance of burglars, including Vernon Dent, his old army buddy, sparks a flashback to the First World War and the French girlfriend they both loved.

Capra claimed that he had suggested the idea of Harry as the 'elf' whom only God can help, succoured by his goodness 'like the Good Soldier Schweik'. There is little resemblance, however, between dreamer Harry and Jaroslav Hašek's shrewd Czech Everyman who mostly pretends to be dumb in order to survive the madness of war, a wholly political creation. Langdon's politics are beyond all politics, like a shrewder film character, Charlie Chaplin. Chaplin's tramp, however, is knowing and cunning, as well as cruel when required. Langdon doesn't understand the concept of cruelty. He recognizes danger, from falling objects, cruel or violent people and the sexuality of women, but his immediate instinct is to run away. He is not entirely without guile, but it is mostly incidental, and if he wins through, it is by circumstance or, as Capra would put it, the intervention of 'God'.

Capra paid tribute to the contribution to the Langdon character of writer Arthur Ripley, and Joyce Rheuban has pointed out the darker shades of the 'noir' films that Ripley directed in later years (*Waterfront*, 1939; *Prisoner of Japan*, 1942; *Voice in the Wind*, 1944). Capra described Ripley, who had come from the New York stage, as 'a theorizer of drama; an analyst; a constructionist. He could spellbind for an hour without anyone discovering what he was talking about. Every picture had to "say" something . . . had to have a beginning, a middle, and end – and a *theme*.' Not a normal procedure at Sennett's studio!

As the chronology shows, the shadows that lurk behind the sadness and melancholy of Langdon predate Ripley's or Capra's appearance on the scene and were most probably present in the stage act, in the disturbed relationship between Harry and wife. One wonders, in the films in which Harry is married (as in similar movies with Stan Laurel), how the character ended up in the married state in the first place. In *Saturday Afternoon* (a Ripley–Capra story), Harry, a factory worker, is married to a wife who from her ironing-board power-base issues orders for him to arrive home dead on time and harangues him when she discovers the stash of coins he has hidden cunningly under the carpet – in two places, so that when she discovers the first, he can take some dimes from the second corner to toddle off to join pal Vernon Dent on a picnic with two loose girls. A call from the house just as he is about to get into Vernon's car leaves him utterly paralysed in the street, caught between freedom and obedience, two

DRESSING
ROOM

CHARLIE CHAPLIN
BETTY COMPSON
FORD STERLING
EVO CHEVIEM
CHAS MURRAY
BEBE DANIELS
HAROLD LLOYD
GLORIA SWANSON

HARRY LANGDON

Harry joins an illustrious line

concepts he cannot comprehend. Later, in a fight which develops when two hunks whom the girls deserted in order to motor off with Vernon and Harry turn up in their own car, Harry is so stunned by their punches that he sits down over the running boards of the cars and remains there when the cars take off in parallel. The rolling asphalt beneath his eyes seems to be his own confuddlement, as the cars, with Harry caught between them, weave in and out of traffic. Eventually a telephone pole catches Harry, who remains wrapped around it, still uncomprehending of the real objects which have intervened in his stupor.

What in the end was Ripley's and Capra's grand theme for Langdon was properly played out in the great feature films made after Langdon's departure from Sennett – *The Strong Man* and *Long Pants*. One feature, *His First Flame*, directed by Harry Edwards, was shot in the Sennett period, and the next, *Tramp, Tramp, Tramp*, also directed by Edwards, did not credit Ripley as writer. (Ripley remained as Langdon's writer for the three silent features Langdon directed himself after parting with Capra – *Three's a Crowd, The Chaser* and *Heart Trouble*.) The Capra–Ripley theme involved finding a fertile balance between social satire, the observation of the absurdities of real life and Langdon's universe of innocent dreams. This is prefigured nicely in one of their last Sennett shorts with Langdon, *Lucky Stars*, of mid-1925.

Harry is introduced as 'Harry Lamb . . . as trusting as a bald-headed man with his first bottle of hair tonic', who is told by a bearded man (Andy Clyde) looking through a telescope that he should 'follow that star and you'll win fame and fortune'. Harry is handed a card, which tells him, 'you are cut out to be a doctor', and 'you will take a long journey and fall in love with a dark woman'. Off Harry goes to the train station, boarding the carriage after a contretemps with a luggage cart reduces his own trunk to a matchstick. Alas, he finds he is on the wrong train. Jumping off, he is hauled back on board and ministered to by a doctor, Vernon Dent – 'Hiram Healey, the biggest quack that ever sold a bottle of colored water for a dollar'. Healey, seeing Harry's wad of bills, declares, 'My boy, Heaven has sent you to me!' And so Harry becomes an assistant to the fake medicine man, mirroring perhaps his earliest experience with Doctor Belcher's Kickapoo Indian Medicine Show – according to legend, his very first gig.

Vending Doctor Healey's Health Herbs in a Mexican town is, however, an enterprise fraught with peril. The local druggist's daughter, Señorita Mazda, sets out to entice him while her Pa puts some fiery stuff into the medicine. The townspeople begin to get conniptions from the balm and Harry and Vernon have to hotfoot it out of town, pursued by a killer mob.

In an earlier scene, as Harry and Vernon enter town, they walk through a deserted street lit by a streetlight and flanked by a saloon. Harry slides into the saloon under the swing doors, emerging with a mug of beer that he puts in the road. The camera remains at a distance from Langdon and we don't follow him into the bar. Harry circles the drink, unsure what should be done with it. Vernon comes up, goes through the swing doors, emerges, pulls Harry away. The whole scene is played in two varying long shots, from the same position. It has no plot function. The two are dressed in frock coats and top hats. Harry abandons the mug of beer in the road. Some strange power has made him go through a lighted aperture to obtain it, but he cannot work out how or why.

When, in the fade-out shot, Harry run–walks down a dark road, out of the town, his trail is marked by exploding medicine bottles. The surrealist Ado Kyrou wrote of Langdon: 'Logical distinctions slide past him; he is coated with sleep and with dreams.' Harry as a child, or even as embryo, arrested at the 'fetal' or 'larval' stage of development, has been noted. What lies behind the pudgy white face, with its pencil eyebrows and little moue of a mouth? What is it that Harry sees when he looks at life, the world, objects, doors, people, wives, friends? It all seems too, too mysterious.

Of all the movie clowns, Langdon is the most difficult to describe in words to those who have never seen him on screen. His art is an accumulation of small gestures: the hesitant rubber-legged steps, the hand to the mouth, or holding on to the brim of his hat as he runs, the way his body often seems to be trying to move in different directions at once. It is reminiscent of Samuel Beckett's near-autistic character Watt (in the book of the same name), of whom Beckett writes: 'Watt's way of advancing due east, for example, was to turn his bust as far as possible towards the north and at the same time to fling out his right leg towards the south, and then to turn his bust as far as possible towards the south and at the same time to fling out his left leg as far as possible towards the north', and so on. Watt proceeds in life along the line of infinite choices, all of which could be taken, had not the best method been to remain in a kind of paralytic limbo. As Beckett had admired the great movie clowns, like Laurel and Hardy, Langdon might well have stuck somewhere in his mind. Or not, as Beckettian, and Langdonian, logic could decree.

Mack Sennett's support of his new recruit, the very antithesis of Keystone chaos, was unstinting, and he promoted his new find to the utmost. The press sheet for *Picking Peaches* already stated:

## CHAPLIN COMPETITOR DISCOVERED

Charlie Chaplin's discoverer, Mack Sennett, has made another find in Harry Langdon.

Sennett's announcement years ago that he had discovered the world's greatest screen comedian was not taken seriously, until Charlie Chaplin's appearance on the screen vindicated all of the Comedy King's extravagant claims for him.

Since the inception of Chaplin's pantomimic action, there have been no discoveries in the line of comedians of any noteworthy importance until the present.

Mack Sennett lays claim to the fact that he has made another most important find, and the only real competitor to the famous Charlie, in the person of Harry Langdon. Sennett even goes so far as to say, 'he is Chaplin's equal'.

This does show remarkable insight on Mack's part, given the initial puzzlement of his writers. Langdon's contract of March 1924 promised him $750 a week for his first six months, $1,000 for the next six, $1,500 for the third segment and $2,000 for the fourth, of a two-year contract. Sennett was putting his money where his mouth was, and he was not disappointed, until the usual syndrome manifested itself: Start with Sennett, get rich somewhere else . . .

Although Sennett allowed his writers and directors, as well as his actors, a great deal of leeway to develop their stories, he remained in close daily contact with every production, and in the editing process remained very much in control. His fussiness extended to the intertitles, as he insisted on choosing every title from a long list submitted by the titlers, usually Felix Adler and/or A. H. Giebler. For the opening title of *Boobs in the Wood*, for instance, the list to choose from included:

In the Hermitage mountains, where the men are so tough they steal wood alcohol from the trunks of the trees . . .

In the wild Kilmenny Mountains where men drink their wood alcohol straight – from the trees . . .

In the wild Kilmenny Mountains, where the lumbermen break saplings and saps with their bare hands . . .

In the Northwoods, where even the jack rabbits chew tobacoo . . .

In the Northwoods country – where men play mumblety peg with double bitt axes . . .

In the great Northwest – where a tree is a tree and a rock is a rock and a man's a man . . .

In the great Northwoods where Nature makes any family tree look like a daffodil . . . [*etc, etc.*]

The last turned out to be the winner. Even in the simplest matter of a scene of a tough customer at a table complaining to the waiter: 'Say, when do I get my soup?', the titlers went through: 'How about my soup?', 'Where's my soup coming from – Chicago?', 'Hurry up with my soup!', 'Where's my soup?', 'Do I get my soup?', 'Say, you forgot my soup!', 'Hey, I ordered soup an hour ago!', 'How long must I wait for my soup?', 'What do I get – soup or trouble?', 'Bring my soup and make it snappy!', 'I ordered soup!', 'I'm waiting for my soup!' and 'SOUP! SOUP! I want soup!'

The film title had umpteen versions too, among them *Lumber Limbers*, *The Lumber Jack*, *The Lumber Ox*, *Up a Tree*, *Timber Twigs*, *Timber Twisters*, *Buzz Saw and Buckwheat*, *A Buzz Saw Romance*, *Busy Buzz Saws*, *Buzzing Around*, *The Saw Dust Trail*, *Chips and Shavings* and so forth, with *Boobs in the Wood* circled in pencil.

Langdon's last short for Sennett was *Fiddlesticks*, released in 1927 (another Ripley–Capra script), the tale of a dysfunctional son in a family described as 'men of metal – bronze muscles, iron wills and tin heads'. (The set-up bears more than a passing resemblance to that of Harold Lloyd's *The Kid Brother*, which was released earlier that year – everybody in comedy stole from everybody else.) Harry wants to play the cello but his teacher, Professor Von Tempo – Vernon Dent again – gives him a diploma rather than deal with the complaints of his neighbours whenever Harry's bow grates on the strings. Eventually he takes up with a junkman (an unknown actor sporting the most hooked Jewish nose in Hollywood), who discovers that every time Harry plays, people throw things out of their windows. In one marvellous shot, Harry plays inside a wire cage in the street, with the junkman rubbing his hands gleefully as a cascade of junk fills the net over his head. The destruction of a fifty-dollar pianola by a steam-roller Harry has expropriated to carry it away nets them three hundred dollars from the guilt-ridden owner of the vehicle, and Harry returns home in top hat, with cigar, having realized the junkman's appreciative 'There's money in music!' All are reconciled, as long as Harry plays with the windows shut.

By that time, Langdon had decided not to remain a cog in the Sennett machine and, teaming up with director Edwards and Capra (with Ripley following), branched out on his own, striking a distribution deal with First National films. The Capra–Langdon features, as noted above, were the apex of his career and established Langdon in the first rank with Chaplin, Keaton and Lloyd. His later films, however, suffered from his fatal decision to dispense with Capra and direct on his own. By the time sound came, Langdon had declined, and his subsequent films for Hal Roach, Educational Films and Columbia continued the slide. Langdon was, *par excellence*, the silent comedian, a throw-back, in some ways, to the halcyon age of the circus clown with his painted smile and melancholic interior. The cabaret clown in Federico Fellini's *La Dolce Vita*, who performs a poignant trumpet piece with balloons that follow him offstage, could have been played perfectly by Langdon.

Langdon's demise was also hastened by personal conflicts with divorced wives, first his vaudeville partner, Frances, who divorced him in 1928, and then with Helen Walton, wife number two. Their acrimonious alimony suits made him a press target for several years from 1932. He continued making sound shorts and working as a gagman for other comedians, including Laurel and Hardy, appearing as Oliver Hardy's partner in Ollie's only starring solo feature, *Zenobia*, in 1939. But when he died, in December 1944, the *Los Angeles Examiner* summed him up as 'COMEDIAN HARRY LANGDON, WHO HAD RAGS TO RICHES ROUNDTRIP, DIES OF HEMORRHAGE'. It was a vintage piece of verbal Hollywood cruelty. Fellow Sennett alumni Andy Clyde and Chester Conklin were, however, among his pallbearers.

In his early days at Sennett, in November 1924, publicist Agnes O'Malley prepared another of her press releases in the name of the studio's comic stars, quoting Harry Langdon about his passage from stage to screen:

'The advantage of vaudeville is that you can change your act to suit each audience. When you have made a picture, there it is. It has to go just the same for Medicine Hat and Broadway.

'Coming for the first time into screen comedies, a funny man is surprised to find how difficult it is to get stories; you have to have more plot and a more logical and consistent plot than for a high brow drama.

'The odd thing about the whole business of being funny is that the public wants to laugh; but it is the hardest thing in the world to make them do it. They don't want to cry; yet they will cry at the slightest provocation.'

When watching Harry Langdon, it is indeed difficult to figure out where comedy stops and tragedy begins. He was not deft with words, and his poetry was not quite of this world but of a realm on which the surrealists expended enormous efforts and endless manifestos, claiming but never quite possessing, whereas Harry merely stood still and expressed it. Capra remembered him, finally, as an ungrateful dullard, surprised by his own greatness and unwilling to share the credit for his success with others. Sennett wrote of him, in *King of Comedy*:

His shy charm and gentle humor have yet to be matched on the screen. I wish he had stayed with me. He was a quaint artist who had no business in business. He was hurt and bewildered in the end and he never understood what happened to him.

Let us leave him, therefore, sitting on a pavement, staring up at the sky, musing over the advice of the old bearded man with the telescope: 'Follow that star, and you'll win fame and fortune.'

Only a real fool would turn that one down.

CHAPTER TWENTY-FOUR

# The Neglected King of Gags: Billy Bevan (or *the Return of Contagious Nervous Twitching*)

The mid-1920s were the acknowledged heyday of silent comedy's major masterpieces: the great feature-film classics, from Harold Lloyd's *Safety Last* through Chaplin's *The Gold Rush* and Buster Keaton's *Sherlock Jr.*, *The Navigator*, *The General* et al. to Langdon's Capra-directed *The Strong Man*. But despite the ascendancy of the comedy feature, comedy shorts – two- and three-reelers – continued to proliferate, literally in their thousands. Hal Roach swept up Charley Chase, Jimmy Finlayson, Clyde Cook, Edgar Kennedy, Stan Laurel, Oliver Hardy, Mae Busch, Anita Garvin and Vivien Oakland, to name but a few. Larry Semon and Lupino Lane, among many others, ploughed their own furrows. The banishment of Arbuckle was the one gaping hole in this golden age of the clowns; he was allowed to return to directing, under the pseudonym of 'William Goodrich', but not to star again on the screen in the silent era.

Sennett's studio was still the largest comedy stock company, right up until the age of sound. Turpin and Langdon apart, a host of lesser-known 'Clown Princes' turned out films, directed by hard-working craftsmen like Roy Del Ruth, Harry Edwards, Lloyd Bacon and 'Piemaster' Del Lord.

One of the most prolific and popular stars on the lot was the Australian-born Billy Bevan. His official studio biography reads:

Early in life, he took up a stage career in which he was immediately tabulated as a comedian . . . In 1912, he came to America with the Pollard Opera Co., and toured Canada for a year playing the roles of Crookie Scrubs in 'Sergeant Brue' and Ko-Ko in 'the Mikado.' . . . In pictures, Bevan was identified for two years with Universal Comedies, one year with Christie and ten years with Sennett . . .

He is known as 'the gentleman farmer' among the actors in Hollywood.

Billy Bevan at work

He owns a large citrus and avocado ranch at Recondido California, where he has spent his weekends for the last five years. In order to carry on this avocation in a paying manner and not merely as a pastime, he took a course in citrus culture at the University of California. Eventually, he expects to give up acting and together with his wife and daughters make his permanent home on the ranch, as he is typically a man of the great outdoors and loves everything pertaining to it.

His hobbies are hunting, fishing and avocados . . .

Bevan would have had little time for any of these pursuits during his working career at Sennett's, as he appeared in over 110 films, commencing in 1919. If Langdon was the most unusual weave in Mack Sennett's basket of madcaps, Billy represented its most typical strand. A Chaplinesque clown with a small walrus moustache, he often played a layabout but, unlike Chaplin's tramp, gave the impression of a gentleman of leisure fallen on hard times; or took the role of a middle-class busybody, a dispenser of disastrous advice.

A Bevan film was a gag-rich environment, specializing in scrapes, conflicts and chases. Two of his 1921 films, *Be Reasonable* and *Astray From the Steerage*, demonstrated his madness in motion. *Be*

*Reasonable*, directed by Roy Del Ruth, opens with a 'morning after' scene on the beach, the litter man sticking his litter. He jabs into the sand and out pops Billy, who has for some reason been snoozing, like a mole, underground. Billy loiters on with an umbrella gag, getting caught under a windowsill at which a girl is watering plants. Conked with the watering can, he moves back to the beach, observing the bathing girls through a periscope as he moves through the sand. He flirts with a girl, Mildred June, and offers her a necklace he has bought on an instalment plan. She takes it but runs off with the lifeguard, who has rescued her drowning dog, Fifi, while Billy has made a fool of himself by diving off a twenty-foot pier and landing head-first in the sand. (The lifeguard's technique is equally odd, as he pulls out a bicycle hidden in the sand and rides into the waves to make his rescue.)

Next thing we know, Billy is chased by the police as he tries to escape from the Instalment Plan Man. The chase, which draws in huge numbers of cops, prefigures Buster Keaton's seminal *Cops*, which was shot several months later. Backing away from a cop's gun into a cactus, Billy mistakes the cactus spike for a spear and, as it detaches from the plant and sticks in his rear, he rushes in panic into the police station, ready to give himself up. Realizing the error, he runs out of the station again, in and out of patrol wagons and on to a crowded tram, hanging on to its pole above the traffic, just as Harold Lloyd would do in *Girl Shy* three years later, in 1924. Back on the beach, Billy is beaten up by mistake by the father of the lifeguard's wife, who has caught her beefy hubby cosying up with bathing-girl Mildred again. The father, a doddering cripple, throws away his crutches and proceeds to demolish all and sundry with a giant anchor he has pulled loose from its chain.

This is 'back to basics' at Sennett, the original slapstick chaos, Keystone-style, but on a higher budget, with faster and better-shot scenes and a greater density of tricks and jokes. A recurring gag in Bevan films is his entry into a drinks bar – in Prohibition days, remember – and asking for a drink with 'some kick in it'. The soda-jerker pours out some libation and turns a switch, so that the stool the drinker sits on revolves at high speed, delivering the 'kick' that's required.

*Astray From the Steerage*, presumably inspired by Chaplin's 1917 film, *The Immigrant*, has a more socially 'realist' background. Billy, his wife, Louise Fazenda, and their small child have arrived at Ellis Island to become Americans. First, he has to take a 'mental test', administered by a freak's gallery of immigration officials, who strap him to a chair and throw a switch which revolves it at high speed ('to see if his constitution agrees with the country's'). The plot involves an evil Yank, who is trying to smuggle his booze through in the immigrants' luggage. A plethora of luggage gags ensues, with the second reel taken up with the Bevans' arrival (with the smuggler in their trunk) at the home of an insane society lady who has engaged them as servants to watch over her son-in-law. Much running in and out of doors follows, with deranged cops on the smuggler's trail.

'Wait, Hugo, I'll see if Papa's an American yet,' Louise tells her boy as she goes to see if his 'mental test' has been finished. A whole shipload of Sennettees might have been steaming back to Europe, one imagines, had they been put through any such procedure. Bevan's films continued to be manic. Later on, he was often twinned with another prolific Sennett star, Andy Clyde. Clyde had been introduced to the studio by his fellow Scot, Jimmy Finlayson, and stayed behind when Fin moved on. His roster of titles at Sennett's runs to an astonishing 160-plus films. He was a master of make-up, and often wore outrageous beards, but he also appeared beardless in several movies with Bevan. A typical example would be *Wandering Willies*, of 1926, another barrelful of non-stop gags and action. Billy and Andy are two bums (Percy Nudge, 'a tourist', and Dusty Duncan, 'playing hookey from the hoosegow') who are first seen diving for cigarette butts in the park. To get food, Andy conceals himself in a stolen pram and grabs steaks off the tables in the restaurant Billy takes him into. There follows a special-effects trick with 'the freshest oysters you ever saw' (not to be viewed prior to a seafood meal), the oysters leaping out of the soup plate and across panicked diners.

Running from the cops, Billy and Andy hide inside a cow-hide suit, which is taken for dead and sold off to a circus chef for lion meat. The axe cut separates the two tramps and panics the chef. Meanwhile the circus ringmaster, the heavyset Kewpie (sometimes spelled Cupie) Morgan, has evolved a dastardly plan, as exposed by waitress Ruth Hiatt: 'Look, a mortgage on Niagara Falls! We must stop it before he shuts off the water!' The cops are called, and Billy rescues Ruth from Kewpie's clutches by means of a car which jacks up its chassis on a spring to her third-floor window. There follows a vintage police

Complete madness in *Super-Hooper-Dyne Lizzies*

chase which is often extracted to illustrate the much older 'Keystone Kops': the cops rush on in their patrol wagon, fall out and are strung along in a daisy chain that weaves drunkenly across the street, eventually wrapping around a telephone pole. Kewpie and driver pursue Billy and Ruth, in a succession of car overturns and crashes that look as if they would kill even the most skilled stunt-person. Billy's car is eventually reduced to a flat panel, wobbling on shrunken wheels, a precursor of the trick used more than once by Stan Laurel and Oliver Hardy.

A few months before this, Billy Bevan and Andy Clyde appeared together in one of the strangest films produced by Mack Sennett, or any comedy studio, the one-and-only *Super-Hooper-Dyne Lizzies* (1925). The term refers to the 'Tin Lizzie' Ford car that would later be termed a 'flivver'. Clyde plays an inventor, Burbank Watts, who is 'trying to get power for autos from the hot air wasted on radio speeches': in non-Sennettese, using electric power through his Radioscope machine, an early television gadget. Bevan is 'Hiram Case, his helper, [who] got Berlin on the radio by baiting the wave trap with limburger cheese'. Daughter Winnie Watts is the try-out driver and the villain is 'T. Potter Doam, one of the biggest oil cans in the gasoline industry', who wants both to get the girl and to destroy the invention which would put him out of business.

The movie features one of the finest, and most expensive, gags in the canon, Billy Bevan pushing a stalled car along the street, catching on to a series of cars parked in front of it, so that he ends up inadvertently pushing a line of seven motor vehicles around the town square, in and out of a traffic jam, up a steep hill and over a cliff. Only Stan and Ollie created more vehicular destruction, in 1928's *Two Tars*. On the distaff side, Sennett plastered the movie with animated electric-power zig-zags, streaks, snoring Z-Z-Z-Zs, a parrott emitting the words 'Ouch! Ouch! Help!' and so forth. This was to become a bad habit, common in the mid-twenties, but dying out in the last two years of silents. The electric-powered cars run riot, and two tycoons ('promoters who got rich putting Hebrew characters on Mah Jongg sets') offer to invest in Professor Watts's process, with the proviso that 'if that invention can be attached to mouse-traps we'll buy it'.

The whole enterprise seems to have been prepared with a kind of warped precognition of Salvador Dali–Buñuel's surrealist movies, but on a much broader, more vulgar basis than the Spanish intellectuals could have ever hoped to descend to. Watts and his crew celebrate their successful sale with a bizarre fancy-dress party, in which they dress up as devils, skeletons and other ghost creatures, enabling them to rout the villain who breaks in to smash the device. Some highly racist stuff with a black sidekick – reduced to soot when a skeleton confronts him – could have done well to hit the cutting-room floor, but, alas, this too was part of the repertoire in those days.

Much of this can be seen as the return of the 'contagious nervous twitching' which characterized popular comedy shorts from the earliest French Pathé period. Considerations of 'art' were very much in the back seat when the careening Lizzies were getting the laughs and the cash. It has been common wisdom that the Sennett studio had declined so far by this time that it was no longer a serious player in the comedy league. Indeed, money problems were beginning to pile up, but as far as the numbers were concerned, 1925 saw forty-two Sennett films produced, with forty-five in 1926 and thirty-four in 1927. 1928, the year of the major transition to sound, saw a fall to thirty-one productions.

A fair number of these, from 1926, were a new series featuring the 'Smith Family', starring veteran Raymond McKee, who had cut his movie teeth in the early days of companies such as Edison, Kalem, Lubin and Vim, appearing in many of the early solo films of Oliver Hardy. Featuring with him were Ruth Hiatt, Mary Ann Jackson, Andy Clyde as the dysfunctional folks, and a new Sennett dog, 'Cap' or 'Captain'. *Smith's Baby*, *Smith's Landlord*, *Smith's Picnic*, *Smith's Candy Shop*, *Smith's Fishing Trip* and *Smith's Army Life* were churned out, over twenty in all, amiable 'situation' affairs that proved profitable at the box office.

The picture of a continual decline, therefore, is misleading. In early 1928, Sennett released a Billy Bevan vehicle, *The Best Man*, which was the equal of any of the 'sophisticated' comedies audiences were said to be favouring. This was an ensemble piece featuring Andy Clyde, old stalwart Vernon Dent, Alma Bennett, the nicely named Sunshine Hart and many others in the stock company, including a nineteen-year-old new bathing beauty, Carole Lombard. The director was Harry Edwards. Bevan was the fussy and destructive best man to Vernon Dent's highly nervous bridegroom. Arriving late and stepping through a tarry road on his way in to the wedding, his sticky shoes lay a trail of tar on the carpet and his endless fiddling with the groom's collar and pants reduce his pal to an embarrassed wreck at the service. The ring, of course, is stuck in the tar to a fat lady's shoe and the wedding guests are obliged to crawl under the pews to find it. Later that night, Billy manages to set the bridal suite on fire with his cigarette, and in the morning, driving the bride and groom into town, he manages to destroy his car, douse the couple in a flood of water and de-trouser the local police. Stan Laurel could hardly have done a better job.

With any historical research, hindsight can be a dangerous enemy, as we look at events unfolding in their own time, knowing the outcome, and seeing inevitability where chance and error often played their own part. The received wisdom of film historians about the Mack Sennett studio was that, compared to the films of Hal Roach, they remained mired in physical slapstick while Roach developed stories and characters. As Roach himself declared:

Mack was almost 100 percent physical. In the early days, everybody used slapstick. I mean, you kicked a character out of the scene and they fell on their rear end into the next scene. You'd hit them over the head with an anvil – something that would kill them – and they'd only get up mad. That's what was funny about it. But . . . Mack had two things that were wrong. The first was that there were a lot of cartoons that could do slapstick better than you could do it with actors. And the other was the Mack Sennett Bathing Beauties . . . When you put the Bathing Beauties in a movie . . . people stop laughing and you have to start your comedy all over again. That's when we passed Sennett. The exhibitors started paying us more than they paid him, because our movies were funnier. Instead of slapstick, we had stories and tried to work out funny ideas and situations.

The record shows, however, that in these last years of the silent cinema, Sennett's shorts were as popular with audiences as those of Roach, and cartoons had yet to experience the boost that Disney would be the first to profit from – the addition of sound and then colour. Indeed, Sennett did produce seven colour films, between 1927 and 1929. The first of these was a four-reeler, *The Girl From Everywhere*, released in December 1927 and featuring Daphne Pollard, Mack Swain, Dot Farley, Andy Clyde, Carole Lombard and a host of Sennett beauties. A colour sequel, *The Girl From Nowhere*, was made in 1928, along with a spectacular colour flying picture, *Love at First Flight*, oddly credited as including Pepper the Cat, though she was supposed to have died in 1924. (No doubt a reincarnation.) The first and third of these were directed by Eddie Cline, who had co-directed Buster Keaton shorts and would go on to glory with W. C. Fields's *My Little Chickadee*, *The Bank Dick* and *Never Give a Sucker an Even Break*.

On the matter of the devotion to slapstick and Bathing Girls, Sennett is guilty as charged. It is very much part of the canon of film appreciation and criticism that we foreground the art as against the sheer vulgar commerce of most of the entire industry's output. And should we not? Much that is successful is mediocre at best and dire and trashy at worst. But cinema art has a strange way of mutating, as trashy drive-in films of the 1950s are rediscovered by semioticians and scribes. And much that is indelibly art was neglected in its day: Buster Keaton's masterpiece *The General* was a box-office and critical flop in 1927. Hal Roach's 'All-Star' comedies were hardly considered high art in their time, whether they starred Charley Chase, Edgar Kennedy or Laurel and Hardy, a few prescient critics aside. But the craft of the gags was, for the film-makers themselves, the only art to which they aspired.

In this regard, Sennett was not yet willing to give up the crown. And the Bathing Girls were without doubt the glittering gewgaws in the studio's tiara. In effect, they had been around from the start – Mack's very first Keystone film, we can recall, was *The Water Nymph*, with Mabel Normand diving off the Santa Monica pier. Sex and fun (and toe-curling ethnic jokes) were a Sennett signature from day one.

Eddie Cline, oddly enough, once laid a claim to be the progenitor of the Bathing Girls, in an RKO Studio press puff by one Melrose Gower: 'Revealed: How Mack Sennett's Bathing Beauties Sold Fish'. In June 1915, Cline said, he was given a wartime assignment by Sennett to make a film 'which would sell the public the idea of eating more fish'. Filming at Santa Monica beach, with Louise Fazenda and a fish, he turned his camera towards a group of girls in boldly short bathing costumes who just happened to be frolicking there.

Press agents can be most inventive, but of course 1915 was not yet wartime in America and the Sennett Bathing Girls arrived formally with the Triangle–Keystone productions of 1917. They made an early appearance in *Hula-Hula Land*, originally entitled 'Cannibal Story'. They then trotted in and out of Keystone and Sennett movies, appearing with all the stock leading players and in particular with Ben Turpin, whom the studio loved portraying as a stringy rooster surrounded by the fairest chicks in the land. In 1924, according to the *Mack Sennett News Bulletin*, they even formed a club:

Not to be outdone by the other picture girls of Hollywood . . . after taking a pledge of charity, sweetness, pleasure, uncattiness, brain development and stardom ambition, they took a plunge into the Sennett pool and adopted the clever title of 'The Little Dippers'.

It was not till 1926, however, that the girls became foreground rather than background, and an entire series of projects entitled 'Sennett Bathing Girls Story Number XXX' were put into production. Sennett had discovered that the public, rather than rioting for more art, wanted more beautiful girls dressed in shorter and shorter costumes, as Edgar A. Moss, of the Moss Features Syndicate in Washington DC, wrote to Mack Sennett Inc. at 1712 Glendale Boulevard, Los Angeles, on 20 October 1927:

You will please send us at once the photos of the Sennett Girls . . . shown on the back page of the Studio Review just received by us.

We hope you'll send us your snappiest Girl studies as soon as they are released. We can and do use good stuff, but do not care for stale or commonplace photos. The scantier clad, the more they use, it seems. So you see, we must give the newspapers what they want.

We thank you for your co-operation,

Cordially, Edgar A. Moss

Even greater enthusiasm was displayed by letters of request from the *Flint Daily Journal*, *Philadelphia Gazette Democrat*, *The Portage Park Review* in Chicago, *Le Petit Journal* in Montreal and many, many more. The Girls were providing publicity for Sennett where much else had failed in the glut of comedy clowns. Cue the *Calgary Herald* (4 October 1927):

A new record in scanty costumes has been set at the Mack Sennett Studios. During the filming of a bathing girl comedy, as yet untitled, Carole Lombard and some of the other girls appeared in such abbreviated costumes that they had to be glued on to insure their staying in place.

Many of the scenes in the girl comedies, especially those featuring the lack of clothes, are being taken on technicolor film to double their attractiveness.

A typical example of the genre is *The Campus Vamp* of 1928, featuring the full roster of Sennett lovelies, including newcomers Sally Eilers and Carole Lombard. Carole is the popular gal 'whose dad was working her through college', while Sally is the bespectacled nice girl whose boyfriend is being poached by the vamp. The cast also includes petite but feisty Daphne Pollard, who would be a late addition to Laurel and Hardy shorts a few years down the line, as a proletarian student working her way through college as a chambermaid. The two-reeler ends with a baseball game on the beach, in the somewhat bilious two-strip colour process, with ample opportunity for Carole Lombard to expose her limbs cantering through the bases.

In late 1927, Sennett had launched his *Mack Sennett Pathé Studio Review*, highlighting his distributor as well as his lovelies, and hyping his new feature-length production, 'Romance of a Bathing Girl', which would be released in 1928 as *The Good-bye Kiss*:

A radical departure from all previous Mack Sennett comedies. Friendship that ripens into love and leads a bathing girl from the studios of Hollywood to the battle-scarred trenches of France furnishes the theme of this unusual piece of cinematic entertainment . . . The entire resources of the Sennett organization are being utilized in this endeavour.

The original idea, mooted in 1926, had been to include an all-star cast, persuading Gloria Swanson, Phyllis Haver and even Mabel Normand to return to the fold for this big project. But in the event Sennett cast seventeen-year-old Sally Eilers in the main role, another reasonably prescient move, as she would become, as we have seen, a mainstay of his 'Girl' movies, and a star in her own right for a short while afterwards, best known for Frank Borzage's *Bad Girl* of 1931. Johnny Burke, 'erstwhile famous vaudeville monologuist', chosen as the male lead, would travel in a different direction, becoming a songwriter for, among many, Bing Crosby. In a later issue of his *Revue*, in December 1927, Sennett tried to push his new project further into the realm of hyperbole, adding his own personal embellishment:

### OLDEST AND SWEETEST STORY TOLD IN 'THE GOOD-BYE KISS'

'The Good-bye Kiss' –

People, the world over, live that title every day!

The whole world gives 'the good-bye kiss' to a wife – a mother – a sister – a baby – or a sweetheart, and every kiss is different!

Of course, a mother's kiss is nearly always the same – the sweetest of all, perhaps.

Sally Eilers in *The Good-bye Kiss*

Then there is a sweetheart's kiss – different from all the rest because it smacks with romance, adventure and a strange feeling of love . . .

I think 'The Good-bye Kiss' is a picture that all movie fans will like. First, because it is human! Second, because it is ROMANCE! Third, because it has a well-balanced blend of comedy and drama. Fourth, because it is CLEAN!

Sennett was clearly tying himself in knots here. One can almost feel him trying to convince himself that this was the future of his enterprise. But at this point, all of Hollywood was in a swirl, following the October opening of Warner Brothers' partly talking picture, *The Jazz Singer*, in which Al Jolson uttered the immortal 'Wait a minute! You ain't heard nothin' yet!' The talking movie, in historical fact, was a cumulative process, with the Vitaphone synchronized sound system featured in a Syd Chaplin vehicle, *The Better 'Ole*, in late 1926, and Warner Brothers' John Barrymore vehicle, *Don Juan*, showcasing a fully synchronized musical score in February 1927. But *The Jazz Singer* packed the theatres, and within a few months all the studios were committed to the massive task of retooling for the new talkie era.

Hal Roach was one of those who read the writing on the wall quite rapidly. He spent 1928 investing in the new medium and was ready for sound production by the spring of 1929. Sennett, however, had got himself into another financial bind. Since 1926 he had been announcing a new '$2,000,000 Studio' which was initially to be built in Burbank, 'adjacent to the new First National Studio', abandoning and selling the old Edendale plant on Glendale Boulevard. Sennett had spent money on the site and commenced building, but would have to vary his plans so as to accommodate the new technology, rather than spend the minimum necessary to retool his old premises. The *Revue* declared, writing before the impact of *The Jazz Singer*:

According to the architect's plans, the new Sennett Studio, while not the largest, will be the most modern in the industry. Present specifications call for the construction of sixteen buildings, among which are included two mammoth stages, executive offices, dressing rooms, property department, carpenter and machine shops, and laboratory. Wooden construction will give way to concrete and steel . . . One of the most enjoyable features of the new studio will be the swimming pool, which will serve a double purpose. It can be used for the filming of some of the water scenes for the Sennett girls, and as a refreshing plunge for the employees of the lot.

To achieve all this, Sennett, like everybody else, was borrowing from New York bankers, shuttling between East and West quite frequently on long trips to obtain the moolah. Much of his own money, as we have seen, was tied up with the continuing plans for the 304-acre mountaintop upon which the Mack Sennett mansion was to be constructed, with its hanging gardens, irrigated terraces, waterfalls and statues. Hearst was building his own castle at San Simeon, in which to cavort with his comedienne mistress, Marion Davies. Sennett remained alone, it was said, in his twenty-one room 'Westmoreland Mansion', as Frank Capra described it, 'with its umpteen baths and twice umpteen stiff-livered butlers'. There, when mother was not in residence, and presumably if she were, too, he entertained his favourite friends, the gag-men, directors and writers with whom he could dream his fondest movie dreams.

His own potential Marion Davies, Mabel, was absent, having married, apparently in a boozy rush, her fellow actor Lew Cody, who had chased her all over the furniture in the attempted rape scene of *Mickey*. The two had eloped in September 1926 and married on the twenty-sixth, pipping her previous suitor, Paul Bern, who was left far short of the altar. Cast most often as a villainous dandy, a 'devil-may-care man', Cody was famous for high living, lavish parties and drunken escapades. Mabel shot her last two movies, *Anything Once* and *Should Men Walk Home*, in the last two months of 1926 (the second again featuring Oliver Hardy, as a party guest), but soon afterwards she became very ill and was confined to the Santa Monica Hospital for two months. During her confinement, she became fascinated with fortune telling, and after her release she sought succour from spiritualists and numerologists, consulted a Catholic priest and began writing poetry. Mabel was beginning to fade out of the public eye and out of life itself. Mack Sennett lost contact with her.

In August, 1928, Theodore Dreiser interviewed Sennett for *Photoplay* magazine. It was the longest interview Mack had ever given, and was billed as 'The Best Motion Picture Interview Ever Written – The Great American Master of Tragedy Brilliantly Interviews the Great American Master of Comedy'.

Dreiser describes meeting Sennett for lunch at the Ambassador Hotel in New York,

a somewhat stocky and yet well-knit, gray person, with a touch of the careless in his appearance and an eye gray and soft, yet suggesting a forceful, searching intellect behind it and one that might on occasion have a granitic quality; yet with a sagging, half-lackadaisical manner, which, none-the-less, as one might well know, could be a manner only.

The author continues:

But anyone taking Mack Sennett's genial, easy manner for anything but a front or mask behind which lurks a terrifying wisdom and executive ability would be most easily deceived. For, looking at him as he sat there – the bulk and girth of him – I could see the constructive energy and will, the absolute instinct and force, which has led and permitted him to do so ably all that he has done. It was interesting just to feel the force and the intelligence of him, his willingness and determination to give a satisfactory account of himself . . .

Dreiser prompts the mogul to reminisce about his early days, about Biograph, recounting the usual myth about the birth of Keystone, about the actors he discovered, Chaplin and Langdon, about the bathing beauties, and, pressing him further:

'But to return to my first question – your artistic excuse for being – the animating faith that is in you?' I said . . .

He stared unblinkingly, the blue-gray of his Irish eyes fronting me like two milky, unrevealing crystals.

'My artistic reason for being! The faith that is in me! I guess I never thought of those things when I started out, but I can give a fair answer now, I think. Everyone wants to laugh at something. Mostly at other people's troubles, if they're not too rough.'

'But you never thought of that when you started, you say?'

'Oh, I must have – as a comedy idea – but not as a philosophy,' was his prompt reply.

'And you still adhere to it?'

'Something uncomfortable happening to the other fellow, but not too uncomfortable? Yes. Things must go wrong, but not too wrong. And to some fellow that you feel reasonably sure can't be too much injured by it – just enough to make you laugh – not enough to make you feel sad or cry. And always in some kind of a story that could be told very differently if one wanted to be serious, but that you don't want to be serious about, see?' . . .

'And now, what of the future, Mr. Sennett? Any special developments?'

'No, none in particular that I see at the moment. Of course business conditions are changing. We produce more and more films. The public taste is changing. They want better dressed comedians – fewer axes and the like of that, maybe. But apart from that –' . . .

'Never get weary of it all?'

'Oh, I won't say that. For a few minutes, maybe, at times. Not so much longer . . . I can scarcely stay away from the studio. Take this particular trip. I did think I'd like to come here and stay three months or so for a rest or change somehow.

'But here I am – only here three or four weeks and anxious to get back. Habit, maybe.

'You might call it a bad one – my ruling weakness or sin. Well, that's the way it is.' He smiled amusedly and I could see so clearly in his face his love for his work. He will die making comedies.

But here I added by way of finis:

'You don't intend to try any more melodrama, I suppose?'

'Oh, I don't know. I may –' he laughed.

'Or dramas? Or tragedies?'

'No tragedies. That's your game. You can have it.'

'And as for bathing beauties?'

'Well, when the public gets tired of looking at attractive women –'

He stirred, and I rose.

Together we strolled out into the lobby of the Ambassador.

Already a telegram or two for him – a boy with a letter.

'If you want to, and will, come out and stay around the lot for three weeks or a month, and see for yourself. I'll throw everything open to you. You can look round the stages and make friends with the actors and directors, sit in on the comedy-building conferences, interview anybody you like – even me – go out to the homes of those who work for me and see how they live.

'It's an interesting world, and it might make a book –'

'Or a Mack Sennett comedy,' I replied.

'Or a Mack Sennett comedy,' he repeated.

The interview was over.

PART IV

# *His Last Laugh?*

Starring:
All those who were
left behind

# The Shriek of Hollywood

From the *Los Angeles Examiner*, 2 March 1928:

SENNETT PLANS TO FABRICATE BIGGEST PIE
Ingredients Purchased by Hundredweight to Build Non-Tossing Variety at Studio.

If not better, at least bigger pies appear to be on the way in California. Yesterday, for example, ingredients for the biggest pie in the world were purchased.

The ingredients were 300 pounds of prepared flour, 350 eggs, 300 pounds of sugar, 100 pounds of butter and a few other sundries of a similar kind.

The pie will be baked at Studio City, North Hollywood, site of the new Mack Sennett pie throwing and comedy plant, at 2 o'clock Sunday afternoon. The pie will be nine feet in diameter and eighteen inches in depth . . . To bake it a brick and sheet iron oven twelve feet long and ten wide is being built. A tractor will serve to draw the pie from its resting place after the baking process. Mack Sennett himself, together with a squad of his bathing beauties and other screen celebrities, will participate in the pie baking festivities.

All the pie lovers of California, as well as others have been invited to attend by the Central Motion Picture District. The pie will be exhibited in the patio of Grauman's Chinese Theater next week.

The coming of sound was Hollywood's greatest challenge, but as yet it was not a crisis. As in the first heady decade of the commercial cinema, audiences responded to technological innovation and producers' profits rocketed up almost 400 per cent between 1927 and 1929. Unlike the first movie revolution, however, the second came, initially, at the cost of quality. Any movie that talked was a revelation, however poor the sound, or the story. Legends abound of the restrictions of the first clumsy sound booths in which cameras were caged up, the hazards of extraneous sound and the tragedies of film stars with squeaky voices who suddenly found themselves on the dustheap. Stanley Donen's marvellous *Singin' in the Rain* of 1952, with Gene Kelly, portrays this in its most colourful light: the arrogant diva, played by Jean Hagen, having to be voiced by singer Debbie Reynolds.

If this were generally the case, one might expect that audiences would have demanded a return to those wonderful, fluid silent sagas, but, alas, this did not happen. The audiences wanted better Talking Pictures, and would eventually get them, as cameras began moving again, solutions were found for microphone problems and sound recording improved.

1928 was the transition year, in which production dipped as the technical changes were made. Only ten all-talking and twenty-three part-talking movies were released that year, while there were 220 silents (counting feature films only), as against 216 part or wholly talking movies released in 1929 and only thirty-eight silents. By the end of 1929, silent movies were finished, artefacts, mere shadows of history. The film cans containing them were a dead weight in studio warehouses and thousands were cleared into oblivion, their contents sold to be melted down for the cosmetics industry.

Although dramatic films lost the magic of the unique – and universal – art form of the silent movies, they became logically transformed into a more 'realist' mode, at first stage-bound, but eventually more fluid and flexible, working in their own language-based form. The problem with comedy was very different. Comedy movies had been, from their inception, a purely pantomimic art, with additional wise-cracks in intertitles which could be, and often were, added in later releases. The irony of fate was that all the comedians who had come from vaudeville and burlesque, and had had to dispense with their stage repartee, now found they had to learn it all over again, after fifteen or twenty years. And the directors of comedy, so fixated on action, non-stop motion, physical mayhem and gags, had to find a new rhythm.

History has shown that few performers managed the change without damage to the core of their art. Chaplin, trained with Karno's Speechless Comedians, could not even contemplate words. His Tramp was a globally understood character. Words could only shrink him to national borders. He rejected them, and continued plans to shoot his next feature, *City Lights*, like his previous films, in pantomime, with an added musical score. It was not until the end of the

1930s, with *The Great Dictator*, that Adolf Hitler forced Charles Chaplin to speak.

Keaton, equally versed in pantomime from his manic days in vaudeville with his family, parents Joe and Myra and his two siblings, found a niche, but fate foreclosed on his independence at the threshold of the sound age, when his producer sold his contract to MGM. Langdon languished, Lloyd soldiered on for a few years, and other comedians slipped and staggered, fatally slowed down. The sole beneficiaries among the silent clowns were Laurel and Hardy, whose success was not dented at all. As luck would have it, they had hit on a formula which depended far less on action gags and far more on the characters they inhabited onscreen. Fans would laugh the moment Stan and Ollie appeared. They could stand and glare at each other, and that would be enough. Spoken dialogue only added another dimension of nonsense to their view of a nonsensical world.

There would be new comics – established vaudevillians whose own talents had been unsuited to the age of silent clowns: the Marx Brothers, classically present in 1929 in the film of their stage madness, *The Cocoanuts*, and Mae West, who had scandalized Broadway and was about to scandalize Hollywood, as far as Will Hays would allow. Of this breed, only one, the most veteran of vaudevillians, who had made a minor mark in the silents, would be relaunched by Mack Sennett's new talkie studio: the ex-juggler and Ziegfeld Follies star, William Claude Dukenfield, alias W. C. Fields.

In 1928, however, there was no reason for Sennett to feel downcast. The giant pie inaugurated his studio, to which all operations were being transferred from the old Edendale lot. There appeared to be ample funds to complete this process. As the bankers in Wall Street watched the rising profit figures of the new talkies, they opened their coffers and showered the movie studios with gold. This was the time of the Big Bull Market, that moment in history when everything seemed possible for rampant capital. Despite a mini-crash in June, the market had rallied, and in November, when Republican Herbert Hoover was elected over the Democrat Al Smith, it went through the roof again, only to fall in December, then rally again, and whoosh up through the spring and summer of 1929. Cautious voices spoke of an inevitable reckoning, but they were scoffed at and told to 'Be a Bull on America' and 'Never Sell the United States Short'.

The pyramid rose ever higher, and everybody got in on the act. Hollywoodians, grand and less grand, harked to the siren advice of their brokers, friends in the know and people who whispered over the luncheon tables that this and that stock was going to take off into the financial stratosphere. Groucho Marx was one of the plebeians who threw caution and money to the winds. Mack Sennett, who spent so much time visiting, wheedling and borrowing from his New York financiers, acted, when in Rome, as the Romans did.

The reckoning came on Thursday, 24 October 1929. Stockholders began to sell instead of buy, panic spread and investors who had bought stock on low margins found their brokers demanding the rest of the sale price and calling in their clients' debts. Millions of shares of stocks were dumped for a fraction of their costs. The money just melted away.

Whatever part of Sennett's personal fortune was invested in stocks was lost overnight. His assets were rapidly reduced to a fraction of their previous worth. The dream of the grand mansion in Hollywoodland evaporated like a puff of smoke. Like so many Americans on that day, he went to sleep rich and woke up, if not poor, at least with his future mortgaged and his long cherished independence curtailed.

As ever, it is not easy to disentangle the financial problems of a particular enterprise in a period of general meltdown. As we have noted, Sennett's post-Triangle operation was marked by a continual shift of distribution from one company to another, and since January 1926 Sennett's films had been distributed by the large Pathé Exchange. In 1927, Sennett's profits began to fall, despite the scanty bathing suits. Some time in late 1928, and not after the Wall Street Crash, as some historians have claimed, Sennett switched his distribution deal from Pathé to a smaller company, Educational Film Exchanges. The Pathé company was in trouble after a range of faulty management moves. Pathé was also distributing Hal Roach movies, the direct competition, something which pleased neither Sennett nor Roach. In the summer of 1927, Roach had taken revenge on Pathé by switching his distribution to the mighty MGM, an alliance which secured him through the shock of 1929. In April 1929, Roach sued Pathé for 'unfair distribution practices' and failing to issue timely accounts. By that date, Sennett had switched to Educational. (Pathé would eventually be gobbled up by RKO Pictures in 1930.)

The Crash itself therefore found Sennett exposed on several fronts: his personal fortune depleted, his distribution in the hands of a minor company and immense debts owing to Wall Street bankers whose self-preservation required that they slit the financial throat of anyone who could not pay them back. In the circumstances, it is astonishing that Mack Sennett was able to carry on at all. But he did, amazingly, increasing the number of his productions: thirty-three films were released in 1931 and forty in 1932. Two full-length feature films – *Midnight Daddies* in 1930 and *Hypnotized*, made in 1932 – were produced (and distributed by another small company, Sono Art-World Wide Pictures).

The New York bankers' response to the plight of the studios in the wake of October 1929 was to insist on new management. Founder-bosses like William Fox and Universal's Carl Laemmle came under heavy pressure. Fox was elbowed out after a lengthy financial strug-gle, and Laemmle hung on until 1935. At Paramount, Jesse Lasky lost his job, while the wily Zukor survived. Other studios made their accommodations and kept their management teams roughly in place. Hal Roach continued to prosper. In the immediate aftermath, it appeared that Sennett had survived, too.

The price of survival, though, was a rapid decline in the quality of the Sennett product. To cut costs, Sennett pared his staff down, returned to directing many of his pictures himself and reduced bud-gets. As far as the cast was concerned, Sennett was left with the 'B' team: Andy Clyde, Harry Gribbon, Vernon Dent, Rosemary Theby, Alma Bennett, Anna Hernandez, Sunshine Hart, Natalie Kingston, Harry McCoy and Anna May the elephant (Pepper and Teddy having long since expired). All were seasoned and enthusiastic performers, but Roach, in the same period, had Stan and Ollie, Charley Chase, Edgar Kennedy, Jimmy Finlayson, Mae Busch, Thelma Todd et al.

Theodore Dreiser was right when he concluded, after his 1928 interview, that Mack Sennett 'will die making comedies'. It was, in the end, in his blood, the sheer pull and push of making movies: the adrenalin rush of motoring through the studio gate with his own name above it, entering into the non-stop 'wailing of bandsaws and planers in the mills, the bursts of shouts and guffaws from shooting "companies" on the open stages, the incessant "beat" of dozens of striking hammers, the wind-whipped flapping and drumming of acres of white cloth sun-diffusers over the open stages', as Frank Capra described his first impressions. Of course, in the time of sound, iron-ically, the stages had to be strangely silent when the shoot was on, and 'Quiet, Please!' became the great *cri de cœur*, just as the raucous interjections of the 'silent movie' directors had to be replaced by a hushed silence. Yet the excitement of it all was still there.

In his private life Sennett remained withdrawn from the public eye. Ironically, the Wall Street Crash coincided with the demise of a pet project probably initiated by Mrs Sinnott, raising hogs on a small ranch adjacent to the new Sennett studio. The hogs, alas, had 'eaten their heads off', and Sennett sold them to a farmer on Ventura Boulevard for $50 cash and a further $200 payable on 23 October. Unfortunately the farmer, Mr C. W. Penterf, defaulted on his note, just ahead of the country defaulting on its own, and Sennett repos-sessed the hogs. By November they had increased by twenty-five head in the usual manner and the farmer sued Sennett for the difference. The dispute was settled in November with Sennett stating that 'pigs is pigs'.

Sennett was also deflected from business woes by the onset of the final act in the saga of Mack and Mabel. After Mabel Normand's whirlwind marriage to Lew Cody in September 1926, she had com-pleted her last film with Roach and then fallen ill again, this time with pneumonia. The doctors finally diagnosed tuberculosis, and, in the words of her biographer, 'over the next three years, despite frequent spells of recovery, Mabel was dying by inches'. The fortune tellers, priests and spiritualists came and went, but Mabel's soul remained in dreamland. After Al Jolson crooned, suggestions were made for Mabel to go on tour promoting the talkies for Hal Roach, but noth-ing came of that. She remained ill through 1928 and was eventually admitted to Pottenger's Sanatorium in Monrovia, California, where her condition could be treated. Even close to the end, the old scandals clung to her, as new witnesses were alleged to have surfaced in the William Desmond Taylor case who had heard a 'motion picture actress' argue with him the day before he was shot. On 2 February 1930, Mabel's father, Claude Glodemir, died, but she was too ill to be told. On the evening of 22 February, she asked for a priest, and that night, in the early hours of 23 February, she died.

Mabel's death certificate lists her cause of death as pulmonary tuberculosis. The certificate was signed by Robert T. Pottenger, head of the sanatorium. No sign of the ailment that had carried off her baby brother – the congenital syphilis of 1898 – was ever publicly diagnosed. The documents attest to Mabel being the victim of a common and deadly disease that could strike in all sectors of the population in that age. And the rest is nagging doubt.

Sennett wrote that from the time Mabel married Lew Cody, he 'never saw her or spoke to her again'. He sent her flowers in the sanatorium, and she was said to have recognized this on her deathbed, saying to her permanent nurse, Julia Benson: 'Those flowers over there . . . they're from Mack, aren't they? He didn't forget me.'

The press reports of Mack's comments were depressingly formal, almost frosty in their clichés:

MACK SENNETT GRIEVED OVER STAR'S DEATH

He was playing golf on the Brentwood Country Club course when the news reached him.

'That is indeed most regrettable,' he said. 'She was a wonderful character. Very generous, and a marvellous little woman. I am deeply pained to hear of her death.'

The newspapers wrote of Mabel's plucky fight for her life in the sanatorium, about her early days as a movie pioneer with Biograph and Chaplin's Keystones:

Mabel Normand will be remembered in Hollywood as a girl of striking contrasts, impulsively reckless, always a tomboy; and one of the greatest screen comediennes that ever sat in the throne of comedy until her star plunged, suddenly and comet-like, into a chaos of scandal, unjust gossip, and illness that ended in death.

Not much soul searching from the gossipmongers of the local and national press, who had cast her into chaos and whooped it up as she floundered about there.

Mabel was buried in a vault in the Calvary Cemetery, by the Church of the Good Shepherd. Honorary pallbearers included Mack Sennett, D. W. Griffith, Samuel Goldwyn, Chaplin, Ford Sterling and Fatty Arbuckle – the Hollywood of the past, its old dispensation, the people who had made the movies what they now were. The *Atlanta Journal* wrote that 'the new Hollywood of microphones and music and dancing chorus girls, was scarcely represented at Mabel Normand's funeral, except by those of the old days who survived into the new' – Marie Dressler, Harold Lloyd and his wife, Mildred Davis,

Louise Fazenda, Mary Pickford, Ben Turpin, Jean Hersholt, Marion Davies, Constance Talmadge, Mae Marsh and other old colleagues. But the famous names were not the only ones present. Hundreds of people from all walks of life crowded outside the church – actors, camera people, electricians, carpenters, costumiers and just plain folks whom she had cheered and entertained over the past two decades.

What were Mack's thoughts as he stood over the casket, before it was consigned to the vault? What did he recall of what had been and what might have been but had been missed in the razzle-dazzle of the rush to achievement, the single-minded pursuit of one dream at the expense of another? Reaching for the gold pot at the end of the rainbow and neglecting the rainbow itself? Or was the dream after all only our own encrustation, a thing of fantasy and hype that concealed other passions, or ordinary failings and mundane ambitions, the daily struggle to preserve the Kingdom of Comedy that was already lost?

# One More Chance
## (or *I Am a Fugitive from a Chain Gag*)

From the *Los Angeles Examiner*, 8 October 1930:

MACK SENNETT ENGAGED? NO!

Are Mack Sennett and Marjorie Beebe, comedy actress, going to get married?

No!

At least that's what Mack Sennett declared last night.

'I don't know how the report got started, but it is untrue,' he said. 'I must say, though, it is the highest compliment paid me in a long time.'

Compliments were indeed thin on the ground, for Mack Sennett or for anyone in Hollywood in the year that kicked off what was to become known as the Great Depression, though the term itself wasn't quite yet in use. Hollywood's moguls, like Sennett, were in denial, making declarations such as 'We are passing through a temporary period of changing values and confusion.' In the words of Paramount Publix president Samuel Katz, 'The firm foundation upon which the United States rests with its free, educated people, its natural resources and national resources, is a permanent, unchanging factor for optimism.' Sez who? As companies laid off more and more workers, and breadlines began snaking round corners in all major cities, movie box-office receipts were plummeting by more than thirty per cent for some studios by 1931. Movie theatres were closing, like their stage counterparts – 4,000 out of 20,000 cinemas shut by 1932. Though most of these were silents, the talkies, which had been born with such high hopes, could not be immune to the ripples of despair and discontent that were spreading across the country.

They could, however, reflect it, and did, with movies that began to exploit the new opportunities provided by spoken dialogue to express these new fears and anxieties. Frank Capra, safely ensconced at Columbia Pictures, was among the first to capture a new vein of socially aware criticism with his satire on religious humbug, *The Miracle Woman* (1931), starring Barbara Stanwyck as a thinly disguised version of the evangelist Aimee Semple McPherson, and his grand mockery of financial craziness in the aptly named *American Madness* (1932), with Walter Huston as the banker who starts lending money to poor people who have no collateral. These dramas were far removed from the whimsical format that would project Capra to classic status in the later 1930s, and were exemplars of a kind of cinema that would be curtailed by the more stringent application of the Hays Code, revised in 1934. It took the censors some time to catch up with the problem of new writers pouring into the movies from less tameable modes of work like the theatre and, especially, journalism. Ben Hecht, Charles MacArthur and Gene Fowler were among those who headed the charge.

Gene Fowler, already renowned as an ace Hearst scribe and wisecracker, took the train west from Long Island to take up residence on Canyon Drive, bashing away at his typewriter to create *State's Attorney* (1931) for his friend John Barrymore, who starred as a whisky-soaked lawyer. Fowler's second movie, *Union Depot*, directed by Alfred E. Green in 1932, featured Douglas Fairbanks Jr and Joan Blondell as two Depression waifs who meet at a bustling train station, a metaphor for a restless nation on the skids. (Green would also direct *Baby Face*, in 1933, the ultimate pre-Hays-Code transgression, with Barbara Stanwyck sleeping her way stage by stage to the top of a great corporation.) Soon Fowler would join with Barrymore, W. C. Fields, artist John Decker and other Hollywood mavericks in a kind of informal boozers' alliance.

It was inevitable, in these spheres, that Gene Fowler would run into Mack Sennett too, no stranger to the soon-to-be-unprohibited sauce. Fowler wrote no scripts for Sennett, his running costs being far too high for Mack to contemplate in his straitened circumstances, but the project of a somewhat embroidered biography was born at an early stage. Fowler began spending time with Sennett, watching his operation, strolling about the studio and sipping the appropriate libations as the King of Comedy recounted his life, the way he wished it to be told.

Having retooled his studio and lost his money at the same time, Sennett had to tread water, finding a cost-effective way to turn out a product that could turn a profit at the worst possible time. The options were narrow. Colour films, still using the limited two-strip process which did not allow the full range of hues, were one of the experiments, with comedies like Andy Clyde's *The Bluffer* and *Bulls and Bears*. The latter was shot both in colour and black and white, though the colour process did not work and the film was released only in black and white. Marjorie Beebe, a sassy blonde comedienne, featured in this film and would be a Sennett staple from then on. The Sennett archives' photographic collection shows that she often accompanied Sennett to film premières and functions, which set the rumour mill rolling. We do not know how she herself viewed this relationship, but it is fairly clear that Sennett saw the situation in decorative terms.

Mack was still residing, as a 'bachelor', at the Westmoreland Place mansion, and at Ocean Front, Santa Monica, plans for the grand palace having been left mouldering in the architect's files. Mother was still providing winter comfort. And there was a yacht, which Mack plied up and down the Pacific coast, and which provided another genre for Sennett sound shorts – fish-films, or documentaries on deep-sea fishing, with titles such as *Trail of the Swordfish*, *Wrestling Swordfish*, *Freaks of the Deep* and *Man-Eating Sharks*. These formed what the studio called a *Cannibals of the Deep* series, also intended for colour, though most were shot in black and white. Veteran Sennett director Del Lord was hired to film marine life near Baja California for these productions.

Like many other producers and directors, it took Sennett a while to figure out how to adapt comedy film-making from pantomime to dialogue, and he lost time and momentum by trying to apply his old method of weighing multiple alternatives for dialogue intertitles to the new format, as he told the *New York Times* in March 1930:

'We rehearse for at least a week before the shooting starts. These rehearsals are held in the completed sets, and a careful check is taken on the running time of each scene . . . Every word of the dialogue is considered before it is accepted. Is it a word that everyone will understand? Does it entirely fit the situation? Is there a shorter word? Sentences also undergo the same inspection. When everything is satisfactory, actual "shooting" starts.'

An early 1929 talkie, *The Bees Buzz*, is typical of this syndrome, with Harry Gribbon, Andy Clyde, Vernon Dent, Barbara Leonard and others standing about stiffly, declaiming their lines, punctuated with some lacklustre activity involving lovers eloping, fiancés pursuing and beehives getting caught in seats of pants. A 1930 release, *He Trumped Her Ace*, with Marjorie Beebe, Dot Farley, Johnny Burke, Bud Jamison et al., is a society 'situation' comedy revolving round a not very dynamic bridge game. Sennett may have fussed over the words, but as they were written by John Waldron, his general manager, with Harry McCoy and Earle Rodney, not Gene Fowler or Ben Hecht, or even W. C. Fields – to come later – this resulted in some pretty tedious scenes. *Racket Cheers*, another sample of high-society flimflam, with Marjorie Beebe, Andy Clyde and Daphne Pollard (who would some years later brain Oliver Hardy with a frying pan in Stan and Ollie's last talkie short, *Thicker Than Water*), displays more scenes of feeble chit-chat. Sennett's return to directing, in this film and others, shows, alas, that the skills he had learned and deployed at Biograph and Keystone did not translate into a facility with the new form. In November 1930, Sennett had to admit to the *Times*:

'Too much talk in talking films, and not enough action . . . I'm going back to the fundamentals of the silent screen comedy and I'm going to stay there. Why, some of our talking comedies have just talked themselves out of being funny . . . Motion pictures are supposed to move . . . We have a wonderful instrument in talk, but we mustn't overuse it. We'll use it as an adjunct to the visual appeal . . .'

By this time, Sennett had released the first of the only two sound features produced by the studio, *Midnight Daddies*, a standard comedy with Harry Gribbon, Andy Clyde et al. The plot was a throwback to the Keystone-era mix-up of a wealthy out-of-towner (Clyde) getting entangled with a bathing beauty who tries to separate him from his money to aid her bankrupt employer, a 'modiste shop' owner (Gribbon). The American Film Institute listing of the categories this film falls into tells us all we need to know: 'Modistes. Fashion models. Cousins. Iowans. Vamps. Dance contests. Bankruptcy. Wedding anniversaries.' It was, by all accounts, a lacklustre affair.

The movie's poor reception discouraged Sennett for a year, but in December 1931 he announced plans for a 'multi-starred supercomedy', a movie of no less than fifteen reels which would feature Clara Bow, Lupe Velez, Jean Harlow, Dorothy Burgess, Edmund Lowe, W. C. Fields and the vaudeville double act of Moran and Mack.

*Hypnotized*: The 'Two Black Crows' with Marjorie Beebe

Sennett would 'endeavor to borrow these players', the studio told the press, for the story, which was Sennett's idea and 'has been written in collaboration with a dozen or more writers over a period of years'.

This project eventually turned up, minus most of its A-list stars, but with Charlie Mack and George Moran, Ernest Torrence, Wallace Ford and the usual suspects – Charlie Murray, Marjorie Beebe (playing in black-face!), Hattie McDaniel (not yet famous for *Gone With the Wind*) and Anna May the elephant, as *Hypnotized*, running a mere seven reels (about seventy minutes' running time). The plotline, involving a circus background and a hypnotist, Professor Limberly, originally intended for W. C. Fields but played by Torrence, was amazingly convoluted, as this brief extract from its summary in the American Film Institute listing reveals:

At the captain's table, when a Russian nobleman's beard catches fire, the captain spritzes him, causing his beard and wig to fall off to reveal that he is really Limberly. He threatens to blow up the ship and throws an object that the others think is a grenade. Egbert catches it and tosses it to the captain, and it gets lodged in a chandelier, then falls into Egbert's pants and out his leg before it is discovered to be an avocado. Egbert upsets Pearl, who throws a knife at him and hits him over the head with a bowling pin. He unwittingly hides in a box to be used in a lion act and finds Limberly already in the box. The box is rolled onto the stage, and after it falls apart during the act, the lion bites Egbert in the pants, while Limberly tries to pull the lion away by the tail. Limberly bites the lion's tail, and the lion knocks Egbert down and lies on him, whereupon Egbert bites the lion's tail and they wrestle . . .

And so forth. The *New York Times* commented that 'this animal submits to more literal tail-twisting than has any other lion in motion pictures. It seems miraculous that several of the players are not clawed and bitten, for this jungle beast is treated in a way that would cause any dog to use its teeth.' Was it perhaps the same animal that Mabel Normand had tugged around the studio on a rope in *The Extra Girl* eight years before, showing both its age and total surrender to the inevitable madness of a Sennett set? Be that as it may, the movie, so heavily touted as a spectacular comeback, was a dismal flop and was rated by *Variety* as 'among the very worst since the entrance of sound'.

As before, Sennett had not mastered the construction and narrative structure of a feature film, and his expert in that field, director Dick Jones, had done his stint at the Hal Roach Studios and gone to the Great Hollywood Retirement Home in the Sky. Like the other veteran practitioners of comedy, Sennett wrestled with the differences and similarities between talkies and silents but failed to find a golden mean. True, the principles of what made people laugh had not radically changed: funny situations, funny characters and gags. The fundamental change, however, as we have seen, was in the sphere of action: in the unwieldy world of early sound movies, nothing could move as fast as it had before, and the wisecrack, not the sight-gag, was king.

As critic Frank S. Nugent wrote in 1935,

Words ruined the old comedy gags. Slapstick was unreal. That's why it was slapstick and that's why it was funny. The minute you put words to it, the minute the slapstick comedians had to talk, they became sensible. You can't mix sense and slapstick. It isn't funny any more.

This would certainly have been true of Ben Turpin, Ford Sterling, Harry Langdon or the early Chaplin, Keaton and Lloyd. The latter learned to speak, but were diminished by it. The new comedians realized that they could sustain the surreal, or 'slapstick', environment as long as their characters, bizarre as they might be, were grounded in reality, even in Groucho-esque masks. The Marxes, Mae West and Fields had tested words for many years on the stage. Stan and Ollie were ever real. But Mack's old hands were articulate when dumb, and dumb when they had to articulate.

Sennett did make one major new discovery in the realm of sound, taking on a young male singer whose act he had caught at Hollywood's Cocoanut Grove early in 1931. Watching the show, Sennett noticed that 'all the stuffed shirts at the Grove stopped dancing and gathered round the bandstand to watch him croon. They came to hear him night after night.' The young man's name was Bing Crosby.

Born Harry Lillis Crosby in Tacoma, Washington in 1903, he had been dubbed 'Bing', legend has it, after his favourite comic strip, 'The Bingville Bugle', while still at school. He began singing in a small combo band while at college, and became a regular crooner with the Paul Whiteman Orchestra in 1926. From that date on, he had recorded dozens of discs, which predated his radio appearances. His first Sennett movie, *I Surrender Dear*, coincided with his first solo radio broadcast, in September 1931. He had in fact made five cameo appearances in movies before Sennett gave him the lead. The two-reel movie anticipated his fame with its Sennettian plot of Bing kissing a girl and being chased by her boyfriend, until she discovers he is the great radio crooner she adores and elopes with him. The movie was a hit and Sennett made five more shorts with Bing before spring 1933: *One More Chance*, *Dream House*, *Billboard Girl*, *Blue of the Night* and *Sing, Bing, Sing*. In the last, Bing was still trying to elope with the girl, against the wishes of her dad and her fiancé, but this time they were helped by a gorilla with, presumably, a mellow taste in melodies.

Bing followed in the footsteps of all those movie stars who chose to 'start with Sennett, get rich somewhere else'. By 1932, Paramount's radio stars film, *The Big Broadcast*, was showcasing his talents at feature length. And the rest, again, is movie history.

In March 1932, Mack Sennett became a US citizen. He took the oath of citizenship in Los Angeles Federal Court before Judge Harry Holizer, apparently just one day too late to vote in the California

primaries. But he was eligible to vote in one of America's most crucial elections in November, which brought the Democratic candidate,
Franklin Delano Roosevelt, to power.

By this time, the Depression had truly taken America by the throat,
and the unemployed were camped in squatters' quarters, the infa-
mous 'Hoovervilles', outside the large cities. One can imagine that
Mack was determined, like so many others, to have his say between
the business-as-usual approach of Hoover and Roosevelt's promise of
bold reforms. In the summer, violence broke out in Washington when
police and troops cleared a demonstration of thousands of war veterans who marched on the capital to demand the payment of promised
war bonuses. The 'Bonus March' ended on 28 July with the squatters' camp torched and two veterans shot dead (Chief of Staff
Douglas MacArthur and Major George S. Patton were in charge of
troops that day). Public outrage at this doomed the Hoover administration.

Bitter times, and tough films continued to express them: films like
*Cabin in the Cotton*, with its tale of class divisions in a southern plan-
tation, and the ultimate Depression film, Warner Brothers' crusading
*I Am a Fugitive From a Chain Gang*, with Paul Muni's unforgettable
retreat into the night at the final fade-out, replying to the cry 'How
do you live?' – 'I steal!' Films featured new types of heroine, no
longer the Bathing Girls simpering on beaches but Barbara
Stanwyck's determined and ambitious schemer, the plucky working
girls of *Gold Diggers of 1933* and Marlene Dietrich in *Shanghai
Express* and *Blonde Venus*, a sultry temptress who gets her own way
– up to a point.

The new comedians, too, attacked adversity with a new ferocity:
Mae West combining the lusty dame and the social rebel with *Night
After Night* in 1932 and *She Done Him Wrong* and *I'm No Angel* in
1933 – a kind of cinematic revenge, one might say, for the victimiza-
tion of the previous generation's 'I Don't Care Girl', Mabel
Normand; or the Brothers Marx, about to make *Duck Soup* and con-
sign all authority to the dustbin of history. Even Stan and Ollie had
plied their trade in the lower depths, as down and out musicians in
*Below Zero*.

Most of Sennett's clowns, however, still capered to older anarchic
tunes: *Candid Camera*, with Franklin Pangborn, still remained wedded to the beach and the world of wayward 'mashing' husbands and

scheming wives. Another film featuring Pangborn, *The Loud Mouth*, was popular enough to be nominated for the 1932 Oscar in the short comedy category (which was won that year by Laurel and Hardy's classic *The Music Box*). *Speed in the Gay 90s* was an attempt at a return to funny gags with vintage motor vehicles, with Andy Clyde as a crazy inventor who is about to be certified because he says men will fly. Andy was Sennett's most popular star now, having been in the business since his British music-hall days. His Scottish burr helped him stand out from the other Sennett talkie actors and he received fan mail from all over the globe. One 'distant admirer' from Kapadia Bungalow, Bombay, wrote to him in what we might today call a 'Peter Sellers' mode:

Dear Friend,

Although I do not know you personally still I have the honour to do so through your successful Screen Career. Myself being a frequent moviegoer I have seen some of your latest talkies and I was simply amazed and enchanted with your fine acting and your mellow voice which records superbly on the talking screen. Moreover your diction was so perfect that I never missed a word of the dialogue which was so perfectly arranged. You are my ideal of what a talking screen star should be, so as a token of your kind remembrance, I would be much pleased if you could send me one of your best autographed photos, which I shall ever cherish in my precious collection . . . Wishing you a topping success in your screen career.

*Sugar Plum Papa*, with Daphne Pollard and Marjorie Beebe, *Alaska Love,* a domestic mix-up in the Frozen North, *The Cannonball*, directed by Del Lord, Sennett's most skilled director, and *Taxi Troubles*, with Andy Clyde and Walter Long as not-very-wisecracking cabbies, brought Andy more fans, though they look pretty sorry affairs to our eyes. In early 1933, Andy became the last of Sennett's veterans to desert the factory and sign a multi-picture deal with Mack's former distributors, Educational Films. According to Kalton Lahue and Sam Gill, Andy had been chafing at the bit since the 'Smith Family' series, in which he was upstaged by Raymond McKee's 'talented but viciously temperamental dog'. Andy walked off the set but the dog stayed, and he was replaced in the series by Arthur Stone, who imitated Andy's make-up. The break came, however, over contracts and Andy's demand for the right to refuse dangerous stunts, which Sennett rejected (what would happen if they all wanted that?). The company soldiered on, with such titles as *Don't Play Bridge With Your Wife* with Marjorie Beebe, *Courting Trouble* with Charlie Murray and *Too Many Highballs* with Lloyd Hamilton and Marjorie Beebe, directed by Clyde Bruckman. The effort was there, but the sparkle was being reduced to a fizzle.

Was this the end of Mack Sennett?

Not yet! Despite it all, there was one more discovery, an ace in the hole that exemplified both the heritage and surreality of the old performers and the ultimate poke in the eye of the righteous. Sennett had one last great service to perform for the cause of Comedy – one last clown to launch, or rather relaunch, into his own orbit.

# 'Figurin' on Goin' Over the Rim Tonight?' (or *The Last Genie in the Box*)

As usual, there are conflicting versions of how Mack Sennett and W. C. Fields, the self-styled 'Great Man' of movie comedy, plighted their transient troth in the winter of 1932. On reflection, it is perhaps strange that they had not worked together before. Fields had appeared in his very first films in 1915, *Pool Sharks* and *His Lordship's Dilemma*, both shorts made on the East Coast for the Gaumont Company but released by Harry Aitken's Mutual Film Corporation. But if Sennett had seen them at the time, he might well have passed them by, as Fields had not yet found his movie persona, at a moment in film history which coincided with Chaplin's rocketing fame.

Fields's own trajectory through life has been oft told and oft lied about, mainly by himself, as he gleefully invented his own 'Dickensian' childhood as a runaway youth, living in the street with a gang of other footloose youths and then breaking into the juggling game by his own ragged bootstraps. In fact, he had begun appearing in Philadelphian Masonic halls with the reluctant assent of his father, the vegetable man, in 1898, setting off to New York with a packed lunch from Mama and swiftly rising through the ranks of small-time burlesque to play the major Keith circuit in New York and national vaudeville. Like Sennett, he considered himself a self-made man, though unlike Sennett, who never left North America throughout his working career, he revelled in the experience he gathered in his 'world tours' between 1901 and 1914.

While Michael Sinnott eked out a living yodelling in the male choruses of Broadway, W. C. Fields was playing the great music-halls of London, Paris, Berlin and Vienna, and as far afield as Cape Town, South Africa and all over Australia – though his own tales of performing for Indian rajahs and the emperor of China were sheer Fieldsian flimflam. He had appeared with Houdini, Sandow the

W. C. Fields – *The Dentist*

Strong Man, Sarah Bernhardt and Busch's Plunging Elephants, diving pachyderms that could have taught Sennett's Anna-May a thing or two. The Great War and German killer ships stopped these trips, but Fields found a second career as one of the stars of impresario Florenz Ziegfeld's spectacular Follies, sharing honours with Will Rogers, Eddie Cantor, Fanny Brice and Bert Williams. On the stage, Fields had begun to write and develop the famous sketches he would bring to the movies, when sound finally enabled him to present the talent he could never fully express in silent films.

Fields's first starring role in a silent feature, after his abortive shorts of 1915, was in *Sally of the Sawdust*, directed by no less than D. W. Griffith in 1925. This was a version of the stage play, *Poppy*, that had given Fields his third career as a Broadway star in his own right. *Sally* and Griffith's second movie with Fields, *That Royle Girl* (now lost), were shot at the Long Island Astoria studios, and so Fields might not have touched base with Sennett at that point, though it is clear that they had become acquainted some time during the Ziegfeld period, perhaps during one of the Follies' Californian tours.

Fields did team up in the late 1920s with one of Keystone's stalwarts, Chester Conklin, in three silent features – *Two Flaming Youths* (1927), *Tillie's Punctured Romance* (1928, a critically panned remake of the 1914 Keystone version) and *Fools for Luck*, also made in 1928. All three films, made at the Paramount Los Angeles studio, are lost, and only the first of them exists as a full script. As box-office failures, they were among the many movies probably melted down for their celluloid materials in the brave new talkie world. This was a blow for Fields, but disastrous for Conklin, who never got the chance to star again, though he appeared in many sound films, including Fields's *Her Majesty Love*, *Hallelujah I'm a Bum* with Harry Langdon (1933) and most famously with Chaplin in *Modern Times* (1936).

Having returned to the New York stage for a brief period before the Wall Street Crash turned most of Broadway's lights off, Fields performed his second coming to Hollywood in the summer of 1931, legendarily motoring across the continent and sauntering into the best Los Angeles hotel he could find, banging his cane on the desk and demanding the bridal suite. Since then, he had starred in two feature films, *Her Majesty Love* for Warner Brothers, directed by William Dieterle, and *Million Dollar Legs*, for supervisor Herman Mankiewicz at Paramount, as the arm-wrestling president of the imaginary kingdom of Klopstokia. This movie was a cornucopia of old Sennett hands – directed by Eddie Cline, featuring Andy Clyde, Vernon Dent, Hank Mann, Heinie Conklin and Ben Turpin as a mysterious spy who lurks, among other places, in portraits. This was swiftly followed by another Paramount film, *If I Had a Million*, supervised by Ernst Lubitsch, an episodic film in which Fields and fellow veteran Alison Skipworth starred in one segment as two old vaudevillians who use her one million-dollar cheque to buy a fleet of cars and ram a series of 'road hogs'.

It was golf, Sennett claimed, that finally brought him and Fields together, at the Lakeside Country Club – though it might well have been the booze, since both were inveterate lovers of the sauce, although Fields was in the world championship league and Mack Sennett merely an amateur player. Sennett wrote, in *King of Comedy*, that Fields moaned to him:

'Mack, I'm fed up with my frivolous existence. Why don't I go out to your studio and do something – anything. Gag, write, direct – any little chore. Money's no object. I just want to be busy.'

Mack replied: 'You've never been in pictures, Bill . . . let's forget the gags and the writing and directing and put you in a comedy.'

Sennett's autobiographical inaccuracies can be fairly staggering. He even took credit for Fields's very first sound picture, the short *The Golf Specialist*, which had been shot by producer Louis Brock for RKO Pictures in 1930. The haggling over Fields's demand for $5,000 a week rings pretty true, though. It may well have been Fields's iron requirement of the highest possible fee for his services that deterred Sennett from hiring him in earlier days. After all, Fields was reeling in $6,000 a week for his performances in Earl Carroll's *Vanities* in 1928.

Despite Sennett's further tales of how he got his gag-writing team together to think up stories for his new recruit – 'For God's sake get a story fast. This actor has already earned $312' – all four of W. C. Fields's short films for the studio were versions of his successful stage sketches.

The first film shot was *The Dentist*, which had begun life as *An Episode at the Dentist*, performed at Earl Carroll's *Vanities* and already written in several versions. As was his wont, Fields lovingly crafted and recrafted his stage skits, adding new ideas, gags and lines all the time. Dr O. Hugh Hurt (later to be Dr Pain), Miss Molar, K. O. Dropp (a prize-fighter), and Mr Foliage, a patient with luxuriant facial hair, to whom the stage-version doctor remarks: 'I'd like to keep all the golf balls I find in here', were revised for the movie. Mr K. O. Dropp was dropped and Fields gave himself a rebellious daughter who wants to marry the iceman ('Get that iceman outa here! I'm going to order a fridgidaire!'). A version of Fields's golf sketch was factored in to the story and the variety of bizarre and masochistic patients, including the bearded wonder, played by old-timer Billy Bletcher, was augmented by the angular Elise Cavanna, whom Fields tugs around the room by her molar as she wraps her legs round his waist – a scene cut from the television transmission version of the movie in the fragile 1950s, though later restored.

Fields's sketches were perfectly formed for Sennett's low-budget sound movies, as they fitted neatly into the two-reel format and took place in limited sets – a couple of indoor rooms and a rudimentary small-town backlot, with some shoddy back-projection thrown in for good measure. This was most apparent in Fields's second Sennett short, *The Fatal Glass of Beer*, again a reconstruction of a *Vanities* sketch, 'The Stolen Bonds'. This has survived, almost verbatim, with some rejigging of the scenes, on the screen. As on the stage, Fields is in a crummy log cabin up in the Frozen North, with pantomime snow thrown in his face every time he opens the door and exclaims dramatically: 'And it ain't a fit night out for man nor beast!' His help-meet in this dire predicament is Ma, Rosemary Theby, a Sennett stalwart, who helps him reminisce about their wastrel son, Chester, who became morally lost in the city after he took 'The Fatal Glass of Beer'. ('Once the city gets into a b-hoy's sy-hystem, he loses his a-hankerin' for the ca-hountry.') Fields wished to play the ballad he intones to Officer Postlewhistle of the Canadian Mounties, who has the misfortune to be its audience, absolutely straight, with its zither accompaniment ('do you mind if I play with ma mittens on?'), but Sennett insisted on shooting flashback scenes of the vital verses – young Chester in the city, taking the Fatal Glass and being kicked in the schnozz by 'a Salvation Army lass' after 'wickedly he stole her tambourine'. This almost sent Fields off the lot in high dudgeon, vowing to make this his final movie for the studio, but Sennett prevailed. A letter from Fields to Sennett reveals his anguish:

I feel rather reluctant to start a new picture until I have an assurance from you that after it is finished you will not make several changes and calmly send word to me that if I do not like it in the approved Sennett form, you will give it to someone else . . . You have been a tremendous success with your formula, but it is new to me and I can't change my way of working at this late stage of the game . . . If the pictures I have made are not what you want tear up the contract . . . I do not believe our business relationships are going to be successful. I wish you would agree to terminate the contract and we continue our friendship of yore.'

Ronald Fields, the great man's grandson, in his filmography of the Fields *œuvre*, relates another instance of the star's grandstanding as he stole a scene from young George Chandler, playing the luckless Chester, who returns home after serving time for stealing a stack of bonds from his employer:

George Chandler . . . recalls that *The Fatal Glass of Beer* was a big break for him. And he was excited over one scene in particular, his return home to 'Ma and Pa'. It was supposed to be a lengthy close-up on him . . . but before filming the sequence W. C. looked around the set and saw a bucket behind one of the cameras. He went over, grabbed the bucket and put it next to his seat.

The cameras started rolling. Chester walked in the door. The cameras started closing in on Chester, but Fields jumped from his seat, put his foot in the bucket, walked around the table so the camera would catch it all, then kicked the bucket off his foot and greeted Chester warmly . . . Chandler said that for over forty years he held a grudge against W. C. for this thievery, and for over forty years he refused to see the film . . .

This appeared to be the reaction of many audiences, too, as reported by theatre owners in various parts of the 'ca-hountry' when the film was released, after being delayed by the Sennett–Fields spat, in March 1933: 'The worst comedy we have played from any company this season. No story, no acting, and on the whole has nothing,' claimed J. J. Medford of the Orpheum, Oxford, North Carolina. (The theatre owners had not liked *The Dentist*, either, J. J. Hoffman of Plainview, Nebraska terming it 'Rotten'; or at best conceding it was funny, but 'rather resented by the dental profession in this town', according to A. B. Jefferis, Piedmont, Mo.) In the context of Sennett history, however, *The Fatal Glass of Beer* was not that outlandish or unusual. In its spoofing of the old Gold Rush tales and pioneering values, not to mention ordinary morality and the integrity of parental–filial duties, it was not that far removed from Ben Turpin's Yukon antics and other inversions of the proper way of telling a story, apart from the fact that it was devoid of all action. 'I'm going out to milk the elk,' says Fields, as he exits the cabin into the poorest back-projection scene in history, with stock-shot moose rushing by helter-skelter. 'Figurin' on goin' over the rim tonight,' he tells his Mountie friend, but the journey is distinctly cheesy. It all hies back to some of Fields's oldest vaudeville tricks, when he played the blazing antipodes in Melbourne in full sleighing costume before doing his billiards act, back in 1903. 'They won't take my lead dog, Balto . . . cause I et him. He was mighty good with mustard.'

In the end, Fields and Ma throw Chester back out in the snow in disgust on hearing that he threw away all the 'tainted bonds' he had stolen and 'came back to live with you and Ma for the rest of my life'. 'Come back to sponge on us!' cries Pa, cracking a water pitcher over his head. He stands over his useless offspring, in the doorway: 'And it ain't a fit night out for man nor beast.' He starts back, but no snow hits him in the face this time.

Sennett and Fields did not throw each other out, but the next, and last, two films they made together were in Fields's more 'realist' vein, returning to the small-town ambience of *The Dentist* with *The Pharmacist* and *The Barber Shop*.

*The Pharmacist* was a return to older stage material, 'The Drug Store', originally a segment of Fields's stage revue *The Comic Supplement*, written with J. P. McEvoy in 1924 and then reprised in the *Ziegfeld Follies of 1925*. He had first filmed it, as a silent sketch, in his 1926 feature, *It's the Old Army Game*. Fields, as pharmacist Dillweg, presides over a perfectly magic emporium, vending the old Smith Brothers' Cough Drops, cake à la mode, bizarre toys ('Old Moscow in winter?') and an eclectic shelf of books: 'Read *Mother India*? *Sex Life of the Polyp*? *The Rover Boys* . . .' Upstairs is the standard Fields family: wife Elise Cavanna, a brattish small daughter and older exemplar, Ooleota, whose boyfriend is one of Fields's favourite foils, the shambling if amiable Cuthbert, played by Grady Sutton: 'I never knew a Cuthbert in my life that wasn't a sissy. When I was a kid I licked every kid in school called Cuthbert.'

In his world of small annoyances and even smaller ambitions, Mr Dillweg can transform the most trivial transaction into a matter of cosmic frustration: the man who wants to buy a stamp from the middle of the sheet, setting off a veritably industrial job with the scissors. Unable to give change for a hundred-dollar note, Dillweg allows his tormentor to walk free from the shop, with the added bonus of a giant vase which is given away free with every purchase. In a flurry of activity at the end of the film, two crooks who have been exchanging shots with the police outside burst in, but Cuthbert, who is in the store phone booth, opens the door and knocks one of them out. He is acclaimed as a hero and Dillweg has to allow him to marry his daughter after all.

Fields's first two Sennett films had been directed by Leslie Pearce and Clyde Bruckman respectively, but the third and fourth were directed by Arthur Ripley, who, after his work with Harry Langdon, knew how to help comedians whose forte was character rather than action. The deft hand is apparent in the last of Fields's Sennett quartet, *The Barber Shop*, another gem of small-town satire. This was an amalgam of ideas which had originated in the old vaudeville sketches, now strung together in a new form, with a kind of tribute to family roots.

The barber, Cornelius O'Hare, who sits in front of his shop, greeting passers-by but offering caustic comments about them to his friend sitting next to him, echoes W. C. Fields née Dukenfield's own mother, who, family lore tells, did this daily.

'Hello, O'Hare, whadayaknow?'

'Not a thing, not a thing . . . (aside) That lunk tells his wife everything he knows . . . Good morning, Mrs. Scroggins. How's Mr. Scroggins?'

'He ain't feeling so well this morning.'

'That's too bad. (aside) Guess he was on one of his benders last night again . . . how he can drink that raw alcohol and live, I don't know . . . fine Mayor he is . . .'

As a clincher, Fields named the town in the movie Felton, after his mother's maiden name.

Once again, there is a dysfunctional family: wife Elise Cavanna and this time a small boy, Ronald, who regales Papa with one of Fields's oldest stage puns from the nineteenth-century minstrels McIntyre and Heath.

'Why is a cat's tale like a long journey? . . . Because it's fur to the end . . .'

'Very good, Ronald . . . eat your spinach . . .'

Barber O'Hare is as dangerous an operator as The Dentist, shaving more than hairs off a customer's face.

'That a mole?'

'Yes, I've had it all my life.'

'You won't have it any more.'

Another customer asks, 'What is that dog doing in here?' only to get an unsettling answer.

'That's a funny thing . . . the other day a man was in here . . . the razor slipped and I cut his ear off . . . the dog got it . . . ever since he's been hanging around . . .'

A fat man enters the steam room and emerges perfectly shrunk, crying out: 'I'll have the law on you for this!'

Not to dispense with formula, a denouement involving crooks is inserted, with O'Hare daydreaming about apprehending the thieves who have robbed the town bank, but when the crook whose face is in the newspaper turns up for a new look, the barber runs away on a completely spurious circulation of the back lot only to arrive back in time to knock over the crook, who is already groggy, having been beaned by son Ronald's baseball. In the last shot, a man who previously left his fiddle behind in a closet together with O'Hare's own cello finds the instruments have given birth to a pile of baby violins. 'Lena, how could you?' O'Hare protests. But all objects are ornery beasts in Fields's world. Forget about the Depression, Fields was saying – life is a madhouse, come what may.

The Sennett films enabled Fields to be the character he had longed to be, but couldn't, in silent films, as the medium lacked his gravelly, muttering voice. Unlike his three previous outings in Talkieland, these films allowed Fields to try out his sketches in their purest form, unspoiled by imposed plots, extraneous characters or the often toe-curling love interest that bedevilled every comedian in feature films. These were distilled Fields and, despite all the screaming and yelling, the complaints and peevish letters about interference, Sennett gave Fields his space and let him curve along his own peculiar and unique path. From this point on, Fields advanced into the heartland of Paramount Pictures and his string of 1930s classics, from *International House* through *You're Telling Me*, *The Old Fashioned Way*, *It's a Gift* and the iconic *Man on the Flying Trapeze*, all made between 1933 and 1935, not to speak of his seminal appearance as Mr Micawber in *David Copperfield*, also in 1935.

W. C. Fields's *The Barber Shop* was the last film released by Mack Sennett productions. It bears the number 477 in the list of 'Mack Sennett Comedy series'. The date of release was 28 July 1933. We do not have a record of when the film was actually shot, so we cannot tell if it was the last Mack Sennett film ever made. It was certainly among the last productions of the new Sennett studios. The old Edendale studio, sadly enough, had blown down in 1932, in an unusual Los Angeles storm. The entire lot was reduced to wreckage, and the steel girders holding the buildings together had collapsed on top of the wooden walls.

The death rattle of Mack Sennett Comedies was the familiar croak of misplaced distribution and the ghostly clanking chains of debt. In February 1932, Sennett had signed a new distribution deal with Paramount Publix, on the face of it a much stronger partner than the minuscule Educational Films. What Sennett did not know was the extent of the downturn experienced by Paramount and the state of their own debts. Soon after this deal, Jesse Lasky, who had founded the business sixteen years earlier with Adolph Zukor and Cecil B. De Mille, was fired from his own studio, though Zukor, as we have noted, hung on. Paramount Publix Corporation went into receivership in January 1933. Sennett's distributor had gone formally bankrupt.

On the face of it, this would not have necessarily been a death blow, as Paramount's 'Voluntary Petition in Bankruptcy' was a legal move to conserve its total assets (which stood at over 150 million dollars) from multiple ongoing law suits. Paramount continued to produce and distribute short films under different headings – though not with Sennett, as it was switching the making of its shorts to studios on the East Coast.

The films were still released after January, but it was too late for Sennett to recover from this latest blow. Shorts in general were facing an uncertain future, as, to combat Depression blues, movie owners had for some time been offering a double feature for the price of one, dropping out the traditional short. Hal Roach had figured this out, and produced five Laurel and Hardy features by the end of 1933, all released by MGM. Sennett's big feature, *Hypnotized*, had, however, eaten so much money and disgorged so little income that it may have been enough to sink the company on its own. Sennett's operation had been highly 'leveraged' since before the Wall Street Crash and the creditors were now lining up, finally howling for their cash. Even the occasional successful movie could not make a difference now. Sennett had run out of options and could not pay his bills.

The end came in a crescendo of small-time legal moves: On 31 October, Leon Schlesinger of Pacific Title and William Hornbeck, Sennett's long-term editor, petitioned the US District Court to 'appoint a receiver in equity for Mack Sennett, Inc.'. On 7 November, Smith Bros., Cinema Props and S. C. Shine filed an 'involuntary petition in bankruptcy' in the Southern District of California, for claims of just over $4,000. On 13 November, *Variety* announced that:

Various actions have accumulated in Federal Court on the status of Mack Sennett, Inc. in proceedings for bankruptcy or distribution of assets through equity. A petition presented asking that John Waldron, general manager of the Sennett studios, be named temporary receiver in Sennett's own filing, with debts listed above $1,000,000, was taken under advisement by Federal Judge George Cosgrave . . .'

A few days later, as Sennett did not respond to a subpoena in the bankruptcy proceedings, he was automatically ruled a bankrupt by Judge Cosgrave. On 13 December 1933, the press announced:

Hollywood, Dec. 12. – Mack Sennett, who for 30 years gave a nation most of its belly laughs, is broke.

The pioneer movie producer, master gag man of them all, the screen 'father' of Harold Lloyd, Ford Sterling, Chester Conklin, 'Fatty' Arbuckle and a host of other fun-makers, today filed in Federal Court a voluntary petition in bankruptcy. He listed his liabilities at $925,681 and his assets at $1,600.

Six months before, the newspapers had announced, in small-point headlines, the death of Roscoe C. Arbuckle, after a decade of forced anonymity:

## FATTY ARBUCKLE LIES DEAD IN CHAPEL, BUT NO EAGER CROWD COMES TO LOOK

In the same 'gold room' at Campbell's Funeral Church where thousands of women battled to view the body of Rudolph Valentino, screen hero, the body of Roscoe 'Fatty' Arbuckle, once a leading comedian, was placed in state yesterday.

But no such mob as sought to see the 'great lover' was expected at the bier of the rotund comedian, once more widely known to movie fans that [sic] was Valentino . . .

*New York American*, 30 June 1933

The Hearst press traduced Roscoe even in his death, as the *New York Times* revealed the next day that about a thousand people had filed past the coffin in the church at Broadway and 66th Street, adding that 'every station in life was represented, including overalled workmen, taxi drivers and young children'.

Arbuckle had just made a series of sound two-reelers and was being promised a miraculous return in a feature film for Warner Brothers. But he died of a heart attack in a hotel bedroom in New York at the age of forty-six, at about the same time that Mack Sennett, in Hollywood, was producing his own last independent comedy film.

# His Busted Trust

And he didn't live happily ever after.

What happens to a man whose life, for a quarter of a century, was full of zeal and activity, the power to create and to enable creativity, to make things happen and achieve his dreams, when, suddenly, it all disappears and the underpinnings of all that dynamic tumult, the daily hustle and bustle of work, are pulled away at the age of fifty-three?

'How does it feel to lose everything you've worked for all your life?' Mack wrote. 'How does it feel to lose a leg? It hurts.'

The formal announcement of the 'collapse of his fun-factory' found Sennett in New York, no doubt recollecting that other crisis of the Triangle company and trying to wrest one last reprieve for his business from the banks. But they had rung down the curtain finally this time.

Sennett wrote that he was glad his mother was in Canada when the studio was closed, unaware of his financial ruin. 'I spent a gentle three months with her, and then she died, peacefully, in her sleep,' he related. But even in this, Mack could not engage with reality. Mrs. Sinnott's death did not occur for another three years. She had a longer fade-out, and Mack a far longer twilight still.

He did not give up immediately. In March 1934 he was still telling the press about plans to 'use his own experiences in a story which will mark his return to film activity'. The idea was for a movie recreating the classic days of the discovery of Chaplin and the story of the making of *Tillie's Punctured Romance* and other Keystone films: 'How the romance of Gloria Swanson and Wallace Beery grew, how Mary Pickford tried to sell Sennett's scenarios . . . and the development of Harold Lloyd and other stars . . .' In short, more mythical flimflam.

'Sennett,' the Associated Press reported, 'who gave up pictures more than a year ago, when his company ran into financial difficulties, has about completed negotiations for the release of his future pictures. He believes the film, which he is temporarily calling "My Twenty Years in the Movies," will be different enough and unusual enough to make auspicious his return to production.'

But no amount of dancing around the totem-pole of wishful thinking could make those dry bones come alive again. Mack had other problems as well, in the immediate aftermath of his bankruptcy, as he had been involved in a motoring accident on 11 January which killed his friend and leading actor of the 1932 feature, *Hypnotized*, Charles E. Mack. Charles Mack's partner, George Moran, was also in the car, which was being driven, allegedly at high speed, by Mrs Mack. Both Moran and Sennett sued Mrs Mack after the accident, Sennett alleging that he had suffered back and chest injuries and lost the fees he would have made making two pictures, whatever they might have been. Neither plaintiff managed to collect from the unfortunate widow, but it was an ugly symptom of desperate times.

Gene Fowler's biography of Sennett, *Father Goose*, was published by Covici-Friede Publishers in New York in 1934, and Fowler arranged for payment of the royalties from its sale to Sennett. Fowler had recounted all Sennett's myths and added some of his own, to spice up the brew. Fowler's deepest wish was to establish himself as a novelist, though his forte, after fifteen years of journalism, was as Hollywood's most skilful script doctor. He would be handed scripts that had become hopelessly tangled by incompetence, intoxication or failed collaboration and would type out his own revisions at great speed, producing a bankable property, such as *Jesse James*, *White Fang* or *The Earl of Chicago*.

Fowler's 'novelized' biography was a kind of dry run for his masterly evocation of his close friend John Barrymore, *Good Night Sweet Prince*, to be published in 1943. It abounded with such descriptions as his portrayal of Mack's attempted farming ventures, relating one incident in which our hero returns from a golf game:

One morning he came from the links to find a commotion at his vegetable market. His Italian vendor was screaming. Sennett, clad in plus fours and hob-nail shoes, ran to the stands to find a cub bear wrecking the vegetable bins. This animal had been appearing in a picture on a neighbouring stage, had smelled Sennett's maple syrup and had broken loose.

Sennett charged the bear and booted it in the rump with a hobnail brogan. The terrorized bear retreated. The Italian, thinking it was chasing him, also began to run. Sennett accepted both their resignations and began to lose faith in his farming projects.

As Fowler came to the end of his narrative, he had a different explanation for the demise of Sennett's enterprise than the mundane financial nemesis:

The advent of sound and the collapse of the world's economic structure found Sennett with his back to the wall, but still full of fight. Then came a thrust from nowhere, a sudden and unexpected stab which Sennett, like Caesar in the Forum, accepted as the unkindest cut of all.

The animated cartoon was a new and popular toy – especially to a world in despair. It preserved and accentuated a thousand-fold all the illusions of slap-stick. The pen was mightier than the bed-slat. By the exercise of a few thousand strokes of a cartoonist's quill, a whole animal kingdom of stars came into being . . .

These charming imps cost but little, were not given to fits of temper and knew not the weaknesses of the flesh. They worked for no salary, and for the sheer fun of it; they would never grow old . . .

A nimble rodent has become the world's hero. In the eyes of Mack Sennett, he must always remain a scraggly mustachioed villain whose mischief will never be undone.

Who killed Cock Robin?

'I did,' said Mickey Mouse.

On 25 May 1933, Walt Disney had encapsulated the anxieties of the Depression, and offered what would become a familiar Waltish solution with the première of his short cartoon *Three Little Pigs*, featuring the tunesome refrain of 'Who's Afraid of the Big Bad Wolf', the two unwise little pigs who build their houses of straw and wood and the good one who builds his with the bricks, presumably, of Roosevelt's New Deal. Disney's first Technicolor short, *Flowers and Trees*, had been released in July 1932, with Disney pioneering the three-strip process, far superior to anything Sennett or anyone else could have produced in colour before. (Non-animation three-strip Technicolor was first used in 1934.) With sound, lush colour and gags untrammelled by human limitations, the cartoons were revitalized.

Mickey Mouse had been born, in black-and-white with music, in July 1928, with *Steamboat Willie*, so Sennett had given him a good run for five years. The pen would never, in fact, be mightier than the human puss, but it was, indeed, often much cheaper. By 1933, exhibitors were paying between $12,500 and $25,000 for a two-reel short, which could have cost over $40,000. At W. C. Fields's prices of five thousand per week, or even half that, deficit margins were greater. Gone were the days of Keystone's starting salaries of $150 or $250 a week, rising to $2,000 for a true star. In the job market, Mickey Mouse, Pluto, Donald and all were cut-rate, non-unionized scabs. The record shows, moreover, that another animated rival was stealing Sennett's thunder under Paramount's own distribution banner – New York's home-grown starlet, Betty Boop.

In reality, Mack Sennett had built his house with bricks, but as it happened, straw was easier to tear down, move and use for reconstruction. The truth was that the parade had indeed gone by. Sennett was not defeated by sound. Always ready for challenges, he could and did master the technical side of the transition to the new talkies. It was not the form but the content of the movie dreams that defeated him. To recognize this is to understand Sennett's character, the creative cogs that drove the engine of Keystone and the subsequent Mack Sennett Comedies.

Griffith and Sennett, the Don Quixote and Sancho Panza of the early film pioneers, had much in common as well as much that appeared to divide them. Despite the great difference in their backgrounds – as the son of a defeated Civil War officer and the son of a farmer turned wage-earning labourer – they both viewed the world as a domain of unceasing struggle between opposing moral forces. Griffith viewed the stark class divisions between people through a moralist's glass: great wealth begat greed which begat human exploitation; poverty led to moral degradation and the collapse of human solidarity. The bridge between these worlds was love: marital love, parental love, the love of siblings, and a desire for purity and a return to a primal innocence, a paradise lost. Griffith's moral tragedy was, and is, that this view was sullied by racism and his belief that the essential innocence of black people was degraded by their desire for equality.

Sennett experienced the struggle that Griffith observed from outside as a participant, an employee in the works, however brief his sojourn at hard labour, and, for five crucial years, as a down-at-heel jobbing actor. America's turn of the twentieth century, in its harsh New York environment, gave him a front-row seat for the show of dog eat dog. Where Griffith railed against this, Sennett revelled in the fight, imbibed great gulps of the anarchy of the lower depths, and made it into art. Not as social protest, but as a heightened vision of the absurdity of the same struggle. Men with fat paunches and top hats are ripe for a fall; policemen are incompetent and visibly insane; lovers are plain mad; every person with the slightest authority – such as a fleapit hotel owner wanting to exercise his droit de seigneur on any female guest – wants to abuse his position; and the only balm is the dream world of the girls on the beach, bouncing their beach balls from one to the other, or caressing the hero's fevered brow.

The moral force that Sennett opposed to Griffith's social evangelism was Freedom: freedom to abandon convention; freedom to be vulgar; freedom to kick the rich man in the tummy; freedom to drive at high speed, wreck cars and demolish property; freedom to fly in aeroplanes, for both men and women (preferably upside-down); freedom to beat up anybody with a sour face; freedom to belch; freedom to throw rotten fruit at rotten performers; freedom to question the laws of logic and the rationality of science. All through the catharsis of comedy.

When Sennett leaned away from comedy, as he allowed in Mabel Normand's little-Cinderella-who-will-win-her-prince movies, he was even more mawkish and sentimental than Griffith. And what remains morally taboo in Sennett's *œuvre* is notable: murder, personal theft, coveting one's neighbour's wife or ox (or dog), being really beastly to Ma and Pa, or to the clergy – in short, the Ten Commandments; and of course, no one would have the temerity to insult the American flag. Where Sennett had the edge on Griffith was his treatment of minorities: blacks, Jews, Turks or Chinese people could, and should, be lampooned, but on roughly equal terms with anybody else.

What neither Sennett nor Griffith could admit, in their art, was the hidden power of sex, the shadowy impulses of the soul and the spirit, moral ambivalence and self-destructiveness of desires. Theirs was, in the main, a pre-Freudian world, despite the fact that they worked in a medium which was perfectly positioned to represent these lights and shadows and which was directly accused, as we have noted, of expressing these subversive ideas.

When Paul Muni retreated into the darkness, at the end of *I Am a Fugitive from a Chain Gang*, he exemplified the deeper fears and anxieties that both Don Quixote and Sancho Panza had glossed over. These ideas came into the cinema by means of technical developments in film lighting, composition, camera placement and movement. They came initially from Scandinavian film-makers and then from the movies produced in Germany and bracketed as 'Expressionist' cinema. Lighting for mood (which Griffith and others had experimented with, too) became the method by which the camera lens could look behind the activity of the actors into their 'soul', their innermost thoughts, their unconscious mind. These techniques would become a favoured method for cinematographers and directors to tell more ambivalent tales, transforming genres such as the thriller or gangster film into fables of light and shadow and even infecting the old-fashioned western with elements of moral doubt, flawed heroes and tentative villains. In contrast, Keystone and Sennett films are invariably soaked in sunlight, or the strong, even illumination of studio lights.

Two actors, whom Sennett had discovered, were able to express the darker shadows behind their physical action in comedy: Chaplin and Harry Langdon. It was the mark of Chaplin's genius that, even in his Keystone apprenticeship, there are unmistakable signs of his ability to use pantomime to express complex thoughts. It was not for nothing that clergymen objected at an early stage to his hold on the public, commenting on his base vulgarity, his bad manners and bad example to youth. (The same clerics also objected to Theda Bara 'at all times and in all circumstances'.) 'Charlie Chaplin is more to some people than Almighty God,' said Father Watt, an English priest 'recovering from wounds after a year spent on the battlefield' (quoted in the *Toledo Blade*). Chaplin lurched around in a drunken stupor, kicking the men and pawing the ladies in paroxysms of gratuitous violence and lust. In a world of chaos, I'll do anything for a bit of 'aggro' and a fuck, said the unspoken leer that Chaplin had imported from the world of the eternal English proletarian lout. Langdon stood still in the frame, and directors like Harry Edwards and Frank Capra allowed the camera to roll on as he decided whether to remain asleep or wake up, whether or how to scratch a persistent itch, or how to respond to such unfathomable things as a pretty girl's sudden kiss. Both Langdon's deep melancholy and Chaplin's satyr's leer derived from the oldest repertoire of traditional clowning, from Nat Wills, Dan Leno and Joseph Grimaldi, but the old clowns had long anticipated Freud and the serious savants of the subconscious soul.

Sennett's instincts were visceral and immediate; he sensed talent without stopping to analyse it; he hired first and asked questions afterwards. It was not, as we have established, that he was the rough-hewn clod of his own self-made image, for, as we have seen, he was well educated and well read, like many show people who liked to present their unshaven souls to the public. But like a good Catholic father, he had a vast brood of children, a proliferating family that had to be treated with some modicum of equality. Even when Kessel and Baumann were pleading with him, in the hot days of Triangle (SIG) creation, to hire Chaplin back 'regardless of cost', he lacked the inclination, as well as the means, to achieve this. Capra's naked Sennett, leaping into his tub to think up the latest gags chomping his cigar in the suds, may have been a mythical exaggeration, but the lust for gags and jokes was authentic.

In 1935, Sennett's hopes of a comeback were briefly boosted by a directing assignment of five short films for Educational Pictures. These five titles, unearthed by the Italian Sennettist, Davide Turconi, included one of Buster Keaton's lackluster talkies, *The Timid Young Man*, released in October. The other films, *Ye Old Saw Mill*, with Franklin Pangborn, *Flicker Fever*, *Just Another Murder* and *Way Up Thar*, released between August and November, were a quickly fading echo. The Sennett studios had already been sold by the receivers to Mascot Pictures, producer of matinee serials. Later in the year, Monogram Pictures moved to the site, both companies financed by former tobacco mogul Herbert J. Yates, who then merged them as Republic Pictures, producing a string of second-feature Westerns and dramas, as well as most of Hollywood's sound-era serials, among them *Flash Gordon*, *The Lone Ranger*, *The Adventures of Captain Marvel* and *Fighting Devil Dogs*. Sennett's other remaining real estate was sold off, too, along with the Westmoreland mansion, long emptied of its platoon of butlers.

Mack returned, for a while, to Canada, to Mrs Sinnott's farm near Danville, Quebec. Local lore recalls that Sennett had begun visiting his mother's farm regularly during the summer since 1928, sometimes staying at a local hotel with one or two women, presumed to be actresses, who accompanied him on these trips. It is not clear whether Marjorie Beebe was one of these companions. Some locals recalled that the women appeared more interested in each other than in their employer, but their precise place in the puzzle remains unclear, despite the digging of local historians. In 1935, Sennett returned to stay with his mother on his own.

Mrs Sinnott had not remained idle after it became clear that her son's plans to install her in his dream-palace had fallen through, although she was in her eighties. She had purchased more property around the old Curley farm at Shipton, which turned out to have a rich vein of asbestos and, it was claimed, signs of oil. When Mack's enterprise failed it was, ironically, the old ancestral homestead which provided him with some means of support.

The older locals in Danville remember the returning homeboy from Hollywood sitting on the terrace of his mother's house, watching the fields, in a mostly silent reverie. Compared to the buzz of the studio, or virtually anywhere else, Richmond County was not a place where much happened. Then, as now, the roads stretched from horizon to horizon, with an occasional car or truck going by.

On 15 September 1936, the *Sherbrooke Daily Record* noted:

### DEATH CLAIMED MACK SENNETT'S MOTHER TODAY

Ninety-Year-Old Mother of Noted Screen Personality Passed Away This Morning on Old Sennett Homestead at Tingwick.

Death today claimed a pioneer resident of this district and the mother of a noted screen personality when Mrs. John Sinnott passed away from the effects of a paralytic stroke suffered six weeks ago. Mrs. Sinnott was the mother of Mack Sennett, popular comedian in the days of the silent movies.

A very smart and active lady until she was stricken more than a month ago, the deceased passed away at the old Sinnott homestead between here and Shipton – a property which had been in the Sinnott family for more than a century . . . Mack Sennett had been with his mother two weeks prior to her death this morning . . .

Left to mourn her loss are two sons, Mack Sennett, who was born Michael Sinnott, and John Sinnott, of Montreal; a granddaughter, Mrs. Max Holden, of Barre, Vt; two brothers, Messrs. John and Michael Foy, of Tingwick, and one sister, Mrs. M. Dorin, of Long Island, N.Y.

Funeral arrangements have not yet been completed, but interment will take place in Northampton, Mass., where Mr. Sinnott and two children are buried.

Thus the great matriarch passed away, aged eighty-eight, according to reliable records, having seen her son come full circle from the dreamer of his teens in the last decade of the nineteenth century to the introspective companion of her last days.

Was she, rather than Mabel Normand, the only woman in his life for whom he really cared deeply, Mack's Quebecois roots counting for more than his Hollywood round-trip, in the end? Quebec historian Pierre Pageau appears to think so, having written:

*C'était la femme la plus importante dans sa vie, celle qui n'a jamais ecrasé ses rêves. Musicienne, elle l'avait encouragé à devenir chanteur. Mme Foy-Sinnott se fera vers la fin appeler Sennett comme son fils.*

*La Presse*, Montreal, 8 June 1996

But there are a few other clues we can glean, from Mack Sennett's 'afterlife', to cast light, in the prolonged period of his enforced retirement, on the deposed king as he passed into the shadows.

# His Hereafter

Sennett remained in Richmond County for a few weeks after his mother's death, tending to the family's affairs, and then returned to California. He began living in apartment-hotels, paying an inexpensive rent and waiting for something that did not happen. Louise Brooks, in her 1974 memoir, *Lulu in Hollywood*, describes how she used to see him hanging around in the Roosevelt Hotel, where she was living in 1936:

Almost every day, from about noon, he would sit in the lobby for a couple of hours, smoking his cigars, watching the people go by. He was then only fifty-one [*in fact, fifty-six*] – a big, healthy wonderfully handsome and virile man. How could he have allowed himself to be discarded to die on the Hollywood rubbish heap? Although he spoke to no one, he was never bored. As he followed with keen and unembarrassed attention my flights in and out of the hotel, I wondered what thoughts lay behind the expressionless mask he wore in public. Now I know he was practicing the art of paying attention. In his book, speaking of working for D. W. Griffith in New York, he says, 'I learned all I ever learned about making pictures by standing around watching people who knew how.' Anyone who has achieved excellence in any form knows that it comes as a result of ceaseless concentration. Paying attention.

Paying attention for no apparent reason seemed to become Mack Sennett's new rationale. Gene Fowler's son, Will, a teenager at that time, who was tasked with chauffeuring his father and his boozy companions, W. C. Fields, John Barrymore, Decker et al., across Los Angeles, since they assumed (wrongly) that he was not drinking, remembers a brief lunch meeting with Sennett in the Roosevelt lobby. 'He was a melancholy man,' Will said. 'I remember he took his cigar, clipped off the end, dunked it in his coffee and sucked it.' Mack took his simple pleasures as they came.

He never married. He never, in any recollection, shared a residence with a woman, although there were close male companions. 'Loyal friends who relieved some of the arid loneliness', in the words of researcher Robert Giroux. One such was Jack Mulhall, one-time silent screen star, who had appeared with Mabel Normand in *Mickey* and *Molly O'* and featured in Sennett's mythology as the man he socked in the puss as an alleged rival for Mabel's straying affections.

Mack was then domiciled at the Garden Court Apartments, 7021 Hollywood Boulevard, right next to Grauman's Chinese Theatre and across the way from the Roosevelt Hotel. This was not by any mark a poorhouse, and the accommodation was comfortable if not spacious. Mack was living in the eye of the creature which had made him, and which he had helped to make. He did not remain without honour: In 1938, at the annual Oscars ceremony held on 10 March, the Academy of Motion Picture Arts and Sciences awarded him an honorary Oscar for his contribution to film. The statuette was handed to him by W. C. Fields and Academy President Frank Capra. The young man hired fourteen years before and the second-chancer of the Fatal Glass of Beer had done good, as had so many other Sennett alumni.

In 1939, Twentieth Century Fox boss Daryl Zanuck gave Mack a job in a segment of *Hollywood Cavalcade*, a nostalgia-fest directed by Irving Cummings, in which Don Ameche brings Alice Faye to the old Hollywood, featuring Buster Keaton, Chester Conklin, Al Jolson, Rin-Tin-Tin and Mack Sennett, introducing 'old-time Sennett comedy routines and formulas. Views of filmmaking in the days when a pie was worth five jokes, and when Keystone Cops whirled recklessly through traffic to save distressed maidens, are hilariously reproduced,' quoth *Variety*. Some of the original Kops were decidedly creaky by this time, and were lucky not to do themselves serious injury.

No further movie work followed from this. In December 1940, Hollywood luminaries unveiled a memorial plaque for Mabel Normand at the Republic Studio. This must have been a wrenching moment for Mack. The roll-call of names that turned up on Friday evening, the twenty-seventh, included eighty-seven old Sennett hands, from Harold Lloyd, Harry Langdon, Frank Capra, W. C. Fields and Bing Crosby to Edna Purviance, Edgar Kennedy, Slim Summerville, Chester Conklin, Al St John and every surviving Kop. Mae Busch, Sennett's alleged nemesis, was there, as were Polly Moran, Minta

Durfee, Marjorie Beebe, Carole Lombard and the oldest-timers of all: Fred J. Balshofer, founder-member of the original Kessel and Baumann outfit, J. S. Blackton, one of the founders of Vitagraph, and Colonel William Selig, who had set up the first studio in California, back in 1910. Stan Laurel, Oliver Hardy, John Wayne and John Ford paid tribute to the old Hollywood, in the name of the new.

The looming war, however, would usher in an even newer movie world. *Citizen Kane*, despite its awesome troubles, set a new benchmark for Hollywood's art. The male face of the cinema was Bogart, not Valentino. Joan Crawford and Rita Hayworth replaced Mary Pickford and Mabel Normand. Hitchcock had arrived from England to bring Freud directly into the pictures. While Mack Sennett sat in the lobby of the Roosevelt, dunking his cigar in his mocha java, the Japanese had attacked Pearl Harbor and Americans shipped out to fight in their hundreds of thousands in Europe, Asia and North Africa.

Comedy was still taking place, but its face would soon be neither Kops, nor Stan and Ollie, nor W. C. Fields or Mae West, but the low-down clattering of Abbott and Costello. Sennett would probably have hired them if he had had the chance. They were popular and made the troops and battered civilians laugh, so why not? But nobody was making offers.

In August 1948, the actors' club, the Masquers, gave Sennett a 'testimonial' dinner at their headquarters, with six of the original Kops masquerading in their old uniforms outside, directing the traffic. Hank Mann, Heinie Conklin and Jimmy Finlayson posed with Sennett and Phyllis Haver. Harold Lloyd, Hal Roach, Jesse Lasky and other bigwigs and not so bigwigs attended. *Variety* described Mack as 'the earlyday laughmaker, now retired'. Sennett, aged sixty-eight, regaled his admirers with recollections of the old 'Keystone bookies' myth.

His claim to the Kops was one thing Mack was not willing to give up, as he was suing the producers of a Broadway musical, *High Button Shoes*, for using both his name and that of the Kops without his permission. He sued for $250,000 and won $100,000, most of which was, of course, devoured by his lawyers. The judge ruled that Sennett did after all have some property on the term 'Mack Sennett Bathing Beauty', as a sign of a certain generation. Not, alas, the present one.

In March 1949, the California Country Club provided its premises for a 'Mack Sennett Alumni and Remember When Association' bash on St Patrick's Day, once again with old Kops and 'bathing queens':

After a few rounds of drinks and dinner the custard pie ingredient was stirred in by Del Lord, who threw a huge whipped cream cake at Billy Bevan while Monta Blue was preparing to introduce Sennett . . .

Blue extolled Sennett as the greatest teacher of timing in show business. He said, 'There was always a race between Tom Ince and D. W. Griffith to see who could put most thrills into a picture. Then along came Sennett, and where Ince and Griffith pushed one guy over a cliff, Mack pushed nine. We love you, Mack. You're a lousy golfer but you make great pictures.'

The mention of Griffith was poignant, as the great pioneer of the movies had been laid to rest the year before, at the end of July 1948, the service held at Hollywood's Masonic Temple and attended by a small crowd of old-timers. Louis B. Mayer and Sam Goldwyn were honorary pallbearers, but Hollywood had buried Griffith long before. His own last attempt at a comeback had been as a consultant for a Hal Roach movie, *One Million B.C.*, in 1939, of which he was reputed to have directed a couple of scenes. As rebuffed as the cave man, he had spent his last years alone, drinking, and died of a cerebral haemorrhage in his apartment-hotel. Mack would have looked at the flower-strewn casket with the most sombre reflections.

So bring on the custard pies! 1949 also saw the fruition of a project long mooted – a compilation film of Keystone and Sennett productions. Entitled *Down Memory Lane*, it was released by Eagle Lion Films in August, and incorporated footage from later sound shorts such as *Sing, Bing, Sing* and Fields's *The Dentist*. Another project, a biographical picture 'developed' by Paramount, to tell the tale of Mack and Mabel, was often cited and as often postponed. John Lund was supposed to play Sennett, with Betty Hutton as Mabel, as the 'King and Queen of Comedy'. Paramount announced on 18 April that 'the project is on the schedule as one of the most important productions ever undertaken by the studio, and it promises to be one of the greatest in the history of the screen'. But the film languished long in 'development', and was never made.

Sennett still dispensed his views whenever opportunity knocked, informing the *Hollywood Citizen-News*, in the run-up to the release of the compilation film in 1949, that:

Sennett honoured by his peers

## CHEESECAKE WAS CHEESECAKE IN 1918, SAYS MACK SENNETT

The white-haired producer says you can see more in this age of atom bombs and French bathing suits. But you can't trust what you see.

'When you looked at my girls,' he snorted, 'you knew what you were look-ing at was all theirs. Nowadays, with these falsies and things, a man doesn't know what to believe in . . .

'My girls,' he said with a reminiscent gleam in his eye, 'had effeminate shapes. They were pleasingly plump and rounded all over, and they had hips, by golly . . .'

In 1950, Sennett was again celebrating, this time his seventieth birthday, which for some reason was set at 30 April instead of the real date of 17 January. *Variety* reported on the event at White Oak Park: 'Oldsters mostly sat around and yakked about the good old days although there was horseback riding for those still limber enough to clamber aboard . . .'

Mack was still limber enough to be planning future projects, including a book, entitled 'The Quince', which he described as 'a Mack Sennett comedy in novelized form'. Doubleday publishers were apparently interested, and the leading characters, according to Sennett, were

J. Wallace Twist, a romantic and likeable show-off, Jack Ransome, a suave and shrewd bogus genealogist; Charlie Wellington, young and personable, but predatory; Mary, a co-ed whose heart beats only for Johnny, a young aviation cadet, and a friendly police dog, a singing crow, an ornery black cat and an heroic bullfrog.

In the event, clearly Doubleday passed.

Sennett was not, however, ready yet to give up on Paramount's foot-dragging over the 'Mack and Mabel' story, regaling the *Daily News* of 14 February 1950 with his favoured version of the tale which was to be the basis for the film:

'Mabel and I met when we were both extras at the old Biograph studio in New York more than 40 years ago . . . It was a sweet romance, boy and girl stuff. Once I gave her a little $2.50 cameo ring. You never heard such raves. It was the most wonderful thing to her . . .

'I was too busy making both of us big successes . . . too busy working to romance her or take her out. I had 16 movie companies under me and whenever she wanted to see me I had a business appointment. You can't expect a beautiful girl to sit home and let those beautiful clothes stand in the closet . . .'

After 'seven or eight years' of being a 'movie studio widow' Mabel quit both Sennett's heart and his movies. She later married one of his actors, Lew Cody. She died soon after, in 1930.

Sennett never married.

Today the comedy king, white haired and jolly, lives alone in Hollywood's oldest apartment house on busy Hollywood Boulevard. His jaunty figure is a familiar sight on the street he helped to make famous.

But if Sennett had to do it over, he said, he would trade some of that fame for love. He would rewrite the script of their romance and give it a happy ending.

'I wish I'd married her,' he said.

But Sennett had already rewritten the script, several times . . .

In 1951, at a ceremony held at the Academy of Motion Picture Arts and Sciences, Sennett handed the Academy's librarian, Margaret Herrick, an immense collection comprising his companies' records, saved both from the wreck of Triangle–Keystone and the Sennett studios, the production files, scripts and 40,000 stills that form the present-day archive. Much of this had been in storage, but some of it was apparently kept in his apartment, a living memory through which he riffled and meandered during the long, lonely hours. The archive was so immense that it would take decades to organize and catalogue, to the frustration of many early scholars. The Academy awarded Sennett a life membership, and a 'gold lifetime certificate', an honour he shared only with Bob Hope and British movie mogul J. Arthur Rank.

In 1952, he set off on a unique visit to France, to the Cannes Film Festival, for a special screening of vintage Sennett shorts, all silents, which 'drew belly laughs from an audience representing 39 countries'. Inevitable quips about bathing girls and swimsuits followed, with Sennett pronouncing 'French Bikini Isn't Sexy . . . the French girls show too much . . . But Sennett finally admitted that while he was on the Riviera he had worn dark glasses. "This may have colored my feelings," he said.'

In 1954, for some reason, he was celebrating his sixty-ninth birthday, though he had fairly and squarely celebrated his seventieth four years before. Mack seemed to be getting younger and younger. He was the subject of one of Ralph Edwards's successful if cloying *This Is Your Life* shows, appearing on live television with old friends Harold Lloyd, Jack Mulhall and the Kops represented by the two Conklins and Hank Mann, the oldest memorialist being Fritzi Scheff, a musical actress who remembered him from the chorus of *Mademoiselle Modiste* of 1906. Sennett's fury at being tricked into this jamboree, rather than the fake programme called 'So You Want to Publish a Book' which he thought he was in for, is palpable during the first ten minutes of the show. This was not a man who liked surprises.

Later in the year, Doubleday finally published a Mack Sennett book, not 'The Quince' but the autobiography written with Cameron Shipp, *King of Comedy*. The *Los Angeles Times* wrote, in November 1954:

Mack Sennett is the sad clown of legend. He was an awkward, outsize boy with big feet who had ambitions to sing grand opera and even dance. But he was condemned to make people laugh at his ungainly, rumpled person and at the amazing comedies he and his helpers literally slapped together.

As ever, 'when the legend becomes truth, print the legend'.

But the real Mack Sennett was, in fact, fading out. Royalties from the book were not spectacular. Like almost everyone else in Hollywood, he had the tax man on his tail, and eventually settled in

1956, paying $500 on liabilities of about $10,000 claimed from 1949 and subsequent years. The revenue's report was quoted in the *L.A. Times* on 9 May 1956:

'The taxpayer reports his age as being 75; however, taxpayers' attorney indicated that it is probably closer to 80,' the report continued. 'Taxpayer's income includes $227 received annually from the 20th Century retirement fund. Taxpayer is also employed on occasions by various studios, which provides him with the funds for a modest living existence.

Sennett's assets were listed as several outdated motion picture shorts and it was noted that he had neither an automobile nor a television set. A camera received in an appearance on the television program This Is Your Life was 'sold to realize cash.'

Sennett lives in a $125-a-month furnished apartment on Hollywood Blvd., the report continued, and 'does his own cooking.'

In 1957, Sennett had a prostate operation and then returned to his apartment. He still claimed to be working on his novel, now tentatively titled, after his mother's old motto, 'Don't Step on My Dreams'. He was trying to sell the work to comedian Jackie Gleason as a film property, 'an ideal motion picture vehicle for you and Art Carney to satisfy the public's thirst for humor that will be so sadly lacking in the months to come, not only on television but the screen as well'. A secretary, Joe Madison, was also helping him to type out new scripts, or so he claimed to the *Los Angeles Examiner*:

'I have a whole new career in that thing,' he said (pointing to a typewriter near a window of his living room) . . . he is rewriting his old classics in modern dress for a new generation of film fans 'who prefer good wholesome comedy to horror pictures and distressing social dramas staged against the background of a worried world.'

Alas, the fans had moved on. But Mack was rewriting the old Mabel Normand vehicle *Molly O'* as '*When Grandma Was a Girl*, with the opening scene in a modern television studio. Then we flash back to the lovely casual days before the world began to get the jim-jams.' Working with his secretary, 'from 9 in the morning till noon, six days a week', Sennett continued to revisit his dreams.

A syndicated piece, by journalist Vernon Scott, appeared in August 1958:

## COMEBACK DREAM STIRS MACK SENNETT

HOLLYWOOD – Mack Sennett, one-time king of the movies who luxuriated in mansions with gold bathtubs, lives today in a small apartment overlooking a gasoline station . . . in near poverty.

More powerful in his day than Cecil B. DeMille, Sam Goldwyn and Jesse Lasky combined, Mr. Sennett spends his time feeding pigeons . . .

Cheery and hopeful at 78, Mr. Sennett sat in the lobby of the apartment building (primarily a haven for elderly women) and explained, 'I'd invite you up to my suite, but the afternoon sun gets terribly warm on the balcony.'

There is no balcony.

He was dressed in a shiny, bespotted brown suit. His necktie was splattered with food, but Mr. Sennett's eyes were alert and merry . . .

'Someday they're going to make a picture of my life,' he went on. 'It will be a story about comedy and laughs. I always trusted myself on picking talent.'

The old man kept decrying modern comedy, and producers who have their mind on 'big productions, on spectacles, on murder, on seduction'.

On 26 April 1959, an article by *New York Times* writer Murray Schumach took up the story:

Sennett lifted his hat politely as an elderly lady passed the piazza in front of the apartment hotel where he lives.

'It's all very well and good to try for gag lines. But you have to know when not to talk. Now Bill Fields, when he worked for me, he knew about that. Our writers would work out a situation. Bill would do the lines, and then, when he came to the topper, he would go into pantomime and hit them right in the belly.

'Bill was a man who knew that chuckles have to build up to a belly laugh. We don't have the belly laughs any more. And people can get tired of nothing but polite chuckles. Damn tired.'

The famous producer of about 1,000 movies paused to let a noisy truck go down the street.

'Next thing', he resumed, 'is sympathy. Now Charlie Chaplin. Everybody thinks of him for his pantomime. And he is great. But he had an instinct for sympathy . . .

'I remember one day we were working on a movie and Ben Turpin came over to me and said: "I'm supposed to be the hero, but at the end of the movie this other guy gets the girl. What do I get?"

'"You get sympathy," I told him. "That's what you get."'

Sennett was being looked after by his secretary–companion, Joe Madison, and his literary agent, Reece Halsey, and Halsey's wife. By his eightieth birthday, on 17 January 1960, he was too frail to take care of his physical needs and Halsey arranged for him to be admitted to the Motion Picture Country Home in Woodland Hills. According to Mrs Halsey: 'He fought tooth and nail against being taken there . . . He was cussing all the way. Once there, though, he was delighted.'

Mack made the best of a new audience. He showed his fellow patients a print of *Tillie's Punctured Romance* and talked again about the old days. By July, he was planning again, telling UIP hacks about a new television series in the making:

'It'll all be shot new – no old film clips . . . The girls will wear the newest bathing suits. The Kops will be the same. But the bathing suits are the eye-catcher. After all, who'd want to look at a girl in an old-fashioned bathing suit? You've got to keep young and up with the times.

'My show will have only one purpose – to make people laugh. There'll be beautiful girls to look at and plenty of action. And with a young fella like me around, things will keep hopping.'

On 5 November 1960, at 2.45 a.m., Sennett died at the hospital of a coronary thrombosis, following unsuccessful surgery. One of his last acts, in August, had been to add his voice to those protesting at the fact that Charlie Chaplin's name was not included among the 1,500 brass stars being embedded in the sidewalk of Hollywood Boulevard. The business people footing the bill objected to Chaplin's politics. Sennett could still 'rumble up a storm', declaring:

That's ridiculous . . . This is a matter of art, not politics. Charlie was the greatest comedian we ever had on the screen. I might add that I don't know anything about politics. I'm not a Communist. I'm an Irish Catholic.

A requiem mass took place at the Church of the Blessed Sacrament in Hollywood, attended by all the usual suspects: Louise Fazenda, Hank Mann, Chester Conklin, Del Lord, Frank Capra, actors, directors, producers and writers. Agent Reece Halsey told the press that 'Sennett was dictating a plot for a Broadway play up until a half hour before they rolled him into surgery.' Interment was held back because his brother, in Canada, was suggesting that he should be buried in the family plot in Northampton, Massachusetts. But in the event he was buried in the Holy Cross Cemetery. The *Los Angeles Mirror* added, after Reece Halsey's remarks:

Paramount Studios owns the rights to Sennett's life story but has never been able to work out a satisfactory story line, mainly because of a lack of 'love interest'.

It was the Old Man himself, as he was affectionately known to two generations of movie people, who suggested a theme.

'How come', he said to the writers, 'that I never fell in love and married?'

He gave them the question but he never supplied the answer.

# CHAPTER THIRTY

# Epilogue
## (or *Mabel Won By a Bear*)

In the end, it was a Broadway musical, *Mack and Mabel*, that tried to retrieve the mislaid 'love interest' and present Mack Sennett to a new generation. Opening in October 1974 on Broadway, it only lasted sixty-six performances before closing, but had a better run in a London revival in 1995, playing for eight months. Originally starring Robert Preston and Bernadette Peters, the show struggled with its inevitably unhappy ending, which no amount of mythologizing could avoid. Mack sang about 'when movies were movies and you paid a dime to escape', and Mabel sang that 'time heals everything but loving you', as she declined into the world of scandals and drugs. But it was difficult to make a great love story out of two people who had plenty of opportunities to get together but didn't.

The question has been posed for long enough. What, in the end, is the answer?

The vital clues, I believe, lie in the quoted press cuttings of Mack Sennett's ongoing plans for a comeback, which veered between ideas for new scripts, reconstructions of the old and the most promising project, which almost got off the ground but eventually fell away: scripting his own life as fiction.

The lifelong romance of Mack and Mabel is, I am convinced, an invention. In Mack's public comments, the idea of this unrequited love as the main theme of his life appears for the first time in 1950, as part of his attempts to provide a proper narrative for Paramount's projected bio-picture.

'It was a sweet romance, boy and girl stuff,' Sennett told the press, referring to the earliest days. When Mack met Mabel, she was, it is true, a teenager, only seventeen years old, but he was already twenty-nine. Most witnesses of the period who knew them both, like Minta Durfee, affirmed that Mack and Mabel had been

Ford Sterling between Mack and Mabel – *Barney Oldfield's Race for Life*

linked romantically for several years before the Mabel–Mae Busch
bust-up of 1915.

In the context of the times, though, this could have meant several
things: that they were lovers as we understand it today, having sexual relations; that they were living through a long, unrequited engagement, which did not involve sex; or that despite their 'steady' status,
each was having affairs with other people, and eventually they
arrived at a stage where there was no point pretending any different.

We can revisit my speculations about Mabel's possible anxiety
about the death by venereal infection of one of her baby brothers –
and about Mack Sennett's sexual orientation. A man who never married, appears never to have shared a residence with a woman, was a
renowned 'bachelor' who lived with a succession of male companions including an ex-boxer who was his valet and various friends
who shared the capacious rooms of the Westmoreland mansion, and
whom so many people affirm was a 'man's man' who enjoyed all the
manly pursuits of golfing, fishing, hiking, smoking cigars in the bath
and hawking into spittoons, inevitably invites speculation that he
was, in our modern term, gay. The speculation is increased when one

realizes how conveniently the myth of Mack and Mabel provides a heterosexual shield: Mack never married because he only ever loved one woman and pined for her, after her death, for ever more.

Who can look into a human heart, even someone we think we know closely, let alone a person we have never met, who died over forty years ago, and whose defining moments, emotionally, intellectually, artistically, were lived forty years before that?

The myth could be true, but that is highly improbable. Ben Turpin, whose deep love for his suffering wife was evident, who accompanied her in her crippled state to Catholic shrines to pray for miracle cures, and who could truly be said to have had a love of his life, nevertheless married another woman after Carrie's death and enjoyed her companionship in his later years – much the more common pattern.

The paper trail on Mack's private life reveals, despite his obsessive protection of that privacy, three women linked to him romantically, apart from Mabel – Mae Busch, Phyllis Haver and Marjorie Beebe, all three actresses in his employ. These links were nevertheless tenuous, found in obscure sources or isolated reports and the scattered oral tales of sexual peccadilloes, which do not amount to a great deal. The Sennett Bathing Girls could have been a classic casting-couch pool, though one might think more would have been made of this during twenty years of press attention, in a period when Hollywood's 'sins' were sure-fire circulation builders. The evidence that Mack employed his 'droit de seigneur' frequently is thin to non-existent. Like many other such movie set-ups, there was a great deal of emphasis on the prevention of easy liaisons of this kind. Nevertheless, hanky panky will out, even when we remind ourselves that sexual mores were somewhat different BC – Before Contraception protected umarried women from the consequences of casual sex. To note another relevant fact, Mabel had no children and the only intimation of a pregnancy remains the rumour about her miscarriage of a child by Samuel Goldwyn, sourced only in oral gossip.

The paper trail, such as it is, also fails to support the 'gay' theory. All the male companions linked to Sennett as residing with him, or close buddies, carry the usual trail of wives. There remain the tendrils of gossip, like the tale of Chaplin's bearding of Mack about his 'queer' nature, quoted by Canadian author Charles Foster. Foster, who interviewed Sennett one year before his death, in 1959, did not raise this issue with the ailing Mack. But he does tell another curious story, claiming that Mack, in the presence of Reece Halsey, his friend and literary agent, and 'after more than a few glasses of Scotch', confessed to Foster that he had been the killer of William Desmond Taylor. 'It was me they saw leaving the house,' Foster quotes Mack saying. 'I stayed there for about an hour after I shot him, looking for things that might incriminate Mabel. I found some letters she had written but I daren't tell her I had them.' Foster continues:

Reece asked him why he had killed Taylor. Sennett opened his eyes and said clearly, 'Because he was a bloody queer [homosexual] and stole Mabel by giving her drugs,' he said. Then he closed his eyes and fell asleep. When he woke up he claimed to have no memory of what he had said. 'I knew nothing about the murder. Absolutely nothing.'

In the spirit of the hall of mirrors that has characterized our search for the real amid the made-up, this muddies the waters even further. Like Socrates, we end up humbly offering that we only know that we don't know.

None the less, the reader is entitled to the author's personal conclusions, even if only in the form of a hunch. After peering into the murky crystal ball, and following the cat's cradle of evidence and obfuscation, I have become convinced that Sennett, while indulging in occasional heterosexual dalliances, was essentially homosexual in his inclinations, though how active a 'gay' life he led in his secluded mansions, when mother was absent, we genuinely cannot know. This did not of course preclude tender feelings, love or passion for Mabel Normand, though it clearly precluded a commitment to a marriage or long-term liaison with any woman. In the absence of a 'smoking gun', apart from the Keystone moment of Mack rearing up from Mae Busch, *déshabillé*, to confront Mabel's blind rage, and Stuart Heisler's breathless eavesdropping at the editing table, one is left, in the end, with the kind of verdict common in the Scottish legal system: 'not proven'.

Does it matter? Apart from the urge to categorize, honour or stigmatize, or the plain inevitable curiosity about 'who does what to whom', what effect might the pinning down of Mack Sennett's sexual orientation have on our story?

As an outsider, a person much aware of his own nonconformity in more than one regard, Sennett viewed the world through his own peculiar prism – as outsiders do, seeing in predictable social mores something basically alien. What is taken for granted seems absurd, both in reality and art. The open question itself is paradoxically revealing about the true nature of the man. Sennett wrote, at the end of his book, *King of Comedy*:

I wanted to tell about the comedies and how we made them, and about the funny fellows and pretty girls who acted in them. They are a lost breed. Their like may never walk, tumble or prat-fall again. Most of all I wanted you to meet Mabel Normand.

But it is clear that Mack's image of Mabel Normand was as much a fantasy as the image he constructed to portray himself. This was the image preserved by her friends, such as Minta Durfee, who, in her eighties, was telling interviewers: 'I can't rave enough about her . . . she was a little imp, and she was a lot of fun . . . a remarkable, wonderful girl . . .' A lost child in the dark, slimy forest.

But Mabel was not, in reality, Cinderella, and Mack Sennett was never Prince Charming. Toughened up in the world of work and years in the chorus, living in the accommodations of impecunious actors in the harsh world of early twentieth-century New York, he became apprenticed to the most ambitious workhorse in the history of early motion pictures, D. W. Griffith, the man who more than anyone else made a novelty art form into America's most powerful cultural force. Mabel herself would not have remained long an innocent in this world of endless possibilities, if indeed she was as innocent as she was portrayed in her early career as a 'Gibson Girl' model. Success did not come to the meek, and her burning ambition derived from a strong inner core. By 1916 – aged twenty-four! – she had her own studio, short-lived as it turned out to be. Her life off-set was a renowned swirl of luxury living, parties on yachts, diamonds and swanky clothes, not to speak of her illicit drug needs. An imp perhaps, but no shrinking violet.

Mack and Mabel were business partners of a kind, as well as friends or lovers, and determined fellow travellers along the road of making up the movies as they went along. Historical timing had handed them a tremendous opportunity which they seized with enormous energy and passion. This passion for the movies, was to prove, to use the unavoidable cliché, 'bigger than both of them', and they surrendered to it completely.

Orson Welles called the film studio 'the greatest train set' an adult child could have, and one can imagine the impact of being present at the very moment these toy factories were expanding into industrial plants. It was this, I suggest, that was Mack Sennett's true love: The business, the craft and the art.

If Sennett was consumed by a lust, it was a lust to create, to enable the men and women he gathered together to turn his private fantasies into those celluloid dreams. It was this that caused him to wander about in his dotage, blinking, along Hollywood Boulevard, before the brass stars were fixed in, telling anyone who would listen about the way gags worked. Better than money, better than sex, the buzz of turning up every day, to orchestrate the symphony of chaos, play fantastic tunes on all these raggedy instruments, the power to make base metals into gold.

As his empire grew, Mack simply grew apart from Mabel. Clearly, in public they did plan marriage, postpone and re-plan it, and perhaps the Mae Busch incident did mark the end of this delusion, or perhaps Mack and Mabel were already living separate lives at that point. In any case, as we have seen, the grand Triangle Conspiracy was taking up most of Mack's attention by then.

Mabel, shrewd as she was, could see that Mack's professional attention was defused in many directions. He was concerned with his ensemble, hiring more actors, staff and crews. She bargained for her studio, but it was still an auxiliary in the Keystone–Triangle plan. The bottom line was that this was an issue of power, power to control her creativity as a separate force. Sennett could not, in the end, provide it, and so she moved on elsewhere.

Did Mabel love Mack? Minta Durfee had no doubts: 'She never loved any man but Mack Sennett!' But it was a strange love, that swirled away in different directions, so fragile that it could be derailed completely by one casting-couch sin. Once again, nothing is impossible, but we are left with too many improbabilities, too many contradictory strands. In any case, once Mabel left Keystone for Goldwyn, her life was entangled in other spheres, among people who might attend Sennett's dinner parties but were not his inner circle of wisecracking gagsters and laughsmiths.

Gay or straight, besotted or business-minded, assassin of William Desmond Taylor or geriatric fantasist, there is no doubt that Mack loved Mabel. He loved her, primarily, as he loved all his performers.

He loved talent, and provided the wherewithal to his beloved actors to enhance it. He wanted money for the talent, not the talent for the money. This, above all, was his downfall. Despite all his railing about Harry Langdon being an actor who should never have tried to be a businessman, he was temperamentally in the same boat. For twenty years, he managed to keep the business balls in the air, to weave and duck and see his way through, but this defeated him in the end. He had his ruthless moments, his strategic withdrawal from Triangle's breakdown, sacking staff, ordering 'cheap and speedy stories regardless of quality', his cutting of corners after the Wall Street Crash, but these were in the end sacrifices – borne, as these ever are, by other people – to preserve the core idea.

In the end, it was all or nothing for Sennett. Despite the mumblings about writing scripts and novels, and the guest appearances and occasional consultation jobs offered by friends who wanted to help him out of a hole, there was no working existence for Mack Sennett except as Mack Sennett, King of Comedy. And if there was no working existence for Mack Sennett, there was no Mack Sennett, only a ghost, walking up and down Hollywood Boulevard, tipping his hat to old ladies and cops on the beat, attending anniversaries, receiving awards, eulogized as the icon of an age that had died out long before his own demise.

On 17 December 1982, a small ad appeared in the pages of *Variety*:

MACK SENNETT ADMINISTRATION BUILDING
FOR LEASE

ALLEN REALTY INC. Call for appt.

2,200 sq. ft., $2,000 Month. Historic old office building overlooking Ventura Blvd. (Ventura Blvd. Address). Originally an estate home in the 30s, later a school, and now tastefully restored as production offices. 50' Executive Office Suite with Cathedral Beams, Fireplace, and indoor rock spa grotto. Control Air and Heat, full Kitchen, 2 Baths., and 8,000 sq. ft. of private grounds with fruit trees and huge rock waterfall. Drive by 12528 Ventura Blvd. – don't you dare disturb the mad film maker who is moving out next week.

# Coda

Good night, troupers

## A HAREM KNIGHT (1926)
Starring Ben Turpin
Selected titles confirmed by Sennett:

- It happened in Barabia - where Variety is the Spice of Love
- While the police awaited an inspiration - the Rajah worked up a perspiration
- Petunia - the Rajah's sister - someone had put concrete in her beauty cream
- Kiss them - love them - then detour - that was Rodney St. Clair
- 'My brown eyed fawn - Allah be praised!'
- 'I warn you, that spank will be heard around the world!'
- 'Get out of my clothes and beat it while I'm still reasonable!'
- 'It was Saturday night in the Harem -'
- Like most married men, the Rajah loved solitaire -
- 'My Lord, there comes from the Nile one who shall make thee sit up and percolate -'
- 'Keep me no longer in suspense - remove the seven veils!'
- 'Draw, Rajie! Don't stand there looking like an overstuffed sofa!'
- 'They must have eaten my jumping beans!'
- 'As the bride said when her husband fell into Niagara - that's over.'

'Sir, breakfast is served - and the wife is waiting!'
'The wife? Whose wife?'
'Yours, sir - you forget you were married at dawn!'
'You're crazy - nothing like that ever dawned on me!'
'Papa, why do you keep Mama waiting?'
'Oh, death! Where is thy sting?'

# WEBER AND FIELDS STORY (1916) – rough synopsis:

The rear of a middle class house is shown and Weber and Fields enter.

They are hoboes and are trying to steal a pie that has been placed on the back window sill. They are stopped by a dog and the farmer with a gun shooting out of window drives them away . . .

At another house Weber and Fields are promised five dollars by an old maid if they will take her pet cat Minnie down to the beach and drown it, as she is moving and will not trust the cat to anyone else . . .

Weber and Fields are shown trying to drown the cat. There is an argument about drowning the cat. Fields shows Weber how to put cat in bag with paving stone enclosed. To do this he practises on Weber putting the rope around his neck. Both kiss cat goodbye. Neither has the heart to drown it. They wonder: 'HOW WILL WE KNOW THE CAT IS DROWNED?'

Weber tells Fields that it is very important that the cat is really drowned as they will not get the money if it turns up alive. He reminds Fields that every cat has nine lives. They are in a quandary how to tell the cat is drowned when Weber says: 'PUT ME IN THE BAG; WHEN THE CAT IS DROWNED I'LL PULL THE STRING AND YOU CAN DRAG ME OUT.'

Fields puts Weber in bag with the cat. Ties the neck of the bag with rope. Attaches the end of the rope to handle of car, sits on other end, pushes bag overboard and awaits results . . . He watches shoreline but doesn't notice string is being pulled, suddenly sees it and pulls bag out of water. Weber's head still with hat on appears. Weber spits water out and says: 'IT AIN'T DEAD YET.'

Fields ties the string around Weber's neck by a single stroke closing the bag around his neck. He then pushes Weber under water again by pressing on his hat . . .

# A DASH OF COURAGE, 1916
Working title: Chloroform story.
Starring, Gloria Swanson, Wallace Beery, Harry Gribbon . . .

'THE APPLE OF THE PUBLIC'S EYE' is the opening sub-title used to introduce Wallace Beery as the Chief of Police. He is surrounded by the police, who carefully assist him to dress, and with a nail file start to manicure his nails. After he is properly groomed, he reads to his men from a newspaper, the

following: 'OLD POLICEMAN'S HOME FUND. GRAND RALLY
PROMISED. HON. HENRY COOPE DUE ON DAY TRAIN WILL PAY
FIRST VISIT TO HOKUM CENTER TO LOOSEN OUR CITIZEN'S PURSE
STRINGS WITH HIS ELOQUENCE.' The chief then orders the men
to decorate the station in honor of the expected arrival, and
sitting behind his desk he reads the paper. Pursuant with his
orders the police start decorating the station house, and Burg
starts to nail flag on the desk. The nail is driven thru the
wood into Chief's knee, the Chief takes fright and starts
bawling out the cops . . .

     (later)

  . . . the auto comes to a long flight of steps and runs down
same, striking a wall at the bottom and exploding. Policemen,
Gribbon and Gloria are blown up in the air and go flying
through the clouds. Bob is on his wheel riding along calling
up in the air to Gloria. Gloria falls from clouds, and lights
on Bob's handle bars. Convicts and Woodward ride up to Bob.
The fake police fall from the clouds to the ground, also
Gribbon. The convicts take off under arrest. Opperman,
Woodward, Bob and Gloria congratulate each other on their several escapes. Woodward makes Bob a money present, and FADE
OUT.

# FATTY AND MABEL ADRIFT
Synopsis, 1916.

| | |
|---|---|
| Roscoe Arbuckle . . . . . . | A Farm Hand |
| Mabel Normand . . . . . . . | His Sweetheart |
| Frank Hayes . . . . . . . . | Her Father |
| May Wells . . . . . . . . . | Her Mother |
| Al St John . . . . . . . . | A Neighbors Son |
| (Wayland Trask . . . . . . | Chief Crook) |
| (Glen Cavender . . . . . . | Real Estate Dealer) |

Mabel has biz taking biscuits from stove, puts them on table
and goes to window, looks out and watches sunset. Roscoe is on
beach with dog, fishing, biz of catching large shark, he
fights on beach with it, dog joins the fight, shark and Roscoe
fall, he gets up, shark jumps back into sea, dog chases it,
swims out, in water, Roscoe calls him back, Roscoe goes to
house, followed by dog, Mabel meets them on porch and all go
in to table where Roscoe has biz of trying to bite hard bis-
cuit, can't be done, Mabel tries, breaks plate.

# CODA

Meantime St John comes down street, goes to Roscoe's window and looks in, biz of dog seeing St John and barking at him. Roscoe goes out and catches him and they fight, and Roscoe throws St John out and he falls in water, Mabel meantime in house, comes out with dog. Meantime St John throws rock which hits Roscoe, Roscoe sics dog on St John, who runs, chased by dog. Dog returns to Roscoe and Mabel and they go in house.

Meantime St John goes to café where he is held up by two crooks who take him into cave. In ante chamber in cave Trask is on, biz of eating dynamite etc, when he sets off and sees St John and two crooks. Crooks push St John into ante chamber and St John tries to get away but Trask grabs him. Trask gives him card, St John hires him for dirty work, Trask sends John and two crooks off with tools. Meantime it starts to rain and St John and crooks start for cottage thru rain.

Meantime Roscoe and Mabel in cottage discover storm which is howling and Mabel has biz of going to bed, Roscoe kissing her goodnight etc, and she takes dog to bed with her, Roscoe reading, then puts out light and also goes to bed, but later is awakened by storm and he and Mabel watch lightning flashes thru window, etc., to point where Roscoe pulls down shades and he and Mabel go back to bed and sleep.

Meantime St John and crooks arrive outside and have biz in rain of cutting away supports under house and it is pushed and floated out to beach, where waves carry it out into ocean.

Meantime St John and two crooks go back to and enter cave, where they see St John pay off Trask, and at sight of the money they decide to trim St John and have biz of getting him into poker game.

Meantime the house floats out to sea, and Roscoe suddenly awakens inside to find the bed floating around the room, he looks around and Mabel's bed floats in along side of his, they awaken and look out of window and suddenly discover they (are) out in ocean. Wild biz of fright follows and Roscoe gets over the idea of sending dog back for help. He dives around and secures cloth and pencil and writes note and ties it to dog's collar and sends dog swimming out window.

Meantime St John and crooks are playing cards and St John steadily wins from the crooks.

Meantime the dog swims to shore and starts running toward Hayes house.

Meantime on house Roscoe and Mabel climb to roof and cut their way thru to top.

Meantime Hayes and Wells have gone to bed and dog runs in and jumps against door. Hayes awakens and goes out and lets dog in,

he finds note on collar and awakens Wells, he and Wells get on
tandem bycycle and start for town for help, first phoning the
cops who rush to water and get in motor boat and start to
rescue.

Meantime Mabel and Roscoe hail a passing ship which does not
pay any attention to them.

Meantime Cavender, a real estate agent (who has sold the
cottage to Hayes as a wedding present for Roscoe and Mabel) is
sitting on his yacht when Wells and Hayes ride in and are
rescued from water as they ride off wharf. Cavender is told

trouble and he takes Wells and Hayes on his boat and starts
out to rescue.

Meantime in cave St John has won all the coin from the two
crooks, and Trask, in his part of cave, carelessly tosses a
cigar away which falls into barrel of powder and explodes,
blows side of cave out which falls thru next set on two crooks
and Trask, and St John recovers money Trask took from him,
when rock from roof falls in and knocks him out.

Meantime Cavender's boat and two police boats rush past each
other in water and police boat sinks, when Cavender's boat
arrive(s) at the floating cottage and Mabel and Roscoe are
rescued.

## MABEL AND BEAR (undated)
Synopsis:

Mabel is going to the picnic. First lover comes and whistles,
comes in and Mabel and himself depart for picnic. Second lover
comes and Mabel's mother tells him Mabel has gone to the picnic. He follows. At picnic boy in party finds field mouse and
when Mabel and first lover are sitting near tree, boy puts
mouse in lover's pocket. Mabel playfully puts her hand in and
the mouse frightens her. She gets mad at first lover and sends
him away. He meets his rival going to the girl with a big box
of candy, gets the candy and goes back to the girl with the
candy as a peace offering. Lays it on the bench and tells her
that when she makes up with him he will give it to her.
Meantime second lover slips up and exchanges the mouse for the
candy. Lover gives her the candy and the mouse jumps out for
the second time. She gets mad at first lover and second steps
in and gets solid. First wanders away and finds boys playing
with bear skin. Gets boy to put on the bear skin and scare his
rival. Boy goes to rival and Mabel and rival deserts. Mabel
phones for constables. Rival is laughing at second lover for
being scared at the fake bear when a real one comes along and
takes after him. Real bear chases crowd and constables.
Another bear chases Mabel. Second lover has given the candy he
took out of box and she feeds the bear on this and wins him
over. Both rivals see Mabel won by a bear.

THE END

308

# Notes on Sources

## Abbreviations

AMPAS-SC, Sennett Collection, Margaret Herrick Library, Academy of Motion
    Picture Arts and Sciences, Los Angeles.
BFI, British Film Institute Library, London.
BLT, Bruce Long's 'Taylorology'.
NYPL, New York Library of the Performing Arts, New York.
NYDM, *New York Dramatic Mirror*.

## Prologue: That Rag Time Band

### Page

xi    'the greatest monument . . .' Gene Fowler, *Father Goose*, Covici
       Friede Publishers, New York, 1934, p. 370
xi    'look well from all sides . . .' architectural plans, AMPAS-SC
xii   'All creative intellectual work . . .' *Mack Sennett Weekly*, 2.12.1917,
       AMPAS-SC
xii   'There is no form of American industry', ibid, 4.9.1917, AMPAS-SC

### PART I: HIS HIDDEN TALENT

## Chapter One: Trail of the Pioneers

4    'Well furnished by good maple . . .' *Tread of Pioneers, Annals of
     Richmond County & Vicinity*, Richmond County Historical Society,
     Richmond, Quebec, 1968.
4    'The beautiful little spring . . .' ibid
5    'The Sinnots and the Foys . . .' etc, Mack Sennett, *King of Comedy*,
     Doubleday & Co., New York, 1954, Mercury House, San Francisco,
     1990, p. 14.
5    'I mooed on lonely roads . . .' ibid, p. 18
6    'There is no American who, as a boy . . .' *Motion Picture Classic*,
     November 1918, NYPL
7    'As a result . . .' Mack Sennett, *King of Comedy*, ibid, p. 17
7    'Naturally a great deal of attention . . .' Pierre Pageau, 'Mack Sennett
     au Quebec', *Journal of Film Preservation*, 58/59, 1999
8    'All the kids yelling at us . . .' Gene Fowler, *Father Goose*, ibid, p. 46

## Chapter Two: 'You Mean the Sinnott House Is Noisy?'

9    'A Falstaffian Portuguese . . .' etc, *Father Goose*, ibid, p. 22
10   'In my day, it was commonplace . . .' Mack Sennett, *King of Comedy*, ibid, p. 19
11   'This kid . . . will never be a singer . . .' ibid, p. 21
11   'The people of Northampton . . .' *The Northampton Book, 300 Years in the Life of a New England Town 1654–1954*, The Tercentenary Committee, North Mass., 1954
12   'Raw Materials for the Mount Tom . . .' *The Look of Paradise, a Pictorial History of Northampton, Mass.* by Jaqueline Van Voris, Canaan, New Hampshire, 1984
12   'Several immense circular tanks . . .' *Picturesque Hampden*, ed. Charles F. Warner, Picturesque Publishing, Northampton, Mass., 1892
13   'I said to Mother . . .' Mack Sennett, *King of Comedy*, ibid, p. 21
15   'Mack Sennett strutted into . . .' Gene Fowler, *Father Goose*, ibid, p. 49
15   'Charlie Chaplin, when he was young . . .' Mack Sennett, *King of Comedy*, ibid, p. 17

## Chapter Three: Ad Lib Comedy Biz

20   'eminent in the delineation of brusque . . .' *Chicago Tribune*, 3.20.1914, NYPL.
20   'close harmony quartet . . .' etc, Mack Sennett, *King of Comedy*, ibid, p. 42
21   'Kindly remove this bumbler . . .' ibid, p. 39
21   'there was a very large chorus . . .' NYDM, 6.14.1902, NYPL
21   'I had met a manufacturer of a tooth-wash . . .' *Billboard*, 8.18.1906, NYPL
22   'This musical comedy . . .' NYDM, 4.9.1904, NYPL
22   'Never give away everything . . .' Mack Sennett, *King of Comedy*, ibid, p. 40
22   'another sweetly sentimental . . .' etc, NYDM 4.20.1907, NYPL
23   'He came in more cautiously . . .' Mack Sennett, *King of Comedy*, ibid, p. 37

## Chapter Four: The State of the Art

25   'Mirror Film Criticisms . . .' NYDM, 7.25.1908, NYPL
25   'The Indian and the Child . . .' NYDM, 8.8.1908, NYPL
25   'There is an excellent . . .' NYDM, 7.11.1908, NYPL
26   'The story is not convincing . . .' NYDM, 8.1.1908, NYPL
26   'He was my day school . . .' Mack Sennett, *King of Comedy*, ibid p. 51
26   'One of our regular 'extra' people . . .' Mrs D. W. Griffith (Linda Arvidson), *When the Movies Were Young*, Dover Publications Inc, 1969, New York, p. 77
27   'burly bear-like figure . . .' Richard Schickel, *D. W. Griffith, An American Life*, Simon & Schuster, New York, 1984, p. 116

28    'dear Mom: I am doing fine . . .' Mack Sennett, *King of Comedy*, ibid, p. 35

30    'It was those Frenchmen . . .' ibid, p. 65

30    'This film appears frivolous . . .' NYDM, 7.11.1908, NYPL

## Chapter Five: Beyond the Curtain Pole

34    'Carpenters had been sent over . . .' etc, Mrs D.W. Griffith, *When the Movies Were Young*, ibid, p. 79

35    'After this picture was exhibited . . .' NYDM, 2.6.1909, NYPL

## Chapter Six: A Dash Through the Clouds

39    'the slaughter still goes on . . .' 'Modernity, Hyperstimulus, and the Rise of Popular Sensationalism', by Ben Singer, in *Cinema and the Invention of Modern Life*, edited by Leo Charney and Vanessa R. Schwartz, University of California Press, 1995, p. 81

40    'Comrades, comrades . . .' *Biograph Bulletin*, 3.13.1911, BFI

41    'London's a strange place . . .' *Toledo Blade*, 11.21.1908, NYPL

42    'The wind blew me into pictures . . .' *New York Evening World*, 3.8.1918, NYPL

43    'struggles as an orphan . . .' quoted in Betty Harper Fussell, *Mabel, Hollywood's First I Don't Care Girl*, Ticknor & Fields, New Haven & N.Y., 1982, p. 23

43    'to visit an aunt of mine . . .' clipping, NYPL

44    'I don't remember much . . .' *Toledo Times*, 9.21.1919, NYPL

44    'to seek her fortune . . .' Betty Harper Fussell, *Mabel*, ibid, p. 27

44    'On that particular day . . .' clipping, NYPL

45    'I worked in whatever Griffith . . .' Mack Sennett, *King of Comedy*, ibid, p. 64

46    'Mabel was like . . .' ibid, p. 110

## Chapter Seven: He Goes Big

49    'Three men were sitting in a hotel . . .' *Mack Sennett Weekly*, 1.1.1917, AMPAS-SC

53    'At It Again . . .' NYDM, 11.6.1912, NYPL

54    'Sergei was in a condescending humor . . .' Gene Fowler, *Father Goose*, ibid p. 138

54    'Hank Hopkins is a "rube" . . .' *Biograph Bulletins*, 7.25.1912, AMPAS

54    'Mack Sennet, director . . .' *Moving Picture World*, 9.12.1912, NYPL

54    'Two western reels . . .' NYDM, 9.11.1912, NYPL

## Chapter Eight: Consternation, et cetera . . .

59    'We did the best we could . . .' Mack Sennett, *King of Comedy*, ibid, p. 89

59    'was used chiefly as a place . . .' *Motion Picture Classic*, 11.1917, NYPL

62    'It has an odor,' the usher said . . .' Mack Sennett, *King of Comedy*, ibid, p. 65

63    'Orphis Noodle . . .' *Indianapolis Star*, 9.21.1909, NYPL

63    'In the spring of 1912 . . .' *Denver Times*, 5.4.1913, NYPL

66    'Mabel Normand is all that . . .' *Motography*, 4.19.1913, NYPL

66    'It's only a picture . . .' clipping, NYPL

66    'Pretty, Dashing Mabel . . .' *Minneapolis News*, 3.11.1913, NYPL

67    'Mack Sennett, director . . .' *Motion Picture World*, 10.26.1912, NYPL

## Chapter Nine: Love, Speed and Thrills – the Keystone Ethos

69    'The strangeness of this world . . .' Rae Beth Gordon, *Why the French Love Jerry Lewis*, Stanford University Press, Calif., 2001, p. 133

70    'a thief robs and kills . . .' ibid, p. 151

71    'probably issued and circulated . . .' *New York Times*, 7.12.1911, BFI

71    'there shall be no sensationalism . . .' *New York Times*, 5.14.1911, BFI

72    'There are certain characters . . .' *Motion Picture Classic*, 11.1918, NYPL

## Chapter Ten: The Clowns: Fatty's Fickle Falls

76    'When I'm tired of watching . . .' *Motion Picture*, 11.1916, NYPL

76    'Mr. Arbuckle was born to fame . . .' *Photoplay Magazine*, 8.1918, NYPL

78    'You are either going to say . . .' David Yallop, *The Day the Laughter Stopped*, St Martins Press, New York, 1976, p. 32

78    'Roscoe Arbuckle, the German comedian . . .' *Los Angeles Examiner*, 4.26.1910, NYPL

78    'China, Japan, India . . .' *Motion Picture*, 9.1914, NYPL

78    'a tremendous man . . .' Mack Sennett, *King of Comedy*, ibid, p. 195

79    'a man with a shock of grey hair . . .' David Yallop, *The Day the Laughter Stopped*, ibid, p. 38

79    'we worked out on the streets . . .' ibid, p. 53

80    'coffin factories, brickyards, lumber mills . . .' *New York Post*, 4.16.1936, NYPL

80    'We figure it out on paper . . .' *Photoplay*, 4.1916, NYPL

81    'Roscoe Arbuckle is doing some tremendous . . .' *Toledo Times*, 7.19.1914, NYPL

84    'Roscoe . . . took the camera . . .' Buster Keaton, *My Wonderful World of Slapstick*, Doubleday, 1960, Da Capo, 1982, p. 93

84    'Mr. Arbuckle has probably . . .' *New York Sun*, 7.29.1917, NYPL

84    'You don't throw like a shortstop . . .' Mack Sennett, *King of Comedy*, ibid, p. 139

85    'These people adored "Fatty" . . .' *Photoplay Journal*, 11.1918, NYPL

# Chapter Eleven: Charlie's Strange Predicament

87    'I left New York for California . . .' *Chicago Herald*, 7.18.1921, NYPL

90    'I had no idea what make-up . . .' *Charles Chaplin, My Autobiography*, Simon & Schuster, 1964, Pocket Books, New York, 1966, p. 148

92    'Father urged me to stay at home . . .' article: Comic Conkling, by Mary McAubrey, undated, NYPL

95    'My Dear Sid . . .' David Robinson, *Chaplin, His Life and Art*, William Collins Sons & Co., London 1985, Paladin Grafton Books, 1986, p. 131

98    'I loved Tillie . . . she was so human . . .' *Chicago Herald*, 9.15.1915, NYPL

99    'Ince and Sennett Coming East . . .' *Moving Picture World*, 8.1914, NYPL

# Chapter Twelve: Love and Money

102    'Words Mean Nothing . . .' *Toledo Blade*, 1.23.1917, NYPL

103    'Supervised By Sennett . . .' clippings, NYPL

104    'The following Monday . . .' Gloria Swanson, *Swanson on Swanson*, Michael Joseph, London, 1981, p. 47

105    'is a fearless little lady . . .' NYDM, 9.9.1916, NYPL

105    'light hair, hazel eyes . . .' *Chicago Tribune*, 3.7.1920, NYPL

105    'I was raised in an atmosphere of roasts . . .' *Motion Picture Classic*, 5.1919, NYPL

106    'the boys seemed to Louise . . .' clipping, NYPL

106    'a fierce-eyed individual . . .' *Motion Picture Classic*, ibid.

107    'The clouds rolled by . . .' *Photoplay*, 8.1915, NYPL

108    'Mabel and I were engaged . . .' Mack Sennett, *King of Comedy*, ibid, p. 103

108    'A Hollywood Newspaper Man . . .' etc, *The Sins of Hollywood, an Expose of Movie Vice*, May 1922, Hollywood Publishing Co., BLT

109    'Pathé blurted out . . .' Gene Fowler, *Father Goose*, ibid, p. 225

111    'Mabel Normand Fighting Death . . .' *Los Angeles Herald*, 9.30.1915, AMPAS clipping

112    'the Nat Goodwin Pier . . .' Betty Harper Fussell, *Mabel*, ibid, p. 80

112    'A Battle Royal . . .' etc, *The Sins of Hollywood*, ibid, BLT

# Chapter Thirteen: Of Mabel, Mammon and Mamma

114    'The new contracts beginning . . .' Letters, AMPAS-SC files.

117    'she is out of danger . . .' *Photoplayers Weekly*, 10.16.1915, NYPL

118    'It is further reported . . .' etc, BLT

119    'the most naïve person . . .' etc, Betty Harper Fussell, *Mabel*, ibid p. 83, 84

119    'Mack's production manager . . .' ibid, p. 84

120    'Mack didn't marry . . .' ibid, p. 85

120    'Personally Mr Sennett is not . . .' *Photoplay Journal*, 5.1920, NYPL

121 'gambling syndicate that tried . . .' Charles Foster, *Stardust and Shadows, Canadians in Early Hollywood*, Dundurn Press, Toronto, p. 328

121 'He gave Phyllis a little hump . . .' interviews with Stuart Heisler, manuscript, courtesy of Joe Adamson, Los Angeles.

122 'I've already broken it to you . . .' *Photoplay*, 1.1920, NYPL

123 'passes each winter with her son . . .' *Los Angeles Examiner*, 6.7.1925, AMPAS

124 '1 lge bread . . .' etc, AMPAS-SC files

## Chapter Fourteen: Bath-tub Perils – Back to the Clowns

128 'Cutting is Real Secret . . .' *Photoplay Journal*, 4.23.1917, NYPL

128 'Heisler: (The story lines) came from . . .' Heisler interviews, ibid.

130 'when a runaway monoplane . . .' etc, BLT

130 'All of you who have for years . . .' Motion Picture, 12.1916, by Pearl Gaddis, NYPL

131 'independent and feminine . . .' NYDM, 9.9.1916, NYPL

131 'the privilege of supervising . . .' etc, contracts files, AMPAS-SC

133 'In order to induce you to enter . . .' AMPAS-SC files

134 'walking on limburger cheese . . .' *Armond Fields*, Eddie Foy, McFarland & Co., 1999, North Carolina, p. 205

## Chapter Fifteen: Mack Sennett and the Triangle of Doom.

136 'Miss Mabel Normand . . .' *Mack Sennett Weekly*, 1.8.1917, AMPAS-SC

136 'Board of Censors . . .' *Mack Sennett Weekly*, 2.5.1917, AMPAS-SC

137 'personally met the elusive Mexican . . .' ibid

137 'Commercial efficiency . . .' ibid, 2.12.1917

138 'Dear Sir, In November 1915 . . .' letters file AMPAS-SC

139 'KEYSTONE FILM CO . . .' etc, telegrams in AMPAS-SC

142 'There will be no difference . . .' *Mack Sennett Weekly*, 7.30.1917, AMPAS-SC

PART 3: HIS UPS AND DOWNS

## Chapter Sixteen: The Eyes Have It: Case History of a Clown – Ben Turpin, Episode One

147 'Drowning out the screeches . . .' Ben Turpin clippings, AMPAS-SC

149 'I joined the Fourth Street German . . .' etc, *The American Magazine*, November 1934, NYPL

150 'My eyes were straight . . .' ibid.

151 'This is a great life . . .' *Motion Picture World*, 4.3.1909, quoted in *Slapstick*, issue 1, 1998, courtesy of Steve Rydzewski

151 'Haw! . . . what sort of funny . . .' quoted in *Slapstick*, issue 2, ditto.

152 'I sat and sat . . .' quoted in *Slapstick*, issue 4, 2001, courtesy Steve Rydzewski

153 'Aw, what's the difference . . .' *The American Magazine*, ibid, NYPL

153 'Since I've been with Sennett . . .' ibid

153 'They say that when Ben cries . . .' Ben Turpin files, AMPAS-SC

153 'to pay loss providing . . .' clippings, NYPL

154 'The Philosophy of Ben Turpin . . .' Ben Turpin files, AMPAS-SC

## Chapter Seventeen: Mabel's Wilful Way

156 'It Is Necessary That We Try . . .' telegrams in AMPAS-SC

156 'I hollered . . .' Mack Sennett, *King of Comedy*, ibid, p. 210

158 'joy powder,' as cocaine was called . . .' Kenneth Anger, *Hollywood Babylon*, Dell Publishing Co., New York, 1975, p. 6

158 'every fool thing you might think of . . .' Mack Sennett, *King of Comedy*, ibid, p. 88

159 'in lieu of unpaid bonuses . . .' Betty Harper Fussell, *Mabel*, ibid, p. 99

160 'saturated the country with sheet music . . .' ibid, p. 101

161 'Los Angeles Athletic Club . . .' telegrams, AMPAS-SC

162 'Just as Mabel Normand . . .' *Los Angeles Times*, 12.28.1918, BLT

162 'Why, all my friends are out here . . .' *Los Angeles Times*, 1.12.1919, BLT

163 'Here is Gloria Swanson . . .' *Motion Picture Classic*, 3.1918, NYPL

163 'Ville de Paris importation . . .' *Motion Picture*, 4.1917, NYPL

163 'I kept Ted half starved . . .' clipping, courtesy of Steve Rydzewski

163 'Who's your friend, Teddy . . .' *Photoplay*, 7.1917, NYPL

164 'Wally, in full villain's make-up . . .' *Swanson on Swanson*, ibid, p. 76

164 'I hated the vulgarity . . .' ibid, p. 78

## Chapter Eighteen: He Did and He Didn't

167 'Gozzi, the famous Italian dramatist . . .' *Motion Picture Classic*, 11.1918, NYPL

168 'Mack Sennett Mack Sennett Studios . . .' etc, Booze file, AMPAS-SC

170 'When you sit down tonight . . .' *Mack Sennett Weekly*, 12.31.1917, AMPAS-SC

171 'Getting Into Rut . . .' *Mack Sennett Weekly*, 4.9.1917, AMPAS-SC

171 'flapper' slang, BLT

172 'the most costly production . . .' Publicity files, AMPAS-SC

172 'Molly O is the personification . . .' *Oklahoman*, 5.14.1922, scrapbook, AMPAS-SC

173 'A day's work with F. Richard Jones . . .' *Los Angeles Examiner*, 6.25.1922, scrapbook, AMPAS-SC

## Chapter Nineteen: Fatty's Fatal Fun

174 'If you are gifted with avordupois . . .' *Photoplay Journal*, 2.1919, NYPL

175 'Fatty Arbuckle Sought in Orgy Death . . .' clippings, NYPL

176 'That's what comes of taking vulgarians . . .' quoted in David Yallop, *The Day the Laughter Stopped*, ibid, p. 145

176 'In all the years . . .' ibid, p. 146

178    'that sacred thing, the mind of a child . . .' quoted in Kenneth Anger, *Hollywood Babylon*, ibid, p. 46

178    'a story for every father and mother . . .' David Yallop, ibid, p. 251

178    'hope that the American people . . .' ibid, p. 253

## Chapter Twenty: Isn't Love Cuckoo?

180    'In spite of the fact . . .' *Los Angeles Record*, 11.12.1921, BLT

180    'we have not been cleaning house . . .' BLT

183    'Mack Sennett Questioned . . .' *Los Angeles Herald*, 2.15.1922, BLT

183    'William Desmond Taylor was playing . . .' *Chicago American*, 2.15.1922, BLT

184    'Sometime ago I guess . . .' *Chicago American*, 2.21.1922, BLT

185    'There are only two . . .' 2.21.1922, BLT

185    'I would be no more surprised . . .' *Chicago American*, 2.20.1922, BLT

186    'Speaking on the sanctity . . .' *Buffalo Express*, 2.20.1922, BLT

## Chapter Twenty-One: A Small Town Idol

190    'six big productions . . .' *Morning Telegraph*, 12.19.1920, AMPAS

190    'of old age at the Cat and Dog Hospital . . .' Mack Sennett News Bulletin, 3.27.1924, AMPAS-SC

191    'eternally tasting . . .' *Life Magazine*, 9.5.1949, p. 73

192    'We have so often seen . . .' quoted in 'Mack Sennett' by Robert Giroux, *Films in Review*, December 1968 issue, p. 17

193    'We Americans like our humor laid on thick . . .' *The Photo-Play World*, undated clipping, AMPAS

193    'Beauty and Truth in art . . .' Tristan Tzara, *Seven Dada Manifestos and Lampisteries*, John Calder 1977, p. 110

194    'We loved Ben Turpin . . .' Luis Buñuel, *My Last Breath*, Jonathan Cape, London, 1984, p. 75

194    'The Story Opens . . .' *The Shriek of Araby* file, AMPAS-SC

195    'Moving pillars and posts . . .' ibid.

197    'Open on an Alpine skyline . . .' Three Foolish Weeks file, AMPAS-SC

198    'What's the good of all the money . . .' clippings, Ben Turpin file, NYPL

198    'I read in the magazines . . .' Ben Turpin file, AMPAS-SC

## Chapter Twenty-Two: A Lover's Lost Control

203    'only big films . . .' *Morning Telegraph*, New York, 12.24.1922, AMPAS

203    'he followed her to Paris . . .' Betty Harper Fussell, *Mabel*, ibid, p.182

203    'Hollywood, April 21 . . .' *New York Morning Telegraph*, 4.22.1923, AMPAS

203    'Mabel Normand must have . . .' quoted in BLT

206    'a little too old . . .' quoted in Betty Harper Fussell, *Mabel*, ibid, p.188

206    '35-year-old oil operator . . .' clipping, 1.2.1924, NYPL

207    'Honest, I never saw the shooting . . .' 1.2.1924, *Chicago Tribune*, BLT

207    'MABEL'S CHAFFEUR WANTED . . .' clipping, 1.3.1924, NYPL
207    'This guy Dines has got a lot . . .' *Chicago Tribune*, ibid, BLT
208    'Charles Chaplin, who starred . . .' clipping, NYPL
208    'permanently as a result . . .' 1.4.1924, *Toledo Blade*, NYPL
208    'As long as Fatty Arbuckle is banned . . .' 1.10.1924, *Toledo Blade*, NYPL
208    'Mack Sennett, producer of . . .' AMPAS-SC
209    'The Inside Dope on Movie Stars . . .' *Sunday News*, 6.29.1924, AMPAS

## Chapter Twenty-Three: His Lucky Star: the Quiet Clown – Harry Langdon

211    'The Mack Sennett Studio . . .' *Frank Capra, The Name Above the Title*, The Macmillan Company, New York, 1971, p. 44
213    'Mack Sennett lay prone . . .' ibid, p. 45
213    'Thou shalt punch the time clock . . .' ibid, p. 47
214    'Sennett sat in the big leather chair . . .' ibid, p. 49
215    'has been a riotous laugh . . .' *New York Telegraph*, 11.11.1911, NYPL, quoted in Joyce Rheuban, *Harry Langdon, the Comedian as Metteur-en-Scene*, Farleigh Dickinson University Press, 1983, p. 24
215    'Well, there he is . . .' *Frank Capra, The Name Above the Title*, ibid, p. 58
216    'While gaiety prevails on the main deck . . .' *The Sea Squawk* file, AMPAS-SC
218    'A child-like man who is lost . . .' Donald W. McCaffrey, *Four Great Comedians*, A. Zwemmer, London, A. S. Barnes, New York, p. 105
218    'the model of one who has attained . . .' Joyce Rheuban, *Harry Langdon*, ibid, p. 55
219    'a theorizer of drama . . .' *Frank Capra, The Name Above the Title*, ibid, p. 59
222    'Logical distinctions slide past him . . .' Joyce Rheuban, ibid, p. 55
222    'Watt's way of advancing . . .' *Samuel Beckett, Watt*, John Calder, 1963, p. 28
223    'Chaplin Competitor Discovered . . .' *Picking Peaches* file, AMPAS-SC
223    'In the Hermitage mountains . . .' etc, *Boobs in the Wood* file, AMPAS-SC
225    'Comedian Harry Langdon . . .' *Los Angeles Examiner*, 12.23.1944, AMPAS
225    'The advantage of vaudeville is . . .' AMPAS-SC
226    'His shy charm and gentle humor . . .' Mack Sennett, *King of Comedy*, ibid, p. 143

## Chapter Twenty-Four: The Neglected King of Gags: Billy Bevan

227    'Early in life . . .' Billy Bevan biography file, AMPAS-SC
233    'Mack was almost 100 percent physical . . .' *Screen Actor Hollywood*, winter 1987, NYPL

235 'Revealed: How Mack Sennett's Bathing Beauties . . .' RKO, Hollywood Features, 6.1938, AMPAS

236 'Not to be outdone . . .' Mack Sennett News Bulletin, 6.2.1924, AMPAS-SC

236 'You will please send us at once . . .' AMPAS-SC

236 'A new record in scanty costumes . . .' *Calgary Herald*, 10.4.1927, AMPAS-SC

237 'A radical departure . . .' *Mack Sennett Studio Review*, Vol. 1 No.1, 10.1927, AMPAS-SC

237 'Oldest and Sweetest Story . . .' ibid, Vol.1 No.3, 12.1927, AMPAS-SC

239 'According to the architect's plans . . .' ibid, Vol.1 No.1, AMPAS-SC

239 'Westmoreland Mansion . . .' *Frank Capra, The Name Above the Title*, ibid, p. 61

240 'The Best Motion Picture Interview . . .' *Moving Picture World*, 8.15.1928, NYPL, BLT

PART 4: HIS LAST LAUGH?

## Chapter Twenty-Five: The Shriek of Hollywood

245 'Sennett Plans to Fabricate . . .' *Los Angeles Examiner*, 3.2.1928, AMPAS

247 'Be a Bull on America . . .' Frederick Lewis Allen, *Only Yesterday*, Bantam Books, New York, 1946, p. 344

250 'eaten their heads off . . . pigs is pigs . . .' clipping, 11.25.1929, AMPAS

250 'over the next three years . . .' Betty Harper Fussell, *Mabel*, ibid, p. 218

251 'never saw her . . .' Mack Sennett, *King of Comedy*, p. 272

251 'Those flowers over there . . .' Betty Harper Fussell, *Mabel*, ibid, p. 228

251 'Mack Sennett Grieved Over . . .' clipping, Mabel Normand file, AMPAS

251 'Mabel Normand will be remembered . . .' ibid.

251 'the new Hollywood of microphones . . .' *Atlanta Journal*, 3.1.1930, AMPAS

## Chapter Twenty-Six: One More Chance

253 'Mack Sennett Engaged? . . .' *Los Angeles Examiner*, 10.8.1930, AMPAS

253 'We are passing through . . .' etc, Thomas Doherty, *Pre-Code Hollywood: Sex, Immorality and Insurrection in American Cinema 1930–1934*, Columbia University Press, New York, 1999, p. 27

255 'We rehearse for at least a week . . .' *New York Times*, 3.30.1930, BFI

256 'Too much talk in talking films . . .' *New York Times*, 11.30.1930, BFI

256 'Modistes. Fashion models . . .' American Film Institute Catalog, 1930, p. 508–9.

256 'multi-starred supercomedy . . .' etc, clipping, 12.9.1931, AMPAS

257 'At the captain's table . . .' American Film Institute Catalog, 1932, p. 980

258   'this animal submits . . .' quoted ibid.

258   'among the very worst . . .' quoted ibid.

258   'Words ruined the old comedy gags . . .' *New York Times*, 5.5.1935, BFI

259   'all the stuffed shirts at the Grove . . .' Bing Crosby website, unattributed.

261   'Dear Friend . . .' Andy Clyde file, AMPAS-SC

## Chapter Twenty-Seven: 'Figurin' on Goin' Over the Rim Tonight?

265   'Mack, I'm fed up . . .' Mack Sennett, *King of Comedy*, ibid, p.265

266   'For God's sake get a story . . .' ibid.

267   'I feel rather reluctant . . .' Ronald Fields, *W. C. Fields by Himself*, Prentice-Hall, Englefield, N.J., 1973, p. 269

267   'George Chandler . . . recalls . . .' Ronald Fields, *W. C. Fields, A Life on Film*, St Martins Press, 1984, p. 97–98

268   'The worst comedy . . .' *Motion Picture Herald*, 7.8.1933, NYPL

268   'rather resented by the dental profession . . .' ibid, 6.24.1933, NYPL

272   'Various actions have accumulated . . .' *Variety*, 13.11.1933, AMPAS

273   'Hollywood, Dec.12 . . .' clipping, 12.13.1933, NYPL

273   'Fatty Arbuckle Lies Dead . . .' *New York American*, 6.30.1933, NYPL

## Chapter Twenty-Eight: His Busted Trust

274   'How does it feel like . . .' Mack Sennett, *King of Comedy*, ibid, p. 274

274   'to use his own experiences . . .' etc, clipping, 3.7.1934, AMPAS

275   'One morning he came from the links . . .' Gene Fowler, *Father Goose*, ibid, p.347

276   'The advent of sound . . .' ibid, pp. 406–7

279   'Charlie Chaplin is more . . .' *Toledo Blade*, 2.12.1916, NYPL

281   'Death Claimed Mack Sennett's Mother . . .' *Sherbrooke Daily Record*, 9.15.1936, courtesy of M. Gilles Geoffroy, Danville, Quebec.

282   'C'était la femme las plus importante . . .' *La Presse*, Montreal, 6.8.1996, ibid.

## Chapter Twenty-Nine: His Hereafter

283   'Almost every day . . .' *Louise Brooks, Lulu in Hollywood*, Limelight Editions, New York, 1985, p. 75

283   'He was a melancholy man . . .' Will Fowler, in conversation with the author

284   'Loyal friends . . .' Robert Giroux, Mack Sennett, in *Films in Review*, January 1969, p. 24

286   'After a few rounds . . .' *Variety*, 3.18.1949, AMPAS

287   'Cheesecake was Cheesecake . . .' *Hollywood Citizen-News*, 7.6.1949, AMPAS

287   'Oldsters mostly sat around . . .' *Variety*, 5.1.1950, AMPAS

287   'The Quince . . .' etc, *Daily News*, 2.20.1950, AMPAS

288   'Mabel and I met . . .' *Daily News*, 2.14.1950, AMPAS

289    'drew belly laughs . . .' *Hollywood Reporter*, 5.19.1952, AMPAS

289    'French Bikini Isn't Sexy . . .' *Hollywood Citizen-News*, 6.3.1952, AMPAS

289    'Mack Sennett is the sad clown . . .' *Los Angeles Times*, 11.28.1954, AMPAS

290    'The taxpayer reports . . .' *Los Angeles Times*, 5.9.1956, AMPAS

290    'an ideal motion picture vehicle . . .' quoted in Robert Giroux, ibid, p. 26

290    'I have a whole new career in that thing . . .' *Los Angeles Examiner*, 9.7.1958, AMPAS

290    'When Grandma was a girl . . .' ibid.

290    'Comeback Dream . . .' *N. Y. World Telegram*, 8.25.1958, NYPL

291    'big productions, on spectacles . . .' etc, Murray Schumach, in *Courier-Journal*, Louisville, Kentucky, 4.26.1959, NYPL

292    'He fought tooth and nail . . .' Robert Giroux, ibid, p.27

292    'It'll all be shot new . . .' *Morning Telegraph*, 7.4.1960, NYPL

292    'That's ridiculous . . . This is a matter of art . . .' *Los Angeles Mirror*, 8.26.1960, AMPAS

292    'Sennett was dictating a plot . . .' *Los Angeles Mirror*, 11.5.1960

293    'Paramount Studios owns the rights . . .' ibid.

## Chapter Thirty: Epilogue

294    'when movies were movies . . .' etc, *Mack and Mabel, Music & Lyrics by Jerry Herman*, book by Michael Stewart, opened 10.6.1974 Majestic Theatre, Broadway.

294    'It was a sweet romance . . .' *Daily News*, ibid, 2.14.1950, AMPAS

297    'It was me they saw leaving the house . . .' Charles Foster, *Stardust and Shadows, Canadians in Early Hollywood*, Dundurn Press, Toronto, 2000, p. 335

297    'Reece asked him why . . .' ibid, p.336

298    'I can't rave enough about her . . .' Interview with Minta Durfee by Don Schneider and Stephen Normand, Mabel Normand website – *www.angelfire.com/mn/hp*

300    'Mack Sennett Administration Building . . .' *Variety*, 12.17.1982, AMPAS

## Coda

303    Segments from archive scripts and files for *A Harem Knight, Weber and Fields Story, A Dash of Courage, Fatty and Mabel Adrift, Mabel and Bear*, AMPAS-SC, Sennett Collection.

# Chronology

Between 1912 and 1933, Mack Sennett produced, by some estimates, over 1,150 films. These were mostly short subjects of one, two or three reels' length (between 10 minutes and half an hour), with some shorter 'split-reel' (4 or 5 minute) subjects at the earliest Keystone period, a variety of four- or five-reel works and a dozen full-length feature films, mostly made in the 1920s. It is not possible in this book to include a full filmography, which awaits a braver soul than I. The Sennett Collection archivists have published *The Films of Mack Sennett – Credit Documentation from the Mack Sennett Collection at the Margaret Herrick Library* (Scarecrow Press, 1998), compiled and edited by Warren Sherk, with the assistance of Samuel Gill, Harry Garvin and Robert Cushman. This includes 855 titles, each one of which has an archival file, though many earlier files, before 1915, contain only a handful of pages, and some photographic files can contain merely one still. From 1915 onwards the list is more robust. Kalton Lahue appended, in *Kops and Custards* (1971) and *Mack Sennett's Keystone, the Man, the Myth and the Comedies* (1972), a list of films produced by Keystone between 1912 and 1917, until the end of the Keystone–Triangle project. The 300 titles that remain unaccounted for derive from lists of titles, many of which might simply be re-titles of films that have indeed been catalogued. The fall of Triangle, in particular, left film packages to change hands among many distributors, renamed and then renamed again.

The following chronology attempts to lay out the dates and periods between which certain key Sennett players were active either in the Keystone films or with the later Mack Sennett Comedies, which will hopefully give the reader some idea of the scope of the Sennett project's achievements, and the contextual dates during which his clowns flourished. The Bibliography should provide appropriate clues as to where movie archaeologists might continue digging for yet undisturbed golden noogets.

1879    24 February: Marriage of Catherine Foy and John Francis Sinnott, in Shipton, Quebec.

1880    17 January: birth of Michael Sinnott.

1896    Enrolment of Michael Sinnott and brothers at Institut Française Evangelique, Point-aux-Trembles.

1897    Emigration of the Sinnott family to East Berlin, Connecticut, USA.

1898    Domicile of Sinnott family in Northampton, Massachussets.

1900–1    (or 1902) Employment of Michael Sinnott at Mount Tom Sulphite Pulp Co.

1902 (?)    Michael and Catherine Sinnott approach to Calvin Coolidge and Marie Dressler.

1902(?)–1907: Employment of Michael Sinnott (Sennett?) in burlesque, travelling chorus shows, singing quartets, male chorus of Broadway shows, allegedly including:

1902    *King Dodo*, starring Raymond Hitchcock (later Sennett employee).

1903    *A Chinese Honeymoon*, running 376 performances.

1904    *A Chinese Honeymoon*, starring Fred Mace.
        *Piff! Paff! Pouf!* Starring Eddie Foy (later Sennett employee), 264 performances.
        *Wang*, 57 performances.

1906    *M.lle Modiste*, 22 performances.

1907    *The Boys of Company B* – first verified credit of Mack Sennett. 96 performances.
        (*Research of performances by Maryan Chach of Shubert Archive, New York.*)

1908    Sennett joins Biograph company as actor, alongside D. W. Griffith; first verified appearance of Sennett and Griffith together, May 1908. First Griffith-directed film, June 1908.

1908–11 Mack Sennett acts in Griffith's Biograph shorts.

1909    15 February: release of *The Curtain Pole*, first film starring Mack Sennett.
        April: release of Griffith's short *The Lonely Villa*, with script by Sennett.
        Mabel Normand joins Biograph company.

1910    Biograph company winters in California.

1911    13 March: release of first film directed by Mack Sennett, Comrades. March – 1912, August, Sennett directs comedies for Biograph.
        Regular featured players: Fred Mace, Mabel Normand, Del Henderson.

1912    July: meeting with Adam Kessel and Charles Baumann forms Keystone company.
        Summer: Sennett shoots earliest Keystone films in New York (Coney Island).
        23 September: First release of Keystone films, the split-reel of *Cohen Collects a Debt* and *The Water Nymph*, featuring Ford Sterling and Mabel Normand.

1912–13 Earliest Keystones feature Fred Mace, Ford Sterling, Mabel Normand, Henry 'Pathe' Lehrman, Alice Davenport, Victoria Forde, Nick Cogley.

1913    24 April: release of first 'Keystone Kops' movie, *The Bangville Police*, directed by Henry Lehrman (split-reel with *A Fishy Affair*, directed by Sennett).

29 May: release of *The Gangsters*, first Keystone with Roscoe 'Fatty' Arbuckle.

3 June: *Barney Oldfield's Race for a Life*, with Mack, Mabel, Ford Sterling.

Other actors in 1913 (and after): Charles Avery, Wilfred Lucas, Hank Mann, Al St. John, Dot Farley, William Hauber, Henry Lehrman, Rube Miller, Edgar Kennedy, George Jeske, Teddy Tetzlaff, Earl Cooper, Charles Haggerty, etc.

1914    2 February: *Making a Living*, first Charles Chaplin picture, released. To December, 34 Chaplin shorts and one feature made at Keystone.* Chaplin films feature: Mabel Normand, Virginia Kirtley, Alice Davenport, Henry Lehrman, Minta Durfee, Chester Conklin, Harry McCoy, Hank Mann, Al St. John, Ford Sterling, Emma Clifton, Sadie Lampe, Roscoe Arbuckle, Peggy Pearce, Edgar Kennedy, Fred Mace, Mack Swain, Joseph Swickard, Gordon Griffith, Alice Howell, Phyllis Allen, Charles Murray, Charles Parrott (later to be Charley Chase), Joe Bordeaux, Slim Summerville, Wallace McDonald, Fritz Schade, Norma Nichols, Cecile Arnold, Vivian Edwards, Jack Dillon.

14 November: Release of *Tillie's Punctured Romance*, first Sennett feature, first comedy feature ever. Directed by Mack Sennett; scenario by Sennett from the play *Tillie's Nightmare*. Starring Marie Dressler, Charles Chaplin, Mabel Normand. Featuring: Mack Swain, Charles Bennett, Charles Murray, Charles Parrott, Edgar Kennedy, Harry McCoy, Minta Durfee, Phyllis Allen, Alice Davenport, Slim Summerville, Al St. John, Wallace McDonald, Joe Bordeaux, G. G. Ligon, Gordon Griffith, Billie Bennett, Rev D. Simpson. Release length: 6,000 feet.

1915–16 Expansion of Keystone studios at Edendale. Director: Del Henderson, Charles Avery, Frank Griffin, Fred Fishbach, Mabel Normand, Roscoe Arbuckle.

New acting recruits: Louise Fazenda, Bobby Dunn, Bill Colvin, Earle Rodney, Eddie Sutherland, Joseph Belmont, Harry Williams, Della Pringle, Polly Moran, May Emory, Cecile Arley, Claire Anderson, Louella Maxam, Dorothy Duffee, Dale Fuller, Ora Carew, Julia Fay, Harry and Eddie Gribbon, Wayland Trask, Hugh Fay, Victor Potel, James Donnelly, Harry Booker, Raymond Griffith, Phyllis Haver, Mae Busch, Mary Thurman, Vera Stedman, Eleanor Field, Anna Luther, Dave Morris, Harry Bernard, Gloria Swanson, Wallace Beery, Teddy the Dog, Glen Cavender, Joe Weber and Lew Fields, Eddie Foy etc.

1915    July: setting up of Triangle–Keystone operation through the Triangle Film Corporation (aka SIG – Sennett-Ince-Griffith).

September, possible date of alleged Mack–Mae Busch sex-romp incident.

1916     Kessel and Baumann sell their original New York Motion Picture Company to Harry Aitken of Triangle. Roscoe 'Fatty' Arbuckle leaves Keystone. **

1917     January: commence publication of the *Mack Sennett Weekly*, runs to 1919. February: death of Fred Mace.

March: Sennett signs Ben Turpin. Turpin titles for Sennett in 1917 include: *A Clever Dummy*, *Lost – A Cook*, *A Pawnbroker's Heart*, *Roping Her Romeo*, *Are Waitresses Safe?*, *Taming Target Center*.

March: D. W. Griffith abandons Triangle company, followed by Thomas Ince.

June: Sennett plots to leave Triangle holding his Keystone imprint while maintaining all his actual assets and studio.

July: Sennett signs distribution deal with Adolph Zukor's Paramount company.

Sennett films released as Mack Sennett Comedies.

Largest number of Sennett films released is in 1917 – archive lists 125 titles.

1918     Only 27 titles released. Turpin titles: *Sheriff Nell's Tussle*, *Saucy Madeline*, *The Battle Royal*, *Two Tough Tenderfeet*, *She Loved Him Plenty*, *Hide and Seek Detectives*.

11 August: release of Mabel Normand feature, *Mickey*, directed by F. Richard Jones, starring Mabel Normand, Lew Cody, Wheeler Oakman, with Minnie Ha Ha (Devereaux), George Nichols, Minta Durfee, Laura Lavarnie, Tom Kennedy.

Cinematographers: Hugh C. McClung, Frank D. Williams and Fred Jackman.

Mabel Normand already working with Goldwyn pictures.

1919     First Ben Turpin feature (5 reels): *Yankee Doodle in Berlin*. Other Turpin titles: *Cupid's Day Off*, *East Lynne With Variations*, *When Love Is Blind*, *Whose Little Wife Are You?* (directed by Eddie Cline) *Uncle Tom Without the Cabin* (dir. Ray Hunt), *No Mother to Guide Him* (dirs. Mal St. Claire and Erle Kenton), *Sleuths* (dir. F. Richard Jones) and *Salome vs. Shenandoah* (dirs. Erle Kenton and Ray Hunt). Billy Bevan joins Sennett comedies. Looming threat of Prohibition – Sennett trawls 'private vaults' for booze stockpile with prop dept.

1920     Ben Turpin titles: *The Star Boarder* (dir. James Davis), *Down on the Farm* (5-reel feature, dirs. Erle Kenton and Ray Grey), *Married Life* (5 reels, dir. Erle Kenton).

Sennett moves to Westmoreland 'mansion' some time between 1919 and 1921.

1921     Ben Turpin titles: *A Small Town Idol* (7-reel feature, dir. Erle Kenton) with Jimmy Finlayson and Phyllis Haver; *Love's Outcast* (dir. J. A. Waldron); *Love and Doughnuts* (dir. Roy Del Ruth). Release of Billy Bevan short, *Be Reasonable*.

September: Eruption of 'Fatty' Arbuckle scandal; trials stretch into 1922.

1922     1 February: killing of William Desmond Taylor, Hollywood's most spectacular scandal. November, release of *Molly O'*, Sennett–

Normand prestige feature, starring Mabel Normand, George Nichols, Anna Hernandez, Albert Hackett, Jack Mulhall. Directed by F. Richard Jones. (Ben Turpin in small part.)

Ben Turpin 1922 releases: *Bright Eyes* (dir. Roy Del Ruth), *Step Forward* (dir. F. Richard Jones), *Home Made Movies* (dirs. Ray Grey and Gus Mains).

1923  Further consolidation of Mack Sennett studios. Sennett switches distribution from Paramount to Pathe Exchange, to handle all short subjects. Release of *Suzanna*, second prestige Mabel Normand film, directed by F. Richard Jones (February 1923), starring Mabel Normand, George Nichols, Walter McGrail, Minnie Ha Ha.

Ben Turpin titles: *The Shriek of Araby* (5 reels, dir. F. Richard Jones), *Where's My Wandering Boy Tonight & Pitfalls of a Big City* (dir. J. A. Waldron), *Asleep at the Switch* (dir. Roy Del Ruth), *The Daredevil* (dir. Del Lord).

September: release of *The Extra Girl*, last Sennett–Mabel Normand feature, Directed by F. Richard Jones, with Mabel Normand, Vernon Dent, George Nichols, Anna Hernandez, Ralph Graves, Charlotte Mineau, Kewpie Morgan, Teddy the Dog.

1924  New Year's Day, 1 January: Mabel Normand–Dines shooting scandal. Normand films barred from exhibition in some states.

First Harry Langdon film for Sennett, *Picking Peaches*, released in February.

Langdon directed at Sennett first by Erle Kenton, Roy del Ruth, Harry Sweet, Harry Edwards. Frank Capra arrives at Sennett studios.

Ben Turpin titles: *Ten Dollars or Ten Days*, *The Hollywood Kid*, *Yukon Jake* (dir. Del Lord), *Romeo and Juliet* (dirs. Reggie Morris and Harry Sweet), *Three Foolish Weeks* and *The Reel Virginian* (dirs. Reggie Morris and Ed Kennedy).

Death of Pepper the Cat.

1925  Second golden era for Sennett: Billy Bevan comedies (*Super-Hooper-Dyne Lizzies,* dir. Del Lord), first Arthur Ripley stories for Langdon (*Boobs in the Woods, His Marriage Wow*), first Capra writing collaborations with Ripley for Langdon (*Plain Clothes, Lucky Stars, There He Goes*, all directed by Harry Edwards). Supporting cast in Langdon shorts: Vernon Dent, Andy Clyde, Natalie Kingston, Peggy Montgomery, Frank Whitson, Charlotte Mineau, Marie Astaire, Jean Hathaway, Claire Cushman.

Ben Turpin titles: *Wild Goose Chaser, Raspberry Romance* (dir. Lloyd Bacon), *The Marriage Circus* (dirs. Reggie Morris and Ed Kennedy). Sennett begins (?) planning for his great Hollywood mansion on the hill.

1926  Smith Family series, with Raymond McKee, Ruth Hiatt, Mary Ann Jackson, Sunshine Hart, Andy Clyde, Polly Moran, Vernon Dent, Bud Jamison, Glen Cavender, William McCall, Irving Bacon, Johnny Burke, Cap the Dog (later Balto and Omar, replacement canines). Series runs through 1929.

Ben Turpin titles: *When a Man's a Prince* (dir. Edward Cline), *A Prodigal Bridegroom* (dir. Lloyd Bacon), *A Harem Knight* (dir. Gill Pratt), *A Blonde's Revenge* (dir. Del Lord).

Harry Langdon title in 1926: *Saturday Afternoon*, dir. Harry Edwards, story by Arthur Ripley and Frank Capra.

September: Mabel Normand marries Lew Cody.

1927     Sennett Bathing Girls come forward center stage; Mack Sennett Studio Review features girls as main attraction. Sennett losing ground to Hal Roach studios.

First box-office hit sound picture, *The Jazz Singer*, opens in October. Death knell begins to sound for silent movies.

Ben Turpin titles: *A Hollywood Hero, Daddy Boy* (dir. Harry Edwards), *The Jolly Jilter, Broke in China* (dir. Edward Cline), *Pride of Pikeville* (dir. Alf Goulding), *Love's Languid Lure* (dir. Lige Conley). (Turpin leaves Sennett for his last silent films.)

Harry Langdon titles in 1927: *Fiddlesticks* and *Soldier Man*, both directed by Harry Edwards, story by Arthur Ripley and Frank Capra.

1928     July: Sennett releases major feature, *The Good-bye Kiss*, with Sally Eilers and Johnny Burke. Announces plans for new studio, in new location. Sennett commits to sound pictures, becoming financially over-stretched. Inaugurates new studio at Studio City, and switches distribution to Educational Film Exchanges.

1929     Sennett begins releasing sound pictures from the new Studio City lot. (Early titles: *The Bees Buzz, The Big Palooka, Caught in a Taxi, The Golfers, Jazz Mammas*.)

Wall Street Crash of October.

Sennett returns to personal directing, cuts staff.

Repertory cast includes, in this period: Andy Clyde, Jack Cullen, Jack Cooper, Blanche Payson, Marjorie Beebe, Daphne Pollard, Dot Farley, Johnny Burke, Bud Jamison, Vernon Dent, Harry Gribbon, Frank Eastman, Marvin Lobach, Florence Roberts, Charles Irwin, Ann Christy, Patsy O'Leary, Julia Griffith, Pat Harman, Ted Strohbach, Fay Holderness, Franklin Pangborn, etc.

1930     Only 24 films released, including first sound feature, *Midnight Daddies*, poorly received.

Death of Mabel Normand, 23 February 1930.

In October, Sennett, photographed stepping out with Marjorie Beebe, denies any thoughts of marriage.

1931     Depression deepens, but Sennett strikes lucky with Bing Crosby. *I Surrender Dear*, two-reeler with Bing, Marion Sayers, Luis Alberni, Arthur Stone and Julia Griffith, features hit songs: 'I Surrender Dear', 'Out of Nowhere' and 'A Little Bit of Heaven'. Sennett produces in quick succession five more Bing Crosby two-reelers: *One More Chance, Dream House, Billboard Girl, Blue of the Night* and *Sing, Bing Sing*.

1932    February: Sennett signs new distribution deal with Paramount Publix.
        March: Sennett becomes U.S. citizen. Andy Clyde is Sennett's most
        prolific star.
        Later in the year Sennett signs W. C. Fields. First Fields–Sennett short,
        *The Dentist*, released in December. Sennett's long-touted 'all-star'
        feature also released in December as *Hypnotized*, directed by Sennett
        and starring Charlie Mack and George Moran, Ernest Torrence,
        Charlie Murray, Wallace Ford, Marjorie Beebe, Maria Alba, Hattie
        McDaniel, Luis Alberni and Anna May the Elephant (as well as the
        long-suffering lion).
1933    Sennett continues production while Paramount announces 'voluntary
        petition in bankruptcy'.
        Release of three remaining Fields shorts: *The Fatal Glass of Beer*, *The
        Pharmacist* and *The Barber Shop*, the latter being the last title formally
        released produced by Mack Sennett studios, 28 July, 1933.
        Death of Roscoe 'Fatty' Arbuckle, 29 June, 1933.
        Court petitions, resulting in Sennett personal bankruptcy in December.
1934    Sennett continues talk of comeback, but nothing materializes.
        Publication of Gene Fowler's embroidered biography, *Father Goose*.
        Studio City premises sold to Mascot Pictures, later to become
        Republic Pictures.
1935–6  Sennett returns to Danville, Quebec, to ageing mother, Catherine
        Sinnott.
1936    14 September: death of Catherine Sinnott at Tingwick.
        Mack moves to Garden Court Apartments, Hollywood Boulevard,
        and begins his long retirement.
1938    10 March: Sennett receives honorary Oscar.
1939    Sennett participates in *Hollywood Cavalcade*, portmanteau picture of
        old Hollywood.
1940    Sennett at memorial for Mabel Normand at the Republic Studio.
1948    Masquers 'testimonial dinner', with six original Kops attending.
        July: death of D.W. Griffith, in Hollywood obscurity.
1949    Mack Sennett Alumni bash on St. Patrick's Day, at California Country
        Club.
        Sennett plans 'Mack and Mabel' bio-picture with Paramount, unmade
        project.
        Release of *Down Memory Lane*, compilation of old Sennett films.
1951    Sennett hands Academy librarian Margaret Herrick collection of his
        records.
1952    Sennett attends Cannes Film Festival.
1954    publication of autobiographical *King of Comedy*, with Cameron Shipp.
1956–9  Comeback dreams variously reported.
1960    17 January: Sennett celebrates his eightieth birthday but frail condition
        necessitates move to Motion Picture Country Home in Woodland
        Hills.
        5 November: Sennett succumbs to illness in hospital.

* Charles Chaplin films made at Keystone (1914): *Making a Living; Kid Auto Races at Venice; Mabel's Strange Predicament; Between Showers; A Film Johnnie; Tango Tangles; His Favorite Pastime; Cruel, Cruel Love; The Star Boarder; Mabel at the Wheel; Twenty Minutes of Love; Caught in a Cabaret; Caught in the Rain; A Busy Day; The Fatal Mallet; Her Friend the Bandit; The Knockout; Mabel's Busy Day; Mabel's Married Life; Laughing Gas; The Property Man; The Face on the Bar Room Floor; Recreation; The Masquerader; His New Profession; The Rounders; The New Janitor; Those Love Pangs; Dough and Dynamite; Gentlemen of Nerve; His Musical Career; His Trysting Place; Tillie's Punctured Romance; Getting Acquainted; His Prehistoric Past.*

** Roscoe 'Fatty' Arbuckle films made for Keystone and Keystone–Triangle, 1913–16:

1913: *The Gangsters; Passions He Had Three; Help! Help! Hydrophobia!; The Waiter's Picnic; A Bandit; Peeping Pete; For the Love of Mabel; The Telltale Light; A New Trick; Love and Courage; House Moving; The Riot; Mabel's New Hero; Fatty's Day Off; Mabel's Dramatic Career; The Gypsy Queen; The Fatal Taxicab; When Dreams Come True; Mother's Boy; Two Old Tars; A Quiet Little Wedding; The Speed Kings; Fatty at San Diego; Wine; Fatty Joins the Force; The Woman Haters; Ride for a Bride; Fatty's Flirtation; His Sister's Kids; He Would a-Hunting Go.*

1914: *A Misplaced Foot; The Under Sheriff; A Flirt's Mistake; In the Clutches of the Gang; Rebecca's Wedding Day; A Robust Romeo; Twixt Love and Fire; A Film Johnnie; Tango Tangles; His Favorite Pastime; A Rural Demon; Barnyard Flirtations; Chicken Chaser; A Bath House Beauty; Where Hazel Met the Villain; A Suspended Ordeal; The Water Dog; The Alarm; The Knock-out; Fatty and the Heiress; Fatty's Finish; Love and Bullets; A Rowboat Romance; The Sky Pirate; Those Happy Days; That Minstrel Man; Those Country Kids; Fatty's Gift; The Masquerader; A Brand New Hero; The Rounders; Lover's Luck; Fatty's Debut; Fatty Again; Their Ups and Downs; Zip the Dodger; Lover's Post Office; An Incompetent Hero; Fatty's Jonah Day; Fatty's Wine Party; The Sea Nymphs; Leading Lizzie Astray; Shotguns That Kick; Fatty's Magic Pants; Fatty and Minnie-He-Haw.*

1915: *Mabel and Fatty's Wash Day; Fatty and Mabel's Simple Life; Fatty and Mabel at the San Diego Exposition; Mabel, Fatty and the Law; Fatty's New Role; Mabel and Fatty's Married Life; Fatty's Reckless Fling; Fatty's Chance Acquaintance; Love in Armor; That Little Band of Gold; Fatty's Faithful Fido; When Love Took Wings; Wished on Mabel; Mabel and Fatty Viewing the World's Fair at San Francisco; Mabel's Wilful Way; Miss Fatty's Seaside Lovers; The Little Teacher; Fatty's Plucky Pup; Fatty's Tintype Tangle; Fickle Fatty's Fall; The Village Scandal; Fatty and the Broadway Stars.*

1916: *Fatty and Mabel Adrift; He Did and He Didn't; The Bright Lights; His Wife's Mistake; The Other Man; The Moonshiners; The Waiter's Ball; A Reckless Romeo; A Creampuff Romance.*

(Full Arbuckle filmography, subsequent teaming with Buster Keaton, etc, in David Yallop, *The Day the Laughter Stopped*.)

# Select Bibliography

**History of the American Cinema Series, University of California Press**

Balio, Tino, *Grand Design, Hollywood as a Modern Business Enterprise, 1930–1939* (Volume 5), 1993

Bowser, Eileen, *The Transformation of Cinema, 1907–1915* (Volume 2), 1990

Crafton, Donald, *The Talkies, American Cinema's Transition to Sound, 1926–1931* (Volume 4), 1997

Koszarski, Richard, *An Evening's Entertainment, The Age of the Silent Feature Picture, 1915–1928* (Volume 3), 1990

Musser, Charles, *The Emergence of Cinema, the American Screen to 1907* (Volume 1), 1990


Allen, Frederick Lewis, *Only Yesterday, the Fabulous Twenties*, Bantam Books, New York, 1946

Anthony, Brian and Edmonds, Andy, *Smile When the Raindrops Fall, the Story of Charley Chase*, The Scarecrow Press, Lanham Md., 1998.

Balshofer, Fred J. and Miller, Arthur C., *One Reel a Week*, University of California Press, 1967

Basinger, Jeanine, *Silent Stars*, Wesleyan University Press, University Press of New England, Hanover and London, 1999

Bergman, Andrew, *We're in the Money, Depression America and Its Films*, Elephant Paperbacks, Ivan R. Dee Publisher, Chicago, 1992

Blesh, Rudi, *Keaton,* Secker and Warburg, London, 1967

Brownlow, Kevin, *Behind the Mask of Innocence*, Jonathan Cape, London, 1990

Brownlow, Kevin, *The Parade's Gone By*, Secker and Warburg, London, 1968

Capra, Frank, *The Name Above the Title, An Autobiography*, The Macmillan Company, New York, 1971

Chaplin, Charles, *My Autobiography*, Simon and Schuster, New York, 1964

Charney, Leo and Vanessa R. Schwartz, editors, *Cinema and the Invention of Modern Life,* University of California Press, Berkeley, Los Angeles, 1995

Crafton, Donald, *Emile Cohl, Caricature and Film*, Princeton University Press, 1990

Curtis, James, *W. C. Fields*, Alfred A. Knopf, New York, 2003

Doherty, Thomas, *Pre-Code Hollywood: Sex, Immorality and Insurrection in American Cinema 1930–1934,* Columbia University Press, New York, 1999

Durgnat, Raymond, *The Crazy Mirror – Hollywood Comedy and the American Image*, Faber and Faber, London, 1969

Everson, William K., *American Silent Film*, Oxford University Press, New York, 1978

Fields, Armond, *Eddie Foy, A Biography*, McFarland and Company, 1999

Fields, Armond and Fields, L. Marc, *From the Bowery to Broadway*, Oxford University Press, New York, Oxford, 1993

Fields, Ronald J., *W. C. Fields, A Life on Film*, St. Martins Press, New York, 1984

Fields, Ronald J., *W. C. Fields By Himself, His Intended Autobiography*, Prentice Hall, Englewood Cliffs, N.J., 1973

Finler, Joel L., *The Hollywood Story*, Octopus Books, London, 1988

Foster, Charles, *Stardust and Shadows, Canadians in Early Hollywood*, Dundurn Press, Toronto, Oxford, 2000

Fowler, Gene, *Father Goose, the Story of Mack Sennett*, Covici Friede Publishers, New York, 1934

Fussell, Betty Harper, *Mabel, Hollywood's First I Don't Care Girl*, Ticknor & Fields, New Haven and N.Y., 1982

Gabler, Neal, *An Empire of Their Own, How the Jews Invented Hollywood*, Crown Publishers Inc., New York, 1988

Garnett, Tay, with Dudley Balling, Freda, *Light Your Torches and Pull Up Your Tights*, Arlington House, 1973

Gilbert, Douglas, *American Vaudeville, Its Life and Times*, Whittlesey House, McGraw Hill, New York, London, 1940

Gordon, Rae Beth, *Why the French Love Jerry Lewis, From Cabaret to Early Cinema*, Stanford University Press, Stanford, California, 2001

Griffith, Mrs D. W. (Linda Arvidson), *When the Movies Were Young*, Dover Publications Inc., New York, 1969 (first published 1925)

Henderson, Robert M., *D.W. Griffith, the Years at Biograph*, Farrar, Straus and Giroux, New York, 1971

Jobes, Gertrude, *Motion Picture Empire*, Archon Books, Hamden, Connecticut, 1966 *

Keaton, Buster, with Samuels, Charles, *My Wonderful World of Slapstick*, Doubleday, New York, 1960, Da Capo Press, New York, 1982

Kerr, Walter, *The Silent Clowns*, Alfred A. Knopf, New York, 1975

Lahue, Kalton C., *Dreams for Sale, the Rise and Fall of the Triangle Film Corporation*, South Brunswick and New York, A. S. Barnes and Company, London, Thomas Yoseloff Ltd, 1971

Lahue, Kalton C., *Mack Sennett's Keystone, the Man, the Myth and the Comedies*, South Brunswick and New York, A.S. Barnes and Company, London, Thomas Yoseloff Ltd, 1972

Lahue, Kalton C., *World of Laughter, the Motion Picture Comedy Short, 1910–1930*, University of Oklahoma Press, 1966

Lahue, Kalton C. and Brewer, Terry, *Kops and Custards, The Legend of Keystone Films*, The University of Oklahoma Press, 1968.

* Unique detailed look at the business history of pioneer Hollywood.

Lahue, Kalton C. and Gill, Samuel, *Clown Princes and Court Jesters*, South Brunswick and New York, A. S. Barnes and Company, London, Thomas Yoseloff Ltd, 1970

Louvish, Simon, *Man on the Flying Trapeze, the Life and Times of W. C. Fields*, Faber and Faber, London, 1997

Louvish, Simon, *Monkey Business, the Lives and Legends of the Marx Brothers*, Faber and Faber, London, 1999

Louvish, Simon, *Stan and Ollie, the Roots of Comedy, the Double Life of Laurel and Hardy*, Faber and Faber, London, 2001

May, Larry, *Screening Out the Past, the Birth of Mass Culture and the Motion Picture Industry*, Oxford University Press, New York, Oxford, 1980

McCaffery, Donald W., *Four Great Comedians*, Zwemmer/Barnes, 1968

Meade, Marion, *Buster Keaton, Cut to the Chase*, HarperCollins Publishers, 1995

Mitchell, Glenn, *A–Z of Silent Film Comedy*, B. T. Batsford Ltd, London, 1998

Mitchell, Glenn, *The Chaplin Encyclopedia*, B. T. Batsford Ltd, London, 1997

Mitchell, Glenn, *The Laurel and Hardy Encyclopedia*, B. T. Batsford Ltd, London, 1995

O'Dell, Paul, *Griffith and the Rise of Hollywood*, Zwemmer/Barnes, 1970

Rheuban, Joyce, *Harry Langdon, the Comedian as Metteur-en-Scene*, Farleigh Dickinson University Press, Associated University Presses, London, Toronto, 1983

Robinson, David, *Chaplin – His Life and Art*, William Collins Sons & Co., London, 1985

Robinson, David, *From Peepshow to Palace, the Birth of American Film*, Columbia University Press, New York, 1997

Robinson, David, *The Great Funnies, a History of Film Comedy*, Studio Vista, 1969

Schickel, Richard, *D. W. Griffith, An American Life*, Simon and Schuster, New York, 1984

Sennett, Mack, as told to Cameron Shipp, *King of Comedy*, Doubleday & Co, New York, 1954, Mercury House Inc., San Francisco, 1990

Sherk, Warren M. (compiler, editor) *The Films of Mack Sennett, Credit Documentation from the Mack Sennett Collection at the Margaret Herrick Library*, The Scarecrow Press Inc., Lanham, Md., and London, 1998

Sklar, Robert, *Movie-Made America, A Cultural History of American Movies*, Vintage Books, New York, 1994

Slide, Anthony, *Early American Cinema*, Zwemmer/Barnes, 1970

Sloan, Kay, *The Loud Silents, Origins of the Social Problem Film*, University of Illinois Press, Urbana and Chicago, 1988

Swanson, Gloria, *Swanson on Swanson, An Autobiography*, Michael Joseph, London, 1981

Wagenknecht, Edward, *The Movies in the Age of Innocence*, Ballantine Books, New York, 1971

Watson, Coy, *The Keystone Kid, Tales of Early Hollywood*, Santa Monica Press, California, 2001

Yallop, David, *The Day the Laughter Stopped, the True Story of Fatty Arbuckle*, St Martins Press, New York, 1976

# Acknowledgements

The essential archive of Mack Sennett's papers, files and photographs is at the Academy of Motion Picture Arts and Sciences' Margaret Herrick Library in Los Angeles, and heartfelt thanks to Barbara Hall, Harry Garvin, Warren M. Sherk, Sam Gill and all personnel at the Special Collections service. Plaudits too to the usual suspects at the New York Public Library's Performing Arts collections, Rod Bladel and all who man the pumps. A very special thank you again to Dave Rothman, genealogist extraordinaire, in California, whose attention to detail overtakes my own cluttered procedures, and who will never let a fact go until it has been squeezed of its tangiest juice. The British Film Institute in London has been of great help in mopping up loose ends, and many thanks to all staff there. Thanks again to Walter Donohue, Richard Kelly et al. at Faber and Faber for supporting my attempts at scholarly work in an entertaining form. Appreciation to Pierre Pageau of Quebec, Mack Sennett scholar and expert on the history and background of our hero's homeland, to his colleague Jean Chabot, to Gilles Geoffroy of Danville, tour guide of the old homestead, to M. Leo Rioux and other memorialists of Danville, Quebec. Thanks to Ms D. Healy of the Societé Histoire de Comte de Richmond, and staff of the Toronto Public Library. Individual thanks to Karen Mulhallen of Toronto, to Will Fowler, chief raconteur of the Golden Age in Sherman Oaks, Cal., to Steve Rydzewski, Glenn Mitchell, David Wyatt, Jack Hardy of Grapevine Video, Alex Bartosh of A-1 Video and Chris Snowden of Unknown Video, to Joe Adamson, Joel Finler, Rick Mitz, Stuart Schaar, Clyde Jeavons, and of course to Mairi, whose endurance of Ben Turpin trivia and Ford Sterling imitations has been well beyond the call of duty.

# General Index

# Index of Films